OXFORD STUDIES IN

OXFORD STUDIES IN METAPHYSICS

Editorial Advisory Board
Elizabeth Barnes (University of Virginia)
Ross Cameron (University of Virginia)
David Chalmers (New York University and Australasian National University)
Andrew Cortens (Boise State University)
Tamar Szabó Gendler (Yale University)
Sally Haslanger (MIT)
John Hawthorne (University of Southern California)
Mark Heller (Syracuse University)
Hud Hudson (Western Washington University)
Kathrin Koslicki (University of Alberta)
Kris McDaniel (Syracuse University)
Brian McLaughlin (Rutgers University)
Trenton Merricks (University of Virginia)
Kevin Mulligan (Université de Genève)
Laurie Paul (University of North Carolina–Chapel Hill)
Theodore Sider (Cornell University)
Timothy Williamson (Oxford University)

Managing Editors
Stephanie Leary (Rutgers University)
Peter van Elswyk (Rutgers University)

# OXFORD STUDIES IN METAPHYSICS

Volume 9

Edited by
Karen Bennett
and
Dean W. Zimmerman

OXFORD
UNIVERSITY PRESS

OXFORD
UNIVERSITY PRESS

Great Clarendon Street, Oxford, OX2 6DP,
United Kingdom

Oxford University Press is a department of the University of Oxford.
It furthers the University's objective of excellence in research, scholarship,
and education by publishing worldwide. Oxford is a registered trade mark of
Oxford University Press in the UK and in certain other countries

© the several contributors 2015

The moral rights of the authors have been asserted

First Edition published in 2015

Impression: 1

All rights reserved. No part of this publication may be reproduced, stored in
a retrieval system, or transmitted, in any form or by any means, without the
prior permission in writing of Oxford University Press, or as expressly permitted
by law, by licence or under terms agreed with the appropriate reprographics
rights organization. Enquiries concerning reproduction outside the scope of the
above should be sent to the Rights Department, Oxford University Press, at the
address above

You must not circulate this work in any other form
and you must impose this same condition on any acquirer

Published in the United States of America by Oxford University Press
198 Madison Avenue, New York, NY 10016, United States of America

British Library Cataloguing in Publication Data

Data available

Library of Congress Control Number: 2014945770

ISBN 978–0–19–872924–2 (Hbk.)
978–0–19–872925–9 (Pbk.)

Printed and bound by
CPI Group (UK) Ltd, Croydon, CR0 4YY

Links to third party websites are provided by Oxford in good faith and
for information only. Oxford disclaims any responsibility for the materials
contained in any third party website referenced in this work.

PREFACE

Oxford Studies in Metaphysics is dedicated to the timely publication of new work in metaphysics, broadly construed. The subject is taken to include not only perennially central topics (e.g. modality, ontology, and mereology) but also metaphysical questions that emerge within other subfields (e.g. philosophy of mind, philosophy of science, and philosophy of religion). Each volume also contains an essay by the winner of the Sanders Prize in Metaphysics, an annual award described within.

K. B. & D. W. Z.

Ithaca, NY, & New Brunswick, NJ

CONTENTS

The Sanders Prize in Metaphysics   ix

INFINITIES

1. On infinite size   3
   Bruno Whittle
2. Whittle's assault on Cantor's paradise   20
   Vann McGee
3. Reply to Vann McGee's 'Whittle's assault on Cantor's paradise'   33
   Bruno Whittle
4. Problems with plurals   42
   Alexander Pruss and Joshua Rasmussen

METHODOLOGICAL ISSUES, OLD AND NEW

5. The unreasonable effectiveness of abstract metaphysics   61
   Daniel Nolan
6. Paraphrase, semantics, and ontology   89
   John A. Keller
7. Analyticity and ontology   129
   Louis deRosset
8. Naturalizing metaphysics with the help of cognitive science   171
   Alvin I. Goldman

GROUNDING, SUPERVENIENCE, AND CONSTITUTION

9. Multiple constitution   217
   Nicholas K. Jones
10. Half-hearted Humeanism   262
    Aaron Segal
11. The coarse-grainedness of grounding   306
    Kathrin Koslicki

12 A universe of explanations 345
   Ghislain Guigon

COMMENTS

13 Return of the living dead: reply to Braddon-Mitchell 376
   Fabrice Correia and Sven Rosenkranz

Author Index 391

THE SANDERS PRIZE IN METAPHYSICS

Sponsored by the Marc Sanders Foundation* and administered by the editorial board of *Oxford Studies in Metaphysics*, this annual essay competition is open to scholars who are within fifteen years of receiving a Ph.D. or students who are currently enrolled in a graduate program. (Independent scholars should enquire of the editors to determine eligibility.) The award is $10,000. Winning essays will appear in *Oxford Studies in Metaphysics*, so submissions must not be under review elsewhere.

Essays should generally be no longer than 10,000 words; longer essays may be considered, but authors must seek prior approval by providing the editor with an abstract and word count by 1 November. To be eligible for next year's prize, submissions must be electronically submitted by 31 January. Refereeing will be blind; authors should omit remarks and references that might disclose their identities. Receipt of submissions will be acknowledged by e-mail. The winner is determined by a committee of members of the editorial board of *Oxford Studies in Metaphysics*, and will be announced in early March. At the author's request, the board will simultaneously consider entries in the prize competition as submissions for *Oxford Studies in Metaphysics*, independently of the prize.

> Previous winners of the Sanders Prize are:
> Thomas Hofweber, "Inexpressible Properties and Propositions", Vol. 2;
> Matthew McGrath, "Four-Dimensionalism and the Puzzles of Coincidence", Vol. 3;
> Cody Gilmore, "Time Travel, Coinciding Objects, and Persistence", Vol. 3;
> Stephan Leuenberger, "*Ceteris Absentibus* Physicalism", Vol. 4;
> Jeffrey Sanford Russell, "The Structure of Gunk: Adventures in the Ontology of Space", Vol. 4;
> Bradford Skow, "Extrinsic Temporal Metrics", Vol. 5;

---

* The Marc Sanders Foundation is a non-profit organization dedicated to the revival of systematic philosophy and traditional metaphysics. Information about the Foundation's other initiatives may be found at <http://www.marcsanders foundation.com/>.

Jason Turner, "Ontological Nihilism", Vol. 6;
Rachael Briggs and Graeme A. Forbes, "The Real Truth About the Unreal Future", Vol. 7;
Shamik Dasgupta, "Absolutism vs. Comparativism about Quantities", Vol. 8;
Louis deRosset, "Analyticity and Ontology", Vol. 9;
Nicholas K. Jones, "Multiple Constitution", Vol. 9;
Nick Kroll, "Teleological Dispositions", forthcoming in Vol. 10.

Enquiries should be addressed to Dean Zimmerman at: dwzimmer@rci.rutgers.edu

INFINITIES

1. On infinite size

Bruno Whittle

Late in the nineteenth century, Cantor introduced the notion of the 'power', or the 'cardinality', of an infinite set.[1] According to Cantor's definition, two infinite sets have the same cardinality if and only if there is a one-to-one correspondence between them. And what Cantor was able to show was that there are infinite sets that do not have the same cardinality in this sense. Further, since he equated the cardinality of a set with its *size*, he took this result to show that there are infinite sets of different sizes: and, indeed, this has become the absolutely standard understanding of the result. The aim of this paper, however, is to challenge this standard understanding—and, more generally, to argue that we do not, in fact, have any reason to think that there are infinite sets of different sizes.

I should underscore that I am not, in any way, going to challenge Cantor's *mathematics*: my arguments are aimed solely at the standard account of the *significance* of this mathematics. But I trust that the interest of the challenge is nevertheless clear: for, without this claim about significance, Cantor *cannot* be said to have established that there are different sizes of infinity.

The plan for the paper is as follows. In §1 I will give an initial argument against the claim that Cantor established that there are infinite sets of different sizes. This initial argument will proceed by way of an analogy between Cantor's mathematical result and Russell's paradox. Then, in §2, I will give a more direct argument against the claim that Cantor established that there are infinite sets of different sizes. Finally, in §3, I will consider objections to the arguments; and I will also consider what the consequences are, if they work.[2]

---

[1] See, e.g. Cantor (1883).
[2] I said that Cantor's equation of the size of a set with its cardinality has become absolutely standard. However, I should note that there *have* been challenges to this equation: in particular, there have been attempts to develop alternative accounts of infinite size on which two sets can be of different sizes even if there is a one-to-one

1. AN INITIAL ARGUMENT

The aim of this section is thus to give an initial argument against the claim that Cantor established that there are infinite sets of different sizes.

I should start by stating (what I will refer to as) Cantor's account of infinite size. Thus, as I said in the introduction, according to Cantor's notion of cardinality, two infinite sets have the same cardinality iff there is a one-to-one correspondence between them. Further, Cantor equated the cardinality of a set with its size. Together, these claims thus yield the following account of when two infinite sets are of the same size.[3,4]

(C1) For any infinite sets A and B, A is the same size as B iff there is a one-to-one correspondence from A to B.

Further, according to Cantor's notion of cardinality, the cardinality of A is at least as great as the cardinality of B iff there is a one-to-one function from B to A.[5,6] Thus, once again equating claims about

correspondence between them; see, e.g. Mancosu (2009) and the work cited there. As will become clear, the challenge that I will raise in this paper is of a very different sort: it is a challenge to the claim that if two infinite sets are the same size, then there is a one-to-one correspondence between them, whereas the challenges just mentioned are to the converse of this claim. A thorough discussion of these alternative challenges is, unfortunately, beyond the scope of this paper. However, one reason why one might be *somewhat* sceptical about their prospects is that we do *seem* to be in possession of a very good argument for the claim that they challenge (i.e. the claim that the existence of a one-to-one correspondence between two sets entails that they are of the same size); see §2 (although see Mancosu (2009) for a dissenting evaluation of a similar argument). In contrast, I will argue that the best arguments for the claim challenged *here* can in fact be shown to fail. However, I should also note that everything that I will say here could easily be made compatible with the success of these alternative challenges, if it turns out that they are successful.

[3] A function from A to B is a one-to-one correspondence iff: (i) any two members of A are sent to different members of B; and (ii) every member of B has some member of A sent to it.

[4] Cantor proposed not only (C1), but also its generalization to *all* sets (whether infinite or finite). For simplicity, I will initially focus only on the claim for infinite sets. But the claim for finite sets will be discussed further in §3.2.

[5] A function from B to A is one-to-one iff any two members of A are sent to different members of B.

[6] An alternative definition would say that the cardinality of A is at least as great as the cardinality of B iff there is an onto function from A to B; where a function from A to be B is onto iff every member of B has some member of A sent to it. These two definitions are equivalent, given the axiom of choice (which says that for any set C of

cardinality with claims about size (as Cantor did, and has become standard), we get the following.

> (C2) For any infinite sets A and B, A is at least as large as B iff there is a one-to-one function from B to A.

So by 'Cantor's account of infinite size' I will mean this pair of claims, (C1) and (C2).

Now, given this account of infinite size, to establish that there are infinite sets of different sizes, it suffices to establish that there are infinite sets A and B without a one-to-one correspondence between them. And this Cantor did with the following groundbreaking result.[7]

> *Cantor's Theorem.* *For any infinite set A, there is no one-to-one function from the powerset of A to A.*

The proof of the theorem is then as follows.

Proof. Suppose that f is a one-to-one function from P(A) into A, and consider C = {x ∈ A: ∃y ∈ P(A) such that f(y) = x and x ∉ y}. But now consider f(C). And suppose first that f(C) ∈ C. Then (by the definition of C, and the fact that f is one-to-one) it follows that f(C) ∉ C. So f(C) ∉ C. But then (by the definition of C again) f(C) ∈ C: which is a contradiction.

So that (allegedly!) is how Cantor established that there are different sizes of infinity. The aim of this section, however, is to give an initial argument against the claim that Cantor really established this. This initial argument is in terms of Russell's paradox, and the basic idea is as follows. There is a very close analogy between the proof of Cantor's theorem and the derivation of Russell's paradox: indeed, they are really just the same argument in slightly different settings. And, similarly, there is a very close analogy between the following two claims: (a) the claim that Cantor established that the powerset of A is always larger than A; and (b) the claim that the reason for—or

---

disjoint sets, there is a set D that contains exactly one member of each member of C). For the purposes of this paper, I will assume that these two definitions are equivalent (but nothing that I will say will make essential use of this fact).

[7] If A is a set, then the powerset of A is the set of all of A's subsets. I will use P(A) for this set.

the diagnosis of—Russell's paradox is that there are more pluralities than there are objects. Indeed, the analogy between Cantor's proof and the paradox is so tight that it would seem that these two claims must stand or fall together. However, what I will give is an argument *against* the claim about Russell's paradox; and this will thus give an initial argument against the claim about Cantor's result.

I will start, then, by giving the derivation of Russell's paradox. This is the proof of a contradiction from Frege's Basic Law V, which (in slightly updated form) is as follows; here (and throughout) uppercase 'X', 'Y', etc. range over pluralities, while lowercase variables range over objects; thus, in the law, 'ext' is a term intended to denote a function from pluralities to objects (and 'ext' stands for extension; so the idea is that ext(X) is the 'extension' of X).[8]

(V) $\forall X \forall Y(\text{ext}(X) = \text{ext}(Y) \leftrightarrow \forall z(Xz \leftrightarrow Yz))$

Thus, (V) says that ext is a one-to-one function from pluralities to objects (X and Y are the same plurality iff for any z, Xz iff Yz; so (V) says that ext(X) = ext(Y) iff X and Y are the same plurality). What the paradox shows, however, is that there can be no such function. For consider the plurality R, consisting of those objects x such that: for some plurality Y, ext(Y) = x and x is not in Y. First suppose ext(R) is in R: then (by the definition of R, together with the fact, from (V), that ext is one-to-one) ext(R) is not in R. So ext(R) is not in R. But then (by the definition of R again) ext(R) *is* in R: which is of course a contradiction. That, then, is the derivation of the paradox.

Clearly, the argument here is essentially just that of the proof of Cantor's theorem (with the plurality R defined here in just the same way that C was in that proof, and playing the same role in the argument). Thus suppose (in accordance with orthodoxy) that Cantor's argument does indeed establish that, for any infinite set A, A has more subsets than members. Then, presumably, what Russell's paradox shows—what the reason for the paradox is—is that there are, similarly, more pluralities than there are objects. And, assuming Cantor's account of infinite size, that is indeed a very

---

[8] Frege's original version of the law was about concepts rather than pluralities. I am stating it in terms of pluralities since these seem to raise fewer distracting issues. However, to remain relatively close to Frege's original version I will (inessentially) assume that there is an empty plurality (i.e. a plurality X such that for any z, $\neg Xz$).

natural diagnosis of the paradox. But—natural or not—we will see that it cannot be right: and we will see this by considering a variant of the paradox that is so similar to the original that it must have the same diagnosis; but, *also*, it will be completely clear that the diagnosis of the variant has nothing to do with size; and, in that case, it will follow that the diagnosis of the original *similarly* cannot have anything to do with size.

So the first thing is to give the variant paradox. Now, (V) attempts (in effect) to assign a distinct object to each plurality (i.e. each plurality is assigned an 'extension', and (V) says that distinct pluralities get distinct extensions). But now suppose that—inspired, perhaps, by the suggested diagnosis of Russell's paradox—we rein back our ambitions, and try instead merely to assign every *definable* plurality its own object. That is, suppose that all we try to do is to assign a distinct object to every plurality that is defined by a formula of our language. Thus, instead of (V), we propose the following; here $\varphi(z)$ stands for a formula of our language (and so (V*) is a schema, with a different instance for each different formula).

(V*) $\forall X(\forall z(Xz \leftrightarrow \varphi(z)) \rightarrow \forall Y(\text{ext}(X) = \text{ext}(Y) \leftrightarrow \forall z(Xz \leftrightarrow Yz)))$

So (V*) is, in effect, the restriction of (V) to definable pluralities. And, if the problem with (V) was that there are more pluralities than objects, then presumably (V*) will be entirely unproblematic: because clearly there are not more *definable* pluralities than objects, because there are no more definable pluralities than there are formulas to do the defining; thus, since formulas just *are* objects, there are no more such definable pluralities than there are objects; and so (V*) should not be problematic in the way that (V) was.[9]

But unfortunately (V*) *is* problematic and in just the same way that (V) is. That is, we can derive a paradox from (V*) in just the same way that we did from (V). For consider the plurality R, defined just as before: i.e. let R be the plurality of those objects x such that for some plurality Y, x = ext(Y) and x is not in Y. Then, as before, we

---

[9] In case one is unconvinced by the claim that formulas are objects, one could give a version of this argument using merely the fact that there will be a one-to-one correspondence between the formulas of our language and the natural numbers, together with the fact that if there is a one-to-one correspondence between two sets, then they are of the same size. (The latter is the direction of Cantor's account that I will *not* challenge; indeed, I will give an argument for this direction of the account in §2.)

have ext(R) is in R iff it is not: for suppose first that ext(R) is in R; then (by the definition of R, together with the fact that R is defined by the formula $\exists Y(z = \text{ext}(Y) \wedge \neg Yz)$, and the fact that ext is one-to-one for definable pluralities) we get that ext(R) is not in R; so ext(R) is not in R; but then (by the definition of R, again) we get that ext(R) *is* in R; so contradiction.

Thus, even if we restrict attention to definable pluralities, we still get a paradox. And, further, the paradox involves essentially the same argument that Russell's original paradox did. That is, the variant paradox is *extremely* similar to the original. And, given that, they are presumably going to have the same (or very similar) diagnoses. But—as we have seen—the diagnosis of the variant cannot have anything to do with size (because there are *not* too many definable pluralities to allow each to get its own object). And so it seems that the diagnosis of Russell's original paradox similarly cannot have anything to do with size. But (as we also saw above) the idea that Russell's paradox *should* be diagnosed in terms of size would seem to stand or fall with the claim that Cantor established that there are different sizes of infinity. So we seem to have an initial argument against the claim that Cantor established that there are different sizes of infinity.

That, then, concludes the work of this section. In the next section I will try to give a more direct argument against the claim that Cantor established that there are different sizes of infinity.

2. A MORE DIRECT ARGUMENT

So, the aim of this section is to give a direct argument to the effect that we are not justified in believing Cantor's account of infinite size (i.e. (C1) and (C2) of §1). Thus, the first question to ask is: what reason might we have for believing this account?

And one thought one might have here is the following.

> Surely (C1) simply states *what it is* for two infinite sets to be of the same size; and, similarly, surely (C2) simply states *what it is* for one infinite set to be at least as large as another. That is, surely the right-hand-sides of (C1) and (C2) simply unpack what it is for the relation mentioned in the left-hand-side to hold. So—similarly—surely we can justify our belief in (C1)

and (C2) simply by reflecting on the nature of these relations mentioned in the left-hand-sides.

So perhaps there is a very simple and easy account of why we should believe Cantor's account? Unfortunately, though, tempting or not, this thought is hopeless. For the size of a set (infinite or otherwise) is an intrinsic property of that set: that is, it is a property that a set has purely in virtue of what *it* is like; it is *not* a property that it has in virtue of its relations to distinct sets, or to functions between it and such sets.[10] Thus, for two sets (infinite or otherwise) to be of the *same* size is simply for them to have a certain sort of intrinsic property in common; it is *not* for these sets to stand in some sort of relation to certain functions between the two sets. So (C1) does *not* state *what it is* for two sets to be of the same size. And, for analogous reasons, (C2) does not state what it is for one set to be at least as large as another.

Of course, this is not to say that (C1) and (C2) cannot still be true; but they cannot, it seems, be seen to be so simply by reflecting on the nature of the same-size relation, or on the nature of the at-least-as-large-as relation. So, I ask again: what reason might there be for believing Cantor's account of infinite size?

It is perhaps useful, at this point, to separate out the different directions of the claims of the account (and perhaps also to reproduce the claims).

(C1) For any infinite sets A and B, A is the same size as B iff there is a one-to-one correspondence from A to B.
(C2) For any infinite sets A and B, A is at least as large as B iff there is a one-to-one function from B to A.

In each case, the left-to-right direction goes from a claim about size to a claim asserting the existence of a function; while the right-to-left direction goes (of course) from the functional existence claim back to the claim about size. And, actually, we seem to have pretty good reasons for believing the latter directions of the account (i.e. the function-to-size claims). Consider, for example, the function-

---

[10] To put this last point slightly more carefully: the size of a set depends only on which members a set has; it does not depend on its relations to sets *other than its members*, or on its relations to functions from it to other sets, etc.

to-size direction of (C1); this can apparently be argued for as follows.[11]

> Suppose first that A is some infinite set, let x be some member of A, and let y be some object that does *not* belong to A. Now let A* be the result of removing x from A, and replacing it with y. Surely A* is the same size as A: for the *size* of a set does not depend on *which* members it has, just on *how many* it has; and so swapping one member for another should not affect size.
>
> But now suppose that B is some other set, and that there is a one-to-one correspondence from A to B. In this case, B is, in effect, the result of simultaneously replacing each member of A with a distinct object. And, just as in the A* case (and for similar reasons), it seems that B must thus be the same size as the set one started with; that is, it seems that A and B must be the same size here.

Thus, we seem to have good reason to believe the function-to-size direction of (C1); and a similar argument can be given for the corresponding direction of (C2) (but this time using the principle that a set is at least as large as each of its subsets).

But now what about the size-to-function directions of (C1) and (C2)? Ideally, at this point in the paper I would consider the best arguments that been given for these. Unfortunately, however, it is hard to find *any* arguments for these directions of the claims.[12]

Before one has thought much about infinite sets, one might be tempted to argue as follows. Suppose that A and B are infinite sets, and suppose (for the sake of argument) that they are the same size. Then surely one can just *construct* a one-to-one correspondence from A to B: simply first choose some member of A, then choose

---

[11] For a similar argument, see Gödel (1947: 176).

[12] For one very striking failure to give such an argument, see (again) Gödel (1947). Gödel starts the paper by asking if Cantor's account of infinite size is 'uniquely determined'. He then proceeds to give an argument for the function-to-size direction of this account (his argument is similar to that which I have just given). And he then concludes from this that Cantor's account *is* uniquely determined—without any apparent recognition of the fact that he has (in effect) just argued for a biconditional by arguing for one direction of it. Similarly, set theory textbooks typically present Cantor's account with very little in the way of accompanying argumentation (e.g. Hrbacek and Jech (1999) simply mention a case involving theatregoers and seats, and then say that Cantor's account is 'very intuitive' (1999: 65–6)).

a member of B to send it to; then another member of A, and another member of B to send it to, and so on. Surely (the thought would go) if A and B are *really* the same size, then this will eventually yield a one-to-one correspondence: for if one runs out of members of A before one runs out of members of B (say), then surely that just shows that A is *smaller* than B (and similarly if one runs out of members of B first).

Unfortunately, though (although this argument looks fine in the finite case), it is of course hopeless in the infinite one. For, even if A and B are both the same set (e.g. the set of natural numbers), there is no guarantee that simply choosing members will lead to a one-to-one correspondence (e.g. suppose that one chooses members of 'A' in the obvious order, i.e. 0, 1, 2, etc. but that one chooses members of 'B' in the order 0, 2, 4, etc.; then one will obviously not end up with a one-to-one correspondence from A to B). So the idea that simply choosing members will lead to a one-to-one correspondence, as long as A and B are the same size, is hopeless.[13]

So that argument won't work. But it is not, I take it, that proponents of Cantor's account think that these size-to-function claims must simply be taken on faith. Rather, the thought (I take it) is that they are sufficiently obvious that we are entitled to believe them, even in the absence of any explicit argument (and I must confess that is what I thought, when I first learnt set theory). But *why* should it seem obvious that if a pair of sets stand in a certain size-relation, then there should exist a certain sort of function between them—especially in light of the fact that it is far from obvious how to actually construct such a function? The implicit thought, surely, is something like the following (what I am about to say is about (C1), but it could easily be rephrased so as to be about (C2)):

> Let A and B be infinite sets, and suppose, for the sake of argument, that there is no one-to-one correspondence between them. Well, what possible reason could there be for *why* there is no such function? The only possible reason, surely, is that the two sets are of different *sizes*—for what else could be relevant

---

[13] I will discuss an attempt to strengthen this argument, using the fact that every set has a least well-ordering, in §3.1 (but I will argue that the modified argument also fails).

here? That is, if there is no one-to-one correspondence between A and B, then they must be different sizes; but that is logically equivalent to the relevant direction of (C1) (i.e. that if A and B are the same size, then there *is* such a function).

Thus, I suggest that the reason *why* the size-to-function claims seem obvious is because of something like such an inference to the best explanation: i.e. the thought is that if there *isn't* a one-to-one correspondence between two sets, then the only possible (and hence the best!) explanation is that one set must be bigger than the other.[14]

What I will argue in the rest of this section, however, is that—natural as this thought may be—it is mistaken. For (I will argue) in the paradigm cases of pairs of infinite sets without a one-to-one correspondence between them, there *is* a better explanation for why there is no such function; so the upshot will be that we should no longer believe Cantor's account of infinite size (because the reason that it seemed obvious turns out to be a mistake).

In making my case, for the sake of definiteness I will focus on the set of natural numbers, N, and its powerset (but similar points could be made about any infinite set A and *its* powerset). Thus, what I will argue is that there is an explanation of why there is no one-to-one correspondence between N and P(N) that is better than that which uses the hypothesis that one is larger than the other.

So what is this better explanation? Well, the thought is simply as follows. Here is a completely banal and general fact of mathematical life: there are very often 'connecting principles' between mathematical domains, D_1 and D_2, which say that for every object d_1 of D_1, there is an object d_2 in D_2, that is related to d_1 in a certain way; and these principles are often pretty self-evident to anyone who understands the natures of the domains D_1 and D_2. So, to illustrate, here is an example where $D_1 = D_2 = P(N)$.

(1) For every set of numbers A, there is another set of numbers B, that contains precisely the numbers that are not in A.

---

[14] I will take for granted here that it makes sense to talk about explanations of mathematical facts (of course, if it doesn't make sense, then that would seem to make things even worse for Cantor). For a discussion of such explanations, see Mancosu (2011).

This, surely, is pretty self-evident to anyone who knows what sets of numbers are. Another example where $D_1 = {}^N N$ (i.e. the set of functions from N to N), and $D_2 = P(N)$, is as follows.

> (2) For any function f from N to N, there is a set of numbers A, that contains precisely those numbers that f sends to 0.

Again, surely pretty self-evident to anyone who knows what the domains D_1 and D_2 are. And now here is another example, where $D_1 = {}^N P(N)$ and $D_2 = P(N)$.

> (3) For any function f from N to P(N), there is a set A that contains precisely those numbers that are not members of the sets that they are sent to by f.

Again, this principle is surely pretty self-evident to anyone who knows what functions from N to P(N) are, and also what sets of numbers are. But it turns out that this last principle gives us a completely sufficient explanation for why there is no one-to-one correspondence from N to P(N): for why, in particular, there is no onto function from N to P(N).[15] This explanation, starting with (3), is as follows. Let f be any function from N to P(N). Then, by (3), there is a set A containing precisely those numbers that are not members of the sets they are sent to (by f). And so suppose that for some n, f(n) = A; and suppose, to begin with, that n is in A. Then, by the definition of A, n is not in f(n), i.e. n is not in A: so it turns out that n is not in A, after all. But then, by the definition of A again, it follows that n is in A: which is a contradiction. So, given only the connecting principle (3), we can completely explain why there can be no onto function from N to P(N) (and thus why there cannot be a one-to-one correspondence from N to P(N)).

What I now want to argue is that this is in fact a *better* explanation than any in terms of the sizes of N and P(N). But I should first just make clear that this really is a *different* explanation. Actually, though, that is relatively obvious. For the explanation that I have

---

[15] The explanation I am about to give corresponds to the proof of an alternative version of Cantor's theorem (i.e. the version that says that there is no onto function from N to P(N)). The points that I will make could also be put in terms of an explanation corresponding to the proof of the version of the theorem in §2; however, it is slightly simpler to focus on the explanation that I do.

proposed starts from a fact connecting functions from to N to P(N) (on the one hand) and members of P(N) (on the other); and this is simply a very different fact from the (alleged) fact that P(N) is bigger than N (for the latter, as we have seen, concerns only the intrinsic properties of N and P(N), and not functions between them); thus, the two explanations start from very different facts, and so they are different.

But—one might respond:

> OK. The explanation that you have proposed really *is* different. But only because it is incomplete: yes, it starts from something that is not (in and of itself) about size; but this starting point must itself be explained; and surely *that* explanation will bottom-out at a fact about the relative sizes of N and P(N).

This response is not very promising, however. For, while it may be correct that my explanation is incomplete (i.e. perhaps (3) must, as the respondent contends, itself ultimately be explained), nevertheless, it is hardly plausible that this explanation should take us back to the sizes of N and P(N). For, surely, whatever this ultimate explanation of (3) is going to look like, it is going to be essentially similar to the ultimate explanations of other connecting principles, such as (1) and (2). And surely one does not want to say that every connecting principle from D_1 to D_2 must ultimately be explained in terms of the sizes of the domains D_1 and D_2 (or anything along those lines). Rather, it is surely much more plausible to say that these principles are explained by what sorts of things the members of the domains are (facts about the conditions for their existence, for example). For instance, in the case of each of (1–3), the ultimate explanations are plausibly all going to start from the fact that for any property of numbers, there is a set of numbers that contains precisely the numbers with that property.[16]

Thus, the proposed explanation of why there is no one-to-one correspondence from N to P(N) really does seem to be an alternative explanation to that in terms of size. But is it *better*? Well, *of course* it is: because it only uses things that we are committed to anyway

---

[16] This basic fact about sets of numbers may *also* explain *how many* such sets there are, but that in no way tells against what I am saying: for what is crucial is simply that this basic fact is not in and of itself a fact about size.

(i.e. the connecting principle (3); for it is not as if, if we accept that P(N) is larger than N, then we would give up on (3)). That is, the proposed explanation is clearly more economical than that in terms of size. And, thus, since the only reason we could find for believing Cantor's account in the first place was a sort of inference to the best explanation, it would seem to follow that we do not, in the end, have any reason to believe that account.

3. OBJECTIONS AND CONSEQUENCES

In this section I will consider objections to my arguments; and I will also consider what the consequences are, if the arguments work.

3.1. Least well-orderings

Now, in §2 I considered an argument for Cantor's account based essentially on the following thought: surely if A and B are the same size then one can simply *construct* a one-to-one correspondence between them, i.e. by successively choosing members of the two sets. But I rejected this argument as hopeless: because even if A and B are the very same set, there is no guarantee that the proposed construction will yield a one-to-one correspondence. One might, however, be tempted to respond as follows.

> OK, unlike in the finite case, it is not true that *any* way of choosing members will yield a one-to-one correspondence. But every set has a least well-ordering.[17] And as long as one chooses the members of A and B in line with least well-orderings of the sets,[18] then, as long as they really *are* of the same size, one will

---

[17] A well-ordering of A is a relation $\prec$ on A that is anti-symmetric (if $x \prec y$ then not $y \prec x$), and such that every non-empty subset of A has a $\prec$-least element (i.e. for every subset X of A, there is $x \in X$ such that for every $y \in X$, if $y \neq x$ then $x \prec y$). The domain of a relation $\prec$ is the set of things x such that for some y, $x \prec y$ or $y \prec x$. And a relation $\prec$ is isomorphic to a relation $\prec'$ iff there is a one-to-one correspondence f between the domains of $\prec$ and $\prec'$ such that for any x and y in the domain of $\prec$, $x \prec y$ iff $f(x) \prec' f(y)$. Finally, $\prec$ is the least well-ordering of A iff for any well-ordering $\prec'$ of A, $\prec$ is isomorphic to an initial segment of $\prec'$.

[18] i.e. as long as for some least well-orderings $\prec_A$ and $\prec_B$ of A and B, respectively, one first chooses the $\prec_A$-least member of A, and sends it to the $\prec_B$-least member of

end up with a one-to-one correspondence. So Cantor was right after all!

Unfortunately, however, this response simply begs the question. For what this response is simply *taking for granted* is that if A and B are the same size, then their least well-orderings will be isomorphic. For if these well-orderings are *not* isomorphic then the construction described will not yield a one-to-one correspondence. But what is being taken for granted is then *stronger* than what we are trying to prove: because an isomorphism between $\prec_A$ and $\prec_B$ (where these are well-orderings of A and B, respectively) *is* (among other things) a one-to-one correspondence between A and B. Thus, the proposed argument simply begs the question.

3.2. What about the finite case?

An alternative objection focuses on the version of Cantor's account for finite sets. For (the objection goes) surely *this* version of Cantor's account is correct (i.e. surely for any *finite* sets A and B, they are the same size iff there is a one-to-one correspondence between them). But one might then worry that if my argument works in the infinite case, then it will work in the finite case too: giving the unacceptable result that we are not justified in believing even the finite version of Cantor's account. In fact, however, there is no need for concern here. For, as I have already hinted, it is actually clear how this version of Cantor's account can be supported. For, in the finite case, one *can* simply give the argument that is 'hopeless' in the infinite case: because given *finite* sets of the same size A and B, one *can* always construct a one-to-one correspondence between them simply by choosing successive members of them. Thus, in *this* case, there is no need to fall back on an inference to the best explanation, and, similarly, there is no danger that my challenge will generalize in the way that we were worried about.

B; and one then chooses the second $\prec_A$-least member of A, and sends it to the second $\prec_B$-least member of B; and so on.

3.3. Significance

A different sort of worry one might have about my arguments concerns not their cogency but their significance. For, one might think something like the following.

> OK, perhaps you're right that Cantor did not actually establish anything about *size*. Still, he did introduce a rich and fruitful mathematical concept (i.e. *cardinality*). And why should we really care if his results are about *size*, as opposed to being merely about cardinality (which one might call 'size*')?

I must admit that I find this line of thought incredible: when I learnt (or came to believe!) that Cantor had shown that there are different sizes of infinity, I thought that it was one of the most exciting mathematical results I had ever encountered. I would not have been anywhere near as excited if all I had come to believe was that Cantor had provided a new technical notion (with certain similarities to the notion of size, perhaps) and shown that there are infinite sets which this new notion puts into different categories. Surely I am not alone in feeling this way!

Another way to put essentially the same point is this. Cantor's theorem surely belongs to a general category of mathematical results whose significance in large part depends on their connection to pre-theoretic notions. Another good example of such a result is that of Kurt Gödel and Alonzo Church to the effect that the set of arithmetical truths is not computable (i.e. that no computer could output precisely the true sentences of the language of arithmetic).[19] Now, the way in which the Gödel-Church result is actually *proved* is by providing some precise mathematical definition of computability, and then showing that the set of arithmetical truths is not computable in this sense. But it is surely obvious that the significance of the technical result depends in very large part on the adequacy of the definition of computability (i.e. on whether it is really coextensive with the pre-theoretic notion). And it is surely similarly obvious that the significance of Cantor's result depends in very large part on the adequacy of his technical notion of size (i.e. on whether or not what I have been calling his account of infinite size is correct). But, if that is right, then the significance of *my* conclusion should also

---

[19] For this result, see, e.g. Boolos and Jeffrey (1989: 176).

be clear (because it gets to the heart of the significance of Cantor's fundamental result!).

3.4. Consequences

So much, then, for objections. I want to end the paper by saying something about what the consequences are, if the arguments that I have given are correct. And the first natural question to ask here is of course this: so are there, after all that, different sizes of infinity? For, if we accept that Cantor did not succeed in answering this question, then it is of course very natural to ask what the answer really is. Now, giving any sort of definite answer is well beyond the scope of this paper. However, I do want to suggest that—while we work on that!—the most reasonable view to take is that there is exactly *one* size of infinity. For this is clearly the simplest hypothesis, and, if the above arguments work, then Cantor did not give us any reason to prefer an alternative. Of course, I am not suggesting that we are entitled to believe this one-size hypothesis with anything like the certainty that previously we thought that we were entitled to believe Cantor's hypothesis. But the simplicity of the former does seem to give it a good claim to being our best working hypothesis.

I want to make one further point about the picture that emerges, if my arguments are correct. And I will for the sake of definiteness once again focus on N and P(N) (but similar points could be made about any infinite set and its powerset). Now, what Cantor *did* of course establish is that there is no one-to-one correspondence between N and P(N). But what I have been arguing is that this does not tell us anything about the sizes of the sets, because the reason *why* there is no such function is not that the sets are of different sizes; rather, the lack of such a function is due to basic connections between, on the one hand, functions between N and P(N), and, on the other, the members of P(N) (cf. (3) of §2). That is to say: on the picture that emerges (if my arguments are correct), these functions cannot be used to *measure* N and P(N) because there is a basic connection between the functions and the sets that gets in the way. So, if I am right, then one way to think about the situation is this: these functions are simply not the 'independent observers' that Cantor needed them to be.

Thus, I hope to have shown that, for all we know, there is only one size of infinity.[20]

Yale University

REFERENCES

Boolos, G., and R. Jeffrey (1989). *Computability and Logic*. Third edition. Cambridge: Cambridge University Press.

Cantor, G. (1883). 'Foundations of a General Theory of Manifolds: A Mathematico-Philosophical Investigation into the Theory of the Infinite.' W. Ewald (trans.) in W. Ewald (ed.), *From Kant to Hilbert: A Source Book in the Foundations of Mathematics, Volume II*, 1996: 881–920. Oxford: Clarendon Press.

Gödel, K. (1947). 'What Is Cantor's Continuum Problem?' in his *Collected Works: Volume II, Publications 1938–1974*, S. Feferman et al. (eds), 1990: 176–87. Oxford: Oxford University Press.

Hrbacek, K., and T. Jech (1999). *Introduction to Set Theory*. Third edition. New York: Marcel Dekker.

Mancosu, P. (2009). 'Measuring the Size of Infinite Collections of Natural Numbers: Was Cantor's Theory of the Infinite Inevitable?' *Review of Symbolic Logic* 2: 612–46.

Mancosu, P. (2011). 'Explanation in Mathematics.' In E. Zalta (ed.), *The Stanford Encyclopedia of Philosophy*, Summer 2011 edition. <http://plato.stanford.edu/archives/sum2011/entries/mathematics-explanation/>.

---

[20] For comments and discussion I am extremely grateful to George Bealer, Cian Dorr, John Hawthorne, Øystein Linnebo, Alex Paseau, Agustín Rayo, Zoltán Gendler Szabó, and Tim Williamson, and also to audiences at Bristol, Oxford, and Yale.

2. Whittle's assault on Cantor's paradise

Vann McGee

Bruno Whittle aims to drive us from the paradise[1] created by Cantor's theory of infinite number. His principal complaint is that Cantor's proof that the subsets of a set are more numerous than its elements fails to yield an adequate diagnosis of Russell's paradox.

Frege (1893, §20) proposed that the function *ext* that takes a concept to the object that is its extension satisfies the following basic law:

(V) $(\forall A)(\forall B)(ext(A) = ext(B) \leftrightarrow (\forall x)(A(x) \leftrightarrow B(x)))$,

which breaks down into two principles:

(Va) $(\forall A)(\forall B)(ext(A) = ext(B) \rightarrow (\forall x)(A(x) \leftrightarrow B(x)))$.
(Vb) $(\forall A)(\forall B)((\forall x)(A(x) \leftrightarrow B(x)) \rightarrow ext(A) = ext(B))$.

(Va) is harmless enough, but (Vb) leads directly to a contradiction. Russell's (1902) derivation of the contradiction exactly mimics Cantor's (1891) proof that the subsets of a given set are more numerous than its elements. In the derivation of the contradiction from (Vb), Cantor's diagonal set becomes the Russell set.

To emphasize the analogy between Cantor's proof and Russell's, we are sometimes told that the failure of (Vb) shows that there are more concepts than there are objects. More precisely, there are more first-level concepts of one argument—functions taking objects to truth values—than objects. The derivation of an inconsistency from (Vb) is directly analogous to the proof of the theorem of Cantor that Boolos (1997) calls "Not 1-1": There isn't any injection from the power set of a set to the set itself. Russell's analogous result is that there isn't any injective second-level function taking the first-level one-argument concepts to objects (treating first-level concepts as identical iff the same objects fall under them). Within the framework

---

[1] Defying an earlier assault on Cantor's theory, Hilbert (1926, p. 376) declared, "No one shall be able to drive us from the paradise that Cantor created for us."

of Frege's hierarchy of functions and concepts, this is a natural way of saying that there are more concepts than objects, but taking Frege's hierarchy for granted is a rather large presumption.

Not Onto is the other version of Cantor's s theorem: There isn't a surjection from a set onto its power set. This too has a Russellian analogue, telling us that there isn't a surjective map taking objects to concepts. Suppose, *per impossible*, that f were such a map. Then the relation F defined by:

$$F(x, y) =_{\text{Def}} y \text{ falls under } f(x)$$

will satisfy the condition:

($\ddagger$) $(\forall A)(\exists x)(\forall y)(A(y) \leftrightarrow F(x, y))$.

If, conversely, F were a relation satisfying ($\ddagger$), then the function f given by:

$f(x) =_{\text{Def}}$ the concept satisfied by all and only the objects that bear F to x

would be a surjective map taking objects to concepts. Thus Russell's conclusion that there can be no such map can be reformulated as a theorem of second-order logic:

$\sim (\exists F)(\forall A)(\exists x)(\forall y)(A(y) \leftrightarrow F(x, y))$.

Assuming the availability of a pairing function, this theorem can be rewritten as a theorem of the logic of plurals, which Boolos (1984) and (1985) has argued convincingly—at least I was convinced—is innocent of burdensome ontological commitments. The rendering into English is painfully awkward: There aren't any pairs such that, for any objects, there is an object such that they are the objects paired with it. Undeniably barbarous, this usage provides a method for expressing the idea that there are more concepts than objects without having to pay for a lot of expensive metaphysical machinery. With the method in place, I'll go back to talking about Fregean concepts, sparing your ears further insult.

Terminological niceties aside, it's hard to see how the analogy between Cantor's proof and Russell's is useful as a explanation of where Frege went wrong. It's not as if Frege ever said to himself, "Postulating (Vb) is unproblematic, since there aren't more concepts than objects." Professor Whittle (this volume) attacks Cantorian set theory on the grounds that Cantor's theorem fails to provide an adequate diagnosis of what went wrong in the *Grundgesetze*. I think he can fairly be accused of setting up a straw man. No one ever thought that an appeal to Cantor's theorem offered an adequate diagnosis of Russell's paradox.

The standard diagnosis, to the extent there can be said to be one, points to two divergent conceptions of *class*; see Levine (1994). The *logical* conception understands classes as formed from predicates by abstraction. The *combinatorial* conception sees classes as formed from objects by collection.

Frege was the foremost proponent of the logical conception. For him, to say that Traveler is an element of the class of horses is just another way of saying that Traveler is a horse. Classes are logical objects. If we are entitled to use the word "horse," we are entitled to talk about the class of all horses. The transition from "Traveler is a horse" to "Traveler is an element of the class of horses" is as innocuous as the transition from "Mary chased John" to "John was chased by Mary."

The natural first response to Russell's paradox is to judge that the logical conception of class is inconsistent, but that response is too hasty. Whitehead and Russell (1927) devised an ingenious answer to the paradox that retained the logical conception, albeit in a watered-down form. In the end, they want to deny that there are any classes, but they at least want to defend talk of classes as a legitimate manner of speaking, whose literal content is given by replacing talk about classes with talk about propositional functions. If we're talking class talk, we'll say that every well-formed open sentence has an extension, but the open sentence "x is a class that doesn't contain itself" isn't well-formed, because a properly constructed language won't allow circular reference. The attempt to convert "$x \notin x$" into primitive notation produces a "formula" of the form "$\sim x(x)$," which isn't grammatical. It should be noted that this response to the paradox makes no appeal to Cantor's theorem.

Principia Mathematica is a lovely Baroque structure that is rarely visited nowadays. Contemporary sensibilities prefer the sleek, expansive lines of ZFC. ZFC regards a set as an object, produced by gathering together other objects. The idea of creating a set by gathering together a bunch of objects, one of which is the very set being created, makes no sense. Nor does the idea of forming a set s by collecting a bunch of objects, some of which contain s. The repudiation of such misbegotten collections, which is codified in the foundation axiom, gives us our defense against Russell-style antinomies. It's surprising that the addition of the foundation axiom to Zermelo's axioms made people more secure that their theory of sets was consistent. After all, the addition of a new axiom can never repair an inconsistent system. The explanation is that the new axiom came with a diagnosis. The error that underlay all the set-theoretic paradoxes surveyed in *Principia* was the postulation of sets that aren't well-founded. Once we realize that there are no sets that aren't well-founded, the paradoxes disappear. Of course, we have no proof that our theory of sets is consistent—the second incompleteness theorem still constrains us—but we at least have the assurance that the particular road that led Frege to ruin has been blocked off. Notice that what closed the road was the repudiation of non-well-founded sets; it wasn't Cantor's theorem.

On a combinatorial conception of sets, the inconsistency of (Vb) shows that it's not the case that, for any things, there is a set consisting of just those things. The comprehension principle,

$$(\exists \text{ set } x)(\forall y)(y \in x \leftrightarrow \varphi(y)),$$

has to be restricted somehow. Set theorists typically go on to say that one restricts the comprehension principle so as to ensure that the sets form a well-founded hierarchy. There is, however, a well-regarded alternative,[2] which contends that things form a set unless there are too many of them. This limitation-of-size principle enters into the standard axioms with the replacement principle, which, when formulated in plural logic as a single axiom, tells us that, if the As are the same or fewer in number than the Bs, then if the Bs form a set, the As do too. On the limitation-of-size conception, the reason the Burali-Forti (1897) paradox doesn't lead to a contradiction is that the ordinals are too numerous to form a set. The reason Russell's paradox doesn't lead to ruin is that the sets that don't contain themselves are more numerous than any set. What's important to note here is that the diagnosis is that, for certain concepts, the objects

---

[2] Limitation of size was introduced by von Neumann (1925) as an alternative motivation for standard set theory, and it was further developed by Aczel (1988) as a rival to the standard theory of sets.

that fall under the concept are too many to form a set. The fact that the concepts are more numerous than the objects is irrelevant.

(V) introduces a new term into the language, but it doesn't count as a definition. A definition is specific, and (V) leaves unanswered such questions as whether the moon is an extension. While not defining "*ext*," (V) aims to give its most important property. The effort fails, alas, as (V) lapses into inconsistency. Does (V*), Whittle's restricted, schematic version of (V), fare better?

(V*) $(\forall X)((\forall z)(X(z) \leftrightarrow \varphi(z)) \rightarrow (\forall Y)(ext(X) = ext(Y) \leftrightarrow (\forall z)(X(z) \leftrightarrow Y(z)))$.

The answer depends on how we implement the schema. We start with a countable language $\mathcal{L}$ and extend it to a language $\mathcal{L}_{ext}$, obtained by adding a new second-level function sign "*ext*," whose use is governed by (V*). Sentences obtained from the schema by substituting appropriate open sentences for "$\varphi(z)$" are taken as axioms, meaning postulates that partially define the new term.

Precisely which substitutions for "$\varphi(z)$" are "appropriate" is a matter of some delicacy. If we take the permissible substitutions to be open sentences of $\mathcal{L}$, (V*) is harmless. We can get a model of (V*) by taking "extensions" to be natural numbers, stipulating:

$ext(X) =$ the least n for which there is a formula $\varphi(z)$ with Gödel number n that is satisfied by all and only the Xs, provided there is such a formula;
$= 0$, if there is no such formula.

Note that, because it makes use of the notion of satisfaction, this definition takes place in the metalanguage, not in $\mathcal{L}$.

(V*) doesn't define $ext(\varphi(\hat{x}))$. It doesn't even give complete identity conditions for $ext(\varphi(\hat{x}))$, since it doesn't answer the question whether $ext(\varphi(\hat{x}))$ is identical to the moon. It does, however, give useful partial identity conditions. We can think of (V*) as the principle we get from (V) by restricting it to concepts definable in $\mathcal{L}$. (V) is an *abstraction principle*,[3] a rule that pairs, in a one-one fashion, certain objects, identified by an abstraction operator, with the equivalence classes of a certain equivalence relation. In the present

---

[3] See Hale and Wright (2004) and Fine (2008).

case, the appropriate equivalence relation is coextensiveness,[4] and the operator is "*ext*." In general, we are able to introduce an abstraction operator so as to satisfy an abstraction principle just in case the equivalence classes are not more numerous than the available objects. This presumes, of course, that the abstraction operator is new to the language. Because concepts are more numerous than objects, postulating (V) leads to inconsistency. Because, assuming the domain of $\mathcal{L}$ is infinite, the concepts definable in $\mathcal{L}$ aren't more numerous than the objects in the domain of $\mathcal{L}$, (V*) is harmless.

So far, so good for (V*), but things turn out quite differently if we allow "*ext*" to appear within the open sentence we substitute for "$\varphi(z)$." Such permissiveness results in a kind of circularity. (V*) is intended to partially specify what "*ext*" means by providing partial identity conditions for the objects in its range. To know what it tells us about the identity conditions for $ext(\varphi(\hat{x}))$, we have to know what $\varphi(z)$ means, and, if "*ext*" is part of $\varphi(z)$, to understand $\varphi(z)$, we have to already understand what "*ext*" means. The circularity is vicious. Under the permissive understanding of "appropriate substitution," (V*) is inconsistent. This inconsistency doesn't strike me as paradoxical. We gave the intended meaning of a new term by laying down a bunch of conditions that were to govern its use, and these conditions turned out to be inconsistent. It's not unlike introducing a function sign "f" by laying down conditions that f is required to satisfy, one of which is the condition that f is to assign to 0 a value equal to $f(0) + 1$.

The ambivalent status of (V*) is strongly reminiscent of Richard's (1905) paradox. Cantor showed that, for any numerical listing of real numbers, there will have to be some real numbers that aren't on the list. Richard focused his attention on a special case of Cantor's proof. If we list the expressions that define real numbers—by this, I mean expressions that uniquely specify some particular real number—in alphabetical order, Cantor's proof shows us that there are real numbers that aren't defined by any of the expressions on the list. What's more, Cantor's construction actually uniquely specifies a real number that's different from every number specified by a listed

---

[4] If we suppose, naturally enough, that concepts are the same if the same objects fall under them, coextensiveness for concepts is the same as identity. But Frege was careful to apply the identity relation only to objects.

expression. Cantor's construction defines a real number that has no definition!

The standard response to Richard's paradox begins by noting that any inquiry whether a real number can be defined by a linguistic expression should start with the question, "Defined in what language?" For a given countable language $\mathcal{L}$, we can enumerate the real numbers definable in $\mathcal{L}$, and we can define a real number r, different from every number on the list. The definition of r isn't given in $\mathcal{L}$, however. r is defined semantically, and the semantic theory of $\mathcal{L}$ is developed, not in $\mathcal{L}$ itself, but in a metalanguage richer than $\mathcal{L}$ in expressive power. Once we take account of the language-relativity of definability, what looked like a manifest absurdity—a definition of a real number that isn't defined—is seen to be a garden-variety example of a something defined in the metalanguage that cannot be defined in the object language. König's (1905) antinomy about the least undefinable ordinal and Berry's antinomy[5] about the least integer not definable in fewer than twenty syllables have a similar dissolution: "Definable in $\mathcal{L}$" isn't definable in $\mathcal{L}$.

The standard response, which is due to Tarski (1935), is fine as far as it goes, but it doesn't go nearly as far as we'd like. Richard asked about real numbers that were definable in French, and the prospects of devising a metalanguage adequate to the semantics of a natural language are dim. The semantical paradoxes—Richard's paradox, Epimenides' paradox, and the others—are an urgent philosophical problem, but they aren't a problem that can be fairly laid at Cantor's door. Grelling's paradox[6] is so very similar to Russell's paradox, and König's paradox is so very similar to Burali-Forti's, that the thought that the paradoxes have to have similar solutions is difficult to resist. But we should resist it. Although the problems are similar, the available solutions are quite different. Attempts at a unified solution have had disappointing results. Mathematical success has been obtained by following Ramsey's (1925) strategic advice and developing set theory on its own, without tying its fortunes to philosophy or semantics. Russell's paradox lies on the set-theoretic side of Ramsey's divide, the contradiction engendered by the permissive reading of (V*) on the semantic side. The fruitful path in the past

---

[5] p. 66 of Whitehead and Russell (1927).
[6] Grelling and Nelson (1908).

has been to resist Whittle's insistence that, because the two contradictions are so similar formally, they require the same response.

Under a logical conception of set, Ramsey's advice is risky. Sets are understood as predicates in extension, and the semantic paradoxes show that our commonsense understanding of predication is deeply troubled. "Predicate" is sometimes used to refer to linguistic items—we talk about the subject and the predicate of a sentence—and sometimes to refer to the abstract entities (properties or attributes or propositional functions or whatever) that the linguistic items represent. Grelling's paradox asks about linguistic predicates that don't satisfy themselves, and König's paradox asks about linguistic predicates that are satisfied by a unique ordinal. Set theorists who follow the logical conception think of predicates in a way that isn't language-bound. On the more abstract conception, for there to exist a predicate P, it is enough that there could be a language with a phrase that expresses P; no one has to actually speak the language. The two ways of thinking of predicates are so intimately connected that we should have to be very lucky for an inconsistency that afflicts one of the notions not to infect the other.

On the combinatorial conception, there is no special connection between set theory and semantics. Of course, we use language to talk about sets, but we also use language to talk about butterflies, and nobody thinks that the semantic paradoxes pose a special problem for lepidoptery. Cantor was an adherent of the combinatorial conception of sets—arguably its first adherent—and it would be overly harsh to condemn his theory of infinite numbers because he hasn't solved the liar paradox.

Cantor showed that it isn't possible to give a numerical listing of the real numbers. For any proposed listing, there will be real numbers that are left off the list. The same argument shows that, for a given countable language $\mathcal{L}$, even though there is a numerical listing of the expressions of $\mathcal{L}$ that define real numbers, no such listing is definable in $\mathcal{L}$. Again, the argument shows that, whereas there is a numerical listing of computer programs that calculate total functions from the natural numbers to the natural numbers, no such listing can be generated by a computer program. Cantor's argument is quite versatile. Indeed, the go-to method among descriptive set theorists to show that a hierarchy doesn't collapse is Cantor's diagonal technique. Something I want to emphasize is that the fact that Cantor's argument can be repurposed for evidence uses is no evidence that it didn't succeed in its original aim of showing that the subsets of a set are more numerous than its elements.

We have a variety of ways of assessing sizes. When we ask about the size of a body, we could be asking about its length or its circumference or its weight or its volume. When we say one pop star is bigger than another, we could mean that she sells more songs or fills more seats or inspires more imitators or has a greater influence on fashion. The most general measure of the size of a set is its cardinal number, but Lebesgue measure and Baire category are also ways of assessing the size of a set. To ask which is the true notion of size would be frivolous.

We don't have a numerical measure of a celebrity's fashion impact, but most ways of thinking about sizes come equipped with numerical measures. We answer a "How long?" question by giving a length in inches. We answer a "How heavy?" question by giving a weight in pounds. We answer a "How many?" question by giving a cardinal number. Cantor was the first to realize that we could ask "How many?" questions about infinite collections and get a sensible and useful answer.

Notions of size are, it seems to me, tied inextricably to size comparisons. To ask meaningfully about the size of a thing, whether it's a body or a set or some other sort of thing, we have to have an understanding of when something else would be the same size as it, and when something else would be larger or smaller. The idea that size is an intrinsic property of a thing and that we can inquire about the size of a thing just by looking at the thing itself, in isolation from everything else, with no consideration of what would be required for something else to be bigger, smaller, or the same size, baffles me.

There are a variety of number systems on the mathematician's shelf, but the two most prominent, historically, have been the real numbers, which we use to measure continuous magnitudes, and the natural numbers, which we use to measure discrete magnitudes. Cantor aimed to extend the techniques of discrete mathematics so that they could be applied to infinite sets, but he encountered a striking divergence. Within the domain of the finite, the same numbers can be used both to answer "How many?" questions and to mark positions in a sequence. Once we pass beyond the finite, the same numbers won't serve both purposes, so we need to distinguish cardinal numbers, which measure sizes, from ordinal numbers, which mark positions.

Using numbers to measure the sizes of infinite sets was a dramatic departure. Hitherto, such measures had only been applied to finite sets. Extending arithmetical methods to an enlarged domain will inevitably involve some departures from familiar ways of doing things, and it will also require making choices. We can't expect the familiar rules to give us perfect guidance in an unfamiliar setting. It was Cantor's plan to adhere as nearly as he could to the ways of doing arithmetic that were familiar from the finite case, but adhering as nearly as he could didn't mean complete conformity. The following principle has served us infallibly in counting finite sets, and Cantor proposed to extend it to infinite sets:

Cantor's principle. If the As and the Bs can be put into one–one correspondence, then they are the same in number.

As long as we're talking about finite sets, Cantor's principle can coexist peacefully with:

Galileo's principle.[7] If every A is a B but not every B is an A, then there are fewer As than Bs.

Taking it for granted that, if there are fewer As than Bs, then the As and the Bs aren't the same in number, the two principles cannot both be maintained once we start measuring infinite sets.

Galileo's principle gives us a highly specialized but sometimes very useful way of comparing the sizes of sets. Thus the Borel sets of real numbers are defined by saying that they constitute the *smallest* collection that contains the intervals and is closed under countable unions and countable intersections. If "smallest" here meant smallest in terms of cardinality, this proposed definition would have failed to pin down a unique set of sets. Instead, it would result in a $2^{(2^{\aleph_0})}$-way tie. The definition only makes sense if "smallest" is taken to mean "smallest under the inclusion partial ordering." I daresay no one, not even the most dedicated Cantorian, will condemn the definition of "Borel set" for utilizing an incorrect standard of size comparison. The Cantorian position has to be that

---

[7] From Galileo (1638).

Cantor's principle gives a legitimate notion of sameness of size, one that can be coherently employed for worthwhile purposes even when the sets being measured are infinite. The contention can't be that the principle gives us the only legitimate method of comparing the sizes of infinite sets. This is not anomalous. Height isn't the only legitimate way of measuring a person's size.

Galileo foresaw the path that Cantor went down, and he warned us to stay off it. Violations of Galileo's principle were, he thought, such a manifest absurdity that we must avoid ascribing numbers to infinite totalities.

Whittle follows Cantor in allowing numerical measures of infinite sets, but he rejects both Cantor's principle and Galileo's, proposing instead:

Whittle's principle. Two sets have the same number of members if and only if either their members can be put into one–one correspondence or both are infinite.

He advances this principle, which lies well outside the mainstream, only as a working hypothesis, but, speaking bluntly, I have trouble seeing what work the hypothesis is suited for.

One is awestruck by the audacity of what Cantor did. For nearly all our intellectual history, the authoritative view has been that there is no actual infinite, either in nature or in mathematics. The view originated in Aristotle's response to Zeno's paradoxes, but it persisted long after Zeno's puzzles had lost their terror. Cantor boldly proposed that not only is the infinite actual, we can measure it numerically. His proposal required renouncing Galileo's principle, which put him in a direct confrontation with both common sense and the authority of Galileo. Nonetheless, he persisted, following Cantor's principle where it led him, even when it led him to places far removed from what our experiences with the arithmetic of the finite would have led us to expect.

Cantor's audacity paid off handsomely, yielding a lucid theory that is marvelously fruitful mathematically. In particular, the partition of infinite sets of real numbers and sets of sets of real numbers into those that have cardinality $\aleph_0$ and those that have cardinality greater than $\aleph_0$ has become one of the central ideas of modern mathematical analysis. We saw it above in the use of countable unions and countable intersections to define the Borel sets. The theory of degrees of uncountability has proven much less useful outside set theory, but it's central to set theory. Indeed, it's not a great oversimplification to say that Cantor's theory of infinite ordinal and cardinal numbers is the principal subject matter of set theory.

One person's courage is another person's recklessness, but my own attitude is keenly to admire Cantor's intellectual courage and, eschewing skepticism, to accept his theory of infinite numbers as the great advance it appears to be.

Massachusetts Institute of Technology

REFERENCES

Aczel, Peter (1988). *Non-well-founded Sets*. Stanford, CA: CSLI.
Boolos, George S. (1984). "To Be Is to Be a Value of a Variable (or to Be Some Values of Some Variables)." *Journal of Philosophy* 81: 430–49. Reprinted in Boolos (1998, pp. 54–72).
Boolos, George S. (1985). "Nominalistic Platonism." *Philosophical Review* 94: 327–44. Reprinted in Boolos (1998, pp. 73–87).
Boolos, George S. (1997). "Constructing Cantorian Counterexamples." *Journal of Philosophical Logic* 26: 237–9. Reprinted in Boolos (1998, pp. 338–41).
Boolos, George S. (1998). *Logic, Logic, and Logic*. Cambridge, MA, and London: Harvard University Press.
Burali-Forti, Cesare (1897). "Una Questione sui Numeri transfiniti." *Rendiconit del Circolomathematico di Palermo* 11: 154–64. English translation by Jean van Heijenoort in van Heijenoort (1967, pp. 104–11).
Cantor, Georg (1891). "Über eine elementare Frage der Manningfaltigkeitslehre." *Jahresbericht der Deutschen Mathematiker-Vereinigung* 1: 75–8. English translation by Shaughan Lavine in Lavine (1996, pp. 99–102).
Fine, Kit (2008). *The Limits of Abstraction*. New York: Oxford University Press.
Frege, Gottlob (1893). *Grundgesetze der Arithmetik*, v. 1. Jena: Hermann Pohle. English translation by Philip A. Ebert and Marcus Rossberg. Oxford: Oxford University Press, 2013.
Galilei, Galileo (1638). *Dialogue Concerning Two New Sciences*. English translation by Henry Crew and Alfonso de Salvio. New York: Dover, 1954.
Grelling, Kurt, and Leonard Nelson (1908). "Bemerkungen zu den Paradoxien von Russell und Burali-Forti." *Abhandlungen der Fries'schen Schule* II. Göttingen, pp. 301–34.

Hale, Bob, and Crispin Wright (2004). *The Reason's Proper Study*. Oxford: Oxford University Press.

Hilbert, David (1926). "Über und Unendliche." *Mathematische Annalen* 95; 165–90. English translation by Stefan Bauer-Mangelberg in van Heijenoort (1967, pp. 367–95). Page references are to the translation.

König, Julius (1905). "Über die Grundlagen de Mengenlehre und das Kontinuumproblem." *Mathematische Annalen* 61: 156–60. English translation by Stefan Bauer-Mengelberg in van Heijenoort (1967, pp. 145–9).

Levine, Shaughan (1994). *Understanding the Infinite*. Cambridge, MA: Harvard University Press.

Ramsey, Frank Plumpton (1925). "The Foundations of Mathematics." *Proceedings of the London Mathematical Society* 25: 338–84. Reprinted in Ramsey, *The Foundations of Mathematics* (London: Routledge and Kegan Paul, 1931), pp. 1–61, and in Ramsey, *Philosophical Papers* (Cambridge: Cambridge University Press, 1990), pp. 164–224.

Richard, Jules (1905). "Les Principes des mathématiques et le Probleme des Ensembles." *Revue Générale des Sciences Pures et Appliquées* 16: 541. English translation by Jean van Heijenoort in van Heijenoort (1967, pp. 142–4).

Russell, Bertrand (1902). Letter to Frege in van Heijenoort (1967, pp. 124–5).

Tarski, Alfred (1935). "Der Wahrheitsbegriff in den formalisierten-Sprachen." *Studia Philosophica* 1: 261–405. English translation by J. H. Woodger in Tarski, *Logic, Semantics, Metamathematics*, 2nd ed. (Indianapolis: Hackett, 1983), pp. 152–278.

Van Heijenoort, Jean (1967). *From Frege to Gödel*. Cambridge, MA, and London: Harvard University Press.

Von Neumann, John (1925). "EineAxiomatisierung der Mengenlehre." *Journal für die reine und angewandte Mathematik* 154: 219–40. English translation by Stefan Bauer-Mengelberg and Dagfinn Føllesdal in van Heijenoort (1967, pp. 393–413).

Whitehead, Alfred North, and Bertrand Russell (1927). *Principia Mathematica*, 2nd ed. 3 vols. Cambridge: Cambridge University Press.

Whittle, Bruno (forthcoming). "On Infinite Size." *Oxford Studies in Metaphysics*. New York: Oxford University Press.

3. Reply to Vann McGee's 'Whittle's assault on Cantor's paradise'

Bruno Whittle

I would like to start by thanking Professor McGee for his interesting and thoughtful response to my paper, 'On Infinite Size' (OIS). Naturally, however, I would also like to say a few things in reply.

In OIS I offer two arguments each aimed at establishing that we are not justified in believing that there are infinite sets of different sizes: an initial argument in terms of Russell's paradox in §1, and a more direct argument in §2. I will refer to these as the 'initial' and the 'direct' argument, respectively. I will start with a discussion of the direct argument, and then move on to the initial one.

The direct argument aims to establish that we are not justified in believing Cantor's account of infinite size, by which I mean the following pair of claims.

(C1) For any infinite sets A and B, A is the same size as B iff there is a one-to-one correspondence from A to B.
(C2) For any infinite sets A and B, A is at least as large as B iff there is a one-to-one function from B to A.

Our only justification for believing that there are infinite sets of different sizes would seem to be based on this account. Thus, if we are not justified in believing this account, then we are not justified in believing that there are infinite sets of different sizes. I will describe the version of the direct argument aimed at establishing that we are not justified in believing (C1), but a similar argument could be given for (C2).

I began by arguing that (C1) is not an analysis of the same-size relation. That is, it does not tell us *what it is* for infinite sets to be of the same size. Why? Because the size of a set—whether infinite or finite—is an intrinsic property of that set. It is a property the set has purely in virtue of what it is like; specifically, in virtue of which members it has. Thus, what it is for A and B to be the same size is for them to share a certain sort of intrinsic property. It is *not* for there to exist a certain sort of function between the sets (in typical cases, neither A nor B will contain a function between the sets).

This point can of course be made without using the word 'intrinsic'. The essential point is simply that the same-size relation is one that holds between a pair of sets purely virtue of which members they have; it does not hold in virtue of the existence of a function between the sets (except in the unusual case where the sets happen to contain such a function). For example, the same-size relation holds between {0, 1} and {2, 3} purely in virtue of which members these sets have; it does not hold between them in virtue of the existence of a function between them. Similarly, this relation holds between ω and $\omega + 1$ (assuming that it does so hold) purely in virtue of which members these sets have, not in virtue of the existence of a function between them. Thus, (C1) of Cantor's account is not an analysis of the same-size relation.

This means that our reason for believing (C1) cannot come simply from reflecting on what it is for two sets to be of the same size. Why then is (C1) widely believed? In particular, why is the size-to-function direction of (C1) widely believed? (By the size-to-function direction of (C1) I mean the claim that for any infinite sets A and B, if they are the same size, then there is a one-to-one correspondence from A to B.) This direction is the crucial one when it comes to establishing that there are infinite sets of different sizes. But arguments for this direction seem rather thin on the ground. (There are arguments for the function-to-size direction of (C1): see §2 of OIS. And these seem sufficient to justify our belief in this direction of (C1). It is only our justification for the size-to-function claims that I aim to challenge in OIS.)

The version of (C1) for finite sets is true. However, many claims true of finite sets fail for infinite ones (e.g. the claim that a set is always larger than its proper subsets), and so this does not seem sufficient to justify belief in the size-to-function direction of (C1). But perhaps whatever justifies our belief in the finite version of this claim will extend to the infinite one? Our belief in the finite version seems justified by the fact that given two finite sets of the same size, if one successively chooses members of the two sets, then the result will be a one-to-one correspondence (for if this process does not result in a one-to-one correspondence, i.e. if one runs out of members of one of the sets before that happens, then this would show that there is a one-to-one correspondence between the 'exhausted' set and a proper subset of the other one; which would in turn show that the exhausted set is smaller). However, this justification will not extend to the infinite version of the claim: since given two infinite sets of the same size (e.g. two copies of the natural numbers), successively choosing members may *not* result in a one-to-one correspondence (e.g. if one chooses members of one of the copies in the 'wrong' order).

But why then is the infinite version of the claim widely believed? As I said, arguments seem rather thin on the ground, but my best guess is that this claim is widely believed because of something like the following line of thought: if there does *not* exist a one-to-one correspondence from some infinite set A to another B, then the only possible reason is that A and B are different sizes. This would seem to give us: if there is no one-to-one correspondence from A to B, then A and B are not the same size; which is the contrapositive of the size-to-function direction of (C1). If I am correct about this, then our justification for believing the size-to-function direction of (C1) is an inference to the best explanation: it is the thought that if there is no such function, then the only possible explanation—and hence the best!—is that the sets are of different sizes.

I argue, however, that this inference to the best explanation fails: because in the paradigm cases of infinite sets such that there is no one-to-one correspondence between them, i.e. sets and their powersets, there is a better explanation of why there is no such function. This superior explanation is very straightforward (and closely related to the proof of Cantor's theorem): it starts simply from the principle that for any function f from a set D to its powerset P(D), there will be a subset of D containing precisely those $d \in D$ such that $d \notin f(d)$. This explanation of why there is no one-to-one correspondence from D to P(D) is different from that in terms of the sizes of D and P(D): the principle about functions and subsets of D just stated is clearly not in and of itself a principle about the sizes of D and P(D). Further, it does not seem that this principle must itself be explained in terms of the sizes of D and P(D)—any more than the following principle must be explained in terms of the sizes of D and P(D): for any subset E of D, there is a subset G of D containing precisely those members of D not in E. In each case, the principle is explained simply by the fact that for any property, there is a subset of D containing precisely the members of D with that property; the principle is *not* explained by the sizes of D, P(D) or any other sets. Finally, this explanation seems clearly superior to that in terms of size: it is more economical, since it uses only principles that we are committed to anyway. Thus, it is not in fact the case that if there is no one-to-one correspondence between two sets, then the explanation must be that they are of different sizes. This means that the thought that seemed to justify our belief in the size-to-function direction of (C1) is mistaken, and we appear to be left without any justification for this belief.

There are two points that McGee makes that might be thought to bear on this argument (although it is only the second point that is *clearly* a criticism of it). The first point is that although I talk in OIS of 'the size' of a set, there are in fact multiple notions of size applicable to sets—just as there are multiple notions of size applicable to physical bodies (e.g. volume, length, and mass).[1] Thus, consider the following two sets of points in $\mathbb{R}^3$: S1, the set of points less than one unit from the origin; and S2, the set of points less than two units from the origin. According to one perfectly legitimate notion of size (i.e. volume), S1 is smaller than S2. But there is a one-to-one correspondence from S1 to S2: and so according to another notion, they are the same size. It is thus an oversimplification to talk of *the* size of a set without making clear which notion one means. However, I trust that it was clear that when I spoke of the size of a set in OIS I meant the notion that one has in mind when one asks 'How many members does it have?', rather than the notion one has in mind when one asks 'How much space does it occupy?', for example; and this is what I will continue to mean by the size of a set here.

This might prompt a related worry, as follows. How can we be sure, even once we restrict attention to notions of size relevant to 'How many?' questions, that there is a single determinate such notion, especially when it comes to infinite sets? But if there is *not* a single determinate such notion, then might we not be justified in believing Cantor's account on at least one 'sharpening' of our indeterminate notion (i.e. on at least one determinate notion that 'sharpens' our indeterminate one)? However, while I don't think we

---

[1] See McGee (2015: 28).

can be *sure* that we have a single determinate such notion of size, I think that this worry can be straightforwardly answered. For it would appear that all of the claims made in these arguments would hold for any sharpening of the relevant notion. For example, it seems that on any such sharpening, the size of a set must be an intrinsic property of it; and similarly, it would appear, for all the other claims made in these arguments. But then these arguments would seem to establish that we are not justified in believing the size-to-function direction of (C1) under *any* sharpening of the relevant notion.

The second point that McGee makes—which I take it is intended as a criticism of the above direct argument—is as follows:

Notions of size are, it seems to me, tied inextricably to size comparisons. To ask meaningfully about the size of a thing, whether it's a body or a set or some other sort of thing, we have to have an understanding of when something else would be the same size as it, and when something else would be larger or smaller. The idea that size is an intrinsic property of a thing and that we can inquire about the size of a thing just by looking at the thing itself, in isolation from everything else, with no consideration of what would be required for something else to be bigger, smaller, or the same size, baffles me. (2015: 28)

As I have indicated above, it seems clear to me that the size of a set is an intrinsic property of it. Here McGee seems to object to this claim on the basis that it entails that 'we can inquire about the size of a thing [in this case a set] just by looking at the thing itself, in isolation from everything else'. However, the metaphysical claim that the size of a set is an intrinsic property of it certainly does not entail the epistemic claim that we can know which size a set has without considering its relations to objects other than its members (or any similar epistemic claim). Thus, it is plausible that having a hairline fracture is an intrinsic property of a foot. But this certainly does not entail that we can know whether a foot has such a fracture without considering its relation to distinct objects, such as MRI machines. In just the same way, the claim that the size of a set is an intrinsic property of it does not entail that we can know which size a set has without considering its relations to objects other than its members. Nor does it entail that we can give an adequate mathematical theory of the sizes of sets without giving a criterion for when two sets are the same size, for example, that mentions objects other than the members of the sets. However, if this is really to be a theory of the *sizes* of sets, then this criterion must track the relevant intrinsic properties (i.e. it must obtain iff the sets in question share a size property). And we are justified in believing on the basis of this criterion that there are infinite sets of different sizes only if we are justified in believing that it does so track the relevant intrinsic properties. What I argue in the paper is that in the case of Cantor's criterion (i.e. in (C1)) we are not so justified in believing this.

As far as I can tell, then, the direct argument emerges unscathed from the points that McGee makes that might be thought to bear on it. However, most of his ire is reserved for the initial argument, so let us now move on to discussing that. This argument aims to establish that Cantor did not establish that there are infinite sets of different sizes. It is in terms of Russell's paradox: i.e. Russell's derivation of a contradiction from Frege's Basic Law V.

The heart of this argument is as follows. I start by arguing that if Cantor established with his theorem (i.e. Cantor's theorem) that there are infinite sets of different sizes, then the reason for—or the diagnosis of—Russell's paradox must be that there are more pluralities than objects. (For simplicity, I formulated Frege's Basic Law V, which I call (V), in terms of pluralities rather than concepts.) Since this was just the initial argument of the paper, I did not spell things out as fully as I might have done, but what I had in mind was the following.

By saying that the reason for, or the diagnosis of, Russell's paradox is that there are more pluralities than objects, I meant that the reason why (V) cannot be true—i.e. the reason why there is no function ext as (V) requires—is that there are more pluralities than objects. But why think that if Cantor's theorem establishes that there are infinite sets of different sizes, then the reason (V) cannot be true must be that there are more pluralities than objects?

Well, what Cantor's theorem directly establishes is that for any infinite set A, there is no one-to-one function from P(A) to A. But why think that this further establishes—i.e. puts us in a position to know—that A and P(A) are of different sizes; in particular, that P(A) is larger than A? It seems plausible that it does this only if the sole reason why there is no such function is that P(A) is larger than A (and if also we know that). For if, for all we know, there might be no such function for some other reason, then why would we be entitled to conclude from Cantor's result that P(A) is larger than A? Of course, it is in principle possible that we might have some very different route from Cantor's result to the fact that P(A) is larger than A, but I have no idea what that might look like—and I have never seen such an alternative articulated. Thus, it seems reasonable to assume that Cantor's result establishes that P(A) is larger than A only if the sole reason why there is no one-to-one function from P(A) to A is that P(A) is larger than A (and if also we know this).

(V) states that ext is a one-to-one function from pluralities to objects.[2] It would seem extremely plausible that if (for any infinite set A) the sole reason why there is no one-to-one function from P(A) to A is that P(A) is larger than A, then, similarly, the sole reason why there is no such function from pluralities to objects is that there are more pluralities than objects. Thus, it would seem that if Cantor's theorem establishes that P(A) is larger than A, then the sole reason why (V) cannot be true—i.e. the diagnosis of Russell's paradox—is that there are more pluralities to objects.

I argue, however, that this is not the sole reason why (V) is true. I do this by considering a variant—in fact a weakening—of (V), (V*). Whereas (V) attempted to assign a distinct object to each plurality, (V*) is a schema that merely attempts to assign a distinct object to each definable plurality—but where 'definable' means definable in a language that contains a term for the function that does the assigning (i.e. 'ext'). (V*) gives rise to a contradiction in essentially the same way that (V) does. Since (V*) is a weakening of (V), any reason (V*) cannot be true is a fortiori a reason why (V) cannot be. But no reason (V*) cannot be true involves size: since there are *not* more definable pluralities than there are objects. Thus, it would seem that at least one reason (V) cannot be true does not involve size (i.e. the—or every—reason (V*) cannot be true). But we saw that if Cantor's theorem establishes that there are infinite sets of different sizes, then the sole reason (V) cannot be true must be that there are more pluralities than objects (i.e. must involve size). Thus it seems that Cantor's theorem doesn't establish this, after all.

[2] Strictly speaking, (V) is a biconditional: one direction states that ext is a one-to-one function from pluralities to objects; the other states that if X and Y are pluralities of the same objects, then ext(X) = ext(Y). Since the latter is presumably a logical truth, I talk as if (V) states simply that ext is a one-to-one function from pluralities to objects. This simplifying assumption could easily be done without if desired.

McGee's main criticism of this argument seems to be as follows:

> Terminological niceties aside, it's hard to see how the analogy between Cantor's proof and Russell's is useful as an explanation of where Frege went wrong. It's not as if Frege ever said to himself, "Postulating [(Va)³] [i.e. the one-to-one-function direction of (V)] is unproblematic, since there aren't more concepts than objects." Professor Whittle [in OIS] attacks Cantorian set theory on the grounds that Cantor's theorem fails to provide an adequate diagnosis of what went wrong in the *Grundgesetze*. I think he can fairly be accused of setting up a straw man. No one ever thought that an appeal to Cantor's theorem offered an adequate diagnosis of Russell's paradox. (McGee, 2015: 21–2)

In fact, I do not anywhere in OIS consider the view that Cantor's theorem provides a diagnosis of Russell's paradox. (I am not sure what that would mean.) What I do consider—and argue against—is the claim that the diagnosis of Russell's paradox is that there are more pluralities than objects. But I hope that I have made clear that far from being a straw man, this seems to be a consequence of the extremely widely held claim that Cantor's theorem establishes that the powerset of an infinite set is always larger than that set.

Indeed—concerning the 'straw man' question—on p. 25 (2015) McGee writes:

> Because concepts are more numerous than objects, postulating (V) leads to inconsistency.

Is this not pretty close to the claim that the diagnosis of Russell's paradox is that there are more pluralities (or in this version: concepts) than objects—at least as articulated above, and as argued against in OIS?

McGee also argues that set-theoretic and semantic paradoxes need not have similar solutions (2015: 26). Does my use of (V*) require that these must in fact have similar solutions? Absolutely not. All I rely on concerning (V) and (V*) is essentially that any reason why (V*) cannot be true is a fortiori a reason why (V) cannot be. Since (V*) is a weakening of (V), this seems hard to deny. And it is of course entirely consistent with this that our theories of definability, truth, etc. should be very different from our theories of sets.

---

[3] McGee has '(Vb)' here, but he clearly means (Va).

It seems to me, then, that the initial argument also emerges pretty much unscathed from McGee's criticisms.

McGee ends his response by declaring that he accepts Cantor's 'theory of infinite numbers [i.e. ordinals and cardinals] as the great advance it appears to be' (p. 31). I should thus end mine by making clear that I too accept Cantor's theory of infinite ordinals and cardinals—and I certainly also regard it as a great advance! It is just that I do not think we are justified in believing that the theory of infinite cardinals is a theory of infinite size. Rather, I think we would do better to regard it simply as a theory of which sets have which sorts of functions between them. So viewed, it is still an important theory—just not of size.[4]

Yale University

REFERENCES

McGee, Vann (2015). 'Whittle's assault on Cantor's paradise.' This volume.

---

[4] Thanks to Zoltán Gendler Szabó.

4. Problems with plurals

Alexander Pruss and Joshua Rasmussen

1. INTRODUCTION

A Russell paradox is generated by one axiom schema for the membership relation $\in$:

SET-COMP. $\exists z \forall x (x \in z \leftrightarrow F(x))$

for any formula $F(x)$ open only in x. (Normally comprehension allows other free variables, but we don't need this.) For suppose we put the Russell formula $\sim(x \in x)$ for $F(x)$ in the schema. Then SET-COMP lets us formally prove a contradiction: there is a z such that $z \in z$ if and only if $\sim(z \in z)$.

Plural quantification is attractive because it promises to avoid Russell paradoxes. However, as McGee and Rayo (2000) point out, plural quantification can actually lead back into Russell paradoxes, given certain assumptions about propositions.[1] We offer a more generalized version of the path to paradox by showing that any theory that makes possible the construction of an appropriate *packaging* relation falls prey to a Russell paradox. We then give examples of widely held metaphysical theories that require such a relation. One response to the argument is to drop certain "obvious" axioms of plural quantification. But we explain why doing that leads to other challenges. In the end, we find that the paradoxes that can result from plural quantification are more widely damaging and harder to tame than has been recognized. We also display formal requirements

---

[1] See also Spencer 2012. Spencer's path to paradox is Cantorian in nature, whereas McGee and Rayo's is Russellian. We are here interested in the Russellian path, though we pay attention to the similarities. The path we take also differs from the paths to paradox marked out by Grim (1991, 1993). Those paths are expressed in terms of universal individual quantification, not plural quantification, and they require assumptions about aboutness and classes that are unnecessary for our arguments.

that any metaphysical framework with a packing relation must meet if it is to have a chance of escaping self-contradiction.

We will first give the general paradox-generating setup, and then show how three families of metaphysical assumptions allow one to instantiate it. We'll close by assessing the aftermath of our arguments.

2. PACKAGING AND PARADOX

In this section, we will mark out a pathway from plural quantification to a Russell paradox. The basic primitives of plural quantification are the quantifiers, $\exists xx$ ("there are some xs, such that") and $\forall xx$ ("for any xs") as well as the primitive $\prec$ ("is one of the") which can occur in the context $a \prec xx$. These primitives allow us to construct the plural analogues of quantifier introduction and elimination rules.

We may begin our journey toward paradox with the following axiom schema:

PL-COMP. $\exists x F(x) \rightarrow \exists xx \forall y (y \prec xx \leftrightarrow F(y))$

for any formula $F(x)$ open only in x. (Again, normally comprehension allows other free variables, but we don't need this.) PL-COMP says that if there is a formula that has a satisfier, then there are some things, the xs, which comprise all and only those things that satisfy it. More simply: if there are *any* Fs, then there are *the* Fs. It is worth noting that PL-COMP makes plural quantification useful in contexts where one might be suspicious of the use of sets, such as when talking about *all sets* or other things that can't be grouped into a set according to modern set theory.

We'll reach a paradox from here only if we have an appropriate *packaging* formula. The packaging formula is a formula $P(x, yy)$ open only in a singular variable x and a plural variable yy. Intuitively, $P(x, yy)$ will say x packages the ys. The thought is that x is an entity that encapsulates the ys according to the particular encapsulation method in the construction. We will consider a number of candidate constructions. An initial example of such encapsulation might be sets: one could take $P(x, yy)$ to say that x is the set of the ys, i.e. $\forall z(z \in x \leftrightarrow z \prec yy)$. The pluralist will not use sets for packaging, of course, for doing so offers no advantage over non-plural, set theoretic quantification. Plus, to avoid a Russell paradox, the pluralist who accepts PL-COMP would need to deny that every plurality has a set.

Nevertheless, for a well-constructed packaging formula, a pluralist might still have reasons to accept a packaging axiom that says that each plurality has a package:

PACK. $\forall xx \exists u P(u, xx)$.

(Here, for a formula $F(x_1, \ldots, x_n)$, where some of these might be plural variables, we write $F(y_1, \ldots, y_n)$ for the result of respectively substituting $y_1, \ldots, y_n$ for the free instances of $x_1, \ldots, x_n$.)

Moreover, a package could be thought to contain exactly one plurality:

UNIQ. $\forall u \forall xx \forall yy((P(u,xx) \wedge P(u,yy)) \to xx = yy)$

where $xx = yy$ abbreviates $\forall u(z \prec xx \leftrightarrow z \prec yy)$. Note that although each package contains exactly one plurality, a plurality may be contained in more than one package.

And, finally, one might suppose that not everything is a package:

NONPACK. $\exists x(\sim \text{Package}(x))$

where Package(x) abbreviates $\exists yy(P(x,yy))$. When packages are abstracta, then $P(x,yy)$ cannot hold for a concrete individual x such as the reader, and so NONPACK is true.

Then PL-COMP, PACK, and UNIQ together let one prove:

PACK-COMP. $\exists x F(x) \to \exists z \forall x(x \lhd z \leftrightarrow F(x))$

for any formula $F(x)$ open only in x, where $x \lhd y$ abbreviates $\exists zz(P(y,zz) \wedge x \prec zz)$. (The context will make clear which packaging formula is used in defining $x \lhd y$. If packaging is done in terms of sets, then $\lhd$ will be the membership relation $\in$.)

We shall give the details of the proof shortly. But first, let's see why this matters.

Let $R(x)$ abbreviate the Russell-type formula $\sim(x \lhd x)$. Plugging this formula into PACK-COMP gives us a Russellian contradiction, *if* $\exists x(R(x))$. Yet, we can show that $\exists x(R(x))$ is just a consequence of NONPACK as follows:

1	$\exists x(\sim \text{Package}(x))$	NONPACK
2	a ❘ $\sim \text{Package}(a)$	
3	$a \in a$	
4	$\exists zz(P(a,zz) \wedge a \prec zz)$	def, 3
5	bb ❘ $P(a,bb) \wedge a \prec bb)$	
6	$P(a,bb)$	$\wedge$-elim, 5
7	$\exists yy P(a,yy)$	$\exists$-intro, 6
8	$\exists yy P(a,yy)$	$\exists$-elim, 4, 5–7
9	$\text{Package}(a)$	def, 8
10	$\bot$	$\bot$-intro, 2, 9
11	$\sim(a \triangleleft a)$	$\sim$-intro, 3–10
12	$\exists x(\sim(x \triangleleft x))$	$\exists$-intro, 11
13	$\exists x(\sim(x \triangleleft x))$	$\exists$-elim, 1, 2–12
14	$\exists x(R(x))$	def, 13

We can now go on to formally derive a contradiction from PACK-COMP as follows:

15	$\exists x R(x) \rightarrow \exists z \forall x(x \triangleleft z \leftrightarrow R(x))$	PACK-COMP
16	$\exists z \forall x(x \triangleleft z \leftrightarrow R(x))$	$\rightarrow$-elim, 14, 15
17	c ❘ $\forall x(x \triangleleft c \leftrightarrow R(x))$	
18	$c \triangleleft c \leftrightarrow R(c)$	$\forall$-elim, 17
19	$c \triangleleft c \leftrightarrow \sim(c \in c)$	def, 18
20	$c \triangleleft c$	
21	$\sim(c \triangleleft c)$	$\leftrightarrow$-elim, 19, 20
22	$\bot$	$\bot$-intro, 20, 21
23	$\sim(c \triangleleft c)$	$\sim$-intro, 20–22
24	$c \triangleleft c$	$\leftrightarrow$-elim, 19, 23
25	$\bot$	$\bot$-intro, 23, 2
26	$\bot$	$\exists$-elim, 16, 17–25

It remains to give the proof of PACK-COMP from PL-COMP, PACK, and UNIQ. That proof is given in the Appendix to this chapter. (Note that our proofs above and in the Appendix are intuitionistically valid: double-negation elimination is never used.)

Pluralists must therefore work with a packaging formula satisfying other axioms or go without packaging. These options, however, have surprising consequences for our understanding of propositions, as we shall see next, since there are plausible constructions of packages that do satisfy the above axioms.

3. METAPHYSICS

We now offer some constructions of P on which PACK, UNIQ, and NONPACK (or slight variants) are plausible. These constructions are built from certain reasonable assumptions about propositions. We thus show that plausible packages for plural quantification cause trouble for various claims about propositions. In doing so, we illustrate certain formal requirements that must be met by any metaphysical framework that includes packaging (such as theories of facts, propositions, states of affairs, collections, and so on). Unfortunately, many current theories fail to meet those requirements.[2] Throughout the arguments, we will be talking about propositions that allow for hyperintensional distinctions (as opposed to Lewis's (1986) propositions considered as sets of worlds): so, for example, the proposition that every dog is a dog is distinct from the proposition that Fermat's Last Theorem is true.

3.1. Plural subjects of propositions

Suppose, first, that propositions are abstract entities that don't depend for their existence upon particular concrete arrangements of (say) ink or sound-waves. Then it is plausible that for any ys there is a plural *de re* existential proposition claiming precisely the existence

---

[2] Rosen (1995) applies an informal version of the Russellian "plurals" paradox to Armstrong's theory of states of affairs. We aim to show that the paradox, in the abstracted form we've presented, affects many other frameworks too.

of these *y*s.³ Where English has a referring expression "*rs*" for the *y*s, say "Jim and Bob" or "the actual world's dogs", this proposition can be expressed by "*rs* exist". But even when English lacks a corresponding referring expression, it is plausible that there will still be such propositions—assuming propositions are irreducible to sentence tokens.

But that's enough to land us in a Russell paradox. For with abstract propositions in hand, we may let $P(x, yy)$ say that x is a *de re* existential proposition claiming precisely the existence of the *y*s.⁴ And in that case, PACK and UNIQ will be true. For: (i) for any *y*s, we've assumed there is a *de re* existential proposition x claiming precisely their existence, and (ii) any *z*s that x precisely claims the existence of are the same as the *y*s. Moreover, the truth of NONPACK is undeniable: there exists a non-proposition—for instance the reader. Thus, by the proof we gave in the previous section, a contradiction results.

One reply is to deny that propositions are independent abstract objects. But even if propositions are concrete things such as sentence tokens or dependent on sentence tokens, there is another route to paradox using PL-COMP. First, let's give it informally. Consider all and only the propositions that don't ascribe existence to themselves. There are those propositions—by PL-COMP. And there is the proposition that they exist. I just stated it. Yet that proposition— the proposition that there are the propositions that don't ascribe existence to themselves—ascribes existence to *itself* if and only if it doesn't. We've again landed in contradiction.

Let us make the above argument more explicit. We stipulate that "$\exists!xxF(xx)$" means "There are unique *x*s such that $F(xs)$", which in turn means "$\exists xxF(xx) \wedge (yy)(F(yy) \to yy = xx)$", where "=" is understood as before. Now suppose $F(x)$ is a formula in our language open only in x that has at least one satisfier. Then, $\exists x(F(x))$. And thus from PL-COMP we have: there are *y*s such that for all x, $F(x)$ iff x is one of the *y*s. Therefore, there are unique *y*s such that for all x, $F(x)$ iff x is one of the *y*s. Now, consider them. They exist. This token of "They exist" expresses a proposition that is *de rebus* about *y*s such

---

³ Spencer (2012) endorses this premise in his Cantorian-style argument against an instance of PL-COMP (i.e. the instance where $F =$ "x exists"). In a moment we will consider some ramifications of rejecting PL-COMP.

⁴ This packaging is implied by Pruss's suggested reduction of collections to propositions (2011, p. 161).

that $F(x)$ iff x is one of the ys. In general, therefore, for any formula $F(x)$ open in one variable we can express, if there is a plurality of satisfiers, then there is, or can be, a sentence, and hence a proposition (perhaps a non-abstract one), about all and only the satisfiers. Now let $F(x) =$ "x is a proposition that is not *de rebus* about objects that include x", and the contradiction results.[5]

We should add that there is nothing particularly special about existential propositions. We could run the construction instead in terms of plural predicative propositions in two ways. First way: fix a property or relation Q, say *concreteness* or *mutual spatiotemporal unrelatedness* or even *acting together*,[6] and say that for any ys there is a plural predicative proposition that precisely attributes Q to the ys (and the attributions don't have to be correct). Alternatively, one could more generally say that for any ys there is a plural predicative proposition that precisely attributes *some* property to the ys. Either way we can generate packages. The second way will presumably result in an infinite number of packages for any given plurality, but the arguments that lead to paradox did not assume that a plurality has only one package.

3.2. Unrestricted fusion and singular de re propositions

Within the context of something like classical mereology, assume unrestricted fusion, in plural formulation:

SUM. $\forall xx [\exists y (y \prec xx) \rightarrow \exists z \Sigma(z, xx)]$

where $\Sigma(z, xx)$ is your favorite formulation of the claim that z is a mereological sum or fusion of the xs. For instance:

$\forall w (z \sqcap w \leftrightarrow \exists x (x \prec xx \wedge x \sqcap w))$,

---

[5] You might notice that the argument requires a semantic assumption: that for any formula open in one variable that is uniquely satisfied, we can successfully stipulate a referring term "D" that designates the satisfiers. We might compare the resulting paradox with the following non-plural, Grelling–Nelson paradox: "non-self-describing" describes itself iff it doesn't. Perhaps a successful solution to the semantic paradox would provide a reason to deny the semantic premise in this formulation of our metaphysics paradox. We leave that open.

[6] Notice that these examples apply differently to a plurality. The xs are concrete just in case each of the xs is concrete. The xs are mutually spatiotemporally unrelated just in case any two of the xs are spatiotemporally unrelated. On the other hand, acting together does not admit of any such easy analysis in terms of individuals.

(cf. Varzi 2009, P.12$_\xi$), where ⊓ is the overlap predicate.[7] It won't do to package up the xs just as their fusion, for different pluralities will have the same package, which will violate PACK: for instance, the plurality a and $b + c$ ("$b + c$" denotes the fusion of b and c) and the plurality $a+b$ and c have the same fusion. We need something a little less direct.

Let $E(x,y)$ say that x is a proposition that *de re* claims of y that y exists. Now we define $P(x,yy)$ to claim that x is a fusion of propositions making *de re* existential claims about individual ys, at least one such proposition for each of the ys. Namely $P(x,yy)$ says:

$$\exists zz[\Sigma(x,zz) \wedge \forall u(u \prec zz \rightarrow \exists v(E(u,v) \wedge v \prec yy))$$
$$\wedge \forall v(v \prec yy \rightarrow \exists u(E(u,v) \wedge u \prec zz))].$$

For instance, if the ys are Bill and Ted, and x is the fusion of the proposition that Bill exists with the proposition that Ted exists, then $P(x,yy)$.

An advantage of the present approach is that it only requires singular *de re* subjects,[8] not the plural ones in the previous construction.

Once again the truth of NONPACK is obvious: not everything is a fusion of propositions. What about PACK and UNIQ? Well, for any yys, there will be a plurality of those zs that are propositions *de re* claiming of individual ys that they exist. And by SUM, there will be a fusion f of those zs. This f packages the ys, and so we get PACK.

Moreover, it is very plausible that, as UNIQ says, if f packages the y, then a singular existential proposition is a part of f if and only if it is a singular existential proposition claiming the existence of one of the ys. For while singular existential propositions may have structure, plausibly they lack *mereological* structure. The most plausible theory where singular propositions would have classical mereological structure is one where the proposition that attributes property Q to x is the fusion of x and Q. But that theory must be false, because if Q and R are distinct properties, then the proposition that attributes Q to R differs from the proposition that attributes R to Q, while

---

[7] Plural quantification is not essential to this version of the paradox. We could instead formulate the SUM axiom as a schema: $\exists x(F(x)) \rightarrow \exists z \Sigma_F(z)$, for any formula $F(x)$ open only in x where $\Sigma_F(z)$ says that z is the fusion of all satisfiers of $F(x)$—e.g. formulated as, $\forall w(z \sqcap w \leftrightarrow \exists x(F(x) \wedge x \sqcap w))$.

[8] For discussions of this approach, see Hudson (2006) and Spencer (2006).

the two corresponding fusions will be identical. (Of course, there are plausible theories on which singular propositions have non-mereological structure. See, for example, Rasmussen (2014: Ch. 4). And for a radically non-classical mereological account, see Tillman and Fowler (2011).)

And if singular propositions lack mereological structure, then the only way a singular existential proposition could be a part of a fusion of singular existential propositions would be by being one of these propositions. This claim shows that if z is one of the xs, then some singular existential proposition claiming the existence of z is a part of f. But then that proposition will also affirm the existence of one of the ys. And so every one of the xs is one of the ys. And the converse goes the same way. Thus, the xs are the ys, which is what UNIQ needs.

As in the previous method, if one doesn't like singular existential propositions here, one can have $E(x, y)$ say that x attributes concreteness to y, or that x attributes some property or other to y, and so on.

This version of the paradox basically follows Lewis's construction of set theory out of a singleton function and unrestricted fusion (Lewis 1991). Lewis escapes the Russell paradox by insisting that some objects (the proper classes) do not have a singleton. The point of our version is to note that a non-Lewisian *de re* singular proposition appears to provide a singleton for any object. Lewis is in the unwelcome position of having to deny that for every object there is a *de re* structured (in his terminology—see Lewis 1986, p. 57) proposition about it. It is very odd to suppose some objects are subjects of *de re* propositions and others are not.

Still, you might wonder if there is a way to avoid the paradox by pursuing a mereological theory of propositions, for mereological theories typically lead a denial of UNIQ.[9] We will consider one such theory discussed by Hudson (2006). His solution, when adapted to our setting, says that some singular existential propositions are fusions of other singular propositions.[10] Specifically, if c is a fusion of a and b, then the proposition ⟨c exists⟩ is a fusion of ⟨a exists⟩ and ⟨b exists⟩. This leads to the denial of UNIQ. Hence, we can escape

---

[9] For example, if x is the sum of a and b, then x is also identical to the sum of x, a and b.

[10] We are grateful to an anonymous reader for the adaptation.

the above formulation of the paradox if we accept this mereological theory of propositions.

Unfortunately, we still aren't home free, for we can tweak the packaging. Instead of packaging the ys into a fusion of singular existential propositions, one for each of the ys, we may instead package the ys into a fusion of negations of singular existential propositions, one for each of the ys. Alternatively, we may package the ys into a fusion of propositions, each of which predicates a non-compositional predicate like simplicity of one of the ys.[11] On either packaging, UNIQ is plausible, even granting Hudson's mereological theory. So, these packages land us back in paradox. Perhaps there is a way to further develop Hudson's theory so that we can escape paradox even on the above packagings. But if so, it's far from obvious what that is. We conclude, then, that these versions of the paradox pose an unsolved challenge for mereological theories of propositions.

3.3. Unrestricted conjunction or disjunction

Suppose that any plurality of propositions has a proposition that is a conjunction of the propositions in the plurality. (If there is only one proposition in the plurality, we stipulate that item trivially counts as a conjunction of the propositions in the plurality.) Then instead of doing packaging with fusions of singular *de re* propositions as in the previous section, we can do it with conjunctions (or disjunctions, respectively) of such propositions. In fact, we can even do this with the same definition of $P(x, zz)$ as long as we reinterpret $\Sigma(x, zz)$ to say that x is a conjunction (respectively, disjunction) of the zs. UNIQ will then require the very plausible claim that if x is a conjunction (disjunction) of ys that are singular *de re* propositions of the right type (say, existential), then all the singular *de re* propositions that are conjuncts of x are among the ys.

---

[11] If P is a compositional predicate, i.e. one such that the fusion of the ys satisfies P if and only if each of the ys satisfies P, then someone who finds Hudson's line of thought plausible may think that $\langle P(c) \rangle$ is a fusion of $\langle P(a) \rangle$ and $\langle P(b) \rangle$ when c is a fusion of a and b.

4. WAYS OUT

We now have several families of routes to paradox. All require plural comprehension or unrestricted fusion, and the existence of propositions. The route of Section 3.1 requires a further controversial condition that for any plurality, there is a proposition (existential or predicative) precisely about that plurality. The route of 3.2, instead, requires unrestricted fusions even of abstract objects, and requires that singular or negative propositions not be mereologically composed. The route of 3.3 requires unrestricted conjunctions or disjunctions.

4.1. No plural quantification

A way to cut most of the problems off at the source is to deny plural comprehension (and also deny SUM-SCHEMA).[12] But unless we want to forego plural quantification entirely, we will want a replacement. In the case of set theory, the replacement for comprehension was a number of axioms most notably including separation: the claim that for any set a and formula $F(x)$, there is the set consisting of all the elements of a satisfying $F(x)$ (unlike comprehension, this doesn't allow a set to be built from scratch). We could likewise have the schema:

PL-SEP. $\forall yy \exists x(x \prec yy \wedge F(x)) \rightarrow \exists xx \forall y[y \prec xx \leftrightarrow (y \prec yy \wedge F(y))]$.

But then we couldn't correctly affirm that the propositions exist, whether propositions are understood as concrete or abstract. For suppose there is a plurality of propositions. Then we can adapt our arguments to use PL-SEP in place of PL-COMP as long as our Russell formula is replaced with $x \prec pp \wedge x \notin x$, where the ps are the propositions. So this way out has a cost: although one could still hold on to the claim that there is a proposition, i.e. $\exists x(\text{Prop}(x))$, one could no longer hold that there are *the* propositions, i.e. $\exists xx(\forall y(y \prec xx \leftrightarrow \text{Prop}(y)))$. This is not very plausible. After all, "The propositions are either spatiotemporally unrelated or spatiotempo-

---

[12] This is the way out Spencer (2012) recommends in response to his Cantorian "plurals" paradox.

rally related" seems to express a truth and to have as its subject a plurality.

Moreover, PL-SEP is nowhere near a sufficient replacement for PL-COMP. Just as in Zermelo-Fraenkel set theory other axioms had to be added beyond separation to make up for the lack of comprehension, here too other axioms will be needed. After all, by itself, PL-SEP is compatible with there not being any pluralities at all. We might, for instance, want to have axioms like:

PL-SING. $\forall x \exists yy \forall z(z \prec zz \leftrightarrow z = x)$
PL-UNION. $\forall xx \forall yy \exists zz(u \prec zz \leftrightarrow (u \prec xx \vee u \prec yy))$.

Together, these imply that for any finite sequence of objects $a_1, a_2, \ldots, a_n$, there is a plurality of $a_1, a_2, \ldots$ and a_n. The concern with this approach is that one is recreating something that is very much like set theory over again, thereby stripping plural quantification of its principal advantage over non-plural set-theoretic quantification. Plus, we still can't affirm that the propositions exist, which is a problem. So, giving up PL-COMP leads to other challenges.

4.2. No propositions

A metaphysically radical way out is to deny that there are any propositions at all (whether concrete or abstract), i.e. to deny $\exists x(\text{Prop}(x))$. This leads to difficulties in accounting for content and the objects of propositional attitudes, and is indeed radical. There are, of course, various ways to try to mitigate the harshness of this move, such as by motivating fictionalism about propositions (see Balaguer 1998 and 2010) or finding an appropriate nominalist or conceptualist replacement (see, for example, Pruss 2011, pp. 274–5; cf. Alston 1986).

4.3. No infinite propositions and no unrestricted fusions

One could try for a more finely-grained response to the methods. A common requirement of Sections 3.1 and 3.3 is the existence of certain "infinite propositions", whether infinite because they have an infinite plurality *de rebus* as their subject or because they are infinite conjunctions (or disjunctions). By denying the existence of such infinite propositions, one undercuts all the paradoxes except those based on unrestricted fusion. For this strategy not to be *ad hoc*, it seems we should simply deny all infinite propositions.

We can also get out of the fusion-based method (3.2) by noting that the hypothesis of unrestricted fusions is perhaps the most controversial of our technical assumptions, and there are independent intuitive reasons to deny that assumption. For instance, one might think that everything is either abstract or concrete but not both, and that abstract things do not have concrete parts and concrete things do not have abstract parts. If one thinks this, then there won't be a fusion of an abstract and a concrete object. Or one might think that mereological concepts of overlap depend on spatial relationships, in which case abstract objects won't have fusions—and it is precisely abstract objects that we need to exclude from fusions.

The weak part of this combination approach is that there in fact is good reason to think there could be infinite propositions. Our best guide to the existence of a proposition of a certain sort is the possibility of a sentence that would express that proposition. But the finite sentence, "The propositions (or, the actually existing propositions) are mutually spatiotemporally unrelated" seems to be an English sentence with an infinite plurality *de rebus* as a subject, and it attributes spatiotemporal unrelatedness to that plurality. Thus it seems precisely to express a proposition of the sort this approach says to be nonexistent. Moreover, one could perhaps have beings whose method of linguistic expression made infinite conjunctions possible. For instance, perhaps, they could just utter an infinite English sentence in a finite amount of time as a supertask. Or perhaps one could have a being that could utter each of infinitely many conjuncts at once, with that being understood to be a conjunction of them, with each conjunct being uttered at a different range of frequencies (this will work better with electromagnetic than sound waves). So cutting out infinite propositions is not cheap.

And even an *ad hoc* piecemeal approach, which allows there to be some infinite propositions but denies that for all xs there is a proposition *de rebus* about the xs, and which allows there to be some infinite conjunctions but denies that all infinite pluralities have a conjunction, runs into the difficulty that we seem to be able to form sentences that seem to express precisely the forbidden propositions.

As we saw in Section 3.1, for any formula $F(x)$ open only in x that has something satisfying it and that can be expressed in English, we can form an English sentence that is *de rebus* about the ys that satisfy $F(x)$. We do this by first introducing a context where such ys are contextually relevant, say by saying "There exist unique ys such that something is one of the ys if and only if it satisfies $F(x)$", and then using a plural pronoun as the subject of a sentence, say "They exist", where the context makes it clear that the pronoun refers to such ys.

4.4. Assessment

The above approaches appear to exhaust the viable options. If plural comprehension is rejected, we have the way out of Section 4.1. If we accept plural comprehension, then either we must deny that there are propositions (4.2) or deny more specifically that there are the special kinds of propositions needed by the two routes to paradox that use infinite propositions (3.1 and 3.3).

The two most principled ways out appear to be to deny plural comprehension (4.1) or to deny that there are any propositions at all (4.2). The former is the less metaphysically radical approach, especially if we introduce plural separation and other axioms mirroring those of set theory, but it does lose us some of the advantages of using plural quantification instead of sets or classes. The other approaches each require denying the existence of some propositions that seem to be expressed by contentful English sentences, while accepting that there are such things as propositions. The results in any case are perplexing and instructive.[13]

Baylor University
Azusa Pacific University

---

[13] Our arguments can be viewed as a development of Russell's own "propositions" paradox given at the end of his *Principles of Mathematics*. Russell (1913, p. 527) confesses to have no solution—not even in terms of his theory of types. He writes, "What the complete solution of the difficulty may be, I have not succeeded in discovering; but as it affects the very foundations of reasoning, I earnestly commend the study of it to the attention of all students of logic." The situation remains. The authors are grateful to Dean Zimmerman for interesting discussions and to an anonymous referee for helpful suggestions that have significantly improved this paper.

APPENDIX: PROOF OF PACK-COMP FROM PL-COMP, PACK, AND UNIQ

The following proof schema, valid for any formula $F(x)$ open only in x, is also intuitionistically valid.

1		$\exists x F(x)$			
2		$\exists x F(x) \to \exists xx \forall y (y \prec xx \leftrightarrow F(y))$			PL-COMP
3		$\exists xx \forall y (y \prec xx \leftrightarrow F(y))$			$\to$-elim, 1, 2
4	aa	$\forall y (y \prec aa \leftrightarrow F(y))$			
5		$\forall xx \exists u P(u, xx)$			PACK
6		$\exists u (P(u, aa))$			$\forall$-elim, 5
7	b	$P(b, aa)$			
8		c	$c \lhd b$		
9			$c \prec aa \leftrightarrow F(c)$		$\forall$-elim, 4
10			$\exists zz (P(b, zz) \land c \prec zz)$		def, 8
11			dd	$P(b, dd) \land c \prec dd$	
12				$P(b, dd)$	$\land$-elim, 11
13				$\forall u \forall xx \forall yy ((P(u, xx) \land P(u, yy)) \to xx = yy)$	UNIQ
14				$(P(b, aa) \land P(b, dd)) \to aa = dd$	$\forall$-elim, 13
15				$P(b, aa) \land P(b, dd)$	$\land$-intro, 7, 12
16				$aa = dd$	$\to$-elim, 14, 15
17				$\forall z (z \prec aa \leftrightarrow z \prec dd)$	def, 16
18				$c \prec aa \leftrightarrow c \prec dd$	$\forall$-elim, 17
19				$c \prec dd$	$\land$-elim, 11
20				$c \prec aa$	$\leftrightarrow$-elim, 18, 19
21				$F(c)$	$\leftrightarrow$-elim, 9, 20
22			$F(c)$		$\exists$-elim, 10, 11–21
23			$F(c)$		
24			$c \prec aa$		$\leftrightarrow$-elim, 9, 23
25			$P(b, aa) \land c \prec aa$		$\land$-intro, 7, 24
26			$\exists zz (P(b, zz) \land c \prec zz)$		$\exists$-intro, 25
27			$c \lhd b$		def, 26
28			$c \lhd b \leftrightarrow F(c)$		$\leftrightarrow$-intro, 8–22, 23–27
29		$\forall x (x \lhd b \leftrightarrow F(x))$			$\forall$-intro, 8–28
30		$\exists z \forall x (x \lhd z \leftrightarrow F(x))$			$\exists$-intro, 29
31		$\exists z \forall x (x \lhd z \leftrightarrow F(x))$			$\exists$-elim, 6, 7–30
32		$\exists z \forall x (x \lhd z \leftrightarrow F(x))$			$\exists$-elim, 3, 4–31
33	$\exists x F(x) \to \exists z \forall x (x \lhd z \leftrightarrow F(x))$				$\to$-intro, 1, 2–32

REFERENCES

Alston, William (1986). 'Does God Have Beliefs?' *Religious Studies* 22: 287–306.
Balaguer, Marc (1998). 'Attitudes without Propositions'. *Philosophy and Phenomenological Research* 58 (4): 805–26.
Balaguer, Marc (2010). 'Fictionalism, Mathematical Facts and Logical Modal Facts' in Hans Burkhardt (ed.), *Fictions and Models* (Germany: Philosophia Verlag), 149–89.
Grim, Patrick (1991). *The Incomplete Universe: Totality, Knowledge, and Truth.* Cambridge, MA: MIT Press.
Grim, Patrick, and Alvin Plantinga (1993). 'Truth, Omniscience, and Cantorian Arguments'. *Philosophical Studies* 71: 267–306.
Hudson, Hud (2006). 'Confining Composition'. *Journal of Philosophy* 103: 631–51.
Lewis, David (1986). *On the Plurality of Worlds.* Cambridge: Blackwell.
Lewis, David (1991). *Parts of Classes.* Cambridge: Blackwell.
McGee, Vann, and Augustin Rayo (2000). 'A Puzzle about De Rebus Beliefs'. *Analysis* 60: 297–9.
Pruss, Alexander (2011). *Actuality, Possibility, and Worlds.* New York: The Continuum International Publishing Group.
Rasmussen, Joshua (2014). *Defending the Correspondence Theory of Truth.* Cambridge: Cambridge University Press.
Rosen, Gideon (1995). 'Armstrong on Classes as States of Affairs'. *Australasian Journal of Philosophy* 73: 613–25.
Russell, Bertrand (1903). *Principles of Mathematics.* Cambridge: Cambridge University Press.
Spencer, Joshua (2006). 'Two Mereological Arguments against the Possibility of an Omniscient Being'. *Philo* 9: 62–72.
Spencer, Joshua (2012). 'All Things Must Pass Away' in Karen Bennett and Dean Zimmerman (eds), *Oxford Studies in Metaphysics 7.* New York: Oxford University Press.
Tillman, Chris, and Gregory Fowler (2011). 'Propositions and Parthood: The Universe and Anti-Symmetry'. *Australasian Journal of Philosophy* 90: 525–39.
Varzi, Achille (2009). 'Mereology'. *Stanford Encyclopedia of Philosophy.* <http://plato.stanford.edu>.

METHODOLOGICAL ISSUES, OLD AND NEW

5. The unreasonable effectiveness of abstract metaphysics

Daniel Nolan

One common style of objection to a metaphysical theory is to claim that even if the metaphysical posits of that theory were correct, they would not (and perhaps could not) explain the phenomena they were posited to explain, or that they would otherwise be useless for theoretical purposes. One early example of this sort of objection, I will argue, can be found in some of Aristotle's objections to the theory of Forms. There Aristotle seems to be objecting that a theory of Forms would be useless, or at least unexplanatory in an important way. I think this aspect of Aristotle's objections generalizes: the same problems seem to arise for any theory that is realist about general properties and relations. This is somewhat ironic, since Aristotle himself seems to be a realist about universals.

The same kind of worry as the one I will diagnose has a contemporary incarnation, though as far as I can tell this contemporary cousin has no direct historical link to Aristotle's objections. The contemporary problem has been more widely discussed in the literature in philosophy of mathematics than the mainstream metaphysics literature: it is one aspect of the discussion about the so-called "Unreasonable Effectiveness of Mathematics". I think the parallel is that in both cases it is hard to see how abstract objects, whether numbers and sets or Forms and universals, can help with our theorizing about concrete, particular, sensible objects. And I will claim that the answers available to this challenge in both the mathematics case and the case of general properties and relations will have important similarities.

A terminological note: I will refer to general properties and relations collectively as "universals" in this paper. ("General" properties and relations as opposed to particular property-or-relation instances, which I will call "tropes".) I will use the expression "Aristotelian universals" when I wish to talk specifically of universals as Aristotle conceives of them.

This paper has three aims. One is to argue that some of Aristotle's arguments against Plato's Forms have affinities with some contemporary concerns about abstract objects. The second is to argue that concerns developed in the philosophy of mathematics about Platonist theories of mathematical objects have clear application to theories of abstract objects more generally, particularly contemporary theories of universals. (Fortunately, I think there are good replies to these concerns in both cases.) The third aim is a more historical one, to offer an evaluation of the arguments of Aristotle's that the paper begins with. The next section discusses some objections by Aristotle to Plato's theory, and the penultimate section of the paper will return to Plato and Aristotle, with a discussion of whether Aristotle's objections are indeed worries for the theory of the Forms, and if so are they any less of a concern for Aristotle's own theory.

1. PUZZLING ARISTOTELIAN ARGUMENTS AGAINST PLATO'S THEORY OF FORMS

Aristotle offers a number of arguments against the "system of Plato", particularly Plato's theory of Ideas of Forms, in *Metaphysics* A 987a–988a, 990b–992a, and some essentially repeated in *Metaphysics* M as well (1078b–1080a, and see also 1086a–b). Some of Aristotle's arguments are puzzling because they seem to attack features of a theory of Forms that cannot be found in Plato's dialogues: a "Great and Small" as a first principle generating the numbers, for example (987b–988a). Some have seen these objections to otherwise undocumented features of the theory of Forms as a sign that Aristotle is attacking aspects of Plato's esoteric doctrines rather than the exoteric doctrines, or that he is attacking aspects of theories of early Academics such as Speusippus or Xenocrates rather than Plato's own doctrines.

Other arguments are puzzling, not for these reasons, but because they seem to apply equally well to Aristotle's own theory of universals as they do to Plato's theory of Forms.[1] It is in this class of

---

[1] Interestingly, Aristotle seems to admit as much about some of these worries in M (1086b), though it is unclear to me how much of his discussion he thinks "presents some difficulty both to those who hold the Ideal theory and to those who do not." (Tredennick 1933, p. 249).

arguments I will be interested: these arguments seem to be designed to show that Forms are not *explanatory* in the way they should be.

The first argument (990b) is presented obliquely—Aristotle seems more concerned here to make fun of the friends of the Forms than to make the argument clearly. Aristotle says:

> In the first place in their attempt to find the causes of things in our sensible world, they introduced an equal number of other entities—as though a man who wishes to count things should suppose that it would be impossible when they are few, and should attempt to count them when he has added to them. For the Forms are as many as, or not fewer than, the things in search of whose causes those thinkers were led to the Forms; because corresponding to each thing there is a [homonymous][2] entity apart from the substances (and in the case of non-substantial things there is a One over the Many), both in our everyday world and in the realm of eternal entities. (990b, 1933, p. 63)

We might wonder whether this objection does apply to the theory of Forms we find in Plato's dialogues. In particular, it is not immediately obvious that there are as many Forms as there are sensible entities—many entities may share the same Form, after all.[3] Provided there are many Forms postulated, though, it probably does not matter much whether there are as many as there are sensible entities. We might also worry about whether Plato saw the Forms as *causes*, but this seems more reasonable when we remember that Aristotle is using αἰτία (cause) to mean something close to what we mean by explanation: and it is surely true that Plato thought the theory of Forms helped explain the sensible world. Finally, we may wonder whether Plato would have agreed with Aristotle that the sensible world was full of substances, in Aristotle's sense: but this does not seem important to the objection, since the thrust of it seems

---

[2] Tredennick translates ὁμώνυμόν as "synonymous" rather than "homonymous", which is idiosyncratic.

[3] Aristotle did have some reasons to think that Plato was committed to the Forms being as many as the sensible entities, or at least "not less than" them. One interesting reason is that Aristotle holds that Plato is committed to "ideal numbers" as well as non-ideal mathematical objects: so there is a Form of One, a Form of Two, a Form of Three, and so on. We might still wonder about whether the cardinality of sensible entities is greater than the cardinality of the number series, but it should be clear why Aristotle would have thought that it has been demonstrated that there are not fewer Forms than sensibles once it has been demonstrated that there would be as many Forms as counting numbers.

to be a challenge for explaining the entities in the sensible world, whether or not they are Aristotelian substances.

These reservations aside, Aristotle is pointing out something initially odd about the theory of Forms. When trying to explain the world around us, Plato postulates another realm of entities and tells us a lot about those other entities. But if anything this might seem to make the overall explanatory project *more* difficult. Now we do not just need a theory of the Forms and explanations of the Forms, but we still have our initial task facing us as well: we have all the explanatory burden we started with, plus a new realm which must also be explained. Interpreted this way, it looks like Aristotle is suggesting that the theory of Forms moves us further away from the goal of our theorizing, rather than closer.

If this is the way to understand Aristotle's complaint, then it would seem to apply to any theory that postulates general properties and relations as well as particular objects. We start with a demand for a theory of shaped and coloured things, just societies, moving particles, or whatever: and then if we go on to in addition postulate shapes and colours, justice, movement, and a panoply of other properties and relations, we may seem to be only multiplying our explanatory tasks rather than resolving the ones we began with. (It is as if, as Aristotle says, we are set to count one group of things, and we introduce another group with as many or more objects in them and then have to count both.) Aristotle himself seems to postulate universals (καθολου), so he also faces this sort of objection: how does postulating these things help us in the explanation of the sensible things we started with, and why does it not just make our explanatory predicament worse?

The second argument of Aristotle's I want to discuss is also one which, I will claim, is based on the complaint that Forms do not help to explain the sensible world, though it is put in terms of arguing that Forms do not "contribute" to sensible things:

Above all we might examine the question what on [E]arth the Forms contribute to sensible things, whether eternal or subject to generation or decay; for they are not the cause of any motion or change in them [the sensible things]. Again, they are no help towards the *knowledge* of other things (for they are not the substance of things, otherwise they would be *in* things), nor to their *existence*, since they are not present in the things which partake of them. If they were, it might perhaps seem that they are causes, in the sense in which the admixture of white causes a thing to be white; but... it is easy to adduce plenty of impossibilities against such a view.

Again, other things are not in any accepted sense *derived* from the Forms. To say that the Forms are patterns, and that other things participate in them, is to use empty phrases and poetical metaphors...[4]

Further, it would seem impossible that the substance of the thing and the thing of which it is the substance exist in separation; hence how can the Ideas, if they are the substances of things, exist in separation from them? It is stated in the *Phaedo* that the Forms are the causes both of existence and of generation. Yet, assuming that the Forms exist, still the things which participate in them are not generated unless there is something to impart motion; while many other things *are* generated (e.g. house, ring) of which we hold there are no Forms. Thus it is clearly possible that all other things may both exist and be generated for the same causes as the things just mentioned. (991a–991b, Tredennick, pp. 70–1)

Aristotle concludes with a complaint that the Platonists have ignored the crucial question of how the Forms cause sensible things: he uses the first-person plural "we" in directing this charge, but commentators agree that he talks about what "we" say because, here at least, he is talking as one of the Platonists/Academics, albeit one criticizing their views:[5]

In general, Wisdom is concerned with the cause of [sensible][6] things, we have ignored this question (for we have no account to give of the cause from which change arises), and in the belief that we are accounting for their substance we assert the existence of other substances; but as to *how* the latter are substances of the former, our explanation is worthless—for

---

[4] Here Aristotle lodges some objections to theories that take the connection between particulars and Forms to be a matter of resemblance or copying, reminiscent of objections to this theory discussed by Plato in the *Parmenides* 132c–133a. Aristotle's own text here can be read as suggesting that Plato does not literally take the connection to be a matter of copying or resemblance (presumably this is why Aristotle says it is merely metaphorical). But in any case the aspect of Aristotle's objection I am concerned with does not require the defender of Forms to maintain anything like a copying or resemblance theory of participation.

[5] In one version of *Metaphysics* A, the version Alexander of Aphrodisias used, Aristotle even says "We say in the *Phaedo*"! (Alexander 1989, p. 115)

[6] Tredennick translates Aristotle here as talking of "visible things" rather than sensible ones: but φανερὸν here might also be better translated as "manifest things", which would produce an aphorism that is less objectionable. (Why would wisdom be any less concerned with things that cannot be *seen*?) I have rendered it "sensible" here, since it is clear from context that Aristotle has in mind the sensible things, particularly substances, about which he has been complaining earlier that the theorists of the Forms do not explain. This is a slightly less literal rendering of the word than either "visible" or "manifest" would be, however.

"participation", as we have said before, means nothing. And as for that which we can see to be the cause in the sciences, and through which all mind and nature works—this cause which we hold to be one of the first principles—the Forms have not the slightest bearing on it either. (992a, Tredennick pp. 75–7)[7]

Again, when reading the four connected passages above, we might be concerned about whether Aristotle correctly characterizes Plato's view of Forms, or at least the view of Forms expressed in his dialogues. Aristotle, here and elsewhere, seems to claim that defenders of Forms reject Forms for artifacts: but this is hard to square with the discussion of Forms of beds and tables in *Republic* 10, for example. Aristotle rejects the claim that ordinary things participate in Forms by being copies of those Forms or similar to those Forms, and while some have interpreted Plato as maintaining that they do, I am inclined to think that at least by the *Parmenides* and the *Sophist* Plato does not hold that view of participation. In any case if Plato did insist on that as part of the theory of Forms that theory faces serious problems, so I am happy to suppose for these purposes that Aristotle is right that participation is not a matter of similarity or copying.

As before, these details do not seem to me crucial to one of the main lines of argument in this passage. The main line of argument is that Forms would not help to explain the sensible objects that they are supposedly related to. Contra Plato, Aristotle thinks that they could not be causes or explanations of motion or generation; of the existence of sensibles, or even of our knowledge of the sensibles. Finally, Aristotle thinks we cannot allow that sensibles depend on the Forms, or are derivative from them. Aristotle seems to be suggesting that Forms cannot explain sensible particulars in any way.

I take the argument about multiplying entities to be explained as a subsidiary way of making this point, or making it vivid: presumably the only way that postulating new entities could be an advance in

---

[7] In presenting this part of 992a as part of the argument of 991a–b, I am making the disputable interpretive assumption that in the second quotation Aristotle has returned to general criticisms of theories of Forms, rather than just criticism of those who make the additional claim that Forms are all numbers. Alexander reads Aristotle this way as well (1989, 120.20–1).

our explanatory project is if the theory produced by this postulation did so well in explaining the original explanandum that it was worth the burden of taking on the challenge of explaining the new entities. Otherwise introducing new things that themselves require some explanation is going backwards.

In one respect the question "what do Forms contribute to sensible things?" is a strange question for Aristotle to be asking. One of the four "causes" Aristotle distinguishes is *formal* causation, and indeed he says elsewhere in the *Metaphysics* (Δ, 1013A) that the cause in this sense is the "form or pattern" (εἶδος καὶ τὸ παράδειγμα) of a thing (or one of the genera of these, or parts of these). Presumably Aristotle is using "form" here in a less technical sense, or at least a different technical sense, than when he is discussing Plato's views. Still, one might think it would have occurred to Aristotle that his Academic opponent might say that Forms explain sensibles in *the way that forms do*, and if Aristotle were prepared to concede this much, it seems he would already have his answer to the question of "what the Forms contribute to the sensible things": on this line of response, they are the formal causes of those things.

One thing that is very plausibly happening is that Aristotle thinks Forms cannot be explanations in all the ways he thinks Plato wants them to be (the overall point of his discussion in *Metaphysics* A is that previous thinkers have gone astray in not properly understanding the four causes). Another thing that might be going on is that Aristotle thinks that Forms, conceived of as Plato conceives of them, fail to have the features that would make them fit to be formal causes, in Aristotle's sense. I suspect that what we have in *Metaphysics* A is a list of objections that Aristotle developed in more detail elsewhere (some other objections to Plato's theory of Forms briefly offered in *Metaphysics* A, for example, do seem to have been developed further in his *On The Ideas*, at least if we are to trust Alexander of Aphrodisias (e.g. 79.4 and 98.23–5 in Alexander 1989)), and without the further detail it is sometimes hard to tell exactly what Aristotle had in mind. Nevertheless, let us examine the two suggestions about what is going on here in turn.

If Aristotle wanted to complain that Plato did not clearly distinguish Aristotle's four causes, that seems a fair complaint. And it is plausible that Plato did not do much to argue, in the *Phaedo* at least, that the Forms are efficient causes of generation and change. Aristotle also seems to be attributing the view to Plato that the Forms are efficient causes: but while Plato in the *Phaedo* can be read as saying the Forms are causes of everything, including generation (*Phaedo* 100), it is not at all clear to me that this is a claim about efficient causation: just as Plato in the *Sophist* seems to be saying that moving things move in virtue of participation in the Form of Motion, it is plausible that Plato in the *Phaedo* is only claiming that Motion is the formal cause of motion. (Aristotle may well reject the claim that there is a general formal cause of motion, but that plays no part in his argument here.) Perhaps Aristotle is reading Plato as claiming that Forms are the *only* causes (as opposed to e.g. the most important Form of cause that was the object of Socrates's search). So let us grant to Aristotle (for the sake of the argument at least) that Plato's Forms are not, in general, good candidates to be material, efficient or final causes of material things. This does not yet capture the full extent of Aristotle's complaint, it seems to me.[8]

Aristotle also seems to think that Platonic Forms would be unfit to contribute to a thing's existence in any way (and would not merely be unfit as a efficient cause of generation of a thing, for example). My conjecture is that Aristotle thinks they are unfit to be formal causes because they are not "in" the objects. If the primary formal cause of a thing is its substance, for example, and if for Aristotle substances must be "in" objects, then if Aristotle is right that Platonic Forms would not be "in" their objects, they cannot serve as the primary formal causes of entities. That Aristotle thinks that substances must be "in" their objects is shown by his assertion that the two cannot be "separated" (Tredennick p. 69): he uses "in" and "separated" as antonyms here.[9]

---

[8] The next page or so contains particularly controversial interpretive claims about Aristotle's views. The connections between form, substance, essence, universals, particulars and sensibles are among the most controversial when interpreting Aristotle's metaphysical doctrines.

[9] See also *Metaphysics* M 1086b, where Aristotle seems to be saying that it is separation in particular (i.e. not being "in") that is the source of some troubles for Plato's theory of Forms. Aristotle seeing the issue of separation dividing him from Plato appears in a number of places in Aristotle's work: see Fine (1984) for a thorough discussion.

That substances are the ultimate formal causes for Aristotle is more conjectural.[10] Aristotle characterizes formal causes differently in different places: the "form or pattern; that is, the essential formula and the classes that contain it" (*Metaphysics* Δ 1013a), the "form or characteristics of the type, conformity to which brings it within the definition of the thing we say it is" (*Physics* B 194b), the "essential nature of the thing in question" (*Physics* B 198a).[11] This last characterization suggests that the primary formal cause is the essence (though broader genuses that the essence belong to are clearly formal causes as well, as can be seen in the first characterization, they seem to be so derivatively). It is a further interpretive leap to claim that essences of substances are the substances themselves, though Aristotle's remarks in *Metaphysics* Z 1028b make it hard to deny that he holds that the substance is at least sometimes the essence.

Even if we allow that the primary or most fundamental formal cause of substances is the substance (which is presumably specified by means of the real definition of the substance), then even if we also grant that Platonic Forms cannot be substances, we still have not got an argument that Forms cannot be formal causes: since even if substances are the primary or ultimate formal causes, Aristotle clearly allows that other entities can be formal causes too, such as the "classes" which contain the essential formula. Aristotle's universals seem to fit in here: they are not substances (see *Metaphysics* Z 1038b–1039b), yet things like "number in general" can be formal causes (*Metaphysics* Δ 1013a), which certainly suggests universals can be formal causes even by Aristotle's lights.[12] Aristotle does seem to think that universals are "in" those entities which fall under them, for what it is worth, but without an argument why this must be so we do not have an argument that the Forms' not being "in" the

---

[10] Frank Lewis is one author who defends the view that Aristotle identified the forms of objects with their substances (Lewis (1991), especially Ch. 6). If that is right, that at least strongly suggests that substances are the ultimate formal causes: it would be at least strange if something other than forms were ultimate formal causes.

[11] Aristotle seems to use "form" in a very wide variety of ways across his writings: see Studtmann (2008) for a range of examples and an interesting suggestion about how they might be unified.

[12] Fine (1993) claims Aristotle identifies his forms with Aristotelian universals (p. 251, n. 33). This goes beyond what I am comfortable claiming: I claim only that Aristotle's universals are candidates to be identified with Aristotle's forms. and in any case Aristotelian universals are supposed to be able to be formal explanations.

sensibles rules them out from playing the formal causal role that universals do.

Again, if I may conjecture, my guess is that Aristotle thinks that the universals are formal causes only derivatively—they can only be formal causes by being downstream of the primary formal causes which are "in" substances. Some evidence for this is the way he apparently contrasts his own view with one according to which universals are "in the truest sense a cause and a principle" (*Metaphysics* Z 1038b, Tredennick p. 377): if universals are not "in the truest sense" a cause maybe they are only a cause secondarily or derivatively. Since Platonic Forms are not downstream of sensible substances in the right sort of way, Aristotle might think that they are unfit to be formal causes even derivatively. He does not present such an argument in *Metaphysics* A (or elsewhere in his surviving works, so far as I know), but such an argument, together with an argument that non-substances can only be formal causes of substances derivatively, would rule Platonic Forms out as candidates to be formal causes. Presumably, of course, there must be *some* entities Aristotle is happy to call "forms" which can be formal causes, in light of *Metaphysics* Δ 1013a and *Physics* B 194b.[13]

As far as Aristotle exegesis goes, it may be important to point out these differences in what sorts of objects Aristotle is willing to allow to be causes and what sorts cannot be. But beyond the goal of understanding Aristotle, we might think that Aristotle is pointing to general kinds of problem here, which both he and the Platonist should try to find satisfactory answers to. One problem is what explanatory role can be played by Forms, or Aristotelian universals, or indeed anything that is supposed to play the role of general properties and relations. We should not rest content, either, with the mere postulation of a type of explanation, "formal explanation", which is such that by definition Forms or universals explain in that

---

[13] Lewis (1991) offers an intricate alternative to this picture, whereby, inter alia, forms are universals and substances, but are not the individual substances, and has an alternative diagnosis of Aristotle's objection here against Plato's theory of Forms. Despite the differences, Lewis's interpretation of Aristotle fits well with the main point I want to make, that Aristotle is presenting challenges that are not only objections against Plato's theory, but which require a response from Aristotle's own view. If Lewis is right, this is a response that Aristotle develops in later books of the *Metaphysics*.

way: we would want some assurance that these explanations are genuine ones.

In fact, there seem to be two connected challenges we can draw from Aristotle's objections. The one made most explicitly is that the Forms do not explain sensible particulars. But only slightly more implicit is the charge that Forms are useless for good theorizing. Aristotle may not have distinguished the two since he seems, in the *Metaphysics* at least, to take the aim of theorizing to be supplying causes/explanations (*Metaphysics* A 992a). The second challenge is more serious, at least in principle: if Forms did not explain, that still leaves open that they might perform some other useful theoretical function, but if they are altogether useless for good theorizing, the case for rejecting them is strong.

I will return to the issue of what Plato and Aristotle can usefully say to defend the explanatoriness and usefulness of Forms or Aristotelian universals, respectively. Before doing so, though, I want to connect these ancient problems with a contemporary problem. Platonists about mathematical objects, in the contemporary sense, believe in the literal existence of abstract mathematical objects like sets, numbers, functions, groups and the rest. They face a challenge to explain why it is that postulating all of these abstract entities helps us in our theorizing about the non-mathematical world, in particular the aspects of the world studied by the natural sciences. In looking for the utility of contemporary postulation of abstract objects, we can look to the debate in philosophy of mathematics to turn up some useful options in helping us to solve the ancient problem. And we can see that at some level of generality the ancient problem is a problem for contemporaries who postulate abstract objects.

2. THE UNREASONABLE EFFECTIVENESS OF PLATONIC MATHEMATICS

This way of understanding Aristotle's objection has important similarities to a puzzle about mathematics raised by Eugene Wigner (Wigner 1960). Let me present a version in my own words. Suppose you were primarily interested in studying the behaviour of physical objects: moving bodies, or electric fields, or water in a pipe, or for that matter populations of animals, growth of wheat, or shopping patterns during the year. It turns out that an amazingly good way to do this is to engage in mathematics, including employing mathematical techniques which were often developed with no thought to the application at hand. How could this change of subject to numbers, functions, equations and the rest help us with wheat growth or predicting which pipes full of water burst?

I should note that this is not the only puzzle raised in Wigner's paper and subsequent discussion: Wigner seems more concerned with the puzzle of how mathematics could have turned out to be *so* useful, in the many ways that it has, for the natural sciences, along with other puzzles about how the practices of the natural sciences have been so successful. Nevertheless, the puzzle of how shifting to an apparently very different subject matter can help *at all* is presumably prior to the question of how it can help *so much*.

This puzzle is a challenge to be addressed by various philosophies of mathematics: those who reject the truth of mathematics are sometimes challenged to explain how it could be so useful if it were not true. But I agree with Mark Colyvan (Colyvan 2001) that it is also a problem for mathematical realists and Platonists (in the mathematical sense): if talk of numbers, sets, equations, functions and the rest is talk of a special realm of abstract objects (i.e. numbers, functions, etc.), and of special relationships those objects stand in (being the domain of a function, or the exponentiation of a number or a variable, etc.), then how does theorizing and reasoning about all that stuff help us with burst pipes and growing wheat?

This looks like a version of Aristotle's first puzzle, as applied to Platonistic mathematics: by postulating a new realm of objects and making claims about them, we have doubled our epistemic and explanatory burdens—now we are set the task not only of finding out all about the concrete particular physical things, but about these abstract mathematical things as well. Viewed like that, it seems we have made things worse, not better.

If one strand of Aristotle's objection is a close analogue of this puzzle about Platonistic mathematics, the Lovers of the Forms might well be comforted. After all, however much we might be puzzled by this feature of mathematics, no philosophers I know of want to conclude that we should stop employing mathematics in the physical sciences (or other sciences, for that matter). We should be confident that somehow mathematics is useful in investigating concrete physical phenomena, even if we remain puzzled how. Likewise Plato might retort that however puzzled we might be by our ability to use reasoning about the Forms to help us understand the physical world, we should not respond to this puzzle by rejecting the existence or usefulness of the Theory of Forms.

Things are not quite this simple, of course. There is no immediate guarantee that Forms will be useful in whatever sense mathematics is useful—the fact that one kind of abstract theoretical posit is worth making is not carte blanche for positing whatever we like. Plato would ideally need to show that Forms are useful in either the same sort of way that mathematics is, or in some alternative way, rather than just rely on being in initially promising company. For now, though, let us worry about contemporary partisans of general properties and relations: they too would need to have some reason to suppose universals are useful in whatever sense mathematics is useful before the fact that the problem arises in the mathematical case should be much comfort to them.

For another thing, there is the issue of whether mathematics and a theory of universals are meant to help us in the same way in grappling with the sensible world. Aristotle seems to be asking about supplying explanations of sensible phenomena, and one might think that mathematics is very useful for prediction and summarizing while doing no explanatory work in the sensible realm, or very little. (See Daly and Langford (2009) for a recent argument that mathematics is not explanatory of physical phenomena.) If we reject the claim that mathematics can explain sensible phenomena, we would need to concede Aristotle's first objection, though we could still look for a useful role for mathematics.

Likewise, even if a defender of universals had to concede that they did no explanatory work, she would still have something worthwhile if she could show they were important for some other theoretical purpose. One way to do this might involve showing that they are good in whatever other way mathematics is supposed to be, though this would not be a trivial undertaking. Mathematics seems to play an important role in predictive sciences, for example (this is one reason engineers get out calculators before building things), and it is less obvious that we need to talk about Forms to do successful prediction. Of course, given the widespread use of talk about properties and relations, perhaps a case can be made for universals here, even though it is a less obvious one.

In any case, I suspect Plato at least would want his theory of Forms to be explanatory, and so will many who postulate universals. They do not seem to be postulated just as aids to prediction or calculation: examining them is supposed to yield understanding of the world around us. So Plato, and many of his contemporary counterparts, would probably want a response to both charges: not only an account of a theory of Forms which shows why it is not useless when trying to grapple with the world of sensibles, but also to show how the Forms and facts about them can explain things in the world of change and decay. A number of contemporary believers in abstract mathematical entities also want to be able to defend the explanatoriness of mathematics as well as other usefulness mathematics might have for theorizing: see Colyvan (2001) and Baker (2005) as examples. Presumably Aristotle is also committed to the explanatoriness of universals (they are hardly *causes* in his sense unless they explain). So it is worth keeping in mind both the challenge involving explanation and the more general challenge involving usefulness.

Another hurdle to be faced by a realist about universals who wants to ride on the coat-tails of mathematics is that the puzzle about the applicability of mathematics only looks analogous to the applicability of a theory of Forms (or other theories of general properties and relations) if we think mathematics is about an abstract realm of special objects and their features in the first place. If it turned out that mathematical Platonism was a bad theory of mathematics (and especially if e.g. one of the rival hypotheses about mathematics explained the amazing applicability of mathematics better), then the effectiveness of mathematics in theories of the physical world would be little comfort to the realist about universals. So it would be a mistake to move too quickly from the undoubted usefulness of mathematics to the conviction that, somehow, theorizing about a realm of abstract entities can be a good part of a theory of things in the sensible world.

So both in the case of Platonistic mathematics, and realism about universals (Forms), it would be useful to have a worked-out response to the charge that these theories are not explanatory, and also to the charge that they are not useful at all in theorizing. I will not try to develop a full response here: instead, I will lay out what seem to me important alternative responses, and indicate where I think the most satisfying sort of response will be found.

3. RESPONDING TO THE USEFULNESS AND EXPLANATORY CHARGES

Whether it was what Aristotle had in mind or not, it seems that we have an interesting objection to theories of general properties and relations here. If my purpose is to come up with a good theory of "sensibles", or particular things in the world of individual things in time and space, how does postulating a realm of abstract universals help? Indeed, why is it not just making the theoretical project harder, since we not only need to account for the entities we started with but for a somewhat mysterious realm of additional entities as well?

As we have seen, there are two versions of this challenge: the stronger one raises the question of what use universals are *at all* when dealing with particular objects, while the second is the more specific challenge of what use they could be in *explaining* anything about particular things. Let me discuss some initial options for responding to these challenges which I do not think go far enough, before ending with some more constructive remarks about how I think the challenges are best faced. I will conclude with a brief discussion of how Plato's theory of Forms and Aristotle's theory of universals fare against our updated challenge: I will argue that Plato's theory of transcendental Forms seems to be able to meet the charge just as well as Aristotle's alternative theory of universals. Indeed, it may be that in some respects it is *Aristotle's* theory that has a harder time of things here.

I shall not discuss in any depth the option of conceding that universals are not of any use in theorizing about, or explaining, particular matters of fact. That response is, of course, an interesting one, as is the response of holding that Platonistic mathematics could not be useful for any other purpose. This sort of response to Aristotle's charge may well also have been historically significant, since Aristotle's rejection of Platonic Forms may have motivated some (e.g. Abelard) to read Aristotle himself as a nominalist, or as something close to one.

The first line of response to our challenge I wish to discuss is a somewhat "conceptualist" response, but not necessarily in the sense of taking properties and relations to be metaphysically dependent on thinking. It is rather that the role of explaining particular entities played by postulating universals is one of explaining intelligent activity: general properties and relations are postulated primarily to help explain thought and language. We might postulate universals as the semantic values of predicates, for example, or as part of a theory of mental content. These seem to be the primary intended roles for Frege's concepts, for example. Postulating universals helps a theory of meaning in a number of ways—one obvious way is by providing referents for abstract nouns ("justice", "piety", "redness", and so on), and being able to quantify over the meanings of predicates has proved invaluable in systematic semantics. Of course, this defence is not uncontroversial: there are alternatives to postulating properties and relations when trying to provide a systematic semantics or a systematic theory of mental content. But postulating general features of the world has a natural home in the prediction and explanation of our use of general expressions and our having of general thoughts.[14]

This line of response is compatible with taking the universals themselves to have no dependence on mind or language: Frege's concepts, for example, are not entities generated by our thought or words. It is rather than the role they play in explaining the sensible, particular world is via explanations of our mental lives and voluntary activity (including communication). A full-dress version of this response would presumably also explain how it is that our intelligent activity can involve universals, but even without this further story, this sort of theory is a response to the charge that universals would be explanatorily idle (or idle in so far as we want to explain particular entities, in any case). Humans and their activities are presumably part of the sensible world, after all.

---

[14] An example both less contemporary and more Aristotelian of employing universals to explain mind and language is that of Aquinas. His account of cognition in terms of a universal being present in one way in the mind and in another way among its instances plays a significant role in his theory of mind, and presumably he would think whether and how a given universal is in a mind can make a difference to what the thinker says and does.

Mind and language are important, of course, and being able to help explain important parts of what we do is a valuable enough contribution to be worth a theoretical postulation or two, in my view. But while this answers the letter of the challenge, showing one way that a theory postulating universals can explain some sensible particular things and events, it still does not go as far as I would like. Theories about mind and language are not the only places where we talk about universals: an engineer who studies geometry does not learn about shapes and figures primarily to apply that learning to *people* thinking about and talking about shapes, but to inanimate objects with shapes and dimensions. In the mathematical case, one use for mathematical knowledge is to predict and explain what mathematicians and other people employing mathematics will think and say: but that does not suggest a puzzle about unreasonable effectiveness in the way that the use of mathematics in physics does. We seem to be concerned about properties and relations in a much wider range of inquiries, so it seems to me that we should not be content to point out their use in theories of mind and language but to see what can be said about their use in theories of particular objects in general.

So if we raise our sights to demand a story about the usefulness, and perhaps even the explanatoriness, of universals and mathematical objects across the board (or at least across the natural sciences), is there anything persuasive for the realist to say? Some things the realist about Platonist mathematical objects may want to say can look like reducing the puzzle of appeal to mathematical objects to the puzzle of appeal to general properties and relations. For example, some try to explain the usefulness of appeal to mathematical structures by pointing to *shared structures* between some mathematical structures and some physical structures. One way to understand this is that it is claiming that some structures in pure mathematics (particular objects in pure mathematics) stand in mathematical relationships with some impure mathematical structures (particular mathematical objects with physical things in their transitive closure). This is, for example, what French (2000, p. 106–7) and Beuno, French, and Ladyman (2002, pp. 504–6) do when offering an explanation of the application of mathematics to physics, with partial homomorphisms between pure mathematical structures and classes of models employed by physics, where the models are themselves impure mathematical structures. But that does little to explain the connection between the mathematical realm and the non-mathematical realm: it rather points out a connection between one piece of the mathematical realm and another. A more tenable approach, it seems to me, is to approach applicability of mathematics to the physical world in terms of relations between general features of mathematical structures and general features of physical structures—e.g. a similarity relationship between a mathematical metric, on the one hand, and a relation between spatiotemporal intervals (or indeed between spatiotemporal relations) on the other. Armed with information about the mathematical structure, together with information about how it is similar to a non-mathematical entity, we can infer information about the non-mathematical entity.

Showing how we can link mathematical entities and non-mathematical entities in this way is a promising approach to showing the usefulness of mathematics, though more would need to be said about why bringing mathematics into our theorizing is more useful than just reasoning about the non-mathematical object directly. But the non-mathematical objects mentioned here are general properties and relations (in this example, relations on spacetime intervals). So if this line of response is taken, justifying the use of mathematics in e.g. the natural sciences by pointing out the connections between mathematics and the general properties and relations of interest to the relevant science, then we are still left with the challenge about universals: how does talking about general properties and relations and their features help us with particular entities: particular wheat crops, burst pipes, cloud chambers, etc.?

Another respect in which the challenges about universals might be seen as intimately connected with the challenges about mathematical objects is that some theorists think the role of universals is played by ordinary mathematical objects: that properties, for example, ought to be *identified* with sets of their instances, and relations *identified* with (ordered or un-ordered) n-tuples of the things which stand in them. I think this is the best way to understand Quine's view: his view is not that there are no general properties and relations, but rather that there are such things, and they are sets (see Quine 1980). If this is right, then connecting other mathematical structures to the general properties and relations of objects of interest is not really breaking out of the mathematical realm at all: it is merely associating one mathematical structure with another. So perhaps the applicability of theories of universals just is the question of applicability of mathematics, above appearances notwithstanding.

So the issues about applicability of mathematics and applicability of universals may receive similar solutions, and indeed may be aspects of the same problem in one way or another. One very general thing to say about the use of postulating universals is that statements of connections between universals, and generalizations about universals, can capture information about particular objects that is very difficult to capture through talking about the particulars directly. It is not that we need universals, in any obvious way, to generalize. "All wheat requires water to grow" is about wheat, and water, but not the property of Being Wheat or the property of Being Water, at least not in any direct way. We can even generalize about wheat and other kinds of crop without dragging properties into it: "cereal plants all require water to grow" generalizes over wheat and other kinds of cereals in some sense, but not by talking explicitly about properties or kinds.

However, some generalizations do explicitly talk about properties or kinds. "More than eight kinds of cereal crop were grown in medieval England," for example. Some of these claims can be paraphrased with some success, if a little clumsily: "there is a set of eight past cereal plants, all grown in medieval England, such that each is different-kinded from the others," or something of the sort, and even the reference to sets is eliminable here. Even here the paraphrase is clumsy. Once we get to claims like "the mass-energy of any closed system is constant", "the area of a circular region is equal to π times the square of the length of the radius", it is harder to paraphrase these successfully without reference to properties and relations or mathematical objects (and maybe areas and lengths, whatever they are) respectively. Claims entirely about properties and relations are available, such as "red is more similar to orange than to blue", and while that is explicitly about colours (apparently general properties), it gives us guidance, together with other things we believe, about what to expect when looking at red and orange and blue things. (This traditional example is due to Pap (1959).)

It is at the very least not easy to come up with systematic paraphrases of many of these useful generalizations that invoke mathematical objects or universals, which preserve their usefulness but which are explicitly only generalizations about particular concrete entities. Nominalists might still disagree about whether paraphrase is feasible, and if it is feasible whether it would be preferable, for at least some important purposes. But we can at least see that helping ourselves to the claims about universals and mathematical objects gives us a grasp on generalizations that have useful consequences about particulars, but where those useful consequences are difficult to sum up directly.

Some nominalists, particularly instrumentalists and fictionalists, may agree that the generalizations in terms of properties and relations or mathematical objects are useful, while still denying that we are justified in believing them true. These fictionalists will not, I take it, disagree with the point I am making here, which is that these particular claims are *useful* in theorizing, even if they try to accommodate the usefulness of the claims without admitting their truth. And this defence of usefulness, remember, is not being deployed here as an argument directly for realism about universals or Platonism about mathematical objects: it is rather being deployed to respond to a charge that it needs to be shown how such postulates are useful. It may be that this account of usefulness is one that non-realists can so far share—a defence available to many views is no less a defence for that.

This might not be the only defence of usefulness available (and I will briefly discuss a more ambitious, albeit stranger, defence below). There remains a question about whether universals, or for that matter mathematical objects, can serve in explanations. It is difficult to resolve this question to everyone's satisfaction, largely because the question of what makes something a good explanation is itself so murky and controversial. The deductive-nomological model of explanations, where an explanation is an argument with a law-statement as a major premise and the explanandum as a conclusion, is no longer popular, and rightly so. But there does not seem to be an orthodoxy yet to replace it. One popular movement has been to treat explanation as giving the (efficient) cause of the thing explained, or more generally causal information about the explanandum, but on closer inspection nearly every such theory of explanation restricts its scope to avoid being a general theory of explanation. (See Jenkins and Nolan (2008) for discussion of this, especially footnote 2 and pp. 113–15.) Whether mathematical entities or universals could explain sensible matters of fact, on simple versions of this picture, depends on whether properties and mathematical objects could be *causes*. Even here, the case is not hopeless, since there does seem to be property causation (heat can cause heatstroke, for example, and plausibly can cause particular events of heatstroke—a doctor can diagnose the patient's vomiting and headaches as due to excessive heat).

On a more sophisticated causal theory of explanation (e.g. Lewis 1986), all that would be required for mathematical entities or universals to play a role in explanation of particular events would be for talk about them to be a useful way of conveying information about the causal history of those events: and mathematics and property talk certainly seem to be useful ways of conveying information about these matters. (Lewis is officially silent on explanations of matters other than particular events, but extending his theory in the obvious way gives a theory where anything is explained by giving information about its causal history, and whatever the drawbacks of such a general theory, it seems at least friendly to mathematics and properties and relations playing a role in explanations.)

Other theories of explanation, such as theories of explanations as unificatory (Friedman 1974, Kitcher 1989) would presumably be friendly to counting mathematical and universals-involving explanations as genuine, since mathematics and property-and-relation talk seem to earn their bread and butter in providing general, unified accounts of the phenomena. Theories that are very catholic about what sorts of information can be invoked in explanations, such as van Fraassen's (van Fraassen 1980, Ch. 6) will easily accommodate, at least in principle, citing properties, relations, and mathematical matters in explanations. Nevertheless, the topic of whether mathematical objects and mathematical claims can do explanatory work remains controversial: though one odd aspect of the controversy is that those hostile to mathematical explanation often describe a role for mathematics that would make it straightforwardly explanatory on several common models of explanation such as Kitcher's or van Fraassen's. (See Daly and Langford 2009, and references therein, for a defence of an "indexing" role for mathematics which they see as supporting the claim that mathematics is non-explanatory. It seems to me that if mathematics played this role, that would *vindicate* the role of mathematics in explanation of physical phenomena.)

Most general theories of explanation vindicate an explanatory role for mathematics, and the same sort of explanatory role is standardly available for universals as well. While the fact that theories of explanation are very controversial means that it is unlikely to be made *uncontroversial* that mathematics or universals can be invoked in genuine explanations, if any of the main contending theories of explanation are on the right track, the prospects are good that the correct theory of explanation will not preclude employing mathematical objects and universals in genuine explanations.

The use of universals to capture information about particulars that is difficult to capture otherwise is an important and to my mind rather compelling argument for postulating them and employing theories that do. (Though to show that we should go beyond mere instrumentalist or fictionalist approaches to talk of properties and relations would require much more argument than I have offered here.) The usefulness of citing properties, relations, and mathematical objects in explanations also seems to me important, though more controversial. But I think there is a third, more Platonic, argument for postulating universals as well: and postulating them in a way that makes objects seem to depend on them rather more than they need to for the previous defence to work. This conception of universals makes them explanatory in a much more metaphysical way than the options so far considered.

This third approach involves the question of whether we can explain predication by appeal to properties. One approach to predication is to take true predications as basic. For example, it might just be a fundamental matter of fact that electron E is negatively charged, with no further metaphysical account forthcoming. Another approach, more traditionally realist, is to supply a further explanation: electron E is negatively charged because it has a property—negative charge, or perhaps a determinate of it such as the property of having $-1e$ charge. It is controversial whether this further explanation is worth having: David Lewis is one who argues it is not (Lewis 1983, pp. 21–4). But it seems to me that there are advantages to explaining a lot of ordinary predication in terms of properties and relations instantiated by entities.

One putative advantage is that we have much less unanalysed predication: we do not need "is negatively charged" or "is negatively charged to degree $-1e$" as undefined primitives in our theory, since it is a matter of standing in the instantiation connection to the relevant property. Since "is positively charged" is likewise explained in terms of instantiation and the relevant property, we have at worst one undefined predicate ("...instantiates...") rather than two. Of course, this supposes that identifying the properties of negative and positive charge (or whichever are taken to be basic) can be done without using primitive predicates that apply to properties and relations themselves.[15]

Another putative advantage is that it does more metaphysical explanation in terms of ontology rather than ideology. There is something in virtue of which two electrons E_1 and E_2 are similar: their shared property. Of course, those who think that it is fundamental that E_1 and E_2 are negatively charged can agree that they share a property—but for that view, it is not *because* they share a property that they are similar: rather, presumably, they share a property because they are both negatively charged. It is a difficult matter to say why we might prefer to explain the world in terms of ontology rather than primitive predicates: sometimes "truthmaker" intuitions are appealed to, or sometimes other arguments are offered, and not just by those sympathetic to this sort of analysis of predication: when Quine argues, in effect, that primitive second-order logic is less preferable than set-theory, one thing that is going on seems to be a preference for cashing out commitments ontologically, though no doubt this is not the only thing going on here.

If trading in primitive predicates for extra ontology is an advantage at all in these sorts of cases, it is plausibly an explanatory advantage. Its motivation seems to be some sort of simplicity consid-

---

[15] A trope theorist might want to claim the advantage of analysing predication without invoking general properties and relations: E_1 being negatively charged could be explained in terms of E_1's relation to its negative charge trope. The trope theorist might still face a challenge of explaining in ontological terms what it is for E_1 and E_2 to share a quality, or their being similar, or similar general matters. But the main point of the discussion in the text is to say that the general properties and relations may be able to do a certain kind of useful explanatory work, not that they are the only means of doing that work: if trope theorists can do that work without the general properties and relations, this point would be unaffected. Thanks to Michael Rota for discussion of this issue.

eration, or something analogous to a simplicity consideration: and it does not seem to be done for the sake of prediction or other non-explanatory goals of a theory. So this final motivation, if accepted, seems to help with the project of showing that postulating universals is explanatory, as well as the project of showing that such postulation is theoretically useful somehow or other.

One challenge to this way of thinking is that this "ontology first" approach still suffers from primitive predication or "unanalysed predication", because of the instantiation predicate (Lewis 1983, pp. 22–3). I have argued elsewhere that, depending on what is required to analyse predication, even instantiation can be analysed ontologically (Nolan 2008): but even if this is not so, this strategy arguably replaces many primitive predicates with one (or one for each grade of relation, if instantiation for properties, two-place relations, three-place relations, etc. must be represented by different predicates). Even if we had to concede that unanalysed predication is unavoidable, it could still be maintained that less is better than more.

It seems to me in the spirit of Plato's position to maintain that objects are just, good, beautiful, etc. because of the Forms they participate in, rather than the other way around. So if this gives a theory some genuine advantage, this is another potential resource Plato has to respond to Aristotle's challenge. It seems to me that Aristotle sees things as being the other way around: things are associated with universals because of the *particular* substances and accidents those things have (or are). If there is an advantage to explaining predicates of particulars through their connections to general properties and relations here, it is not available to Aristotle.

4. BACK TO PLATO AND ARISTOTLE

If we can succeed in showing that postulating general properties and relations is valuable, it might seem at first sight that Plato and Aristotle can claim these virtues for the Forms and Aristotelian universals, respectively. Both can agree that we can capture generalizations about sensibles through talk about Forms/universals that are difficult to capture otherwise; both can agree that a single mathematical structure can illuminate a range of patterns in the physical world via being related to properties and relations instantiated in the physical world; both can agree that an account of psychology and linguistic content can be informed by citing universals. Plato at least may also have wished to take aboard and defend the tentative remarks made about reducing or doing away with primitive predication offered in the previous section. The defences mentioned may well not be the only ways to defend the usefulness and perhaps even explanatory ability of universals, but they are hopefully sufficient, when spelled out in the required detail.

In Plato's case, while these arguments would provide him with some defences of the usefulness and explanatoriness of the theory of Forms, it should be clear that they will not vindicate every use to which he put that theory. I have said nothing here of memory through metempsychosis, efficient causal explanations through the operation of the Demiurge, or various other distinctive places where Forms play a role, or appear to play a role. (How much of the views of his mouthpieces can be attributed to Plato is here, as always, a burning question—I am myself dubious that we should treat very much of Timaeus's myth-reporting as Plato's own theory, for example, despite the long tradition of doing so.)

In Aristotle's case, it is less obvious that these considerations will help him show that universals are explanatory. For Aristotle to coherently count something as an explanation he has to show that it is one of the four kinds of cause, at least if $αιτια$ are seen as "becauses", and Aristotle is correctly interpreted as taking his four to be the only causes (in light of e.g. the passage that Tredennick translates as "these are roughly all the meanings of 'cause' ", *Metaphysics* Δ 1013b, Tredennick p. 213). Aristotle is also limited in apparently thinking that the aim of theorizing is supplying causes (992a): if that is right, then postulating entities that are not causes is at least prima facie beside the point. As we have seen, Aristotle is happy to count universals as formal causes (at least when those universals are "classes" ($γενη$) which contain essential formulae). However, the issue remains whether Aristotle is entitled to do this. If the primary or ultimate formal causes (of substances, at least) are the particular essences or substances, why count the universals as well? This is particularly pressing if the universals are metaphysically posterior and dependent on the individual substances: it seems that the substances would explain the universals and the universals would depend on the substances, rather than the other way around. Entities seem to depend on their causes in the other senses of cause: the statue depends on the sculptor as its efficient cause, depends on its bronze material, and depends on the goal of the sculptor: why should some of its formal causes depend on it? It seems reasonable to have the statue depend on its own particular essence: but why should some class it belongs to because of its essence be a reason it is what it is?

At present I am not sure how serious this challenge is for Aristotle. It is clear he wants universals to be generic causes in at least the formal sense of cause and perhaps in others, and the challenge is to see what compelling pictures that preserve other Aristotelian themes can be constructed which allow this. Perhaps what is needed is an Aristotelian account of the causes of universals—if they are derivative from individual substances, one might expect them to be caused in some sense by those substances, and perhaps establishing room for this will preclude them from being formal causes of the substances.[16] It will be important for this project to get clear on how mathematical objects contribute to causes of sensibles for Aristotle as well, since this might give us an insight into the role of mathematical universals and universals more generally. These troubles for Aristotle need not be trouble for us, however, unless we are Aristotelian enough to accept the straitjacket of an Aristotelian account of explanation in the first place.

5. CONCLUSION

If I am right, the puzzle about the point of postulating some of the abstract objects that philosophers like to invoke is one of the oldest in metaphysics. One focus of this paper has been to outline how some of the objections that Aristotle offers against the theory of Forms are connected to the more general issue of the point of employing theories of abstract objects, whether mathematical objects or properties and relations, as well as to comment on how Plato and contemporary realists about mathematics and universals might respond to these challenges. If it turns out that it is *Aristotle* who faces particular

---

[16] An interpretation like that of Lewis (1991) avoids treating some universals, at least, as derivative from individual substances. The problems I discuss here will still arise for Lewis's Aristotle if he allows for any Aristotelian universals that are not primary substances, especially if he allows for Aristotelian universals that are not substances at all. Lewis's Aristotle also still faces the challenge presented for mathematical entities.

difficulties here, that would be especially interesting, though more would need to be said to settle the issue of whether Aristotle can be shown to be inconsistent on this point.

There are lessons here for Aristotle interpretation (and Plato interpretation, in so far as Aristotle is one of our best sources for Plato's views other than Plato's own dialogues). There is also the lesson that some puzzles raised about mathematical Platonism (e.g. by Colyvan 2001) apply to abstract metaphysical posits more generally, and may need to be addressed in similar ways. Indeed, if anything the question of how postulation of general properties and relations helps us in our theorizing about particular things might be even more pressing than the question about mathematical objects, since at least everyone admits that doing mathematics is *somehow* very useful, whereas there is not even that much agreement about apparent talk about universals. In so far as general properties and relations are thought to be *explanatory* of particular matters of fact, there is a debate to be had about them that is closely connected to the debate about whether information about abstract mathematical objects would explain non-mathematical matters. So some of the lessons of this paper are at least as much about what challenges face theories of general properties and relations, as about what the solutions to those challenges are.[17]

Australian National University

REFERENCES

Alexander of Aphrodisias (1989). *On Aristotle Metaphysics 1* (trans. W. E. Dooley). London: Duckworth.

Aristotle (1933). *The Metaphysics I–IX*. Loeb Classical Library (trans. H. Treddenick). London: William Heinemann. Translations from *The Metaphysics* quoted are the Treddenick translations except where noted.

Aristotle (1936). *The Metaphysics X–XIV, Oeconomica and Magna Moralia* Loeb Classical Library (trans. H. Treddenick and G. C. Armstrong) London: William Heinemann.

Aristotle (1929). *The Physics* (trans. P. Wicksteed and F. M. Cornford), Loeb Classical Library. London: William Heinemann.

[17] Thanks to audiences at ANU, Monash and the 2011 Inland Northwestern Philosophy Conference, and special thanks to Chris Daly, Jason Bowers, and Michael Rota for comments, and Karen Bennett for valuable comments as editor.

Baker, A. (2005). "Are there Genuine Mathematical Explanations of Physical Facts?" *Mind* 114: 223–38.

Bueno, O., (L. French, and J. Ladyman) (2002). "On Representing the Relationship between the Mathematical and the Empirical." *Philosophy of Science* 69.3: 497–518.

Colyvan, M. (2001). "The Miracle of Applied Mathematics." *Synthese* 127: 265–77.

Daly, C., and S. Langford (2009). "Mathematical Explanation and Indispensability Arguments." *Philosophical Quarterly* 59.237: 641–58.

Fine, G. (1984). "Separation." *Oxford Studies in Ancient Philosophy* 2: 31–87.

Fine, G. (1993). *On Ideas*. New York: Oxford University Press.

French, S. (2000). "The Reasonable Effectiveness of Mathematics: Partial Structures and the Application of Group Theory to Physics." *Synthese* 125: 103–20.

Friedman, M. (1974). "Explanation and Scientific Understanding." *Journal of Philosophy* 71: 5–19.

Jenkins, C. S., and D. Nolan (2008). "Backwards Explanation." *Philosophical Studies* 140: 103–15.

Kitcher, P. (1981). "Explanatory Unification." *Philosophy of Science* 48: 507–31.

Lewis, D. (1983). "New Work for a Theory of Universals." Reprinted in Lewis, D. (1999). *Papers in Metaphysics and Epistemology*. Cambridge: Cambridge University Press, pp. 8–55. Page references are to this reprint.

Lewis, D. (1986). "Causal Explanation" in Lewis, D., *Philosophical Papers, Volume II*. Oxford: Oxford University Press, pp. 214–40.

Lewis, F. (1991). *Substance and Predication in Aristotle*. New York: Cambridge University Press.

Nolan, D. (2008). "Truthmakers and Predication." *Oxford Studies in Metaphysics* 4: 171–92.

Pap, A. (1959). "Nominalism, Empiricism and Universals—I." *The Philosophical Quarterly* 9.37: 330–40.

Plato. (1997). *Parmenides, Phaedo, The Sophist*, and *The Republic*. In J. M. Cooper (ed.), *Plato: Complete Works*. Indianapolis, IN: Hackett.

Quine, W. V. (1980). "Soft Impeachment Disowned." *Pacific Philosophical Quarterly* 61.4: 450–1.

Studtmann, P. (2008). "On the several senses of 'Form' in Aristotle." *Apeiron* 41.3: 1–26.

van Fraassen, B. C. (1980). *The Scientific Image*. Oxford: Oxford University Press.

Wigner, E. (1960). "The Unreasonable Effectiveness of Mathematics in the Natural Sciences." *Communications in Pure and Applied Mathematics* 13: 1–14.

6. Paraphrase, semantics, and ontology

John A. Keller

1. INTRODUCTION

Consider the following pairs of sentences:

(1) The average mum has 2.4 children.
(1*) There are 2.4× as many children as mums. [compatible with there being no average mum] (cf. Melia (1995))

(2) I saw myself in the mirror.
(2*) I saw my body in the mirror. [compatible with dualism]

(3) There is a crack in my favorite vase.
(3*) My favorite vase is cracked. [compatible with there being no cracks[1]] (cf. Lewis and Lewis (1970))

(4) Santa Claus does not exist.
(4*) 'Santa Claus' does not refer. [compatible with anti-Meinongianism] (cf. Donnellan (1974))

(5) It's possible for only two things to exist.
(5*) It's possible for only two "ordinary" things to exist. [compatible with compositional universalism] (cf. Lewis (1986))

(6) There is a chair in Ava's closet.
(6*) There are some simples arranged chair-wise in Ava's closet. [compatible with eliminativism about composite objects] (cf. van Inwagen (1990))

(7) A has reason to φ in C.
(7*) φ-ing in C is what A would desire if she had a maximally informed, coherent, unified set of desires. [compatible with naturalism] (cf. Smith (1997))

(8) Red is a color.
(8*) Necessarily, all red things are colored. [compatible with nominalism]

(9) There are no golden mountains.
(9*) There are no golden mountains spatiotemporally connected to me. [compatible with Lewisian modal realism] (cf. Lewis (1986))

(10) Joe freely chose to lie to Mary.
(10*) Joe's choice to lie to Mary was caused by his beliefs and desires. [compatible with determinism]

Thanks to Patricia Blanchette, David Braun, Michael Glanzberg, Lorraine Juliano Keller, Jeff Speaks, Peter van Inwagen, the referees for *Oxford Studies in Metaphysics*, and audiences at the Arché conference on Ordinary Language, Linguistics, and Philosophy, the Creighton Club, and the 2014 Central APA for helpful comments and discussion.

[1] For ease of exposition I assume that cracks are not material objects.

These are examples of *reconciling paraphrases*: paraphrases that are intended to show that two apparently inconsistent claims are in fact consistent. The original sentence in each of the examples is in apparent conflict with the corresponding bracketed philosophical thesis. The second sentence is offered as a paraphrase of the first in order to reconcile it with that thesis—to argue that the apparent conflict between them is *merely* apparent. So anti-Meinongians paraphrase negative existentials in order to argue that they are consistent with there being no non-existent objects; David Lewis paraphrases ordinary truths apparently incompatible with modal realism or compositional universalism; nominalists paraphrase scientific and commonsense truths that apparently refer to or quantify over abstract objects; and do on.

Philosophers sometimes intend their paraphrases to be *revisionary*—to replace something they thought was true but have been led to reject. When we cannot reconcile something we believe with the other things we take to be the case, we often look for such a revisionary paraphrase: a replacement truth in the neighborhood of what we now take to be a falsehood.

Such *revisionary* paraphrases are relatively unproblematic. A growing number of philosophers have come to doubt the legitimacy of *reconciling* paraphrases, however. This is because of the lack of "respectable" evidence that can be provided on their behalf. Specifically, these critics think that in order to be plausible, reconciling paraphrases must be accompanied by evidence that would be of interest to linguists, semanticists, or philosophers of language. Since reconciling paraphrases are almost never offered with such evidence, these critics maintain that such paraphrases can be dismissed as mere wishful thinking. The central thesis of this paper is that this concern is mistaken: for many paraphrases, a lack of such evidence is not even a concern, much less a condemnation.[2]

---

[2] Another prominent worry about reconciling paraphrases is that a symmetry necessary for them to be successful—the symmetry of the "expresses the same claim" relation—necessitates a symmetry sufficient for them to be a failure: the symmetry of the "has the same (unwanted) implications" relation. This objection was raised most famously in Alston (1963), but also appears in Jackson (1980), Melia (1995), Yablo (1998), Burgess and Rosen (2005), Varzi (2007), Shaffer (2009), and Williams (2012). See Keller (forthcoming) for a critical discussion.

2. THE LACK OF SCIENTIFIC EVIDENCE OBJECTION (LSE)

As the above examples indicate, reconciling paraphrases are used in diverse areas of philosophical inquiry. They have been most discussed in connection with Quinean meta-ontology, but there is nothing special about that application. Philosophers use paraphrase to reconcile their theories with the other things they believe: their other philosophical theories as well as the deliverances of non-philosophical inquiry, especially common sense and science. Paraphrase is used to argue that the appearance of inconsistency between two claims is illusory—generated by the way the claims are formulated, and not by the content of the claims themselves. When it is possible to provide paraphrases of apparently inconsistent claims—paraphrases that do not themselves appear to be inconsistent—this gives us evidence that the apparent inconsistency between the claims is misleading. We produce such paraphrases, then, in order to undermine the appearance of inconsistency between the things we believe—typically, to defeat certain reasons for thinking that our philosophical theories are inconsistent with the non-philosophical facts.

Given the role of paraphrase in philosophical inquiry, it may seem surprising how indifferent many philosophers are to how their paraphrases are received by both ordinary speakers and language experts. Many paraphrases seem absurd if offered as reformulations that "say the same thing as" the sentences they paraphrase. For example, (6*) seems to be nothing if not revisionary in spirit. Even upon reflection, most speakers do not agree that (6) and (6*) are different ways of saying the same thing. And this commonsense judgement seems to be supported by the considered judgement of linguists and semanticists. But if (6*) doesn't express the fact expressed by (6), it is hard to see how it could be of any use in reconciling that fact with eliminativism about composite objects.

Accordingly, this and other examples of paraphrase face an objection from the lack of scientific evidence in their favor—henceforth the **LSE objection**. John Burgess and Gideon Rosen put the worry as follows:

there is a total lack of scientific evidence in favor of any such [philosophical] reconstrual as a theory of what ordinary... assertions mean. Or at least, no [philosophers] favoring such a reconstrual have ever published their suggestions in a linguistics journal with evidence such as a linguist without ulterior [philosophical] motives might accept.[3]

This objection has recently been pushed against paraphrases like (5*) and (6*) by Daniel Korman:

One often hears it said in conversation about universalism that the apparent conflict with folk discourse poses no serious problem, for the universalist can just say that the folk are restricting their quantifiers. What I have tried to show is that... this is a substantive semantic hypothesis... for which there seems to be no evidence... [Universalists] are not alone in trying to reconcile [apparently] revisionary metaphysical theories with discourse about material objects. For instance, many philosophers (but no linguists, to my knowledge) have endorsed the semantic hypothesis that such English sentences as 'there are tables in the next room', 'this piece of paper exists now', or 'this tree had fewer branches last year' have two uses in English: a "loose and popular" use on which they say something obviously true, and a "strict and philosophical use" on which they express substantive philosophical claims... there seems to be no... evidence for these semantic hypotheses...[4]

---

[3] Burgess and Rosen (2005), p. 525.

[4] Korman (2007), p. 332. See also Korman (2009) and Korman (2013). Korman's worry about (5) is a straightforward instance of the LSE objection: that there isn't linguistic evidence for thinking that ordinary uses of (5) are implicitly restricted à la (5*). His worry about (6) is that there is no linguistic evidence for the existence of two uses of it: a "strict and philosophical" use where (6) expresses something inconsistent with eliminativism, and a "loose and popular" use where (6) expresses something along the lines of (6*). Since this concern is different than the objection discussed in the main text, let me indicate how what I say there does and does not respond to it. There is a growing consensus that (6) can have these two uses without being ambiguous. Rather, the two uses derive from special features of a certain context where (6) is sometimes uttered: the context of the metaphysics room. Many eliminativists claim that what is expressed by (6) in the metaphysics room is inconsistent with eliminativism, but that what is expressed by (6) in ordinary contexts has the truth conditions of (6*). This paper tries to explain how ordinary utterances of (6) could have the truth conditions of (6*), but it doesn't address the question of why we should believe that (6) is context sensitive in this way, nor the question of why or how the context of the metaphysics room has this effect on the content of (6). For (admittedly partial) answers to these questions, see Dorr (2005), Horgan and Potrč (2008), Fine (2009), Sider (2009), Sider (2012), Sider (2013), and van Inwagen (2014). For criticism see Hirsch (2008) and Korman (2013). Thanks to David Braun for stressing the difference between Korman's worries about (5*) and (6*).

And a similar concern seems to lie behind the following famous remarks by Saul Kripke:

> The philosopher advocates a view apparently in patent contradiction to common sense. Rather than repudiating common sense, he asserts that the conflict comes from a philosophical misinterpretation of common language—sometimes he adds that the misinterpretation is encouraged by the 'superficial form' of ordinary speech. He offers his own analysis of the relevant common assertions, one that shows that they do not really say what they seem to say... Personally I think that such philosophical claims are almost invariably suspect. What the claimant calls a 'misleading philosophical misconstrual' of the ordinary statement is probably the natural and correct understanding.[5]

Examples could be multiplied further—compare, e.g. Timothy Williamson's admonishments about philosophy being properly "disciplined by" semantics in *The Philosophy of Philosophy*.[6] The influence of the LSE objection is pervasive, and deservedly so: the worry it raises is a deep and important one. The crux of the objection is that the claims made by paraphrists are simply not credible, since they lack respectable (scientific) evidence—evidence that would be of interest to semanticists, linguists, or philosophers of language.[7] To put forth a reconciling paraphrase involves making a claim about meaning, but the arguments given in support of typical paraphrase proposals do not meet the argumentative standards of the disciplines that study meaning. Proponents of the LSE objection conclude that such paraphrases are based on nothing more than wishful thinking.

3. WHY CARE ABOUT COMMON SENSE?

One might not see much value in responding to the LSE objection if one does not see any reason to care about reconciling common sense with our philosophical theories. I assume most readers will agree

---

[5] Kripke (1982), p. 65.
[6] Williamson (2007), p. 285.
[7] For the purposes of this paper, I do not distinguish between the evidence relevant to linguistics, semantics, lexicographers, empirically oriented philosophy of language, etc. I also don't worry about how to distinguish the "scientific" evidence appealed to by practitioners of these disciplines from the "non-scientific" evidence typically given by paraphrists. However the distinction is drawn, the relevant premise of the LSE objection is correct: the arguments normally given by paraphrists would not be of interest to typical linguists, semanticists, etc.

that it is good for our philosophical theories to be consistent with *science*—or at least, mature and successful science, which is what I am using 'science' to refer to here. Many examples of paraphrase, however, are attempts to reconcile our philosophical theories with things we believe for non-scientific reasons. And one might wonder why we should worry about reconciling our theories with such "commonsense" convictions. For example, given how unlovely (6*) seems as a paraphrase of (6), why doesn't van Inwagen simply put his theory forward as a *revision* of our ordinary way of thinking?

This is an important question, and van Inwagen's answer to it provides helpful background for the critique of the LSE objection to come. Van Inwagen says the following about why he wants to provide *non*-revisionary paraphrases of sentences like (6):

> there is what we might call Universal Belief: that body of propositions that has been accepted by every human being who has ever lived, bar a few imbeciles and madmen... Is the existence of chairs—or, at any rate, of things suitable for sitting on, like stones and stumps—a matter of Universal Belief? If it were, this would count strongly against my position, for any philosopher who denies what practically *everyone* believes is, so far as I can see, adopting a position according to which the human capacity for knowing the truth about things is radically defective. And why should he think that his own capacities are the exception to the rule?[8]

This is a close variant on the standard account of the importance of respecting "common sense", which is that ordinary convictions constrain our philosophical theorizing because we almost always have more evidence for such convictions than we do for our philosophical theories. A defense of this methodology would be out of place here, but note that van Inwagen *accepts* the existence of "Moorean facts", including the fact ordinarily expressed by (6). Van Inwagen claims, however, that such facts are consistent with his metaphysical theory, since in addition to accepting the *existence* of Moorean facts, he also accepts Moore's view of the *depth*, or lack thereof, of the Moorean facts. As David Armstrong puts it:

> Moore was always ready to insist on what we might call the *shallowness* of truistic or Moorean knowledge. The way he would have put it himself was that while, for instance, it is a truism that there is motion, nevertheless that knowledge could co-exist with ignorance of... the true *analysis* of motion. I will put his point by saying that we can know very well that motion exists,

---

[8] van Inwagen (1990), p. 103.

yet at the same time not know just what the true nature of motion is. Motion is an utterly familiar phenomenon, we know it when we see it, or feel it, but our understanding of it, I think, is very far from complete.[9]

As applied to (6), we might say that it is a Moorean fact *that* there is a chair in Ava's closet, but there is no Moorean fact about how to *understand* or *analyze* that claim—no Moorean facts about the nature of its *truth conditions* or potential truthmakers. To put things in linguistic terms, it may be a Moorean fact that 'there is a chair in Ava's closet' expresses a true proposition, but there is no Moorean fact about *which* proposition it expresses. Hence, there can be legitimate debate about what proposition that is, and what is required for it to be true. So there is room, at least in theory, for van Inwagen to claim that his philosophical theory is consistent with "commonsense" matters of universal belief, such as that there are things on which people sometimes sit. As we have seen, this is what he *does* claim, arguing that the belief ordinary non-philosophers express with 'there are chairs' is not contradicted by his metaphysical theory.

The dialectical importance of van Inwagen's paraphrase lies in the fact that it provides him with a response to (6) and other such apparent counterexamples to his theory. But the cogency of this response rests squarely on the claimed equivalence between (6) and (6*). This is precisely the target of the LSE objection. Sentences seemingly "about" chairs like (6) are not synonymous, in any intuitive sense, with sentences about mereological simples like (6*). And of course no linguist has ever proposed that the two sentences are equivalent in meaning.[10]

Before we go any further, I want to make clear that my goal is not to defend van Inwagen's paraphrases, nor any of the other paraphrases given above. For a variety of reasons, I think that most of them are ultimately unsuccessful. For example, the strategy employed in (3*) doesn't generalize, and (2*) is unnecessary since dualism is false. As regards (6*), I think that it is at best correct if van Inwagen's ontology is correct, and I am skeptical about his

---

[9] Armstrong (2006), pp. 160–1.
[10] As indicated above, Dan Korman has repeatedly pushed this objection against van Inwagen's paraphrases. Related objections are pushed in Mackie (1993), Hawthorne and Michael (1996), and Merricks (2001).

ontology. My goal here is rather to defend the *approach* to paraphrase that lies behind these examples—to show that they do not fail simply because of a lack of linguistic evidence. Of course, they may well fail for independent reasons. I am only arguing that it is not, *in general*, a good objection to point out that there is no linguistic evidence supporting a paraphrase—that the success of a paraphrase is not something to be evaluated solely or even mainly in terms of the linguistic evidence that can be marshaled in its favor.

4. THE ARGUMENT

There are three considerations that significantly blunt the force of the LSE objection. The first is that speakers often fail to say what they mean. The second is that widely-accepted metasemantic theses entail that there is not a delimited range of evidence relevant to the determination of meaning—anything, including metaphysics, can play a role. The third is that successful paraphrases do not need to preserve the semantic contents of the sentences they paraphrase, as long as they preserve their truth conditions.

4.1. Speaker's meaning and semantic content

The first problem with the LSE objection arises from the distinction between semantic content and speaker's meaning. It is widely held that what a *speaker* means—the belief she intends to assert or convey with an utterance—is often different than the semantic content of the sentence she uses to express that belief, even relative to context.[11] Reconciling paraphrases, however, are attempts to resolve apparent conflicts between our *beliefs*. Reconciling the things we *say* is only of instrumental value. If our goal is to reconcile our philosophical theories with the other things we take to be the case, the semantic contents of our sentences are relevant only in so far as they

---

[11] Scott Soames, e.g. writes, "the semantic content of a sentence doesn't always determine what is asserted and conveyed by literal uses of it. Sometimes more than the semantic content is asserted or conveyed, and sometimes the semantic content isn't asserted at all." (Soames (2008)) Similar conclusions have been defended in Kripke (1979), Grice (1989), Bach (2001), Recanati (2004), and Cappelen and Lepore (2005). Jason Stanley is perhaps the sharpest critic of this approach. See, e.g. Stanley (2007a) and King and Stanley (2005).

correspond with the contents of our minds. But what a speaker says is imperfect (albeit important) evidence about what she thinks, even when she's speaking sincerely, since what a speaker intends to communicate is underdetermined by the semantic contents of her utterances. Since we can have evidence about what a speaker believes that goes beyond our evidence about the semantic contents of her utterances, a lack of *semantic* evidence that a speaker intends to communicate φ in uttering S does not entail that we have no *respectable* evidence that φ is the belief she intends to communicate in uttering S.

Consider, for example, (2) and (2*). Avowed substance dualists will say things like 'I saw myself in the mirror', 'I was strapped into my seat'. Does the fact that professed dualists utter such sentences without visible reservation show that they are not dualists after all, or that they are inconsistent dualists? Of course not. When a dualist makes such utterances, she means only that she saw her body in the mirror, that her body was strapped in, etc. If I know that the speaker is a dualist, I will know that is all she means. Dualists who thus speak with the vulgar need not be presupposing a revisionary semantic theory of the first person indexical, however. Rather, their uses of such sentences can be explained by the fact that the dualistically acceptable paraphrases are unwieldy, and that if any confusion arises, it can be easily cleared up. A similar phenomenon occurs when one says things like 'I'm parked in the B lot' in order to communicate that *one's car* is parked in the B lot. As a rule, utterances of 'I' refer to the speaker, and never to her automobile, but familiar Gricean mechanisms explain why 'I'm parked in the B lot' can be used to communicate what it does.[12] As David Lewis once said, "abuse of language makes for easier communication than circumlocution or neologism ... I trust that [my audience] will understand [what] I mean".[13]

---

[12] Stanley (1998) convincingly argues against various attempts to explicate the equivalence between (2) and (2*) *semantically*, but that there are no objections to a semantic treatment of 'I'm parked in the B lot'. Whether 'I'm parked in the B lot' has a literally true semantic content is not central to the above argument, however. My suggestion is that it is possible for dualists to use sentences like (2) as a shorthand way to communicate the content of sentences like (2*), independently of the literal semantic content of (2). But if this is possible, it is very likely actual.

[13] Lewis (1997), fn. 1.

Similar considerations apply to (1)/(1*) and (3)/(3*). If the speaker takes them to be mere stylistic variants, the "linguistic evidence" is irrelevant to whether (3*) is a good paraphrase of (3), or (1*) is a good paraphrase of (1). For example, I have a belief about the proportion of children and mums, and I make decisions about whether to express that belief using (1) or (1*) for purely stylistic reasons. Similarly, I have a belief about my vase's being damaged in a certain way, and my decisions about what sentence to use to express that belief are based on style rather than substance. The most that linguistic considerations can show is that the semantic contents of the sentences I use to express my picture of the world would change if I replaced (1)–(3) with (1*)–(3*). They cannot show that speaker's meaning would not be preserved. In cases (1)–(3), the paraphrist has a certain belief, and from her perspective the starred versions are simply different ways that she might express that belief.

It might be objected that semantics or linguistics tells us that these apparently different ways of expressing that belief are not in fact different ways of expressing it, but subtly different ways of refining, revising, or misstating it. So, for example, by formulating my belief about the vase using (3), I say something that entails that there are cracks, but if I use (3*), I do *not* say anything that entails that there are cracks. If this is the case, then there is no way for me to avoid committing myself to an ontology of cracks unless I stop asserting (3). But then, since the particular (fine-grained) claim I happen to have been asserting is not one I have any special attachment to, there is no cost to giving it up—I only used (3) as a means to express my (coarse-grained) thought about my vase being cracked. If that sentence has baggage that I do not wish to carry, I may simply drop it in favor of another expression that does *not* have that baggage, such as (3*). In other words, even if (3*) does not express the same proposition as (3), they will both serve equally well to express my belief about the vase, and *that is all that matters* for a reconciling paraphrase to be a success. *Mutatis mutandis* for (1) and (1*).

The upshot of all of this is that, even if it can be established that the paraphrase and the original sentence are not *semantically* equivalent, they might still be equivalent in all the ways that matter from the perspective of the speaker—just as good for verbally communicating her conception of the world, and indeed, for telling the whole truth from the perspective of the speaker. Given that there are a variety of different linguistic vehicles that I *regard* as able expressions of some particular thought of mine, determining whether there is a linguistic vehicle that expresses that thought in a way that does not entail anything I reject will be a philosophically important endeavor. While paraphrases in this sense will be semantically revisionary, they will not involve revising my conception of reality. Rather, they will be tools for reconciling the commitments of my discourse with the commitments of my thought.

4.1.1. Speaker's intentions and semantic content

The argument in the previous section assumed that there can be a significant gap between what a speaker means and the semantic content of the sentence she utters, and in particular that the semantic content of (2) in the mouth of a dualist is *not* what she actually means: that she saw her body in the mirror. In this section I will show that the LSE objection fares no better if we relax that assumption.

In order to narrow the gap between speaker's meaning and semantic content—and in particular to maintain that (2) has the same semantic content as (2*) in the mouth of a dualist—we are almost certainly going to have to let speaker's *intentions* make significant contributions to the determination of semantic content.[14] But since the speaker's intentions are often neither determined by nor reflected in the linguistic evidence, it follows that the linguistic evidence does not wholly determine the semantic contents of our sentences. For example, there is not any special linguistic evidence that a dualist means (2*) when she utters (2). If her audience does

---

[14] Wettstein (1984) argues persuasively that speakers' intentions are not needed to account for the reference of standard indexicals and demonstratives. But as the contributions of "context" get more complicated, this becomes a much more difficult thesis to defend. For example, in the accounts of complex demonstratives (like 'that man') in Kaplan (1989a) and King (2001) and in the account of quantifier domain restriction in Stanley and Szabo (2000), speakers' intentions play a significant role in getting us from the conventional meaning of an expression to what is expressed in a given context. Furthermore, speaker's intentions are plausibly responsible for disambiguation. As Bach (2000) argues, "it is hard to see how the context, rather than the speaker's intention, could determine which of several like-sounding sentence he is (intends to be) uttering. If after a terrible round a golfer utters 'I hate my clubs', the sentence he is uttering could, if he so intended it, contain the word 'club' meaning social group. Of course, this won't be obvious to his audience, who will misidentify the sentence as one containing the word 'club' meaning golf stick." (fn. 14).

not know the speaker is a dualist—and if they themselves take materialism for granted—they will naturally think that she believes that she "literally" saw herself in the mirror. But an audience that knows the speaker is a dualist will interpret her *à la* (2*).

Why will the dualist's audience interpret her in that way? One plausible explanation is that they will be guided by a principle of charity: a presumption of truth or reasonableness. Such a principle would take *everything* we know about both the speaker and the world into account, since what is true or reasonable to believe depends on the totality of the evidence. So, if charity is an interpretational constraint, there isn't a special delimited set of linguistic data that is privileged with respect to finding correct interpretations. Anything and everything might be relevant.

In fact, a presumption of truth or reasonableness will plausibly direct us to accept certain paraphrases, at least if we grant for the sake of argument that the corresponding philosophical theories are correct. For example, if eliminativism is correct, interpreting sentences such as (6) *à la* (6*) will maximize the number of truths spoken. Less obviously, such an interpretation would maximize reasonableness as well. For what evidence do the ordinary folk (or scientists, for that matter) have that eliminativism is false? By all appearances, they don't have *any*: it is not an empirical claim, and we can safely assume that most non-philosophers are unfamiliar with the relevant metaphysical arguments. Hence, a presumption of reasonableness would yield the conclusion that we should not interpret non-philosophers to be taking a stand on this matter of abstruse metaphysics when making casual or even scientifically informed pronouncements about what there is. We should rather interpret such utterances as being neutral between the various competing theories of composition. This in turn supports van Inwagen's paraphrases, since they are neutral with regard to theories of composition. Independently of whether there are chairs, there are certainly simples arranged chair-wise.[15]

---

[15] Accepting van Inwagen's paraphrases does require us to take a stand on a matter of abstruse fundamental physics, however: for his paraphrases to work, matter must be fundamentally particulate rather than "gunky". (See Sider (1993)) If there were paraphrases that remained neutral on the metaphysics *and* the physics that would be ideal. Unfortunately there aren't.

4.1.2. Hard and easy cases

So the LSE objection fails in cases (1)–(3). There seems to be an important difference between examples (1)–(3) and (5)–(10), however. In (1)–(3) and to some extent (4), ordinary speakers will typically grant that the paraphrase "says the same thing" as the original sentence—that they are two different but equivalent ways of "putting things". To ordinary speakers, these paraphrases seem intuitively correct. Linguists might demur, but given that the purpose of paraphrase is to reconcile the things we believe, the speaker's beliefs take priority over linguistic theory. Ordinary speakers, however, do *not* take (5*)–(10*) to be mere reformulations of (5)–(10). Such paraphrases are not pre-theoretically or intuitively correct. So the distinction between speaker's meaning and semantic content does not look like it will be of much use in defending these examples against the LSE objection. It is worth stressing, however, that (1*)–(3*) are not just toy examples—they are real paraphrases put forth by philosophers attempting to show that their picture of the world is coherent. If paraphrase can be vindicated in cases like (1)–(3), the LSE objection fails. What I aim to show in the following sections is that it doesn't only fail in "easy" cases like (1)–(3), but also in "hard" cases like (5)–(10).

4.2. What is "linguistic evidence"?

According to the proponents of the LSE objection, a sufficient amount of *linguistic* evidence is an important prerequisite for the success of a paraphrase. The first problem with the LSE objection as it applies to hard cases like (5)–(10) is that widely held views in semantics and metasemantics hold that the semantic facts are determined (in part) by the truth about metaphysics.[16] Such

---

[16] *Metasemantics* aims to explain how expressions come to have the meanings they have, while *semantics* aims to pair meaningful expressions with their meanings in a way compatible with our knowing them. (See, e.g. Lewis (1970) and Speaks (2011).) One way of thinking about the argument of this section is as an argument for "metasemantic liberalism"—the thesis that the truth of ordinary utterances containing a term are compatible with large degrees of error in our ordinary understanding of that term. See Sider (2013) for a discussion of metasemantic liberalism and its relation to eliminativism. Note that metasemantic liberalism is also consistent with *internalist* conceptions of semantics: see §4.3 for discussion. Thanks to Louise Antony

theories entail that the *total* linguistic evidence goes beyond the kind of "pure" linguistic evidence appealed to in typical linguistics papers—and that the total linguistic evidence may include metaphysical considerations. Standard forms of *semantic externalism* are the most well-known theories of this kind.

4.2.1. Semantic externalism

As a result of work by Saul Kripke, Hillary Putnam, and Tyler Burge,[17] many philosophers have become convinced that the facts about meaning are determined in part by things external to the mind. For example, there is an important sense in which 'water' and 'H$_2$O' have the same meaning.[18] This fact, however, was discovered by chemists, not linguists. And the *reason* this fact was not discovered by linguists is that it is a fact about the world, not linguistic practice. Just so, if, as reliabilists hold, 'Smith knows that Jones owns a Ford' means that Smith's belief that Jones owns a Ford is true, non-gettierized, and the product of a reliable mechanism, then this is a fact discovered by epistemologists, not linguists. And the reason this fact (if it is a fact) wasn't discovered by linguists is that it is a fact about knowledge, not language.[19] But if chemists have discovered a kind of meaning equivalence between 'water' and 'H$_2$O', and if epistemologists have discovered a kind of meaning equivalence between 'knowledge' and 'non-gettierized true belief produced by a reliable mechanism', then it is hard to see why a metaphysician couldn't (in principle) discover a kind of meaning equivalence between 'chair' and 'simples arranged chair-wise'. It might be *false* that there is any such equivalence, of course, but it is not clear why the fact that it does not have *linguistic* evidence in

---

for suggesting that I explore the relationship between the conclusions of this paper and semantic internalism.

[17] See Putnam (1975), Burge (1979), and Kripke (1980).

[18] After all, they have the same intension. Of course, many contemporary Russellians deny that 'water' and 'H$_2$O' have the same semantic content. But this just offers further support for the argument in §4.3.

[19] See Williamson (2007) for a detailed defense of a generalization of this thesis. If you don't think that necessarily equivalent contingent sentences with the same subject mater are semantically equivalent in any interesting sense, you should also deny that paraphrases need be semantically equivalent, in which case the LSE objection has no force. See §4.3.

its favor is any more relevant here than in the knowledge and water cases.

Many "hard cases" of paraphrase are at least partially motivated by such externalist considerations. Paraphrases are typically proposed after a philosopher makes a (purported) discovery about the nature of the world. It is only as a result of her discovery about the world that she then makes a claim about meaning—it is the change in her conception of reality that underwrites the change in her theory of meaning. For example, certain compatibilists claim to have discovered that choices caused by one's beliefs and desires can be both free and determined. As a result, such compatibilists hold that 'Joe freely chose to lie to Mary' means nothing more than that Joe's choice to lie to Mary was caused by his beliefs and desires. If this analysis is correct, it was discovered on the basis of metaphysical theorizing, not semantics. But if the evidence for such meaning equivalences comes from outside semantics proper, a lack of *semantic* evidence cannot be a significant objection to the compatibilist's claim about meaning. The phenomenon of semantic externalism looks like it straightforwardly contradicts a critical assumption of the LSE objection: that the metaphysical facts do not play a role in the determination of meaning. If controversial truths about metaphysics are relevant to the determination of semantic content (because of semantic externalism), then a "pure" semantic theory that ignores the results of metaphysical inquiry will be based on an unrepresentative subset of the evidence. If this is the case, paraphrase proposals that conflict with such "pure" semantic theories may be better supported by the *total* evidence than paraphrases that comport with such theories.

4.2.2. Metaphysical intrusion: Use

But how, exactly, can semantic externalism be used to buttress the kind of "non-scientific" paraphrases given by van Inwagen and others? In the cases discussed above, it is relatively clear how the metaphysical facts bear on the semantic ones: the facts about metaphysics are (partly) determining the facts about use. As a matter of fact, we *use* 'water' to refer to what is in fact H_2O, we apply 'knowledge' to what are in fact non-gettierized true beliefs produced by reliable mechanisms, and we use 'free choice' to refer to actions that are caused by the beliefs and desires of the person who performs them.[20] This illustrates one important kind of 'metaphysical intrusion', whereby semantics is contaminated by metaphysics: the facts about use depend (in part) on the metaphysical facts, and the facts about meaning depend on the facts about use. Hence, the truth about metaphysics will be partly determinative of the truth about semantics.

Let's look at how this would apply to the composition cases. If we assume that Lewis's compositional universalism is true—that for every two things there is a whole composed out of them—it follows that we use our quantifiers restrictedly, just as Lewis claims. If universalism is true, we do not typically *use* 'there is' to quantify over everything there is—indeed we almost never do so. Similarly, if van Inwagen's eliminativism is correct, and there are no non-living composite objects, it follows that we use expressions like 'table' and 'chair' in more or less exactly the way van Inwagen describes—that is, we use them in the presence of and hence presumably to designate what are in fact nothing more than simples arranged table-wise and chair-wise. These are just specific examples of a general principle: in order to determine what the facts about use are, *we have to determine what there is*. If there are no rabbits, the natives do not use 'gavagai' in the presence of rabbits. If there are no undetached rabbit parts, the natives do not use 'gavagai' in the presence of undetached rabbit parts. If all that exists are mereological simples arranged in different configurations, the natives use 'gavagai' in the presence of certain such configurations and in the presence of nothing else.

Hence, if meaning supervenes to any important extent on use, a layman's—or, indeed, a linguist's—judgements about what we mean or are referring to when we utter sentences like (6) or (5) are going to be largely determined by, and hence worth little more than, a layman's or linguist's judgements about the correct principle of composition. What we use our words in the presence of depends on what there is. As Timothy Williamson quipped, "What there is determines what there is for us to mean."[21]

---

[20] Assuming for the sake of argument that H_2Oism, reliabilism, and compatibilism are true.

[21] Williamson (2007), p. 20.

Before moving on, I want to underscore the importance of the hypothetical nature of this defense of Lewis and van Inwagen's paraphrases. I have argued that *if* van Inwagen or Lewis are right about composition, their claims about semantics are much more plausible. Whether composition never, always, or merely sometimes occurs does not make an observable difference. For all the empirical evidence shows, and hence for all any non-metaphysician knows, the actual world *is* a world where universalism or eliminativism is true. Just for the sake of argument, assume that van Inwagen is right about what exists. How could that possibly threaten the truth of our ordinary discourse about tables and chairs? Is our language really so fragile as that? After all, if our world is a van Inwagen world, the word 'chair' was introduced precisely to talk about what are in fact just simples arranged chair-wise. And if this is the case, it seems hard to deny that sentences like (6) will often express truths—it's just that they will express truths more perspicuously expressed by sentences like (6*).[22]

4.2.3. Metaphysical intrusion: Meaning magnetism

A second way in which metaphysics intrudes upon semantics is through the phenomenon of meaning magnetism. According to the doctrine of meaning magnetism, of the different candidate meanings

---

[22] Some think that the problem with (6*) is that it interprets the 'there is' in (6) as a plural quantifier, not that it interprets 'chair' as referring to simples arranged chair-wise. Sider (2013) takes this to be the main obstacle to this sort of paraphrase, and argues that giving up on the view that 'there is' expresses the standard (singular) existential quantifier is a significant price. But that is a price I am afraid we will just have to pay, since this appealing semantics for 'there is' fails for independent reasons. Evidently, 'there is' sometimes expresses a plural quantifier, as in 'There is a family living next door', 'There is a class that meets here at noon', 'There were 24 Allied infantry divisions that fought in the Battle of the Bulge', etc. 'Family', 'class', and 'division' appear to be plural referring expressions: since families, classes, and divisions can change in size, they cannot be identified with sets. (Similar problems beset the idea that they are mereological sums. And if families, etc. are individuals, what individuals could they be if not sets or sums?) But despite the plural nature of their reference, they are grammatically singular, and ordinary English allows them to be (the values of variables) bound by 'there is'. Of course, there are many examples where 'there is' seems to express a plural quantifier, "binding" grammatically plural expressions, such as 'There are students forming a circle on the quad' and 'There are critics that admire only each other'.

an expression might have, certain meanings—the *natural* ones—are intrinsically more likely to be meant than others. Natural meanings "carve reality at its joints": things falling under natural kinds such as *electron* and *green* are objectively similar, as opposed to things falling under non-natural kinds such as *in Arizona* and *grue*. These natural meanings have a "magnetic" effect on the determination of meaning: the magnetic effect of these special meanings can settle indeterminacies in how expressions are used, and can even override use in some cases. So, since *greenness* is more natural than *grueness*, if we find a linguistic community in which 'grün' is often uttered in the presence of things we would call "green", an interpretation according to which 'grün' means *green* is to be preferred to one according to which 'grün' means *grue*, despite the fact that they accord equally well with use. Note that this principle guiding interpretation derives from a principle about meaning: it is the fact that *green* is intrinsically more likely (or "eligible") to be *meant* than *grue* that makes *interpreting* 'grün' as meaning *green* preferable to interpreting it as meaning *grue*.

The doctrine of meaning magnetism might usefully be compared to the idea that simplicity is a theoretical virtue. It is widely accepted that, of all the theories that are compatible with the evidence, certain of those theories—the simple ones—are antecedently more likely to be correct. And indeed, we sometimes prefer a simpler theory to a more complicated one that fits better with the empirical evidence. Meaning magnetism doctrines claim that, just as simplicity is an external constraint on theory choice in general, there is a special external constraint on semantic theory choice: naturalness.

This doctrine has been famously defended by David Lewis and Ted Sider.[23] If true, it provides a reply to Putnam's Model Theoretic Argument for anti-realism,[24] a solution to the New Riddle of Induction and Hempel's Paradox,[25] and a response to Kripke's skeptical

---

[23] See Lewis (1983), Lewis (1984), Sider (2009), and Sider (2012). Davidson's principle of charity serves as sort of an ur-meaning magnetism doctrine: truth is an "external" constraint on the meaning of sentences. This constraint is relatively uncontroversial, at least once it has been qualified in the usual ways.

[24] In Putnam (1977). See Lewis (1983) and Lewis (1984) for how meaning magnetism provides a response.

[25] See Hempel (1945), Goodman (1955), and Quine (1969) for the problem. Sider (2012) argues that meaning magnetism provides a solution.

argument in *Wittgenstein on Rules and Private Language*.[26] Because of these and other reasons, increasing numbers of philosophers are coming to find the doctrine congenial. My aim here, however, is just to illustrate the way in which meaning magnetism makes semantics beholden to metaphysics.

To see this, think about what sort of constraints meaning magnetism puts on semantics. According to the doctrine, the prior probability of a meaning assignment being correct is a function of its naturalness. Interpretations according to which predicates express natural kinds are to be preferred to those that do not. If naturalness is a constraint on meaning, it is plausible that there will be situations where maximizing the naturalness of an interpretation will conflict with the goal of maximizing fit with use. Just as we sometimes accept a simpler scientific theory over a more complex one that fits somewhat better with our empirical observations, so might we accept a semantic theory that assigns more natural meanings over one that assigns less natural meanings but which fits somewhat better with use. Consider theories of the meaning of 'fish' as it was used by our English-speaking ancestors. People once *used* the word 'fish' to refer to animals that lived in the water, and in particular they used it to refer to whales. There are two possibilities for interpreting these ancestors of ours: we can interpret their uses of 'fish' as expressing (and generally correctly applying) the property *animal that lives in the water*, or we can interpret them to have been sometimes mistakenly applying the more natural property *cold blooded aquatic vertebrate with gills*.[27] The doctrine of meaning magnetism says that, all else being roughly equal, we should take the latter route, since the cold blooded and gilled aquatic vertebrates form a much more natural kind than the animals that live in water. And this verdict appears correct: we *discovered*, rather than *decided*, that whales are not fish.

---

[26] In Kripke (1982). See Lewis (1984) for how meaning magnetism provides a response, and Hawthorne (2007) for doubts about some of these applications of the doctrine, at least as it was articulated by Lewis.

[27] The things that have the latter property are much more objectively similar than the things that have the former. This was (roughly) the justification for classifying whales as fish in Linnaeus's *System of Nature* (1776). Contemporary biologists characterize *genera* and *species* by their causal histories and place on the tree of life rather than on the basis of phenotypic traits. In the case of whales, the end result is of course the same.

If you are hesitant to "reinterpret" our ancestors' uses of 'fish' in this way, consider whether you are willing to "reinterpret" their uses of 'people'. Did they not speak falsely when they denied the personhood of black or female humans? Not if 'person' meant *white male landowner*, or some such nonsense. But if we are willing to say that our ancestors were wrong about what it is to be a person, we should be willing to say that they were also wrong about what it is to be a fish. Human beings of all sexes, classes, and colors are now, were, and ever will be persons—such distinctions divide our species in unnatural ways. And whales are not, never were, and never will be fish—lumping together mammalian and other aquatic animals results in a less natural hodge-podge. Both of these examples, then, are cases of naturalness trumping use. For if our ancestors were wrong about whales being fish, then it is wrong to interpret them as meaning *animal that lives in the water* by 'fish', even though that interpretation fits better with the way in which they used the word.

The upshot of meaning magnetism for theories of paraphrase is that, if naturalness imposes an external constraint on semantic theorizing, and if this constraint can trump use, the fact that a paraphrase proposal clashes with patterns of normal use (and with the results of semantic theorizing built upon such data) is not a sufficient reason to conclude that the paraphrase is a failure. For there may be facts relevant to the determination of meaning that these semantic theories are not taking into account: the facts about naturalness. The facts about naturalness, however, depend on the truth about metaphysics. So a semantic theory developed without regard to the results of metaphysical inquiry will be based on a non-representative subset of the evidence.

According to meaning magnetism, a correct theory of meaning must maximize fit *both* with facts about use—the behavior of the linguistic community—*and* facts about non-linguistic reality. If the facts are such that a seemingly outlandish paraphrase is the interpretation that ranks highest with respect to naturalness, then some degree of conflict with use may have to be tolerated.

4.2.4. Concluding remarks about semantic externalism

I have argued in this section that one reason the LSE objection fails in hard cases like (5*)–(10*) is that linguistic meaning (externally conceived) is itself determined in part by the metaphysical facts. If a philosopher accepts a controversial but correct metaphysical theory, this theory may have implications for semantics that will not be recognized by those unconvinced of the truth of the theory. These implications may arise *via* the metaphysical theory implying unrecognized conclusions about use or eligibility—and perhaps in currently unrecognized ways as well. The important point is that there *are* such implications. Even if it is not apparent how metaphysical conclusions could have a *direct* bearing on semantics, these widely accepted ideas about metasemantics show how they can have an *indirect* effect.

There is not, then, a delimited domain of evidence relevant to the determination of meaning. Since the "respectable" (scientific) evidence—the evidence considered by typical linguists, semanticists, and philosophers of language—*is* limited, it follows that some real evidence is not "respectable". And we have seen that metaphysics can provide such non-respectable but real evidence: surprising metaphysical theories can lead to surprising semantic conclusions.

It is worth noting that this conclusion does not conflict with the argument of §4.1. The contrast in §4.1 was not between internalist and externalist conceptions of semantic content, or between semantics and metasemantics, but between semantic content and speaker's meaning—between the "literal" meaning of a sentence (in context) and the thought the speaker intends to communicate when she utters it. This distinction is of course compatible with an externalist conception of the content of that thought. The final problem with the LSE objection, to which we now turn, is something that semantic internalists and externalists alike can endorse.

4.3. Truth conditions and semantic content

The third problem with the LSE objection is that the success of a paraphrase does not hinge on the *semantic* equivalence of the paraphrase and the original sentence or belief, but merely on their *truth-conditional* equivalence. If we use the term 'proposition' to refer to the semantic contents of sentences (in context), we may say that successful paraphrases do not need to express the same proposition, as long as they express propositions with the same truth conditions.

Propositions, or semantic contents, are one kind of "sentential meaning". The proposition expressed by a sentence is a function of the sentence's conventional (linguistic) meaning and the context in which it is uttered. These conventional or linguistic meanings are another kind of sentential meaning,[28] and a third aspect of sentential meaning is cognitive significance. While it is widely hoped that cognitive significance can be reduced to or explained by one of these other kinds of meaning, as of now the relationship between cognitive significance, linguistic meaning, and semantic content is a matter of controversy. The important point for our purposes is that successful paraphrases need not preserve *any* of these kinds of meaning.[29]

The first thing to note is that sameness of linguistic meaning is neither necessary nor sufficient for sameness of semantic content. Sentences with the same linguistic meaning can express distinct contents—e.g. 'I am hungry' said by you and me—and sentences that express the same content can have different linguistic meanings: e.g. 'John is hungry' and 'I am hungry'. In so far as "linguistic evidence" is evidence about linguistic meaning, it is not required for a paraphrase to be credible, since it is clear that successful paraphrases do not need to preserve linguistic meaning.

What is less clear, but no less true, is that successful paraphrases do not need to preserve semantic content either, as long as they preserve truth conditions. According to the widely held view that propositions are *structured*, sameness of semantic content is sufficient, but not necessary, for truth-conditional equivalence.[30] On this view, 'My favorite vase is empty' and 'Nothing is in my favorite vase' will be truth-conditionally, but not semantically, equivalent. The two sentences have the same truth condition—they are true in exactly the same circumstances—but structured propositionalists hold they have distinct semantic contents. This is shown (they say)

---

[28] These two kinds of meaning roughly correspond to what Kaplan (1989b) calls *character* and *content*, and (subsententially) to what Frege (1952/1892) calls *sense* and *reference*.

[29] Of course the "purely linguistic evidence", bears on more than just linguistic meaning in this restricted sense: the evidence marshaled by linguists, semanticists, and philosophers of language is often useful for determining semantic content as well.

[30] Structured propositionalism is defended in, e.g. Russell (1903), Salmon (1986), Soames (1987), and Braun (1993).

by the fact that the semantic content of the former, but not the latter, can be combined with the semantic value of 'and so is my favorite jar' to yield something well-formed and meaningful.[31]

Of course, distinct propositions cannot have different truth conditions according to standard forms of *un*structured propositionalism, which identify the proposition *p* expressed by sentence *s* (in context) with the set of possible worlds at which *s* is true.[32] Propositions, on this theory, are less finely individuated than they are on structured propositionalism. However, if unstructured propositionalism is true, sentences with very different intuitive meanings can have the same content, and hence the same truth condition: for example, if David is Ava's father, then 'David is a bachelor' and 'Ava's father is an adult unmarried male' are true in the same worlds. And so on this view there is not even a *prima facie* problem with claiming that paraphrases with very different intuitive meanings have the same content, and so the same truth condition. If anything, one might object that unstructured propositionalism makes paraphrase too easy.

So if unstructured propositionalism is true, the LSE objection fails. But if *structured* propositionalism is true, semantic equivalence and truth-conditional equivalence come apart. If truth-conditional equivalence is all that is required for a paraphrase to reconcile one's philosophical theory with the non-philosophical facts, then the LSE objection fails *no matter what* form of propositionalism is true. And truth-conditional equivalence *is* all that is required for a paraphrase to be successful: if x is consistent with y, and y is true in the same worlds as z, then x is consistent with z, independently of whether y and z have the same semantic content. So truth-conditionally but not semantically equivalent paraphrases can be used to demonstrate consistency.

As far as I know, this fact has never been explicitly acknowledged, although paraphrists sometimes gesture in its direction. Van Inwagen, for example, notes that his paraphrases are not *synonymous* with the sentences they paraphrase, but claims that they still "describe the same fact". He writes:

---

[31] Similarly with 'and my favorite jar is too', etc.
[32] Unstructured propositionalism is defended in, e.g. Stalnaker (1984) and Lewis (1986).

When the ordinary man utters the sentence 'Some chairs are heavier than some tables'... he expresses a certain proposition, and one that is almost certainly true... it does not appear to me to be wholly unintelligible to say that the [paraphrase] "describes the same fact" as the first... For all that, it does not seem right to say that the two sentences are identical in meaning.[33]

It isn't obvious what it means to say that two sentences "describe the same fact", but one way to understand this claim is as an attempt to indicate what kind of meaning or content van Inwagen takes his paraphrases to preserve. He is indicating that while they do not preserve linguistic meaning or cognitive significance, they do preserve an "external" or "worldly" dimension of meaning. I suggest that he is gesturing at the fact that *truth conditions* must be preserved by successful paraphrases.[34] This distinction between the aspects of meaning that successful paraphrases must preserve, and those that they need not, is important: many of the objections to hard cases of paraphrase like van Inwagen's make false assumptions about just this question.

The distinction between truth conditions and other kinds of meaning has played a key role in advancing debates in other areas of philosophy as well perhaps most famously the debate between "tensers" and "de-tensers" in the philosophy of time. As L. A. Paul writes:

Although ordinary language and folk intuition are normally characterized in terms of tensed sentences, the original advocate of the tenseless theory of time (the old tenseless theory of time) held that all tensed sentences (and their tokens) could be translated by tenseless sentences... However, as the result of developments in the philosophy of language in the area of demonstratives and indexicals, it soon became apparent that tenseless sentences could not translate all tensed sentences... As a result, detensers have developed new versions of the tenseless theory of time... Detensers now admit that tensed sentences or their tokens are not translatable into tenseless sentences but argue that, nevertheless, tenseless characterisations of the truth conditions of tokens of tensed sentences can adequately capture the meaning of tensed sentences.[35]

---

[33] van Inwagen (1990), p. 112–13.

[34] While semantic content is more "external" than linguistic or conventional meaning, we've seen that paraphrases needn't preserve semantic content, since (as van Inwagen notes) successful paraphrases can express different propositions than the sentences they paraphrase.

[35] Paul (1997), p. 54. Dean Zimmerman characterizes the dispute similarly: "The new B-theorists are... not nearly so ambitious as the old. They do not see themselves

The fact that tensed sentences can be provided with de-tensed truth conditions—truth conditions that are identical with the truth conditions of tenseless sentences—is now generally thought to be sufficient for tenselessly "accounting for" the facts typically stated in tensed language. Establishing a more demanding kind of *synonymy* between tensed and tenseless sentences is not necessary in order to defend the non-existence of tensed facts. Mere sameness of truth conditions is enough to show that tensed sentences are not needed to tell the whole truth, and hence that the ideology of tense is dispensable.

Modal-reductionist analyses in terms of possible worlds are another example where the distinction between truth conditions and linguistic meaning has proved important. David Lewis held that 'Necessarily, $2 + 2 = 4$' can be analyzed as the claim that it is true in every world that $2+2 = 4$. Such analyses are not plausibly construed as proposals about semantic content, however. They aim, rather, at providing de-modalized (i.e. de-*mystified*) truth conditions for our modal talk. If, as such reductionists hope, the notion of a possible world can be specified without recourse to the ideology of modality, we will then be able to tell the whole truth—including the modal facts—without the use of modal ideology, simply by talking about possible worlds. In order to reconcile the truth of sentences containing modal language with the non-existence of *sui generis* modal facts, what is required is only that every true modal sentence be truth-conditionally equivalent with a non-modal sentence, not that every true modal sentence be *synonymous* with a non-modal one.[36]

---

as in the business of providing tenseless sentences that 'mean the same thing as' tensed sentences, by any reasonable standard of meaning equivalence. The new B-theorists admit that the propositions we grasp include temporally perspectival ones, and that they cannot be traded in for temporally non-perspectival ones without falsifying the phenomena that are to be explained: namely, the nature of propositional attitudes like belief, and of the thought expressed in tensed sentences. But they believe—and I am inclined to agree—that the ability to give... de-tensed truth conditions for an important class of tensed assertions is enough to justify their claim to have given a theory of the most basic sort of temporally perspectival thinking, and to have done so without positing a privileged present." Zimmerman (2005), p. 425.

[36] Zimmerman (2005) discusses the parallels between the modal and temporal cases, and in particular the way in which distinguishing between linguistic meaning and truth conditions is essential for properly understanding both the tenseless theory of time and modal reductionism.

Although the importance of distinguishing between synonymy and truth-conditional equivalence has been recognized in these debates, its significance has not been fully appreciated in discussions of paraphrase. Trenton Merricks, for example, objects to van Inwagen's paraphrases as follows:

> Ask yourself—*why* is eliminativism striking and surprising? It cannot be because of its revisionary practical or empirical consequences; it has no such consequences... Instead, eliminativism is striking and surprising simply because—and this is the obvious answer—it contradicts what nearly all of us believe.[37]

There are two problems with what Merricks says here. First, while it seems plausible that a necessary condition on my being surprised to find that p is that I do not already believe p, there are at least two different ways to not believe p. One is by believing not-p, but another is by being agnostic about p. Lottery winners are surprised to find that they have the winning ticket, even though they presumably did not believe that the ticket was a loser when they bought it. If p is a claim about fundamental ontology, we should take seriously the possibility that ordinary folk and even philosophers who are not metaphysicians do not believe that p is false, but rather have no pre-theoretic opinion about p for one's metaphysical theory to contradict. They may still manage to be surprised by the metaphysical theory, if it was not something they expected to be true. Perhaps most people come reject van Inwagen's theory of composition when exposed to it. (After all, most people are exposed to the conclusion without argument.) But this doesn't have any untoward implications: many true claims about which the folk are agnostic would, if presented to them without argument, be rejected, even if a *Meno-style* line of questioning would lead them to change their minds. Examples will be controversial, but consider 'There is some beer in the fridge', uttered in a context where inspection reveals only a small puddle of beer in the fridge.

The more important problem with Merrick's objection, however, hinges on the distinction between cognitive significance, semantic content, and truth conditions. The difficulty is that it is not even clear that a necessary condition on being surprised to find that p is

[37] Merricks (2001), p. 163.

that we not already believe *p*. Whether this is so depends on how we individuate belief contents. For example, I might be surprised to find that *I* am on fire even though I already believe that John Keller is on fire. Lois might be surprised to find that Clark Kent can fly even though she already believes that Superman can fly. I might, at 3:00, be surprised to find that the meeting is *now*, even though I already believe that the meeting is at 3:00. And so on. In each of these cases, it is debatable whether the *proposition* that is found surprising is a proposition the agent already believes, and hence whether the sentences that express them have the same semantic content. While it seems impossible to be surprised by something *cognitively equivalent* to something one already believes, it is easy to be surprised by something *truth-conditionally equivalent* to something one already believes. For example, 'Clark Kent can fly' and 'Superman can fly' clearly have the same truth condition, independently of whether they express the same proposition. But since all that is being claimed for van Inwagen's paraphrases is that they are truth-conditionally equivalent to the originals, surprise cannot be used to argue against this equivalence. For it may be surprising that sentences with differing cognitive significance are truth-conditionally equivalent.

Of course, the objects of the attitudes are plausibly individuated more finely than by truth-conditional equivalence, and so the above cases will not be ones where one is surprised to learn a proposition one already believes. But to do the work he needs them to, van Inwagen's paraphrases need not express identical propositions as the sentences they are paraphrasing, as long as they express propositions with identical truth conditions. And it is beyond reasonable doubt that we might be surprised to learn something truth-conditionally equivalent with something we already believe: the above examples establish that.

If the claims ordinarily expressed by (6) and (6*) are true in the same circumstances, then (6) is compatible with van Inwagen's theory if (6*) is, independently of their seemingly obvious difference in semantic content. So if (6) and (6*) have the same truth condition, van Inwagen's theory does not contradict the kind of ordinary beliefs one might report using sentences like (6). Of course, for this to be correct, the existence of a composite object in the closet cannot be required for the truth of (6) (uttered in ordinary contexts). For all

I have argued here, this may be false. As I said at the end of §3, I am arguing only that paraphrases like van Inwagen's are not sunk by the LSE objection, not that they ultimately succeed.[38]

4.3.1. An objection

The importance I have assigned to the distinction between truth conditions and semantic content might seem puzzling, given that the aim of semantics is often taken to be the specification of truth conditions, and since the LSE objection is sometimes explicitly formulated in terms of truth conditions. Jason Stanley, for example, has objected to certain nominalistic paraphrases of arithmetic on the grounds that they do not give an adequate account of the truth conditions of arithmetical discourse. According to Stanley, it is a constraint on arithmetical paraphrases that they account for the fact that "we are able smoothly to grasp the truth conditions of novel arithmetical sentences on the basis of our familiarity with their parts."[39] Stanley is discussing fictionalist paraphrases such as 'According to the fiction of arithmetic, there are two primes between 5 and 13', but his objection would apply equally well to other prominent paraphrase strategies. His worry is that such nominalistic paraphrases have utterly alien truth conditions, involving fictionalist operators like 'According to the fiction of arithmetic'. Such truth conditions are not smoothly grasped by competent speakers, since they aren't grasped by competent speakers at all, save a few philosophers with an axe to grind. The sentence 'there are two primes between 5 and 13' *appears* to be ontologically loaded—if its truth condition is ontologically innocent, how would ordinary speakers (or semanticists, for that matter) ever know it? As Stanley puts it, "the defender [of the paraphrase] cannot in principle give a successful account of how we could assign ontologically innocent truth conditions to ontologically promiscuous discourse."[40]

Of course, we might, following Chomsky, endorse semantic internalism and reject the idea that it is the job of semantics proper

---

[38] But see §3, 4.2, and 4.3.1 for reasons why (6) and (6*) may well have the same truth condition (*if* van Inwagen is right about composition), and fn. 4 on the importance of distinguishing between the meaning of (6) in ordinary and metaphysical contexts.
[39] Stanley (2001), p. 41.   [40] Stanley (2001), p. 44.

to specify truth conditions.[41] But if we are working within a truth-conditional framework, Stanley's objection appears devastating, since competent speakers do not recognize the truth-conditional equivalence of typical paraphrases. To respond to the objection, it is necessary to distinguish between two kinds of truth conditions, or at least two ways of grasping a sentence's truth condition. For language to be learnable, linguistic meaning—what's grasped by competent speakers—must be compositionally determined. But such compositionally determined truth conditions are not plausibly identified with the kind of truth conditions of interest to metaphysicians, epistemologists, etc. These more philosophically interesting truth conditions appear to be neither compositionally determined nor grasped by competent speakers. For in what sense of truth conditions do we "smoothly grasp" the truth conditions of sentences like 'Santa Claus does not exist', '2 + 2 = 4', 'Smith knows that Jones owns a Ford', or 'Joe freely chose to lie to Mary'? Certainly not in a philosophically interesting one. Stanley is sometimes explicit about the fact that semantics concerns what he calls the *"intuitive* truth conditions" of sentences (in context).[42] Davidsonian bi-conditionals are statements of such "intuitive" truth conditions: the kind of truth conditions that competent speakers must grasp. But Davidsonian bi-conditionals do not actually specify, in a philosophically interesting sense, the conditions under which a sentence is true. Since I took high school German, I know, for example, that 'Smith weiß, dass Jones einen Ford besitzt' is true if and only if Smith knows that Jones owns a Ford. That might suffice for me to know the *linguistic meaning* of 'Smith weiß, dass Jones einen Ford besitzt'—for me to *understand* the sentence—but it certainly doesn't mean that I know in an articulable sense the conditions under which 'Smith weiß, dass Jones einen Ford besitzt' is true. The most important reason for this is that I do not know in an articulable sense the conditions under which it is true that Smith knows that Jones owns a Ford. If I did, I'd be a famous epistemologist.

On a Davidsonian approach, then, intuitive truth conditions, or what might be called *semantic* truth conditions, have to be

---

[41] See, e.g. Chomsky (2000), Pietroski (2005), and Glanzberg (forthcoming).

[42] (Intuitive truth conditions) appears to be Stanley's label of choice in his more recent work—in both the introduction to Stanley (2007a), and in Stanley (2007b).

distinguished from what I'll call *metaphysical* truth conditions: philosophically interesting specifications of the conditions under which something is true.[43] Being competent English speakers, we know the semantic truth conditions of most English sentences. We are at the same time ignorant of the *metaphysical* truth conditions of most of the things we think and say.

Davidsonian bi-conditionals can be somewhat plausibly taken as statements of semantic truth conditions, since competent speakers will typically know and accept paradigmatic Davidsonian bi-conditionals such as " 'There is a chair in Ava's closet' is true if and only if there is a chair in Ava's closet", " 'Joe freely chose to lie to Mary' if and only if Joe freely chose to lie to Mary", etc. Such bi-conditionals do not, however, tell us everything about what the world has to be like for there to be a chair in Ava's closet or for Joe's choice to be free. Must Joe's choice be undetermined? Must there be a chair-shaped substance in Ava's closet, as opposed to merely some particles arranged chair-wise? Davidsonian bi-conditionals do not even attempt to answer these questions.[44] For this reason, the kind of truth conditions produced by Davidsonian meaning theories cannot be identified with the kind of truth conditions that successful paraphrases must preserve.

On the other hand, the distinction between semantic and metaphysical truth conditions seems to break down if we think of semantic truth conditions *ontologically*, as the set of (perhaps centered) worlds where a sentence is true. This second approach to truth conditions essentially identifies truth conditions with "coarse-grained" unstructured propositions. Now, if truth conditions are sets of possible worlds, there is no room for there to be any sort of ontological distinction between those sets as specified by our semantic theories and by our philosophical analyses: the set of worlds where a sentence is true is the set of worlds where a sentence is true. Nonetheless, it remains the case that the specifications of this set produced by

---

[43] My thinking about this distinction has been influenced by Sider (2012), although Sider's conception of metaphysical truth conditions diverges significantly from the one I defend here.

[44] Note as well that Davidsonian bi-conditionals if taken to be—statements of semantic truth conditions—must be "interpretive". There is no such requirement on statements of metaphysical truth conditions: indeed, in most or all cases, statements of metaphysical truth conditions will *not* be interpretive: after all, we don't know the metaphysical truth conditions for many sentences we *understand* perfectly well.

typical semantic theories will be as philosophically uninformative as Davidsonian bi-conditionals were: i.e. 'Joe freely chose to lie to Mary' is true at the worlds where Joe freely chose to lie to Mary, etc. If we think of metaphysical and semantic truth conditions as sets of worlds, the sets themselves will of course be identical—the only difference will be in the way that we grasp or are acquainted with those sets. So on this way of thinking it would perhaps be better to talk about "semantic knowledge" of truth conditions, as opposed to a deeper kind of "metaphysical knowledge". Semantics aims at producing semantic knowledge of truth conditions, while while our philosophical analyses aim at something more.[45]

Call the set of worlds where 'Joe freely chose to lie to Mary' is true ψ. There is nothing *wrong* with philosophically uninteresting semantic specifications of ψ; I am only arguing that such specifications do not shed much light on the actual conditions of membership for that set. And likewise with the set of worlds where (6) is true. Rather obviously, 'There is a chair in Ava's closet' is true at the set of worlds where there is a chair in Ava's closet, but what is required of a world in order for that sentence to be true at it? To describe its truth condition as "the set of worlds where there is a chair in Ava's closet" leaves us in the dark regarding whether there must be a single chair-shaped entity in the closet, or whether (6) might be true if in the closet there are nothing but simples arranged chair-wise.

Appreciating the distinction between semantic and metaphysical truth conditions is critical for understanding the conditions for a paraphrase to be a success, since, as we saw above, successful paraphrases must only have the same (metaphysical) truth conditions as the original.[46] Proponents of the LSE objection, however, seem to have something like linguistic meaning, semantic content, cognitive significance, or semantic truth conditions in mind as what a successful paraphrase must preserve. These are all much more transparent

---

[45] Devitt and Sterelny (1999) argue that the meaning of a sentence is "its mode of presenting its truth condition" (p. 114). Perhaps semantic knowledge of truth conditions requires only that the speaker grasp the truth condition under *some* mode of presentation, while metaphysical knowledge requires grasping the truth condition under a metaphysically perspicuous mode of presentation.

[46] Even this is too strong. Extensional equivalence between referring expressions is enough in certain cases—specifically, when that extensional equivalence is guaranteed by the other parts of one's theory. For example, 'My daughter is playing' and 'Maggie is playing' are (for me) simply two different ways of describing the same fact. See §4.1.

to competent speakers than metaphysical truth conditions, since metaphysical truth conditions aren't transparent at all. We certainly do not grasp them simply in virtue of understanding a sentence. But the equivalence of metaphysical truth conditions is what matters for evaluating the kind of paraphrase proposals under consideration in this paper. If I do not believe that there are φs, the challenge I face is to tell the whole truth without saying anything that entails that φs exist. If I have specified exactly which world is actual, there is a reasonable sense in which I have told the whole truth, or at least the whole contingent truth. But for the purposes of specifying which world is actual, all that is required of (6*) is that necessarily, (6*) is true if and only if (6) is. You might think that, since necessary truths may have intuitively distinct metaphysical truth conditions, equivalence of metaphysical truth conditions requires something more fine-grained than necessary equivalence, such as logical equivalence. Perhaps so, but it is clear that full-blown *semantic* equivalence is not required. Many semantically inequivalent sentences are necessarily (and even logically) equivalent.[47]

Please note that this argument is no indictment of semantics. As noted above, learnability concerns must constrain our theories of linguistic meaning, since linguistic meanings are what language users learn. Normal language users, however, have little or no idea what is metaphysically required for the truth of the sentences they understand. So (knowledge of) linguistic meanings cannot plausibly be identified with (knowledge of) metaphysical truth conditions.

The distinction between metaphysical and semantic truth conditions has recently been defended by Sarah-Jane Leslie. She writes:

I would suggest that these worldly truth specifications—these descriptions of how the world must be for the sentence to be true—should not be mistaken for semantically derived truth conditions... [If] a dispositionalist theory of color is correct...'Bob is red'...is true if and only if Bob is experienced as red by standard observers in standard conditions. This is a specification of the circumstances in the world that must obtain for 'Bob

---

[47] i.e. many sentences that express distinct structured propositions have the same intension—and indeed, many sentences that express distinct structured propositions are logically equivalent. For example, 'All green things are green' and 'All red things are red', are logically but not semantically equivalent. Plausibly, but more contentiously, so are 'My favorite vase is empty' and 'There is nothing in my favorite vase'.

is red' to be true. Such a specification does not tell us anything about the semantically derived, compositionally determined truth conditions for 'Bob is red'... for Bob to be experienced as red by standard observers in standard conditions, there must exist standard observers to experience him as such... metaphysically speaking, the truth of 'Bob is red' entails the existence of standard observers. It is in no way part of semantic competence to recognize that the truth of 'Bob is red' entails that there exist standard observers, however. This is not plausibly a semantic entailment, but merely a metaphysical one.

The semantic truth conditions for 'Bob is red' may well be no more than Red(Bob). This respects the compositional structure of the sentence... For this reason, and others, it is very often desirable to simply disquote individual expressions when giving semantic truth conditions. Any further analysis of individual expressions very often belongs to metaphysics rather than to semantics.[48]

Some might worry that the distinction between semantic and metaphysical truth conditions is spurious, a desperate move made only by metaphysicians who have painted themselves into a corner. If Leslie is correct about there being reasons for drawing such a distinction that are internal to semantic theorizing, this concern is mistaken. The arguments of semantic internalists like Chomsky, who do not even think that knowledge of *semantic* truth conditions is the product of mere linguistic competence, provide further evidence that the distinction can be motivated within linguistic theorizing itself.

Before moving on, I would like to briefly discuss how the conclusion of this section meshes with the idea that there are Moorean facts, such as the fact that things move. Armstrong, following Moore, held that this fact was "shallow"—that we could be sure that things move while being ignorant of the true "analysis" of motion. One

---

[48] Leslie (2008), pp. 43–4. Leslie remarks in another paper that the distinction "is quite intuitive, though it is rarely drawn." (Leslie (2007), p. 386.) The intuitiveness of the distinction is evidenced by the fact that a variety of similar distinctions have been defended in the literature: in addition to Sider (2012), see, e.g. Hawthorne and Cortens (1995) (between two goals of paraphrase), Hawthorne and Michael (1996) (between two conceptions of logical form), and King (2002) (again between two conceptions of logical form). Williams (2010) gives a "theory of requirements" that closely resembles a theory of metaphysical truth conditions (see also Williams (2012)), and a distinction between semantic truth conditions and metaphysical truth*makers* is defended in Cameron (2008a) and Cameron (2008b). As Leslie indicates, these defenses have been largely, and lamentably, ignored. (I thank Stephen Neale for drawing my attention to this aspect of Leslie's work.)

way of thinking about this would be to say that while we know the semantic truth condition for 'The Earth is moving'—and know that it is satisfied!—we may yet be ignorant of that sentence's metaphysical truth condition. Semantically, 'moving' is a predicate—it takes only one argument. We know, however, that from a deeper scientific or metaphysical perspective, motion is a relation. The Earth is moving relative to some frames and at rest relative to another.

But how, we might ask, did the semantically *predicative* phrase 'moving' become associated with its fundamentally *relational* application condition, given that we only became aware of the relational nature of motion long after the meaning of 'motion' was established? That's a fascinating and difficult question of metasemantics, and I won't pretend that I know its answer.[49] But I want to close this section by noting that *whatever* the answer is, a similar answer presumably explains how, if a dispositionalist theory of color is correct, 'Bob is red' became associated with its metaphysical truth condition—and if van Inwagen is correct, how (6) became associated with the truth condition reflected by (6*).

5. CONCLUSION

Let me briefly summarize what I have argued in this paper. There are three reasons why paraphrases advanced without the support of "scientifically respectable" linguistic evidence may still be correct. First, in cases where speaker meaning and semantic content diverge, it can be granted that philosophers often do not have linguistic or otherwise scientific evidence for their paraphrases. This is irrelevant to the success of those paraphrases, however, since the goal of a reconciling paraphrase requires only that it preserve speaker-meaning—the belief that the speaker intends to communicate with her utterance. Furthermore, only one aspect of speaker meaning must be preserved at that: the paraphrase must have the same metaphysical *truth conditions* as the paraphrased. If this point is conceded, the LSE objection loses its force, since metaphysicians, not semanticists, are the relevant experts when it comes to determining whether two sentences have the same metaphysical truth

---

[49] Although I suppose it has something to do with semantic externalism, naturalness, and use.

conditions. For example, it is metaphysicians, not semanticists, who are in a position to authoritatively speculate about whether, say, 'Joe freely chose to lie to Mary' is true in the same worlds as 'Joe's choice to lie to Mary was caused by his beliefs and desires'—or whether 'there is a chair in Ava's closet' is true at the same worlds as 'there are some simples arranged chair-wise in Ava's closet'.

This point about truth conditions holds even when speaker meaning and semantic content do not diverge, since even if a speaker utters a sentence that expresses exactly what she means, not every aspect of meaning needs to be preserved by a paraphrase—sameness of truth conditions is enough. And again, it is metaphysicians, not semanticists, who are experts about sameness of (metaphysical) truth conditions.

Finally, we've seen how semantic externalism casts doubt upon a key assumption behind the LSE objection: that there is a special class of respectable, linguistic (as opposed to metaphysical) evidence which should carry most or all of the weight in our evaluations of paraphrase proposals. Because the facts about use partly determine the facts about meaning, and the metaphysical facts partly determine the facts about use, there is no principled way to delimit a domain of evidence untainted by metaphysical considerations. For example, if van Inwagen's metaphysical theory is correct, this will push us towards accepting his theory of the metaphysical truth conditions of (6). Considerations of this kind will only be amplified if naturalness is a constraint upon semantic theorizing, since the facts about naturalness are metaphysical facts. For these reasons, revisions in our metaphysical theories will often lead to revisions in our semantic ones—or at least, revisions in our theories about the metaphysical truth conditions of our sentences.

If all this is correct, there is a good explanation of the fact that philosophers do not typically offer semantic evidence in support of their paraphrase proposals: they are not making claims about the semantics of the sentences we utter. Rather, they are making claims about the metaphysical truth conditions of the *things we believe*. As we have seen, such metaphysical truth conditions are distinct from linguistic meanings or semantic contents. We all know what 'Smith knows that Jones drives a Ford', 'Joe freely chose to lie to Mary', etc. *mean*, linguistically speaking. What we do not know, with sufficient clarity, is what it takes for them to be true.

Whatever respectable "scientific" evidence we have concerning linguistic meaning, we are largely in the dark about the metaphysical truth conditions of our talk and thought. Platonsim, Aristotelianism, Cartesian Dualism, Reductive Physicalism—not to mention Leibniz's monadology and various forms of monism—all paint radically different pictures of what is required by the truth of, say, 'There is a chair in Ava's closet'. If the metaphysical truth conditions of this sentence were transparent, it would be transparent which (if any) of these theories was correct. But it isn't, so it ain't.

The lack of scientific evidence objection, then, is a failure. Neither semantics nor any other science is first philosophy—semantic inquiry must be conducted in tandem with metaphysics and philosophy more generally, not prior to it.

Niagara University

REFERENCES

Alston, William (1963) "Ontological commitments." *Philosophical Studies*, 14: 1–8.
Armstrong, D. M. (2006) "The scope and limits of human knowledge." *Australasian Journal of Philosophy*, 84(2): 159–66.
Bach, Kent (2000) "Quantification, qualification, and context: A reply to Stanley and Szabó". *Mind and Language*, 15(2–3): 262–83.
Bach, Kent (2001) "Speaking loosely: Sentence nonliterality." *Midwest Studies in Philosophy*, 25: Figurative Language: 249–63.
Braun, David (1993) "Empty names." *Noûs*, 27: 449–69.
Burge, Tyler (1979) "Individualism and the mental." In Peter French, Theodore E. Uehling, Jr., and Howard K. Wettstein, editors, *Midwest Studies in Philosophy IV: Studies in Metaphysics*, pp. 73–121. Minneapolis: University of Minnesota Press.
Burgess, John P. and Gideon Rosen (2005) "Nominalism reconsidered." In Stewart Shapiro, editor, *Oxford Handbook of the Philosophy of Mathematics and Logic*, pp. 515–35. New York: Oxford University Press.
Cameron, Ross P. (2008a) "There are no things that are music works." *British Journal of Aesthetics*, 48(3): 295–314.
Cameron, Ross P. (2008b) "Truthmakers and ontological commitment." *Philosophical Studies*, 140: 1–18.
Cappelen, Herman, and Ernie Lepore (2005) *Insensitive Semantics: a defense of semantic minimalism and speech act pluralism*. Malden, MA: Blackwell Publishing.

Chomsky, Noam (2000) *New Horizons in the Study of Language and Mind.* Cambridge: Cambridge University Press.

Devitt, Michael, and Kim Sterelny (1999) *Language and Reality: An Introduction to the Philosophy of Language.* Cambridge, MA: MIT Press, 2nd edition.

Donnellan, Keith (1974) "Speaking of nothing." *The Philosophical Review*, 83: 3–31.

Dorr, Cian (2005) "What we disagree about when we disagree about ontology." In Mark Kalderon, editor, *Fictionalism in Metaphysics*, pp. 234–86. Oxford: Oxford University Press.

Fine, Kit (2009) "The question of ontology." In David J. Chalmers, David Manley, and Ryan Wasserman, editors, *Metametaphysics*, pp. 157–77. Oxford: Oxford University Press.

Frege, Gottlob ([1892]1952) "On sense and reference." In Peter Geach and Max Black, editors, *Translations of the Philosophical Writings of Gottlob Frege*, pp. 56–78. Oxford: Blackwell.

Glanzberg, Michael (forthcoming) "Explanation and partiality in semantic theory." In Alexis Burgess and Brett Sherman, editors, *Metasemantics: New Essays on the Foundations of Meaning.* Oxford: Oxford University Press.

Goodman, Nelson (1955) *Fact, Fiction, and Forecast.* Cambridge, MA: Harvard University Press.

Grice, H. P. (1989) *Studies in the Way of Words.* Cambridge, MA: Harvard University Press.

Hawthorne, John (2007) "Craziness and metasemantics." *Philosophical Review*, 116(3): 427–40.

Hawthorne, John (O'Leary-), and Andrew Cortens (1995) "Towards ontological nihilism." *Philosophical Studies*, 79: 143–65.

Hawthorne, John (O'Leary-), and Michaelis Michael (1996) "Compatibilist semantics in metaphysics: A case study." *Australasian Journal of Philosophy*, 74(1): 117–34.

Hempel, Carl (1945) "Studies in the logic of confirmation i & ii." *Mind*, 54: 1–26 & 97–121.

Hirsch, Eli (2008) "Language, ontology, and structure." *Noûs*, 42(3): 509–28.

Horgan, Terence, and Matjaž Potrč (2008) *Austere Realism.* Cambridge, MA: MIT Press.

Jackson, Frank (1980) "Ontological commitment and paraphrase." *Philosophy*, 55(213): 303–15.

Kaplan, David (1989a) "Afterthoughts" In Joseph Almog, John Perry, and Howard Wettstein, editors, *Themes from Kaplan*, pp. 565–614. New York: Oxford University Press.

Kaplan, David (1989b) "Demonstratives." In Joseph Almog, John Perry, and Howard Wettstein, editors, *Themes from Kaplan*, pp. 481–563. New York: Oxford University Press.

Keller, John A. (forthcoming) "Paraphrase and the symmetry of meaning."

King, Jeffrey C. (2001) *Complex Demonstratives: a quantificational account*. Cambridge, MA: MIT Press.

King, Jeffrey C. (2002) "Two sorts of claim about 'logical form'." In Gerhard Preyer and Georg Peter, editors, *Logical Form and Language*, pp. 118–131. Oxford: Oxford University Press.

King, Jeffrey C., and Jason Stanley (2005) "Semantics, pragmatics, and the role of semantic content." In Zoltan Szabo, editor, *Semantics vs. Pragmatics*, pp. 111–64. Oxford: Oxford University Press.

Korman, Daniel Z. (2007) "Unrestricted composition and restricted quantification." *Philosophical Studies*, 140: 319–34.

Korman, Daniel Z. (2009) "Eliminativism and the challenge from folk belief." *Noûs*, 43(2): 242–64.

Korman, Daniel Z. (2013) "Fundamental quantification and the language of the ontology room." *Noûs*.

Kripke, Saul (1979) "Speaker's reference and semantic reference." In P. French, T. Uehling, and H. Wettstein, editors, *Contemporary Perspectives in the Philosophy of Language*, pp. 6–27. Minneapolis: University of Minnesota Press.

Kripke, Saul (1980) *Naming and Necessity*. Cambridge, MA: Harvard University Press.

Kripke, Saul (1982) *Wittgenstein on Rules and Private Language*. Cambridge, MA: Harvard University Press.

Leslie, Sarah-Jane (2007) "Generics and the structure of the mind." *Philosophical Perspectives 21, Philosophy of Mind* (1): 375–403.

Leslie, Sarah-Jane (2008) "Generics: Cognition and acquisition." *Philosophical Review*, 117(1): 1–47.

Lewis, David (1970) "General semantics." *Synthese*, 22: 18–67.

Lewis, David (1983) "New work for a theory of universals." *Australasian Journal of Philosophy*, 61: 343–77.

Lewis, David (1984) "Putnam's paradox." *Australasian Journal of Philosophy*, 62: 221–36.

Lewis, David (1986) *On the Plurality of Worlds*. Oxford: Basil Blackwell, Oxford.

Lewis, David (1997) "Do we believe in penal substitution?" *Philosophical Papers*, 26(3): 203–9.

Lewis, David, and Stephanie Lewis, (1970) "Holes." *Australasian Journal of Philosophy*, 48: 206–12.

Mackie, Penelope (1993) "Ordinary language and metaphysical commitment." *Analysis*, 53(4): 243–51.
Joseph, Melia (1995) "On what there's not." *Analysis*, 55: 223–9.
Merricks, Trenton (2001) *Objects and Persons*. Oxford: Clarendon.
Paul, L. A. (1997) "Truth conditions of tensed sentence types." *Synthese*, 111(1): 53–72.
Pietroski, Paul M. (2005) "Meaning before truth." In Gerhard Preyer and Georg Peter, editors, *Contextualism in Philosophy: Knowledge, Meaning, and Truth*, pp. 255–302. Oxford: Oxford University Press.
Putnam, Hilary (1975) "The meaning of meaning." In Keith Gunderson, editor, *Language, Mind and Knowledge*, volume 7 of *Minnesota Studies in the Philosophy of Science*, pp. 131–93. Minneapolis: University of Minnesota Press.
Putnam, Hilary (1977) "Realism and reason." *Proceedings of the American Philosophical Association*, 50: 483–98.
Quine, W. V. O. (1969) "Natural kinds." In *Ontological Relativity and other Essays*, pp. 114–38. New York: Columbia University Press.
Recanati, François (2004) *Literal Meaning*. Cambridge: Cambridge University Press.
Russell, Bertrand (1903) *The Principles of Mathematics*. London: Routledge.
Salmon, Nathan (1986) *Frege's Puzzle*. Cambridge, MA: MIT Press.
Schaffer, Jonathan (2009) "On what grounds what." In David Chalmers, David Manley, and Ryan Wasserman, editors, *Metametaphysics*, pp. 347–83. Oxford: Oxford University Press.
Sider, Theodore (1993) "Van Inwagen and the possibility of gunk." *Analysis*, 53: 285–9.
Sider, Theodore (2009) "Ontological realism." In David Chalmers, David Manley, and Ryan Wasserman, editors, *Metametaphysics*, pp. 384–423. Oxford: Oxford University Press.
Sider, Theodore (2012) *Writing the Book of the World*. New York Oxford University Press.
Sider, Theodore (2013) "Against parthood." In *Oxford Studies in Metaphysics*, volume 8, pp. 237–93. Oxford: Oxford University Press.
Smith, Michael (1997) "In defense of *the moral problem*: A reply to Brink, Copp, and Sayre-McCord." *Ethics*, 108: 84–119.
Soames, Scott (1987) "Direct reference, propositional attitudes, and semantic content." *Philosophical Topics*, 15: 47–87.
Soames, Scott (2008) "Interpreting legal texts: What is, and what is not, special about the law." In *Philosophical Essays, Volume 1*. Princeton, NJ: Princeton University Press. Presented at the Law, Language, and Interpretation conference at the University of Akureyri.

Speaks, Jeff (2011) "Theories of meaning." In Edward N. Zalta, editor, *The Stanford Encyclopedia of Philosophy*. Summer 2011 edition. <http://plato.stanford.edu/entries/meaning/>.

Stalnaker, Robert (1984) *Inquiry*. Cambridge, MA: MIT Press.

Stanley, Jason (1998) "Persons and their properties." *The Philosophical Quarterly*, 48(191): 159–75.

Stanley, Jason (2001) "Hermeneutic fictionalism." In Peter French and Howard K. Wettstein, editors, *Midwest Studies in Philosophy XXV: Figurative Language*, pp. 36–71. Oxford: Basil Blackwell.

Stanley, Jason (2007a) *Language in Context: Selected Essays*. New York: Oxford University Press.

Stanley, Jason (2007b) "Semantics in context." In *Language in Context: Selected Essays*. New York: Oxford University Press.

Stanley, Jason, and Zoltan Gendler Szabo (2000) "On quantifier domain restriction." *Mind and Language*, 15: 219–61.

van Inwagen, Peter (1990) *Material Beings*. Ithaca, NY: Cornell University Press.

van Inwagen, Peter (2014) "Inside and outside the ontology room." In *Existence: Essays in Ontology*. Cambridge: Cambridge University Press.

Varzi, Achille C. (2007) "From language to ontology: Beware of the traps." In Michel Aurnague, Maya Hickmann, and Laure Vieu, editors, *The Categorization of Spatial Entities in Language and Cognition*, pp. 269–84. John Benjamins Publishing Company.

Wettstein, Howard K. (1984) "How to bridge the gap between meaning and reference." *Synthese*, 58: 63–84.

Williams, J. R. G. (2010) "Fundamental and derivative truths." *Mind*, 119 (473): 103–41.

Williams, J. Robert G. (2012) "Requirements on reality." In Fabrice Correia and Benjamin Schnieder, editors, *Metaphysical Grounding: Understanding the Structure of Reality*, pp. 165–85. Cambridge: Cambridge University Press.

Williamson, Timothy (2007) *The Philosophy of Philosophy*. Oxford: Blackwell Publishers.

Yablo, Stephen (1998) "Does ontology rest on a mistake?" *Proceedings of the Aristotelian Society*, Supp. 72: 229–61.

Zimmerman, Dean W. (2005) "The a-theory of time, the b-theory of time, and 'taking tense seriously'." *Dialectica*, 59: 401–57.

7. Analyticity and ontology

Louis deRosset

Let's start with a story. A carpenter formulates a plan to make a table. She assembles some wood, shapes the pieces, and joins them according to the plan. What has the carpenter accomplished? How has she changed the way things are? She formulated and executed a plan, shaped some wood, and has more generally done what in the literature is called "arranging particles table-wise" in a certain spatiotemporal location L.[1] She has also produced a table in that location. We might summarize the import of this development thus:

EXISTENCE   There is a table in L.

What's more, this table is, it seems, distinct from (and irreducible to) the microphysical effects of the carpenter's efforts. The table's distinctness from and irreducibility to those effects is attested by a difference in persistence conditions. The table could survive the passing of all of these effects together; under the right circumstances, the table would exist despite the fact that the particles which in fact make it up enter into a radically different arrangement. Thus, the carpenter has added to the furniture of the world. We might summarize the import of this claim by:

DISTINCTNESS   The table in L is distinct from and irreducible to any congeries of particles.

At least, that's how matters appear to be.

Let's suppose we take these appearances at face value, and acknowledge that the table exists and is distinct from any congeries of particles that make it up. It would appear that we thereby add an

---

[1] The story I am telling makes some physical assumptions. In particular, it assumes that the wood from which the table is produced is made of particles, rather than, say, atomless gunk. I think the arguments of this paper would be unaffected if the physics of the story turned out to be false.

additional entity to our ontology. The addition may be warranted by the arguments for **EXISTENCE** and **DISTINCTNESS**. If so, then we don't run afoul of Occam's Razor by "multiplying entities beyond necessity." We are, however, "multiplying entities." Other things being equal, the universe is less sparsely populated for containing both the table and its particles than it would be if it contained only the particles. At least, that's how it appears.

Authors whom I will call *analyticity theorists* argue that appearances are misleading because the existence of a table in location L is analytically entailed by the existence and arrangment of the particles there.[2] According to this view there is a specification of the existence and features of the particles which is such that it is analytic that if that specification is satisfied, then a table exists in the region where those particles are found. In short,

> **ANALYTICITY** The existence of a table in L is analytically entailed by some appropriate specification of the arrangement of particles in L.[3]

Something similar goes for other artifacts. In fact, claim analyticity theorists, the point generalizes to other entities, including works of art, rocks, mountains, and even properties, events, and numbers.[4]

Obviously the claim that the existence of a table in the relevant location is analytically entailed by the existence and arrangment of particles in that location relies on the notion of analyticity. Analyticity theorists are (among other things) thereby obliged to defend analyticity from the criticisms of Quine and others. They have taken this challenge up with enthusiasm. Their efforts won't be

---

[2] David Lewis has suggested that appearances are misleading for another reason: that mereological composition is ontologically innocent. Lewis's view is beyond the scope of this paper. See (Yi, 1999) and (deRosset, 2010, §6) for criticism of Lewis's contention.

[3] The qualifier 'appropriate' is inserted to ensure that the specification in question does not *trivially* entail that the particles in L compose a table; for instance, 'the particles in L are arranged in such a way as to compose a table' would be an inappropriate specification. If pressed for a clearer account, we may assume that an appropriate specification is acceptable not only to the analyticity theorist, but also to theorists (e.g. van Inwagen (1990)) who accept the existence of the particles but deny the existence of tables.

[4] See (Thomasson, 2007), (Hale and Wright, 2001). Given **DISTINCTNESS**, the analyticity theorist requires the possibility of analytic entailment unaccompanied by reduction.

the focus of our discussion. Instead, let's give analyticity theorists the full measure of analyticity the view requires: assume that the Quinean criticisms can be put to rest, and that **ANALYTICITY** is true. We'll focus on the further claim made by analyticity theorists, that these analytic entailments buy an "ontological free lunch." On this view, accepting the existence of the table incurs no ontological commitments beyond those incurred by accepting that the particles exist and have the right arrangement. Admitting the existence of the table is "no addition to being." This idea is aptly expressed by Amie Thomasson:

> If claim ϕ analytically entails claim ψ, then competent speakers can infer the truth of ψ merely by knowing the truth of ϕ and knowing the relevant meanings of terms (and being competent reasoners). But if this is the case, then clearly ψ requires no more of the world for its truth than ϕ already required—sufficient truth-makers in the world for ϕ are also sufficient truth-makers in the world for ψ, they just make a new claim ψ true. (Thomasson, 2007, p. 16)

The claim, then, that will be our focus, the *doctrine of analyticity in ontology*, asserts a connection between analyticity and ontological parsimony:

DAO If P analytically entails the existence of certain things, then a theory that contains P but does not claim that those things exist is no more ontologically parsimonious than a theory that also claims that they exist.

This paper argues that **DAO** faces counter-examples. If the counter-examples stick, then analyticity does not buy an "ontological free lunch." Even if the existence of a table is analytically entailed by the existence and arrangement of its particles, so long as the particles and the table are distinct, the table is "an addition to being." The objection is closely related to the familiar complaint that, according to **DAO**, we can, implausibly, "define things into existence."[5] Analyticity theorists have argued that this complaint is misplaced, denying that they are committed to the claim that, e.g. the existence of any table *results from* the analyticity of any sentence. The analyticity theorist thinks, just as we do, that tables exist in

---

[5] See (Bennett, 2000, p. 56), for a contemporary attempt to press the objection.

virtue of the existence and features of their particles,[6] so no amount of linguistic legislation can conjure a table into existence. Even so, I will argue, there is a way of reconstructing this familiar complaint so that the underlying idea is correct. One source of the complaint is the idea that there is a sense in which the existence of a table in a given location is a *substantial further fact*, over and above the existence and arrangement of particles there and the rules governing 'table' talk; that's why, on this reconstruction of the complaint, the table can't be defined into existence. I will argue that this underlying idea is essentially correct. Despite **ANALYTICITY**, we have no reason to deny that the existence of a table in the relevant location is a substantial further fact in the relevant sense: **ANALYTICITY** does not imply that the table's existence is an "ontological free lunch."

I begin by specifying in §1 some assumptions concerning analyticity and ontological parsimony that are required, both to properly understand the import of **DAO** and to carry out the arguments against it. Then in §2 I state the case against **DAO**. I discuss responses on behalf of the analyticity theorist in §§3–4. Finally, I close in §5 by sketching the picture of metaphysical inquiry suggested by the arguments.

1. ANALYTICITY AND PARSIMONY

Anayticity theorists claim that there is some specification of the existence and features of the particles in location L that analytically entails the existence of a table there. Let's suppose that $p_1, \ldots, p_n$ are the particles in L and abbreviate the specification in question by saying that $p_1, \ldots, p_n$ are "arranged table-wise." Then the analyticity theorist's claim is that

(1) If $p_1, \ldots, p_n$ are arranged table-wise in L, then there is a table in L.

is analytic.

What does it mean to say that (1) is analytic? The notion of analyticity is notoriously difficult to specify clearly. For present purposes,

---

[6] See (Thomasson, 2007, pp. 63–8) for a more extended response.

we will understand the idea liberally: A sentence ϕ is *analytic* iff it is entailed by true sentences $\psi_1, \psi_2, \ldots$ such that failure to accept any ψ_n constitutes some measure of linguistic incompetence.[7] Call a sentence *foundationally analytic* iff it is true and failure to accept it constitutes some measure of linguistic incompetence. Given our understanding of analyticity,

(2) If Mark Twain is a bachelor, then Mark Twain is unmarried

is analytic, since

(3) No bachelor is married

is, plausibly, foundationally analytic in English. With the notion of analyticity in hand, we may define a notion of analytic entailment: a sentence ϕ *analytically entails* a sentence ψ iff the material conditional $(\phi \Rightarrow \psi)$ is analytic. Thus,

(4) Mark Twain is a bachelor

analytically entails

(5) Mark Twain is unmarried.

I hope that this specification is liberal enough that the analyticity theorist's claims concerning what is analytic in English are plausible. The specification lacks some of the alleged features of analyticity which theorists have found problematic. For instance, it does not require that analytic sentences are true *in virtue of* the rules governing our language; see (Boghossian, 1996). It also allows analytic truths that are surprising and informative. In fact, this specification allows that some analytic truths are so long that no human being could entertain them. It does not require that analytic sentences

---

[7] We may not, however, infer from the fact that a speaker fails to accept one of the ψ's that she is linguistically incompetent *simpliciter*, nor that she fails to understand any expression of her language. The idea, instead, is that she falls short of utterly perfect linguistic competence. Presumably, all of us, even those of us competent in English, fall short of perfect competence. The other day, for instance, I was surprised to learn from the American Heritage Dictionary that 'meretricious' connotes something like 'ostentatious'. I hope nonetheless to be counted as competent *simpliciter* in English, and even competent *simpliciter* with 'meretricious'. What's more, nothing in the specification rules out the idea that these departures from perfect competence are theoretically motivated. Thus, the criticisms of (Williamson, 2007, Ch. 4) seem to me not to apply.

follow from definitions of any sort, nor, more generally, from any specification of necessary and sufficient conditions for the extension of any term. It does not explicitly rely on any notion of synonymy, though undoubtedly some arguments to the effect that there is no such thing as synonymy may also undercut the presumption that there is such a thing as a foundationally analytic sentence—a sentence, that is, whose non-acceptance constitutes some measure of linguistic incompetence; see (Quine, 1951). It does not rely at all on any claim concerning the metaphysics of meanings, conceptual containment, or the like. It does not require or even suggest that analytic sentences are about the meanings of our words or about language, rather than about the extra-linguistic world. It does not require that anyone who fails to accept an analytic sentence, or even a foundationally analytic sentence, fails to understand some of the expressions contained therein. More generally, it does not rely on any strong relation between accepting a sentence and understanding it; see (Williamson, 2007).

Our specification of analyticity is not, however, too liberal. No analytic sentence is false, since anything entailed by true sentences is itself true. And, it seems, there are plenty of true sentences that are not counted as analytic by the specification; for instance,

(6) If Mark Twain is a bachelor, then Mark Twain is famous

is true but does not follow from truths whose acceptance is required for perfect competence in English. Likewise,

(7) If Mark Twain is a bachelor, then the author of *Huckleberry Finn* is unmarried

is not analytic on this account, since failure to accept

(8) Mark Twain = the author of *Huckleberry Finn*

does not constitute any measure of linguistic incompetence.

Our specification of analyticity is murky in crucial ways. First, it relies on a notion of entailment which has not been clearly specified. Second, it relies on the idea that failure to accept a certain sentence constitutes some measure of linguistic incompetence. I have emphasized (see n. 7) that being incompetent to some extent needn't imply being incompetent *simpliciter*. Thus, the notion in question bears an indirect relation to everyday judgments concerning speakers' linguistic incompetence and may for this reason be somewhat elusive.[8] Third, something will need to be done about ambiguity, both lexical and structural, in order to deliver an answer to the question of whether (uses of) these sentences

> (9) If Twain drove a ship onto the ground at the side of a river, then he drove a ship onto a bank
> (10) If Twain gave Crane a dollar, then he received money

are analytic. These are only examples of ways in which our conception of analyticity is unclear. These examples can undoubtedly be multiplied. I will be assuming, however, that the analyticity theorist can meet any reasonable demands for clarification that may arise. Nothing that follows will turn on any particular way of clearing things up.

Our specification of analyticity has an important epistemic upshot. In principle, speakers may come to know the truth of an analytic sentence by logical reasoning from sentences which, when considered, should be accepted by dint of linguistic competence. In this sense, competent speakers, on the basis of their competence and logical acumen, may reason their way to the conclusion that an analytic sentence is true.[9] Thus, our specification of analyticity captures a methodological thread running through analyticity theorists' writing: analytic truths in my language may in principle be known solely by reflection on what my terms mean (together with an application of logical acumen).[10]

I think it's useful to have this rough and ready specification of a notion of analyticity in hand for the arguments that follow, but I don't think the arguments against **DAO** depend crucially on its correctness. In those arguments I will be working with cases in which analyticities are established by what I will call *linguistic stipulations*; linguistic stipulations are stipulations concerning what

---

[8] (Williamson, 2007, pp. 90–2).

[9] In what follows, I will make no distinction between knowing the truth of an analytic sentence, and knowing the truth that sentence expresses; see (Donnellan, 1977), (Jeshion, 2001), and (Hawthorne and Manley, 2012) for discussion. In fact, I will indulge in use-mention sloppiness, since detailed attention to the distinction will not be relevant to the arguments and would be distracting.

[10] See especially (Boghossian, 1996) and (Thomasson, 2007).

an introduced term is to mean. Every linguistic stipulation has a *content*, given by what is stipulated to be the case. For instance, if I make the linguistic stipulation

> (11) I hereby stipulate that: 'π' is a name that refers to the number (if there is one) which, for any circle, expresses the ratio between the circle's circumference and its diameter

then the content of my stipulation is given by the clause that follows the colon. A linguistic stipulation *succeeds* (alternatively, *is successful*) if, as a result of the stipulation, its content is true.[11] An assumption of these arguments is that, under the right conditions, linguistic stipulations succeed, and thereby introduce analyticities into the language. I will assume in particular that if a linguistic stipulation succeeds, then the result of "disquoting" its content yields a non-metalinguistic analyticity. Suppose, for instance, that I make the stipulation (11). The content of that stipulation is a metalinguistic claim concerning the name 'π'. My assumption is that, given the success of the stipulation, the correlative non-metalinguistic claim

> (12) If there is a number that expresses the ratio between the circumference and diameter of a circle, then π is the number that expresses the ratio between the circumference and diameter of a circle

is analytic. Even if the particular way I have chosen to articulate the notion of analyticity is rejected, so long as sucessful linguistic stipulations give rise to non-metalinguistic analyticities of the sort I have suggested, the arguments of this paper will apply.

DAO implies that a theory is no less ontologically parsimonious for asserting the existence of a table in a certain location than it is for claiming that the particles in that location have the right arrangement. This claim crucially relies on the idea of *ontological parsimony*. The expression 'parsimony' is clearly metaphorical. What does this metaphor come to? That's a tough question, and one I won't pretend to answer here in full.

---

[11] There are various ways in which a linguistic stipulation may fall short of success. For instance, the stipulation (11) fails if no term is added to the language, since in that case 'π' would not be a name. That stipulation also fails, however, if 'π' is thereby introduced in the language, but it isn't a name, or it is a name but refers to a boy.

We have two clues to guide us, however. First, there is the widely recognized link between comparative parsimony and the application of Occam's Razor: other things being equal, Occam's Razor favors a more parsimonious theory. A vitalist theory that appeals to the existence of *elan vital* is less ontologically parsimonious than a modern biochemical theory that does without it. Similarly, Avogadro's hypothesis that oxygen molecules are composed of two oxygen atoms bonded together is favored by Occam's Razor over a competing hypothesis that they are composed of 34,000 oxygen atoms bonded together.[12] So, we have some insight into how Occam's Razor applies. The notion of parsimony on which these insights rely is the very notion employed by **DAO**.

Second, the analyticity theorist's claim about ontological parsimony is supposed to be an instance of the more general claim that if *P* is analytically entailed by some sentences, then *P*'s truth "requires nothing more of the world" than does the truth of those sentences. So we can also use our insights into what the truth of a sentence or theory "requires of the world" to assess **DAO**. These insights may be hard to come by in some cases; the question of what Quantum Mechanics "requires of the world" is very difficult. But they are easy to come by in other cases, especially when what's at issue is the comparative question of whether one theory requires more of the world than another very similar theory, rather than the non-comparative question of what a theory requires of the world full stop. For instance, the truth of

(13) Snow is white

requires less of the world than the truth of

(14) Snow is white and grass is green.

I think it evident that (14) requires more of the world for its truth than does (13). But if an argument is needed there is one available. I will assume that requirements for the truth of these sentences are given by what their terms refer to and which properties their

---

[12] Avogadro's hypothesis was required to account for the ratios of volumes of oxygen gas and hydrogen gas to water vapor observed in combustion. See (Nolan, 1997) for discussion.

predicates express.[13] The truth of (14) requires that grass have a certain property, the property *being green*, which is expressed by the predicate 'green'. (13) does not impose this requirement. The requirements for (13)'s truth are satisfied or not according to whether snow has the right color; the requirements for (14)'s truth are satisfied or not according to whether snow has that color and also grass has a certain other color. For this reason, the requirements for (13)'s truth are satisfied and the requirements for (14)'s truth are not in worlds at which grass is purple but snow is still white. So, the truth of (14) imposes a requirement on the world—that grass be green—that (13) does not.

Insights concerning the ontological parsimony of a given theory are just a special case: the parsimony of a theory is given by what the truth of the theory requires of the world *with respect to what there is*. So, a theory that asserts only

(15) There are more than 7 billion prime numbers

is more parsimonious than a theory that asserts

(16) There are more than 7 billion prime numbers and there are more than 7 billion human beings.

I think it evident that (16) requires more of the world than (15) with respect to what there is. But if an argument is needed there is one available. I assume that the requirements for the truth of these sentences are given by which properties their predicates express. The truth of (16) requires that there be more than seven billion instances of a certain property, the property *being human*, which is expressed by the predicate 'human being'. (15) does not impose this requirement. There are a wide variety of plausible views concerning what is required for the truth of (15), but no plausible view ties the satisfaction of these requirements to any particular count of the total human population. For this reason, the requirements for (15)'s truth are met and the requirements for (16)'s truth are not in worlds in which our arithmetical theories are true, but there are fewer than 7 billion human beings.

---

[13] Nominalists, who dispute the cogency of the idea that predicates express properties, are invited to substitute here their favorite replacement for the disputed idea.

I will call the requirements of the world *with respect to what there is* a theory's *ontological commitments*.[14] Since ontological commitments are just a special case of requirements on the world,

GAO If P analytically entails Q, then $(P \wedge Q)$ requires nothing more of the world than does P

is a generalization of **DAO** to which the analyticity theorist is also committed. In what follows, I will offer putative counter-examples to both **DAO** and its generalization **GAO**. The counter-examples will be of essentially the same sort. I hope thereby to show that the problems with **DAO** have nothing to do with any peculiarities of existential claims.

Here, in summary, is an upshot of **DAO** as I am proposing to understand it. Suppose we are given a theory T. T has certain ontological commitments; that is, T imposes certain requirements on the world with respect to what there is. Let T^+ be the result of closing T under analytic entailment. According to **DAO**, T^+ and T have the same ontological commitments. Even supposing other things are equal, considerations of ontological parsimony do not favor T over T^+. The judicious use of Occam's Razor would never leave T and T^+ on different sides of the cut. For instance, T might be a theory exhausted by the claim we have abbreviated as '$p_1, \ldots, p_n$ are arranged table-wise in L' that details the existence and relevant features of particles in a particular location L. According to **ANALYTICITY**, (1) is analytic, so T analytically entails that there is a table in L. Thus, T^+ will contain the claim **EXISTENCE**, according to which there is a table in L. Nevertheless, T^+ has just the same ontological commitments as T; it requires nothing more of the world with respect to what there is than does T. More generally, T^+ requires nothing more of the world than does T.

---

[14] This use of the term "ontological commitment" differs from Quine's seminal treatment. According to Quine, the ontological commitments of a theory are given by what must be taken to be among the values of the theory's variables (under appropriate regimentation) for the theory to be true. Suppose, for instance, that we are given an appropriately regimented theory of artifacts whose truth requires that there be a table in L. According to Quine's treatment, the existence of such a table is among the ontological commitments of the theory. The present treatment, by contrast, is neutral. If the analyticity theorist is right, then the existence of the table needn't be among the ontological commitments of the relevant theory of artifacts.

In standard cases of analyticity, this upshot of **DAO** is very plausible. Suppose we are given a sociological theory according to which there are unmarried males. If we add to that theory the claim

(17) There are bachelors

we seem to have added nothing to the theory's commitments. This is a case in which the analytically entailed claim does not require the existence of anything distinct from the individuals already mentioned by the theory. But more interesting applications of **DAO** are also very plausible. Suppose we have a theory that says that Joe is a husband, but never explicitly mentions Joe's spouse. If we add to that theory the claim

(18) There is an individual married to Joe

then the resulting theory requires no more of the world than does the original theory, despite the fact that Joe's spouse was never explicitly mentioned by the original theory. Thus, the existence of something may be required for the truth of a theory even if it is never explicitly mentioned by the theory. In both of these cases, the enriched theories simply slap labels onto things whose existence the more austere theories already required. The enriched theories may be more explicit about their commitments. They may usefully enable us to say more with fewer words. But they impose no further requirements on how the world is than their less explicit counterparts.

2. THREE STIPULATIONS

Despite the plausibility of **DAO** in standard cases of analyticity, I will argue that it faces counter-examples, in the form of analyticities introduced into the language as a result of successful linguistic stipulation.[15] It is widely acknowledged that not every attempt at linguistic stipulation succeeds. Perhaps the most famous such example is 'tonk'.[16] If the stipulation governing the use of 'tonk' were

---

[15] The arguments of this section owe a substantial debt to Kripke's (1980) discussion of linguistic stipulations that give rise to a priori contingencies.

[16] A. N. Prior (1960) imagined that 'tonk' is stipulated to obey one of the introduction rules for disjunction and one of the elimination rules for conjunction:

$P \vdash (P \text{ tonk } Q)$ $(P \text{ tonk } Q) \vdash Q$

to succeed, then everything would analytically entail everything. Analyticity theorists have reacted to the possibility of bad stipulations of this sort by endorsing necessary conditions on successful stipulation that the stipulations governing 'tonk' and its ilk fail.[17] I will argue that there are linguistic stipulations that plausibly pass all of the necessary conditions, and are intuitively successful to boot, but which still pose a problem for **DAO** and **GAO**.

There are a number of different conditions that theorists have proposed as necessary for successful stipulation. It will be useful to focus our discussion on just one, which is highly plausible and easily motivated. In general, it is plausible to think that a linguistic stipulation succeeds only if there is a consistent way to assign truth conditions to sentences containing the introduced term that makes the content of the stipulation true; call this *Stevenson's constraint* on linguistic stipulation.[18] Stevenson's constraint is attractive. It is plausible to think that the function of linguistic stipulations is to introduce a new expression in such a way as to enable the interpretation of sentences that include it. If Stevenson's constraint is violated, then there is no coherent way to interpret sentences containing the erstwhile new vocabulary, since there is no coherent way to assign truth conditions to such sentences. So it seems that passing Stevenson's constraint is a necessary condition for a linguistic stipulation to fulfill its function.[19]

To illustrate the application of Stevenson's constraint, suppose I attempt to introduce the sentential operator 'it is verdantly the case

---

[17] This strategy is followed in practice by analyticity theorists and articulated explicitly by (Hale and Wright, 2001, pp. 132–7). See also (Thomasson, 2007, pp. 171–2) and (Boghossian, 2003, p. 244).

[18] Stevenson (1961) originally pointed out that there is no truth table one may assign to 'tonk' that makes the proposed introduction and elimination rules valid

[19] There are many other proposed constraints on successful stipulation. Belnap (1962) proposed that stipulations succeed only if the proposed rules of inference that are stipulated to govern the new vocabulary are *conservative* with respect to the old language, in the sense that the new rules do not permit the derivation of any sentences in the old language that were not already derivable. Hale and Wright (2001, pp. 132–7) endorse a weaker conservativity constraint and propose two additional constraints: (*i*) *Generality*: the stipulation should enable the interpretation of a wide enough range of relevant sentences; and (*ii*) *Harmony*: the introduction and elimination rules should not allow us to infer more (or problematically less) than our warrant for the premises allows us to infer.

that...', by stipulating that it be such that the following introduction and elimination rules are valid:

$P \vdash$ It is verdantly the case that P
It is verdantly the case that $P \vdash$ Grass is green
It is verdantly the case that $P \vdash \Diamond P$

This attempt at stipulation fails Stevenson's constraint. Consider the question of what truth value a sentence of the form 'it is verdantly the case that ϕ' should have when ϕ is true and grass is purple. The proposed elimination rule for 'verdantly' is invalid if the 'verdantly' sentence is true, and the proposed introduction rule is invalid otherwise. So, there's no way to coherently assign truth conditions to the operator that makes the content of the stipulation true.

A simple tweak to the stipulation, however, evades this response. Suppose 'it is verdantly* the case that...' is stipulated to be such that the following introduction and elimination rules are valid:

$P \vdash$ It is verdantly* the case that P
It is verdantly* the case that $P \vdash$ Actually: grass is green
It is verdantly* the case that $P \vdash \Diamond P$

The 'actually' operator here is the operator defined by Kaplan (1989): *actually:ϕ* is true at a world iff ϕ is true at the actual world. Notice that this stipulation appears not to fail Stevenson's constraint. Consider the question of what truth value a sentence of the form 'it is verdantly* the case that ϕ' should have when ϕ is true and grass is not green. It should have the truth value *true*, since, as a matter of fact, grass is green. So, we can coherently assign truth conditions to 'verdantly*' sentences.

If our stipulation concerning 'verdantly*' succeeds, then we face a counter-example to **GAO**. Suppose that we are given a theory T that includes the claim

(13) Snow is white

but does not mention grass at all. If our stipulation concerning 'verdantly*' succeeds, closing T under analytic entailment yields a theory T^+ that also includes the claim

(19) Snow is white and actually: grass is green.

The claims of T^+ would be true if T is; in fact, it is necessary that T^+ is true if T is. But that should not distract us from the important point here: T^+ requires more of the world than does T. We have already seen that

(14) Snow is white and grass is green.

requires more of the world than (13). In particular, (14), unlike T, requires for its truth that grass have the property *being green*. T^+ also imposes this requirement, so we have a counter-example to **GAO**. The argument here relies on the assumption that *actually:ϕ* requires no less of the world—the *actual* world, that is—than does *ϕ*. This assumption is powerfully plausible on its face, and is supported by the fact that the truth conditions for the Kaplanian actuality operator are specified by appeal to requirements on how the actual world is: what's required of the actual world for *actually: grass is green* to be true is just for the actual world to meet whatever requirements there are for *grass is green* to be true.[20] The 'verdantly*' stipulation, if successful, thus gives rise to a counter-example to **GAO**.

The analyticity theorist might reasonably complain that we have misapplied Stevenson's constraint. In assessing whether we can coherently assign truth conditions to 'verdantly*' sentences, we go wrong if we take for granted that, for example, grass is green, and go on to ask whether the sentence is true or false in some counterfactual situation in which grass has some color other than its actual color. Instead, we should consider what truth value to assign the sentence under the supposition that, *as a matter of fact*, grass is not green. In other words, when considering whether we can coherently ascribe truth conditions to sentences in the enriched language in the relevant situations, we do what in the literature is called "considering the situation as actual."[21] Now, suppose that, *as*

---

[20] Notice that *actually:ϕ* requires something different of the actual world for its truth from what it requires of a non-actual world. *Actually:ϕ* requires of the actual world that it meet whatever requirements there are for the truth of *ϕ*. The truth of *actually:ϕ* at a non-actual world w does not impose this requirement on w. The requirement on a non-actual world w is that it be such that some *other* world—the actual world—meet the requirement for the truth of *actually:ϕ*.

[21] (Chalmers, 2002, p. 157).

a matter of fact, grass is purple, and consider the question of what truth value should be assigned to

(20) It is verdantly* the case that: grass is either green or not green.

The proposed elimination rule for 'verdantly*' is invalid if the 'verdantly*' sentence is true, and the proposed introduction rule is invalid otherwise. So, there's no way to coherently assign truth conditions to the operator that makes the content of the stipulation true. Our stipulation fails this construal of Stevenson's constraint.

A slightly different stipulation evades this response. Suppose we stipulate that 'grassgreen' is to be a predicate that expresses the property *being green* if, as a matter of fact, grass is green, and *not being green* otherwise. Our stipulation will meet Stevenson's constraint, on the reading on which it requires that the inferences in question be truth preserving in all situations "considered as actual." Suppose that, *as a matter of fact*, grass is purple, and consider the question of what truth value should be assigned to

(21) Grass is grassgreen.

Since grass is either green or not, the success of the stipulation for 'grassgreen' implies that this sentence is true.[22] This causes no problem for the interpretation of the sentence, however, since our supposition, together with the content of our stipulation, requires that 'grassgreen' express *not being green*. Similar remarks apply to the supposition that grass is *as a matter of fact* green.[23]

So, Stevenson's constraint gives us no reason to think that the supposed stipulation concerning 'grassgreen' is unsuccessful. For this reason, that stipulation gives rise to apparent counter-examples to **GAO**. As before, let T be a theory of snow, and T^+ its closure under analytic consequence. T^+ would then contain

(22) Snow is white and grass is grassgreen.

---

[22] Technically, we may need to add the qualification "if grass exists" to (21) to get a sentence whose truth is implied by the success of the 'grassgreen' stipulation. Here and in what follows I will omit that qualification.

[23] Note that the stipulation governing 'grassgreen' is conservative, harmonious, and general. It's also intuitively successful.

T^+ is true if T is. In fact, we have, plausibly, an a priori guarantee that T^+ is true if T is.[24] But that should not distract us from the important point here: T^+ requires more of the world than does T. Because grass is, as a matter of fact, green, the success of our 'grassgreen' stipulation implies that 'grassgreen' expresses the property *being green*. Once this fact is appreciated, I think it evident that T^+ requires more. But if an argument is needed there is one available. I assume that the requirements for the truth of these sentences are given by what their terms refer to and which properties their predicates express. Because grass is green, the success of our 'grassgreen' stipulation implies that the predicate expresses the property *being green*. Thus, the truth of T^+ requires that grass have the property expressed by 'grassgreen', that is, the property *being green*. T does not impose this requirement. The requirements for T's truth are satisfied or not according to whether snow has the right color and other relevant features. For this reason, the requirements for T's truth are satisfied and the requirements for T^+'s truth are not in worlds at which grass is purple but snow is still white. So, the truth of T^+ imposes a requirement on the world—that grass be green—that T does not.[25]

---

[24] Boghossian (2003) considers the case of the stipulation that 'flurg' be governed by the following introduction and elimination rules:

x is an elliptical equation $\vdash x$ is flurg
x is flurg $\vdash x$ can be correlated with a modular form

Given that it is provable that every elliptical equation can be correlated with a modular form (this is the Taniyama-Shimura conjecture, proved by Andrew Wiles in the course of proving Fermat's last theorem), the analytic entailments supposedly introduced into the language by this linguistic stipulation are plausibly a priori. Boghossian argues (p. 244) that these supposed analyticities do not themselves give rise to an a priori entitlement to the Taniyama-Shimura conjecture, presumably because Wiles's sophisticated proof is not made accessible to us by the stipulation. Notice that this epistemological observation does not immediately bear on the plausibility of **GAO**, which is on its face independent of the accessibility to us of any instance of reasoning. Notice also that it is plausible to think that the stipulation governing 'grassgreen' does give rise to a priori entitlements to the alleged new analyticities, given the relative simplicity and transparency of the reasoning in question.

[25] If it is insisted that analytic truths be necessary (Kripke, 1980, p. 39), then we can tweak the example one last time, by mixing our last two cases. Suppose that 'it is verdantly** the case that...' is stipulated to have the following introduction and elimination rules:

$P \vdash$ It is "it is verdantly** the case that P
It is verdantly** the case that $P \vdash$ Actually: grass is grassgreen
It is verdantly** the case that $P \vdash \Diamond P$

We have two apparent counter-examples to **GAO**, each appropriate to a different understanding of how to apply Stevenson's constraint. Neither of them concern existence claims, so they are not counter-examples to **DAO**. However, cases of essentially the same sort can be marshalled against **DAO**. Suppose we stipulate that 'priman being' is to be a predicate that expresses the property *being a human being* if, as a matter of fact, there are more than seven billion human beings, and *being a prime number* otherwise. The same sort of argument we gave in the case of 'grassgreen' applies here to show that the stipulation will satisfy Stevenson's constraint on the reading on which it requires that the inferences in question be truth-preserving in all situations "considered as actual."[26] There is no problem consistently assigning an interpretation to 'priman being'.

Let T be a theory of arithmetic strong enough to prove that there are more than 7 billion prime numbers. If our 'priman being' stipulation is successful, then the result of "disquoting" the content of the stipulation

(23) If, as a matter of fact, there are more than 7 billion human beings, then something is a priman being iff it is a human being; otherwise, something is a priman being iff it is a prime number

is analytic. As a consequence

(24) If there are more than 7 billion prime numbers, then there are more than 7 billion priman beings

is analytic.[27] So, the closure of T under analytic consequence yields a theory T^+ that contains

---

The argument against **GAO** would then appeal to the claim, deployed in the discussion of 'grasssgreen' above, that *actually*:ϕ requires no less of the (actual) world than does ϕ.

[26] The stipulation concerning 'priman being' also meets Belnap's proposed conservativity constraint, and satisfies Hale and Wright's Generality constraint. It satisfies Harmony, since, as I note below, there is plausibly an a priori guarantee that the theory T^+ (described below) is true if the arithmetical theory T (also described below) is true.

[27] Suppose there are more than 7 billion prime numbers. Either there are more than 7 billion human beings or there are not. If there are, then the priman beings are all and only the human beings and there are more than 7 billion of them. If there are not, then the priman beings are all and only the prime numbers and our supposition implies that there are more than 7 billion of them.

(25) There are more than 7 billion prime numbers and there are more than 7 billion priman beings.

As above, T^+ is true if T is, and there is plausibly an a priori guarantee that T^+ is true if T is. But that should not distract us from the important point here: T^+ clearly requires more of the world than does T. Since, as a matter of fact, there are more than seven billion human beings, the success of our 'priman being' stipulation implies that 'priman being' expresses the property *being human*, and is co-intensional with the predicate 'human', which also expresses that property. Once this fact is appreciated, I think it evident that T^+ requires more. But if an argument is needed there is one available. Since 'priman being' expresses *being a human being*, the truth of T^+ requires that there be seven billion instances of that property. T does not impose this requirement. There are a wide variety of plausible views on what the requirements for the truth of T come to, but no plausible view ties the satisfaction of these requirements to any particular count of the total human population. For this reason, the requirements for T's truth are satisfied and the requirements for T^+'s truth are not in worlds at which arithmetic is still true, but there are fewer than 7 billion humans. So, the truth of T^+ imposes a requirement on the world—that there be seven billion humans— that T does not.[28]

The syntactic form of the 'priman being' and 'greengrass' stipulations is a conjunction of conditionals. I have found that this feature of the case gives some people pause. It is important to realize that this is an entirely typical syntactic form to use when making linguistic

---

[28] To get a case relevantly like the case of 'verdantly**', in which the analytic consequence in question is necessary, we might imagine stipulating that 'it is teemingly the case that . . .' is an operator that obeys the following introduction and elimination rules:

($P \wedge$ there are more than 7 billion prime numbers) ⊢ it is teemingly the case that P
It is teemingly the case that P ⊢ Actually: there are more than 7 billion priman beings
It is teemingly the case that P ⊢ $\Diamond P$

Here, as with 'verdantly**', the argument appeals to the claim that a sentence of the form *actually:ϕ* requires no less of the actual world than does ϕ. More specifically, the claim required here is that *actually:ϕ* has at least as many ontological commitments as ϕ. It is not, I think, as clear that the 'teemingly' stipulation is successful as that the 'priman being' stipulation is successful; see §4.1 below for an argument that the original 'priman being' stipulation gives rise to a necessary analytic consequence that presents a counter-example to **DAO**.

stipulations. For instance, if LeVerrier had been careful, he might easily have stipulated that 'Neptune' is to refer to the planet that causes perturbations in the orbit of Uranus if there is a unique such planet; and to refer to nothing otherwise. In fact, this syntactic form is so common in the specification of functions in mathematics that there are special notational conventions for abbreviating it.

One might think on the basis of the form of the stipulation that the argument against **DAO** depends on a controversial view concerning the meanings of 'grassgreen' and 'priman being', to the effect that those meanings vary depending on how things are as a matter of fact. But the argument does not depend on any particular view of the meanings of those predicates. Consider 'priman being'. One might hold that this predicate means one thing if there are more than 7 billion humans and a different thing otherwise; that the meaning of the predicate is the same in the two cases; or that there are two kinds of meaning for this predicate, one of which is constant and the other of which varies across the two cases; or even that the predicate simply doesn't have any feature that one could sensibly count as a meaning. The argument would be unaffected; it requires only that 'priman being' express one property if there are more than 7 billion priman beings and another otherwise. This requirement, however, is guaranteed, so long as the 'priman being' stipulation is successful, and thus has a true content.[29]

3. QUANTIFIERS AND THE COUNTER-EXAMPLES

So, we appear to have counter-examples to **DAO** and **GAO**, whether Stevenson's constraint is applied by "considering worlds as actual" or by evaluating the truth of sentences at them in the more traditional way. How should analyticity theorists respond?

What they actually say seems not to help with the particular cases we have considered. Defenders of **DAO** have typically focused their efforts on the proper interpretation of quantifiers.

For instance, Thomasson (2007) has defended the existence of tables and other artifacts by arguing that existentially quantified sentences are uninterpretable without a contextually-supplied sortal,

---

[29] Thanks to an anonymous referee for indicating the need for this clarification.

whose associated application conditions carry the relevant associated analytic entailments. Consider, for example, the question of whether, for example, there is a table in location L. Thomasson argues that this question is uninterpretable unless some appropriate application conditions are associated with the sortal 'table'. Thomasson maintains that the question of whether there is a table in the relevant location is then answered by asking whether, in the relevant instance, those application conditions are satisfied.[30] We may suppose that the application conditions for 'table' require that when particles of the right sorts exist and have the right features, then a table exists. Thomasson concludes that the proper semantic treatment of quantificational expressions in English thus implies that

(1) If $p_1, \ldots, p_n$ are arranged table-wise in L, then there is a table in L

is analytic.

Thomasson's view does not provide a successful rebuttal of the apparent counter-examples. On Thomasson's theory, the interpretation of (25) requires that we specify the application and co-application conditions for 'priman being'. Nothing could be easier: because there are, as a matter of fact, more than 7 billion human beings, 'priman being' has the same application and co-application conditions as 'human being'. In fact, that's the reason why (25) incurs ontological commitments that T does not: (25) requires that there be more than seven billion loci in which the application conditions for 'human being' are satisfied. T, by contrast, doesn't impose any such requirement.[31]

---

[30] This is a simplification of Thomasson's view, since she also allows that there are "covering uses" of existentially quantified sentences that appeal, in effect, to disjunctions of application conditions supplied by specifying ranges of sortal terms (Thomasson, 2007, pp. 117–18, 121–5). This complication does not affect the discussion in the main text.

[31] Thomasson might reply that what needs to be supplied are what she calls *frame-level* application conditions, which are the application conditions which I had in mind when I introduced the term 'priman being'. The frame-level application conditions for 'priman being' are also easy to supply, since they are given by the content of the stipulation: 'priman being' applies to something just in case it is human if there are actually more than 7 billion humans and prime otherwise. This condition is co-intensional with the application condition for 'human being'. See §4.3 below for discussion.

It might be thought that Eli Hirsch's (2002) doctrine of *quantifier variance* could be deployed in defense of **DAO**.[32] According to this doctrine, there are multiple candidate meanings for the existential quantifier which are equally good for the purposes of ontology. On Hirsch's view, if the language is changed by the stipulative introduction of new vocabulary so that new existential claims are apparently entailed, charity requires that our interpretation of the quantificational idioms shift to a new candidate meaning, so that the newly entailed quantificational sentences come out true. Imagine for the sake of illustration that ordinary English speakers originally speak a language in which they readily claim

(26) There is nothing other than particles in L.

Charity requires that we interpret them as deploying a candidate meaning for their quantifiers on which they speak truly. Imagine now that they stipulatively introduce the predicate 'table' into their language, so that they readily claim

(1) If $p_1, \ldots, p_n$ are arranged table-wise in L, then there is a table in L.

On Hirsch's view, charity now requires that we shift our interpretion of the quantifiers: speakers are now to be interpreted as deploying a candidate meaning for their quantifiers on which this new sentence is true.

But this view seems not to help with the 'priman being' case. On the Hirsch response, that stipulation requires that our interpretation of the existential quantifier shift so that, given the new quantifier meaning,

(27) There are seven billion priman beings

is entailed by our arithmetical theory. But if the relevant kind of entailment is a priori entailment, the old quantifier meaning will

---

[32] It should be noted that Hirsch himself does not explicitly defend **DAO**. In fact, discussion of analyticity is conspicuously absent from Hirsch's writings on charity, quantifier variance, and related matters. Thanks are due to Matti Eklund for discussion on this point.

do just fine.[33] No shift in our interpretation of quantifiers would help an analyticity theorist with the problem posed by the 'priman being' case. Despite the a priori entailment of T^+ by T, T^+ clearly has ontological commitments that T does not have.

Thus, the particular semantic doctrines concerning existential quantification that are proposed by Thomasson and Hirsch do not appear to provide a way of avoiding the challenge posed by 'priman being'. Instead, their arguments, if successful, just show that (1) is analytic. The analyticity of (1) is something we have been supposing they are right about. The problem targeted by the 'priman being' and 'grassgreen' cases does not concern the question of whether (1) is analytic; the problem concerns the ontological significance of (1)'s alleged analyticity. So, Hirsch and Thomasson's arguments don't speak to the challenge posed by our apparent counter-examples.

There is also a more general reason for thinking that theses concerning the semantics of quantifiers won't provide an adequate defense of **DAO**. There is a fundamental continuity between the case against **GAO** and the case against **DAO**. The continuity of our cases against **GAO** and **DAO** suggest that ultimately the defense of **DAO** must appeal to considerations that go beyond the proper semantic treatment of the existential quantifier. The proposed counter-examples to **GAO** do not involve the use of any existential quantifier, so **GAO** cannot be defended by appeal to any semantic thesis concerning only the existential quantifier. Since the proposed counter-example to **DAO** has essentially the same character, we should similarly expect a reply that goes beyond the semantics of quantifiers.

Suppose, finally, that some quantifier-focused defense succeeds for the 'priman being' case, but leaves the alleged counter-examples to **GAO** untouched. Then the plausibility of instances of **DAO** in focal cases of analyticity would no longer be enough to motivate **DAO**. The burden would be on the analyticity theorist to explain why we should expect the closure of a theory under analytic consequence to impose no new requirements on the world with respect to

---

[33] If instead the relevant kind of entailment is modal entailment, then we would have to appeal either to the example involving 'teemingly' (see n. 28), or to the argument of §4.1 below.

what there is, even though it may impose new requirements on the world in other respects.

4. TWO RESPONSES

What analyticity theorists and their fellow travelers have actually said does not appear to help with the apparent counter-examples to **GAO** and **DAO**. But the arguments that the stipulations in question present counter-examples to the analyticity theorist's view rely on two claims: (*i*) the stipulations generate certain analytic entailments; and (*ii*) the theory T^+ that results from closing a theory T under those analytic entailments requires more of the world than T. Thus, there are two potential avenues of response for the analyticity theorist. We'll discuss the prospects for each avenue of response in turn.

4.1. Analyticity, weak and strong

The first potential response available to the analyticity theorist is to deny that the stipulations really give rise to the problematic analytic entailments that I have claimed. Let's focus on the 'priman being' stipulation. One way to pursue this strategy is to deny that this stipulation is successful. Making this claim presents the analyticity theorist with a challenge: articulate and motivate a condition on the success of linguistic stipulations on which the 'priman being' stipulation is unsuccessful.

There is reason to think that this challenge will be difficult to meet. The 'priman being' stipulation does not just meet the constraints on successful stipulation in the literature (see n. 19). It also seems to be utterly unexceptionable on its face. Kripkean stipulations introducing proper names and natural kind terms provide a familiar model for this sort of stipulation (see n. 15). We can successfully stipulate that 'water' (rigidly) designates H_2O if (as a matter of fact) that's the substance common to such-and-such paradigms, and XYZ if (as a matter of fact) that's the substance common to such-and-such paradigms, and so on. The present case differs only in substituting expressing a property for (rigidly) designating a kind. But this seems an unimportant (and dispensable) difference between the cases. The fact that the Kripkean stipulations succeed provides a powerful reason to think that the 'priman being' stipulation also succeeds.[34] Thus, I suspect that the 'priman being' stipulation would present a prima facie counter-example to any otherwise well-motivated constraint on linguistic stipulation that would serve the analyticity theorist's purposes.

It would be unreasonable to rule out in advance the hypothesis of a lurking flaw in the stipulation; perhaps, after all, there's some subtle contradiction derivable from it. In the absence, however, of any indication of such a flaw, the smart money is on the success of the stipulation.

There appears, however, to be a way of denying that the stipulation gives rise to the problematic analytic entailments while accepting the success of the 'priman being' stipulation: refine the explanation on offer of the notion of analyticity. The argument from the success of the stipulation to the falsity of **DAO** deploys a modal condition on the requirements for the truth of a theory: if it is possible for the requirements for T's truth to be met while the requirements for T^+'s truth are not, then T^+ requires more for its truth than T does.[35] The response is to suggest that the notion of analyticity in play likewise requires a modal specification: analyticities in the relevant sense must be restricted to necessities. The analyticity supposedly introduced by the 'priman being' stipulation that causes all the trouble is the contingent truth:

(24) If there are more than 7 billion prime numbers, then there are more than 7 billion priman beings.

---

[34] The idea of emphasizing the similarity between the Kripkean stipulations and the 'priman being' and 'grassgreen' stipulations is due to an anonymous referee.

[35] Notice that the constraint is stated in terms of the possibilities for meeting the requirements for the truth of the theories, rather than in terms of the theories themselves. This is because there are some theories that impose requirements for their truth on non-actual worlds different from the requirements they impose on the actual world. Thus, $(\phi \wedge actually{:}\phi)$ and $actually{:}\phi$ clearly impose the same requirements on the actual world for their truth: to wit, what's required of the actual world for the truth of either is whatever is required of the actual world for the truth of φ. But, if ϕ is contingently true, then there is a possible world at which $(\phi \wedge actually{:}\phi)$ is false and $actually{:}\phi$ is true. This is because the latter sentence does not impose the same requirements on the non-actual world at which ϕ is false as it does on the actual world; see n. 20. So, $actually{:}\phi$ is true at the non-ϕ world for a subtly different reason from the reason it is true at the actual world. Thanks to David Chalmers for pointing out this subtlety.

On this response, (24) is not analytic in the relevant sense because it is not necessary. Thus, the stipulation is successful and gives rise to new entailments in the language, but it does not give rise to any untoward analyticities.[36]

Here is a way of carrying this idea out. Let's call the kind of analyticity we have been talking about up until now *weak analyticity*. Now define a stronger notion: ϕ is *strongly foundationally analytic* iff it is necessarily true and failure to accept it constitutes some measure of linguistic incompetence; ϕ is *strongly analytic* iff it is modally entailed by $\psi_1, \psi_2, \ldots$, such that every ψ_i is strongly foundationally analytic; and ϕ *strongly analytically entails* ψ iff the material conditional ($\phi \Rightarrow \psi$) is strongly analytic. Intuitively, strong analyticity is just weak analyticity "plus necessity." These specifications ensure that only necessities are strongly analytic. Then the analyticity theorist can revise **DAO** to fit:

DAO$_\square$ If P strongly analytically entails the existence of certain things, then a theory that contains P but does not claim that those things exist is no more ontologically parsimonious than a theory that also claims that they exist.

I have argued that the 'priman being' stipulation gives rise to new weak analyticities in the language, including

(24) If there are more than 7 billion prime numbers, then there are more than 7 billion priman beings

As we have seen, (24) is no strong analyticity, since it is contingent. Thus, while (24) may present a counter-example to **DAO**, it presents no counter-example to **DAO**$_\square$.[37]

The analyticity theorist still faces a counter-example if three further premises are granted. The first is that, if ϕ is necessary, then

---

[36] Thanks to David Chalmers and Wesley Holliday for independently suggesting the need to explore this avenue of defense in detail.

[37] This response comes with a cost: if **DAO**$_\square$ is to be useful for establishing that the existence of a table in location L is an "ontological free lunch" given the existence and arrangement of its particles, the analyticity theorist will need to establish that

(1) If $p_1, \ldots, p_n$ are arranged table-wise in L, then there is a table in L

is not only weakly analytic, but also necessary. See (Cameron, 2006) for discussion.

(28) ($\phi \Leftrightarrow$ actually: ϕ)

is strongly analytic. Instances of (28) in which ϕ is not necessary are weakly foundationally analytic, since failure to accept them indicates some measure of linguistic incompetence with respect to the Kaplanian actuality operator. They fail to be strongly analytic only because they fail to be necessarily true. If ϕ is necessary, then the instance meets this further condition for being strongly foundationally analytic. The second further premise is that if

(29) ($\phi \Rightarrow \psi$)

is weakly analytic, then

(30) (Actually:$\phi \Rightarrow$ actually:ψ)

is strongly analytic. To see that this claim is true, suppose that (29) is weakly analytic, and so there are weakly foundationally analytic sentences $\psi_1, \psi_2, \ldots$ that jointly entail (29). But, for each of these weakly foundationally analytic ψ_i, actually:ψ_i is strongly foundationally analytic.[38] But then

actually:ψ_1,   actually:ψ_2,   . . .

are strongly foundationally analytic sentences that modally entail (30).[39] The third premise we have already used in our discussion

---

[38] *Argument*: (*i*) Since by hypothesis ψ_i is true, actually:ψ_i is necessarily true. (*ii*) Accepting ψ_i but failing to accept actually:ψ_i constitutes some measure of linguistic incompetence with 'actually'. Failing to accept ψ_i by hypothesis constitutes some measure of linguistic incompetence, perhaps with respect to other expressions in the language. Thus, failing to accept actually:ψ_i constitutes some measure of linguistic incompetence, with respect to either 'actually' or some other expression in the language. Claim (*ii*) may have to be qualified in order to take account of the fact that, e.g. stringing a trillion 'actuality' operators onto the front of a weakly foundational analyticity may yield a sentence such that failure to accept it constitutes mortality rather than any measure of linguistic incompetence. Qualifications of this sort will not affect the argument in the main text, which involves very short sentences that may be taken in and assessed at a glance.

[39] *Argument*: $\psi_1, \psi_2, \ldots$ entail (29), so actually:ψ_1, actually:$\psi_2, \ldots$ entail

(31)   Actually:($\phi \Rightarrow \psi$).

Because this sentence is necessarily true, the entailment is modally necessary. Further, it is strongly analytic that the relevant instance of the analogue for 'actually' of the axiom K for '$\Box$'

(32) (Actually:($\phi \Rightarrow \psi$) $\Rightarrow$ (actually:$\phi \Rightarrow$ actually:ψ))

is true.

of 'verdantly*'; it is the plausible claim that the truth of *actually:ϕ* requires no less of the world than does the truth of ϕ.

With these three premises in hand, we can show that **DAO**$_\Box$ faces counter-examples of essentially the same sort as **DAO**. Application of the first premise ensures that

> (33) If there are more than 7 billion prime numbers, then actually: there are more than 7 billion prime numbers

is strongly analytic. Because

> (34) If (there are more than 7 billion prime numbers ∨ there are more than 7 billion human beings), then there are more than 7 billion priman beings

is weakly (but not strongly) analytic, application of the second premise ensures that

> (35) If actually:(there are more than 7 billion prime numbers ∨ there are more than 7 billion human beings), then actually: there are more than 7 billion priman beings

is strongly analytic. And, of course,

> (36) If actually: there are more than 7 billion prime numbers, then actually: (there are more than 7 billion prime numbers ∨ there are more than 7 billion human beings)

is strongly analytic. Thus,

> (37) If there are more than 7 billion prime numbers, then actually: there are more than 7 billion priman beings

is strongly analytic. Closing our arithmetic theory T under strong analytic consequence thus yields a theory T^+ which includes

> (38) Actually: there are more than 7 billion priman beings.

Application of the third premise ensures that the original argument against **DAO** can be used to show that T^+ is less ontologically parsimonious than T. Thus, the success of our 'priman being' stipulation poses a problem for **DAO**$_\Box$, just as it does for **DAO**.

4.2. Metaphysical analyticity

We have just considered two ways of denying that the 'grassgreen' and 'priman being' stipulations give rise to problematic analyticities: deny that the particular stipulations in question are successful, or insist that analyticity of the relevant sort requires necessity. These avenues of response are relatively modest, in that they accept a very basic assumption about analyticity that I flagged in §1: that when linguistic stipulations succeed, the result of "disquoting" their contents are analytic (so long, we might need to add, as they are necessary). More generally, these responses accept that we may discern analyticities by reflection on the meanings of our words, as embodied either explicitly in our linguistic stipulations or implicitly in our practices of day-to-day use and instruction. There is, however, a more radical response which rejects this assumption. This more radical response rejects any explanation of the notion of analyticity that appeals in the first instance to the sorts of things that are typically revealed by reflection on the meanings of our words. On this view, analyticity is not to be explained, for instance, by reference to the conditions or conventions governing our understanding, justification, or acceptance of sentences. Instead, analyticity is to be explained in metaphysical terms. Analyticity of this second sort is often called *metaphysical analyticity*. Weak analyticity, by contrast, is a kind of *epistemic analyticity*.[40]

There are many different explanations we might offer of the idea of metaphysical analyticity as part of an attempt to defend **DAO**. The simplest for our purposes is to identify the metaphysical analyticities as those true sentences whose truth imposes no requirements on the world. If we are given the assumption that anything that is a logical consequence of some premises requires nothing more for its truth than is required for the truth of those premises, then **DAO**'s truth is guaranteed.[41] On this response the arguments against **DAO**

---

[40] This terminology is due to Boghossian (1996). Strong analyticity, which requires both necessity and weak analyticity, is a hybrid.

[41] Suppose that Q is analytically entailed by P. Then the material conditional $(P \Rightarrow Q)$ is analytic. So, the truth of all members of $\{P, (P \Rightarrow Q)\}$ requires exactly what is required for the truth of P. Q is a logical consequence of $\{P, (P \Rightarrow Q)\}$. Applying the principle from the main text yields the conclusion that Q requires nothing more for its truth than is required by P.

go wrong because, as I in effect argued, the 'greengrass' and 'priman being' stipulations fail to induce metaphysical analyticities.

This more radical response concedes something important about the methodological role of analyticity in ontological disputes. Here, in broad brushstrokes, is a summary of the dialectic so far. We may think of analytic truths as having two features. First, they have what I will call *the trappings of analyticity*: the conventions of English guarantee that an analytic truth is entailed by certain sentences such that failure to accept any of these sentences constitutes some measure of linguistic incompetence. Second, they are true. My original argument was against the contention that if, for example,

(1) If $p_1, \ldots, p_n$ are arranged table-wise in L, then there is a table in L

has the trappings of analyticity, then its truth comes for free. I argued that this is wrong: granting that (1) has the trappings of analyticity, its truth may be a substantial further fact, imposing significant requirements on the world, including additional truthmakers for the consequent beyond those required for the truth of the antecedent.

The radical response accepts this conclusion: having the trappings of analyticity does not suffice for being metaphysically analytic. My 'priman being' stipulation gave, for instance,

(24) If there are more than 7 billion prime numbers, then there are more than 7 billion priman beings

the trappings of analyticity. But the truth of (24) imposes a substantive requirement on the world, so it is not metaphysically analytic.

Clearly, nothing in the arguments I have offered tells against the interpretation of **DAO** that relies on this sort of metaphysical analyticity. Still, I think this response gives up an important methodological advantage on which the analyticity theorist relies. Suppose the analyticity theorist engages a radical ontologist who denies that there is a table in location L while accepting that there are particles arranged table-wise there. The analyticity theorist hopes that, on the basis of our grasp of the meaning of the relevant vocabulary, we will recognize that (24) has the trappings of analyticity. The analyticity theorist then invokes **DAO** to argue that the entailed existence claim is "nothing extra." But now suppose, as the radical response concedes, that the trappings of analyticity are insufficient for metaphysical analyticity. Then **DAO** does not apply; to establish that the existence of a table in L requires nothing more of the world than the radical ontologist has already accepted, we need to establish that (24) is metaphysically analytic. Showing that (24) has the trappings of analyticity falls short of what's needed. On the radical response, **DAO** is saved, but it's rendered toothless.

We may think of the argument of this paper as posing a dilemma for the analyticity theorist. Either the analyticity theorist sticks with epistemic analyticity, or she moves to metaphysical analyticity. In the first case, **DAO**, interpreted as involving epistemic analyticity, faces counter-examples. In the second case, **DAO**, interpreted as involving metaphysical analyticity, can't be applied, since metaphysical analyticities aren't discernible by the means to which the analyticity theorist appeals.[42]

There are less radical responses that face essentially the same problem. For instance, I have assumed that the truth of *actually:φ* requires no less of the world than does the truth of *φ*. It might be argued, however, that *actually:φ*, if true, imposes no substantial requirement on the world for its truth, notwithstanding the canonical specification of truth conditions for sentences containing the Kaplanian actuality operator. The analyticity theorist then may contend that the argument against **DAO**$_\Box$ in §4.1 goes wrong in inferring that the truth of

(38) Actually: there are more than 7 billion priman beings.

imposes a substantial requirement from the fact that

(39) There are more than 7 billion priman beings

does.[43] Notice that, on this response,

(40) If actually: there are more than 7 billion priman beings, then there are more than 7 billion priman beings

has the trappings of analyticity but still imposes a substantial requirement. Thus, this way of pressing the response of §4.1 also

---

[42] Thanks to Jonathan Simon and Matti Eklund for discussion on this issue.
[43] Thanks to an anonymous referee for suggesting this avenue of response.

concedes that having the trappings of analyticity is insufficient for metaphysical analyticity.[44]

4.3. Requirements and truth conditions

The second avenue of response accepts that our stipulations generate the relevant analytic entailments, but denies that those entailments are problematic. I have argued, for instance, that the theory T^+, which asserts

(22) Snow is white and grass is grassgreen

requires more of the world for its truth than the original theory of snow T from which it was obtained, on the grounds that, unlike the theory of snow, it requires of the world that grass have a certain color, green. But, a defender of **DAO** might urge, (22) does not impose any such requirement. I have claimed that the requirements for the truth of 'grassgreen' sentences like (22) are given in part by which property 'grassgreen' expresses. On the response we are now considering, requirements for (22)'s truth are not given in that straightforward and plausible way. That leaves us with the question of how they are given. So, adopting this response presents the analyticity theorist with a challenge: articulate and motivate an alternative view of the requirements for the truth of 'grassgreen' sentences on which (22)'s truth requires nothing more of the world than that snow is white.[45]

Such an alternative view is inspired by close attention to the content of the 'grassgreen' stipulation. According to the content of that stipulation, something is grassgreen iff it is green if grass is (*as a matter of fact*) green, and not green otherwise. This gives us a characterization of the requirements imposed by simple 'grassgreen' sentences like (21) that serves the analyticity theorist's needs: a sentence of the form 'α is grassgreen' requires for its truth that the referent of the term α be green if grass is, and not green otherwise. On this view, then, all that is required for the truth of

---

[44] Having introduced several alternatives to my original provisional explanation of analyticity, I propose now to drop them. For the remainder of this paper, I will reserve 'analytic' and its cognates for claims that are weakly analytic.

[45] The truth of (22) may also require the existence of grass; see n. 22.

(22) Snow is white and grass is grassgreen

is that (*i*) snow be white and (*ii*) grass be green iff grass is green. It's plausible to think that this requirement does not go beyond the requirements for the truth of

(13) Snow is white

since (*ii*) is trivially satisfied. If (*i*) and (*ii*) exhaust the requirements for the truth of (22), then the new analyticities introduced by our 'grassgreen' stipulation don't pose any problem for the analyticity theorist.[46]

The view of the requirements for the truth of 'grassgreen' sentences that backs this response is implausible. No doubt, one of the requirements for the truth (in the actual world) of sentences of the form 'α is grassgreen' is that the referent of α be green iff grass is. But there is *another* requirement for the truth of such sentences: the referent of α must have the property, *being green*, expressed by the predicate. If this is not also required for the truth of simple 'grassgreen' sentences, then it's a mystery why, for example,

(21) Grass is grassgreen

is false at a world at which grass is purple, and so is green iff grass is. In general, our view of what is required of the world for simple 'grassgreen' sentences to be true ought to explain why (21) is true in some, but not all metaphysically possible circumstances. The view on which (21) requires only that grass be green iff grass is green doesn't pass muster. What's more, it's a mystery why in a world with green clover but purple grass

(41) Clover is grassgreen

is true, even though clover is not green iff grass is green. The truth-conditions for simple 'grassgreen' sentences are thus left unexplained by the view of requirements for the truth of 'grassgreen' sentences on which the analyticity theorist's response draws.[47]

---

[46] Thanks to Mark Moyer and Wesley Holliday for independently pressing the need to explore this avenue of defense. Notice that this sort of response cannot be easily adapted to the case of 'verdantly*'. But I have already provided the analyticity theorist with a response for that case: the 'verdantly*' stipulation fails Stevenson's constraint on the appropriate way of applying it.

[47] It is plausible, perhaps, to think that the truth of (21) requires that grass be green iff grass is *actually* green; this is the view most naturally suggested by the content of

It would be unreasonable, however, to rule out in advance the possibility of offering a view of requirements that does better, while rendering the analytic entailments engendered by the 'grassgreen' and 'priman being' stipulations harmless to the analyticity theorist. Perhaps, after all, there's some subtle theory of the requirements imposed by such sentences that can do the relevant explanatory work. In the absence, however, of any such theory, the smart money is on the claim that the truth of (21) requires, among other things, that grass be green.

5. ANALYTICITY AND ONTOLOGY

The stipulations we have imagined in this paper are silly. But, if the arguments concerning these stipulations are correct, the lesson they teach is serious. The fact that an existence claim is analytically entailed by some further claims about the existence and features of particles is no reason to think that the existence claim is "lightweight," and imposes no further cost with respect to ontological parsimony. The claim we imagined to have been stated in an enriched language by

(39) There are more than 7 billion priman beings

is analytically entailed in that language by any suitably strong theory of arithmetic. It does not follow that the existence of more than 7 billion *homo sapiens* is "nothing over and above" the arithmetical facts, nor that our existence is an "ontological free lunch." Nor does it follow that whatever worldly condition or entity makes the theory true also makes it the case that there are more than 7 billion *Homo sapiens*, nor that there is any truthmaker for the arithmetical theory that is also a truthmaker for the existence claim.

We should take no comfort in the thought that the stipulations we have discussed are contrived, while the analyticities concerning, for example, 'table' sentences occur naturally. The stipulations we have discussed are just a very explicit way of establishing conventional rules for using the terms in question. The fact that those rules are

---

the 'grassgreen' stipulation. But this requirement clearly goes beyond the requirement for the truth of the theory *T* of snow, as evidenced by the fact that the requirement is not satisfied in circumstances in which grass is purple but snow is still white.

explicitly stated is what makes the examples seem contrived. We may not infer that the rules governing 'table' sentences, unlike the rules governing 'priman being' sentences, buy an "ontological free lunch" just because they arose in the give and take of natural language use, rather than being invented by a philosopher fishing for counter-examples. So, we should say the same thing about the existence of artifacts as we do about the existence of priman beings. We may not infer from the fact that **EXISTENCE** is analytically entailed by

(42) $p_1, \ldots, p_n$ are arranged table-wise in L

that its truth requires nothing more of the world than is required by (42). There may be other reasons for thinking so, but those reasons will need to appeal to something other than analytic entailment.

Suppose that we were utterly convinced by these arguments against **DAO**. What view of the significance of analytic truths for metaphysical inquiry is thereby suggested? The arguments suggest that the utility of analyticity for investigation of extra-linguistic matters is virtually nil. If those arguments are correct, then

(24) If there are more than 7 billion prime numbers, then there are more than 7 billion priman beings

is analytic, and

(43) If there are more than 7 billion prime numbers, then there are more than 7 billion human beings

is synthetic. Further, the 'priman being' example can easily be generalized. Suppose $\Phi(F)$ is a claim that attributes a certain feature to the property expressed by the predicate F. (For instance, $\Phi(F)$ might be the claim that there are more than seven billion F's, or that Obama is F.) Let G be another predicate such that, as a matter of fact, $\Phi(G)$ is true. Then the stipulation

Let H be a predicate which expresses G if, as a matter of fact, $\Phi(G)$ and which expresses F otherwise

if successful, will give rise to the analyticity of

(44) If $\Phi(F)$, then $\Phi(H)$.

It's easy, then, to multiply examples so that, for every synthetic truth of the form *if $\Phi(F)$, then $\Phi(G)$* there is a corresponding analytic truth.

It's hard to see how the distinction we thereby mark between these pairs of conditionals tells us anything interesting about the nature of extra-linguistic reality. This suggests that analyticity by itself has no significant metaphysical upshot, other than that analyticity requires truth. And, since the truth of an analytic sentence may impose exactly the same substantial requirements as the truth of some synthetic counterpart, it's tempting to conclude that the trappings of analyticity by themselves have no significant metaphysical upshot at all.

Suppose we give in to temptation. It's easy to come up with sentences that are true but lack the trappings of analyticity; any synthetic truth will fit the bill. But if the arguments of this paper are on track, then we should expect to find the converse situation, in which a sentence has the trappings of analyticity, but isn't true. We haven't yet come up with any sentences of this sort, but potential examples aren't hard to find. For the bulk of this paper, I have assumed **ANALYTICITY**, which says that the existence of a table in location L is analytically entailed by certain truths concerning the arrangement of the particles in L. Analytic entailment by truths requires truth, so this assumption implies that there is a table in L. That means that the assumption is dialectically inappropriate in the context of the debate between someone who denies and someone who affirms the existence of such a table. So, let's maintain the supposition that

(42) $p_1, \ldots, p_n$ are arranged table-wise in L

is true, but drop the supposition that any such table exists. Furthermore, we'll suppose that the participants in the debate over the existence of tables all speak ordinary English as it actually is, and that the analyticity theorist's claims concerning the norms governing the acceptance of 'table' sentences are correct. If no table exists in L, then

(1) If $p_1, \ldots, p_n$ are arranged table-wise in L, then there is a table in L

is not an analytic truth, since it's not a truth at all. Still, the participants in the debate speak English, so (1) has the trappings of analyticity. That is, (1) follows from some sentences whose rejection would constitute some measure of linguistic incompetence. Now, at least one of those sentences is false if no such table exists. So, if there is no table in L, we have at least one sentence of exactly the sort we are looking for: accepting it is required for perfect linguistic competence, but it is false.

I think that many will find it dizzying to consider the possibility of a situation in which the semantic conventions of a language enjoin acceptance of a sentence which (in that very language) is false. There are three considerations that may mitigate the vertigo.

First, it is easy to imagine how someone might find herself in such a situation. Imagine that someone introduces the 'verdantly' operator into the language, and the operator is taken up by ordinary speakers of the language, who continue to use the operator and to apply its rules in accordance with the original stipulation. These language-users are particularly unreflective, however, and so never consider the possibility that, say, grass is not green, but purple. They teach their children to use the operator in accord with the inference rules, and correct them if they fail to accept

(45) If snow is white, then grass is green

much as a logic teacher might correct a student who fails to accept some slightly subtle logical truth, like

(46) If snow is white and grass is green, then grass is green and snow is white.

Thus, in this community, the conventions of the language, as embodied in both day-to-day use and instruction, appear to enjoin the acceptance of (45). Now just imagine that the members of this community wake up one day to discover that grass has turned conspicuously purple overnight. In this situation (45) isn't true (nor is it necessary, nor a priori), but it still has the trappings of analyticity. The first person who thinks to herself,

(47) Snow is white, but grass is not green

is contravening the conventions of the language, as embodied in day-to-day use and instruction. Still, what she says is true. Given our assumption that (1) has the trappings of analyticity, the denier of the existence of a table in L says we are in fact in a similar situation. The conventions of our language, as embodied in both day-to-day use and instruction, enjoin the acceptance of claims that turn out to be false.

Second, it is important to remember that suffering from some measure of linguistic incompetence is very widespread. In fact, it's almost certainly universal. By itself, failure to attain perfect competence in the use of one's terms does not constitute a very weighty charge against a theorist.[48] Consider again the community of relatively unreflective speakers who use 'verdantly'. We have noted that on the morning that grass turns purple, the first person who thinks to herself,

(47) Snow is white, but grass is not green

is contravening the conventions of her language as embodied in day-to-day use and instruction. So what? Those conventions were established unreflectively in a way that had not taken account of the situation in which she finds herself. If this is the price of being right—of believing the truth—then it seems to me that price is right.

Third, it is important to realize that in such a case there may be and typically is some rearrangement of the conventions governing the language to accommodate the recalcitrant facts. There had better be: so long as the rules governing 'verdantly', 'grass', 'green', and so on, remain in force after the grass turns purple, speakers of the language are doomed to either error or some measure of linguistic incompetence. I have presumed throughout that new expressions may be introduced into a language in such a way that new conventions governing the use of those expressions may be established without altering the meanings of expressions in the old language. That means, for instance, that a new expression 'table' may be introduced into the language without altering the meanings of the expressions used to state the claim that $p_1, \ldots, p_n$ are arranged table-wise.[49] Similarly, I have assumed that the new operator 'verdantly' may be introduced into the language without altering the meanings of either

(13) Snow is white

---

[48] That is, it is not a very weighty charge so long as the measure of the theorist's incompetence is not so large that he fails to understand the terms he is using. See (Williamson, 2007, Ch. 4) for an argument that in the cases we are considering, the incompetence in question is not that large.

[49] Of course, the actual history of the expressions in English does not fit this description.

or

(14) Snow is white and grass is green.

In this sense, the introduction of new vocabulary extends the language rather than merely changing it.[50] But, if adding "verdantly" to the language leaves the other vocabulary as is, then presumably removing it from the language does, too.[51] Thus, when the speakers of the "verdantly" language wake up to purple grass, they aren't just stuck with a choice between error and some measure of linguistic incompetence. There's something they can do: pluck "verdantly", or at least the defective conventions governing its use, out of their language.[52]

Analyticity theorists face the challenge, posed by Quine, of accounting for the alleged fact that there are empirical data that might induce one to withhold assent to any sentence whatsoever, including erstwhile analyticities; the charge is, roughly, that each of our beliefs is in principle revisable in light of recalcitrant experience. In response, defenders of analyticity (Grice and Strawson, 1956) invoke the possibility of revising what one *means* (instead of revising

---

[50] Thus, one way for the analyticity theorist to avoid the arguments above is to insist that the stipulations in question changed the meanings of other expressions in the language so that they no longer mean what they used to mean. The analyticity theorist might claim, for instance, that after the introduction of 'verdantly', the meaning of

(13) Snow is white

somehow comes to express information about the color of grass; or he might claim that after the introduction of 'priman being', the arithmetical vocabulary of our theory of arithmetic somehow comes to express information about human beings. I take this sort of response to be prima facie implausible. What's more, it should provide scant comfort; see n. 51 below.

[51] Alternatively, if adding 'verdantly' to the language changes the meanings of the other vocabulary, so that, e.g.

(13) Snow is white

somehow comes to express information about the color of grass, then presumably removing 'verdantly' from the language can change those meanings back, so that (13) no longer conveys information about the greenness of grass, but is otherwise unaffected. The denier of the existence of tables should argue that, if this model applies to the case of 'table' talk, then English-speakers are obeying the conventions of the language when they affirm that there are particles arranged in the relevant way in location *L*, but what they say is (still) false.

[52] This is just one option. Speakers could, among other alternatives, decide to change what they mean by 'grass', by 'green', or even by 'is'.

what one believes) in the face of the new data. Thus, the meaning of the sentence rejected in one's new idiolect is not the same as the meaning of the sentence accepted in the old language. The present picture is neutral on whether the conventions in virtue of which sentences like

(45) If snow is white, then grass is green

have the trappings of analyticity should be taken to articulate the meaning of "verdantly." Other than that, there is just one thing that the present picture adds: that sometimes revision of such conventions is not just convenient, but *required* by the twin demands to accept only truths and avoid linguistic incompetence. Carnap famously offered a list of pragmatic factors bearing on the question of which language to use:

> The purposes for which the language is intended to be used, for instance, the purpose of communicating factual knowledge, will determine which factors are relevant for the decision. The efficiency, fruitfulness, and simplicity of the use of [the language] may be among the decisive factors (1950, p. 208).

Our argument suggests that there is another decisive factor that is not merely pragmatic: whether the rules of use enjoin accepting falsehoods.

Quine and his followers are naturally interpreted as questioning the existence of a distinction between analytic and synthetic truths. If the arguments of this paper are correct, they should also have questioned its metaphysical significance.[53]

University of Vermont

REFERENCES

Belnap, Nuel D. (1962). "Tonk, Plonk, and Plink." *Analysis*, 22(6): 130–4.
Bennett, Karen (2000). "Composition, Colocation, and Metaontology." In David J. Chalmers, David Manley, and Ryan Wasserman, editors,

---

[53] Thanks to audiences at the Australian National University, the "Art and Metaphysics" conference at Lingnan University, and the 2013 meeting of the Pacific Division of the American Philosophical Association. Special thanks to David Chalmers, Terence Cuneo, Philip Goff, Wesley Holliday, Mark Moyer, Daniel Nolan, Derk Pereboom, Jonathon Simon, Daniel Stoljar, and three anonymous referees for comments and conversation. Finally, thanks to Samantha Berthelette for help in preparing the text.

Metametaphysics: New Essays on the Foundations of Ontology, pp. 38–76. Oxford: Oxford University Press.

Boghossian, Paul (1996). "Analyticity Reconsidered." *Noûs*, 30(3): 360–91.

Boghossian, Paul (2003). "Blind Reasoning." *Proceedings of the Aristotelian Society, Supplementary Volume*, 77: 225–48.

Cameron, Ross (2006). "The Contingency of Composition." *Philosophical Studies*, 136: 99–121.

Carnap, Rudolf (1950). "Empiricism, Semantics, and Ontology." *Revue Internationale de Philosophie*, 4: 20–40. Page references are to the reprint in (Carnap, 1956).

Carnap, Rudolf (1956). *Meaning and Necessity: A Study in Semantics and Modal Logic*. Second edition. Chicago and London: University of Chicago Press.

Chalmers, David J. (2002). "Does Conceivability Entail Possibility?" In Tamar Szabó Gendler and John Hawthorne, editors, *Conceivability and Possibility*, pp. 145–200. Oxford: Oxford University Press.

deRosset, Louis (2010). "Getting Priority Straight." *Philosophical Studies*, 149(1): 73–97.

Donnellan, Keith (1977). "The Contingent A Priori and Rigid Designators." *Midwest Studies in Philosophy*, 2(1): 12–27.

Grice, H. P., and P. F. Strawson (1956). "In Defense of a Dogma." *Philosophical Review*, 65(2): 141–58.

Hale, Bob, and Crispin Wright (2001). *The Reason's Proper Study: Essays towards a Neo-Fregean Philosophy of Mathematics*. Oxford: Clarendon Press.

Hawthorne, John, and David Manley (2012). *The Reference Book*. Oxford: Oxford University Press.

Hirsch, Eli (2002). "Quantifier Variance and Realism." *Philosophical Issues*, 12: 51–73.

Jeshion, Robin (2001). "Donnellan on Neptune." *Philosophy and Phenomenological Research*, 63(1): 111–35.

Kaplan, David (1989). "Demonstratives." In Joseph Almog, John Perry, and Howard Wettstein, editors, *Themes from Kaplan*, pp. 481–563. New York: Oxford University Press.

Kripke, Saul (1980). *Naming and Necessity*. Cambridge, MA: Harvard University Press.

Nolan, Daniel (1997). "Quantitative Parsimony." *The British Journal for the Philosophy of Science*, 48: 329–43.

Prior, A. N. (1960). "The Runabout Inference-Ticket." *Analysis*, 21(2): 38–9.

Quine, W. V. (1951). "Two Dogmas of Empiricism." *Philosophical Review*, 60(1): 20–43.

Stevenson, J. T. (1961). "Roundabout the Runabout Inference Ticket." *Analysis*, 21(6): 124–8.

Thomasson, Amie L. (2007). *Ordinary Objects*. Oxford: Oxford University Press.
van Inwagen, Peter (1990). *Material Beings*. Ithaca, NY: Cornell University Press.
Williamson, Timothy (2007). *The Philosophy of Philosophy*. Oxford: Blackwell.
Yi, Byeong-Uk (1999). "Is Mereology Ontologically Innocent?" *Philosophical Studies*, 93: 141–60.

8. Naturalizing metaphysics with the help of cognitive science

Alvin I. Goldman

1. INTRODUCTION

This paper advances a thesis in the methodology of metaphysics. It argues that empirical findings in cognitive science can play a significant evidential role in an optimal methodology for metaphysics. Metaphysicians therefore have an epistemic interest in being attuned to appropriate evidence from cognitive science. This may even rise to the level of epistemic obligation, because epistemic inquiry in general—of which the pursuit of metaphysical truth is an instance—requires responsible inquirers to heed highly relevant and available evidence.[1] Acquiring cognitive scientific evidence can (sometimes) precipitate rational changes in credence functions that metaphysicians assign to competing theories. However, I do not mean to propose any utterly radical metaphysical methodology or any wholesale replacement of traditional methods. The proposal is conceived of as a supplement to traditional methods rather than a replacement of them.

What is proposed, then, is a partial "naturalization" of the methodology of metaphysics. I distinguish between three main kinds of contrasting methodologies that philosopher-metaphysicians can adopt. The first methodology is to follow the traditional conception of metaphysics as a purely a priori, armchair enterprise. It would find no place for any scientific input into metaphysical deliberation. A second methodology would welcome contributions to metaphysics from physics and other (non-biological,

---

[1] This would not necessarily imply that every metaphysician is personally obliged to consult the cognitive-scientific literature. It would only imply that the community of metaphysicians should be collectively informed of relevant findings and theoretical orientations in cognitive science. The most efficient way to achieve this end might be a division of labor, in which certain metaphysicians are in the vanguard of tracking relevant cognitive-scientific findings and communicating them to other practitioners.

non-psychological) physical sciences; but not from cognitive science. This form of limited naturalization might be defended as follows.

Cognitive science is uncontroversially relevant to the metaphysics of *mind*. Questions about consciousness, the nature and ontological status of phenomenology, the relation between mental states and brain states—all of these questions invite appropriate inputs from cognitive science. When the question is raised, however, about how to do metaphysics in general—precisely the question being raised here—why would cognitive science enter the picture? What kinds of information could cognitive science give us about the "external world"? The customary answer would be: none. So the second methodological position would also exclude cognitive science from playing a significant role.

The second position is compatible, however, with an extensive amount of "partial" naturalization of metaphysics, an approach that has made substantial gains in recent metaphysical practice. Appeals to physics have become fairly routine, or at least not uncommon, in the literature. At the radical end of the spectrum is James Ladyman and Don Ross's book *Every Thing Must Go: Metaphysics Naturalized* (2007). It proposes to infuse metaphysics with physics and essentially abandon everything else—at least the usual types of conclusions and methodologies used by traditional metaphysicians. A less extreme program for infusing physics into metaphysics is Tim Maudlin's *The Metaphysics within Physics* (2007), which describes itself as containing "the outlines of an ontology based on physics" (2007: 3). Yet another example in this category is Jonathan Schaffer's (2010a, b) use of physics to defend a very traditional metaphysical thesis—i.e. monism—by appeal to a detailed account of quantum entanglement. Schaffer traces the roots of monism to Parmenides, Plato, Plotinus, Spinoza, Hegel, and Bradley.

With a few exceptions, there is very little in the literature that supports a general role for cognitive science within metaphysics, including a role in the methodology of metaphysics.[2] More precisely,

---

[2] Over a 25-year period I have periodically tried to make the sort of argument undertaken here, in both graduate seminars and publications (Goldman 1987, 1989, 1992, 2007). In the same period a number of other people have advanced the importance of inputs from cognitive science in pursuing various local parts of metaphysics, including color, time, and moral value especially. Nonetheless, casual conversation with prominent contemporary metaphysicians reveals an abundance of skepticism

few metaphysicians who pursue a *realist* as opposed to a *conceptualist* program of metaphysics display much interest in cognitive science. By "conceptualist" metaphysics I mean the project of delineating the ontology (and ideology) characteristic of naïve human thought, i.e. *folk ontology*. There is a growing literature in this conceptualist vein, concerned with the naïve understanding of metaphysical concepts and phenomena. This approach, which saliently includes work by experimental philosophers, welcomes inputs from cognitive science. (Experimental philosophy might itself be classed as a sector of cognitive science.) But this work is not *realist* metaphysics. It does not display the dominant mission of mainstream metaphysics, which is to characterize the *correct* or *true* metaphysics of the world—as opposed to what is commonsensically *thought* or *said* about these matters. Metaphysicians of the realist stripe might fear that cognitive science material can only be informative about modes of thought, whereas proper metaphysics aims to understand, not thought, but the world's objective character. So they may choose to occupy the second methodological position explained above, which would still exclude cognitive science from the methodology of metaphysics generally. I wish to embrace the realist mission of metaphysics.[3] Nonetheless, I shall argue, even a metaphysics that sails under a realist banner is best conducted with the help of cognitive scientific inputs. This is a third kind of methodology, which I shall defend here.

As mentioned in footnote 2, some other metaphysicians have recently made similar pitches for *selected* areas of metaphysics. My aim is broader: to offer a general template (or two) for metaphysical methodology under which cognitive scientific considerations might become routine or commonplace factors in realist metaphysics, not just isolated or occasional factors, as matters currently stand. It is these proposed templates that comprise the chief innovations of the present paper, not the particular applications of them that are presented.

toward the general methodological thesis of the kind advanced here. So efforts at articulation of the general thesis and defense of it can hardly be classified as mere preaching to the choir.

[3] In the past I have sometimes described this as *prescriptive* as opposed to *descriptive* metaphysics (Goldman 1989, 2007). The original distinction, of course, is due to Strawson (1959).

I start with a brief heuristic rationale for the general idea. Like other types of philosophers, metaphysicians appeal extensively to intuition, experience, and commonsense belief to guide their path in metaphysical theorizing. Most cognitive scientists, however, contend that intuitions are massively influenced by our cognitive system—or "cognitive engine," as I shall call it. They are the products of complex computational operations, or neural circuits, which have formed over eons of evolutionary time. The cognitive outputs are rarely if ever simple read-outs of sensory inputs. Instead, they tend to be artifacts of "biases" or "constraints" wired into our cognitive equipment. In seeking to characterize the world itself, therefore, we had better not ignore the features of the complex systems that mold and shape our perceptual and cogitative experience. This means paying attention to the deliverances of cognitive science, our best if not exclusive source of information about the underlying systems.

To fix ideas, consider a familiar illusion from perceptual science, the Kanisza illusion, found in many elementary perception textbooks. (See Figure 8.1.)

Figure 8.1

This visual display is compellingly seen as containing a vivid white triangle with sharp contours in the foreground. Physically speaking, however, there are no such contours on the page (or screen). In fact the triangle's contours are perfectly homogeneous in color with their immediate white surrounds. The observed sides of the triangle are merely apparent; not genuine marks on the page (or screen). The visual experience of them is created or produced (automatically) by the visual system. Other visual illusions, of course, abound. They testify to the fact that our cognitive engine plays a significant role in shaping or "filling in" what is experienced. So we should not blithely assume that experience reliably signals, or indicates, features of the external world. A more complex approach is needed when we reflectively consider the nature of external reality. Provision must be made for the fact that what appears spontaneously to be features of the external world (*punkt*) may be a highly constructed product of an autonomous cognitive engine, the silent operations of which are hidden from perceptual or introspective view. This is not a new story, but it is still a good—and important—story. It is a significant reason why cognitive science should not be neglected.

This story can be given a slightly more formal statement in terms of a general functional relationship between genuine metaphysical reality, on the one hand, and our pre-philosophical intuitions or apprehensions about objects, properties, and relations that populate reality. Let "CSE" (commonsense experience) refer to the vast set of experiences and representations people have concerning reality, i.e. perceptions, intuitions, and judgments concerning the world (expressed in both natural language and the language of thought, if such there be). Examples include experience (as) of the passage of time, apprehension and/or judgment of object persistence over time, and judgments about the number of clouds currently in the sky. Let "R" refer to reality as a whole, or the class of objects, properties, and relations that (genuinely) populate reality. As previously indicated, a fundamental assumption of cognitive science is that commonsense experience and representations of reality are a function not only of reality itself but of the specific kind of cognitive engine (COGEN) we carry with us in all of our interactions with the world. As a result, relations between reality and our perceptual, intuitional, and cognitive acts cannot be adequately captured by a simple functional schema like (1):

(1) $\text{CSE} = f(R)$.

It should instead assume a form more like (2):

(2) CSE = f(R, COGEN).[4]

Arguably, formula (2) should also be expanded in the direction of (3):

(3) CSE = f(R, COGEN, CUL)

in which CUL is the culture in which the cognizer is embedded. For present purposes, however, formula (2) is instructive enough. If commonsense experience were a function of reality alone (i.e. the "rest" of the reality, minus the brain), the metaphysical investigator might hope that each slice or pattern of experience is a determinate function of (external) reality plus our interactions with it—as suggested by formula (1). If f(R) could be specified, an inquiring metaphysician might be able to make an inverse inference from CSE to R. Even this would be problematic, of course, since there may be no determinate inverse function. The same pattern of experience might be compatible with alternative forms of reality. The situation is more complicated yet, however, if formula (2) rather than formula (1) represents the state of play. If two very different kinds of factors are responsible for a given pattern of experience—both the nature of reality and the character of our perceptual and cognitive equipment—then problems ramify for a seeker of metaphysical reality. If our aim is to infer the nature of reality yet our impressions of reality are initially shaped by our cognitive engine (of which we can never divest ourselves), an appropriate epistemic route to the goal of getting a good grip of reality is to pay careful attention to the "silent" role that the cognitive engine plays in generating cognitive outputs. If this engine uses operating principles that help mold the cognitive outputs, this fact should not be neglected in our inquiry. It might be too easy to misattribute (apparent) properties generated by the engine to reality itself. Whatever evidence can be uncovered, then, about the mind's operating principles should be incorporated into a search for the properties of reality.

An analogy from a very different domain may convey the spirit of the perspective I mean to encourage. If a voter ponders the

---

[4] There is a problem of detail here, because what "R" represents—reality as a whole—already includes the human brain, so there is an unhappy bit of overlap here. (Thanks to Yoaav Isaacs for raising this issue.) For present purposes, however, this messy detail will be ignored, lest it distract us from the main point.

future actions and practices of a political candidate, what kinds of evidence should the voter try to track down and deploy? Only a deplorably naïve voter would rely exclusively and uncritically on a candidate's public statements and promises. An informed voter recognizes the lengths to which campaign organizations go to package their candidate for the electorate's consumption. A voter must look beyond such packaging to infer what lies behind it. The present suggestion is that a savvy metaphysician should do no less. What lies "behind" commonsense intuitions, experiences, and judgments (which metaphysicians use as prima facie guides to the nature of reality) should be probed, including what can be gleaned from the scientific study of the cognitive engine.

This is roughly the story advanced by Kant (on a familiar rendition, at any rate), who also promoted the "critical" study of metaphysics. In our own period, the credo of cognitive science was shaped by the idea that outputs of the cognitive engine are not simple products of an external "stimulus." Focusing on knowledge of grammar, Chomsky (1980) argued for the "poverty of the stimulus." On this view the mind has an innate schematism that places substantive constraints on what kinds of cognitions are generated. This innate endowment accounts for the fact that young children converge on the same grammar, despite encountering a very small amount of data. Not all practitioners of cognitive science endorse Chomsky's precise version of the thesis. Nonetheless, cognitive science broadly embraces an attenuated version of it, to the extent of highlighting the powerful impact of the mind's autonomous structure in generating surface-level cognition. Human cognition is constrained and shaped by a specific set of organs, which channel and give rise to distinctively human kinds of cognitive outputs. This idea should be taken to heart by inquiring metaphysicians no less than they take to heart the fundamentals of modern physics.

2. A BAYESIAN APPROACH TO REVISING METAPHYSICAL CREDENCES

How does this perspective translate into methodological advice for metaphysicians? Disputes in metaphysics are often presented as choices between how to interpret experience and discourse in particular domains. What properties, relations, facts, truths, or states of affairs obtain, hold, or are exemplified in each domain? The options on offer for metaphysical choice are frequently couched in the language of "realism" versus "anti-realism" (within a specified domain). The realism in question is a somewhat different sense than the one referred to in section 1. It is commonly understood as a view that upholds the existence of facts, truth-makers, or mind-independent properties, and which corresponds fairly directly to our naïve conception of the domain. In contrast to realism (in this sense), an assortment of anti-realisms are on offer for many metaphysical domains. Terminologies for the variety of anti-realisms vary from domain to domain and from author to author. Popular terminologies for anti-realisms include eliminativism, nihilism, dispositionalism (or response-dependence), expressivism, fictionalism, projectivism, constructivism, error theories, and so on. I won't try to give precise definitions of each of these terms. In any case, the main purpose here is not to decide which of these alternatives is correct in each domain, but what methodology to use in deciding which is correct. More specifically, what kinds of *evidence* should metaphysicians consult to make optimal choices? More specifically yet, the central question is whether evidence from cognitive science can be particularly helpful or even essential. If so, what kinds of findings from cognitive science might be evidentially relevant to metaphysical choices, and exactly how are they relevant?

In many domains of metaphysical dispute, defenders of realism are confronted with opponents who seek to debunk realism.[5] In meta-ethics realism about moral value is contrasted with various kinds of anti-realism. Philosophers who critique realism—from the perspective of evolutionary theory, for example—often call themselves debunkers. Sharon Street (2006) and Richard Joyce (2006) are debunkers in this sense. They defend anti-realism about moral value, the view that there are no antecedent, mind-independent evaluative facts about which things are reasons for doing things. According to such anti-realists, facts about moral reasons consist in, or rest upon, people's attitudes, attitudes that are the products of

[5] Relevant specifications of realism vary from topic to topic and from author to author. So I won't try to give a general characterization of realism that works for all cases. There is enough unity, however, that the relevant points can be made without a precise definitional commitment.

evolution rather than (for example) the *detection* of things in mind-independent reality.

How might such "debunking" take place? Roger White (2010) notes that many debunking attempts are based on alternative causal explanations of the (realist) beliefs in question. Street and Joyce defend evolution-based anti-realism as an alternative to a realist, detectivist account of moral value. White is skeptical about such debunking attempts.[6] But despite his skepticism, he introduces a simple but instructive example, which I shall modify for purposes of my own argument. Here is White's example:

> That the gas gauge reads Full is evidence that the tank is full. But now I learn that the gauge is stuck and would indicate Full whether the tank is full or not. In this way my belief formation was not sensitive to the truth as the gas gauge on which I based my belief was not sensitive to the contents of the tank. This information undercuts the evidential support of the gauge reading. And if my justification for believing the tank is full crucially depended on this evidence then I am no longer justified in supposing that the tank is full. (2010: 585)

White describes the case in terms of categorical belief rather than credences and categorical support or defeat rather than probabilities. But the story could easily be re-analyzed in Bayesian terms. I want to explore a quasi-Bayesian approach in this section, so let us see how such an approach would work here.

Re-describe the gasoline example as featuring two competing hypotheses: the gas tank is full (H) and the gas tank is less than full (~H). Assume that your friend has just lent you his car on an emergency basis, and you have no idea about its fuel situation. For simplicity, then, assume that the priors you assign to H and ~H are equal: both are .50. Upon entering the car, you consult the gas gauge and see that it says "Full", and take that as an item of evidence. You assess the crucial likelihoods (conditional probabilities) as follows:

(L$_1$) The probability that the gas gauge would read "Full" (F) conditional on the gas tank being full ($P_H(F)$) = 0.9

(L$_2$) The probability that the gas gauge would read "Full" conditional on the gas tank being less than full ($P_{\sim H}(F)$) = 0.1.

---

[6] Metaphysics is not the main target of White's discussion; it is epistemology. But you might say that the primary focus of the present paper is also epistemology, i.e. the epistemology (methodology) of metaphysics.

Given these priors and likelihoods, the posterior probabilities you will assign to H and ~H (given that the gauge reads "Full") are as follows: $P_F(H) = 0.90$ and $P_F(\sim H) = 0.10$. In other words, you regard it as highly probable that the tank is full.

Now you learn that the gas gauge is stuck. The first epistemic effect of this new evidence, we may suppose, is that you revise the likelihoods you associate with the gas gauge reading full.[7] Exactly how such revisions should be made is not obvious in the absence of additional information, but minimally both likelihoods should be modified, presumably in the direction of more intermediate values. Assume you revise both L_1 and L_2 so that $L_1 = L_2 = .50$. In other words:

(L_1') $P_H(F) = .50$.
(L_2') $P_{\sim H}(F) = .50$.

To see how one's credence function should be revised in light of the revised pair of likelihoods, we simply plug the new values into a standard form of Bayes' Theorem. This form and the appropriate values are given here:

$$P_F(H) = \frac{P(H)\,P_H(F)}{P(H)\,P_H(F) + P(\sim H)\,P_{\sim H}(F)} = \frac{(.5)(.5)}{(.5)(.5)+(.5)(.5)} = \frac{.25}{.50} = .50.$$

Thus, having learned about the stuck gas gauge, your new posterior probabilities are $H = \sim H = .50$. Under the assumed credal assignments, the epistemic impact of acquiring the new evidence about the stuck gas gauge is considerable.

This analytical template is what I wish to propose for applying cognitive science to metaphysical disputes (at least disputes of the realism/anti-realism variety). In the foregoing illustration, of course, the new evidence has nothing to do with cognitive science. But in the examples that follow, the evidence of interest will be products of cognitive science. Again, in the foregoing example, the result of acquiring the new evidence pushes the rational cognizer toward agnosticism about the target hypothesis. I do not mean to imply that

---

[7] Orthodox Bayesians do not believe in the updating of likelihood priors. But this is a very natural way to treat the kinds of examples I want to discuss here. Readers who have a strong preference for orthodox Bayesianism can re-do the analysis by updating posterior probabilities of H and ~H with the new evidence.

cognitive scientific findings will always breed agnosticism (equal credences vis-à-vis competing theories). Nor do I mean to suggest that such findings would be decisive for settling the metaphysical dispute. I only suggest that suitable cognitive scientific findings can force a rational metaphysician to adjust his/her credences in light of those findings. Such findings will be *relevant evidence* for credal adjustments vis-à-vis the metaphysical hypotheses in question. This is one template for the central thesis I mean to defend in this paper.

I shall next apply this template to four problems in metaphysics. To effect these applications, several kinds of substitutions need to be made. Instead of the gas-tank hypotheses H and ~H, we would need rival hypotheses of a metaphysical kind. I am specifically interested in pairs of metaphysical hypotheses, or theories, that compete as accounts of designated metaphysical phenomena. One would be a realist theory and the other an anti-realist theory. The metaphysician's initial evidence bearing on the theories would be a set of ordinary experiences, intuitions, or beliefs about the domain that each theory tries to accommodate in its own way. A basic assumption here is that such experiences, intuitions, and beliefs are examples of evidence that metaphysicians (legitimately) use when weighing competing metaphysical theories. Finally, I shall identify cases in which cognitive science has (already) found evidence that (by my lights) should influence the credences or credence functions assigned to the likelihoods that link theories and experiential evidence, on the model of the stuck-gauge evidence in White's example. In principle, my points could be made with non-standard metaphysical theories of my own devising and purely invented cognitive scientific findings. But, wherever possible, I shall work with actual metaphysical debates between realist and anti-realist alternatives and with actual cognitive-scientific findings. Of course, such empirical findings are always open to debate and interpretation. But I seek to use examples with pretty legitimate scientific standing.

3. FIRST ILLUSTRATION: THE PASSAGE OF TIME

The metaphysics of time, since McTaggart (1908), has been dominated by two competing theories: the A-theory and the B-theory. The A-theory is commonly taken to imply that tense is real, that there is something privileged about the present, and (often) that time *flows* or *passes*, a notion entirely absent from the B-theory. One lively example of a realism/anti-realism debate is precisely the debate over the reality or unreality of temporal passage. Arguments on behalf of this conclusion vary, but many philosophers contend that we perceive such passage in our perception of change. Thus, Richard Schuster (1986) writes:

> Let me begin this inquiry with the simple but fundamental fact that the flow of time, or passage, as it is known, is given in experience, that it is as indubitable an aspect of our perception of the world as the sights and sounds that come in upon us, even though it is not the peculiar property of a special sense. (1986: 695)

L. A. Paul (2010) introduces her treatment of the topic as follows:

> We all know what it is like to have [passage-of-time experiences]. Reflection on the qualitative character of such an experience suggests that events occurring now have a characteristic property of *nowness*, responsible for a certain special "feel," and that events pass from the future to the present and then into the past. The question that I want to explore is whether we should take this suggestion to support an *antireductionist* ontology of time, that is, whether we should take it to support an ontology that includes a primitive, monadic property of nowness responsible for the special feel of events in the present, and a relation of *passage* that events instantiate in virtue of literally passing from the future to the present and then into the past. (2010: p. 333)

What Paul calls "antireductionism" (with respect to time) is a view that takes both passage and nowness to be real; it is obviously the *realist* position in the debate. What she calls "reductionism" is the *antirealist* position. It claims that there is no such property as passage (or nowness; but we'll focus on passage). According to antirealism, we just inaccurately experience the world *as* having this property. What evidence can the competing sides invoke to support their respective cases?

Antireductionists rely on the force of the experiences themselves. There must be some sort of physical flow, they say, that we detect via our experience as of passage. The problem for reductionists, says Paul, is to provide an account of why (or how) we have such temporal experience despite there being no ontologically real passage. "It is absolutely essential for reductionists to be able to provide an alternative, reasonable explanation of why we have temporal experiences as of nowness and passage" (2010: 339). She proceeds to offer cognitive science-inspired explanations of how we might have such experiences despite there being no such things as nowness or passage.[8]

She first appeals to the familiar phenomenon (within cognitive science) of *apparent motion*. Blinking dots in rapid succession on opposite sides of a screen give rise to an illusion of a dot moving back and forth across the screen. And in the *cutaneous rabbit* experiment a series of appropriately spaced taps (e.g. taps at the wrist, near the elbow, and the upper arm area) produces an illusion of an object moving continuously along one's arm. The "color phi" experiment reports an analogous illusion. Extrapolating from these cases, she suggests, the reductionist can argue that our illusion-creating brain is quite capable of working with a static universe to produce experiences that suggest passage and flow though in reality there are no such phenomena.

Similarly, another opponent of "real" temporal flow, Robin Le Poidevin (2007) appeals to the "flash-lag" experiment to explain a nonveridical experience of temporal flow.

Subjects are presented with a small dot moving across a screen. At some point during the dot's transit, another dot appears briefly directly above or below the other dot: this is the 'flash'. A significant number of subjects report that they saw the moving dot *ahead* of the flashed dot, in the direction of movement. The flash appears to lag behind (McKay 1958). But it does not really do so, so why the illusion that it does?

[I]t takes time for the brain to register what is going on in the outside world. When information is registered about changing objects, and especially about rapidly moving objects, it is already slightly out of date. So we have evolved to compensate for this lag. The brain makes an adjustment to the information it has received about the position of a moving object, and makes a projection based on information concerning the object's velocity and direction. When we see the object, we see it, not in the position it was in when light from it hit the retina, but in the position the brain estimates that the object must be in by the time that information is registered. What we see, once more, is a projection, based on a prediction... Contrasted with this 'predictive' model is the 'postdictive' model... As with the predictive model, however, the suggestion is that the brain is imposing an interpretation on the data. (Le Poidevin 2007: 94)

Thus, both Paul and Le Poidevin offer explanatory stories to defend anti-realism. I completely accept the relevance of such

---

[8] In more recent work Paul (forthcoming) explores a similar theme with respect to time's "arrow". This additional topic, however, is beyond the present purview.

explanatory factors. But as an analytical device I instead propose Bayesianism (as contrasted with explanationism) as a more illuminating and perspicuous account of how metaphysicians should proceed, epistemologically, in the realism/anti-realism debate. What's the connection between the two?

Suppose that anti-realism is true: passage is not ontologically real. If under this supposition there would be no psychological or brain-based explanation of our having experiences as of passage (despite its ontological unreality), it would be entirely reasonable for metaphysicians to assign a very low number to the conditional probability (likelihood) of our undergoing passage experiences if anti-realism were true. On the other hand, if there were a plausible potential explanation of why or how we would undergo passage experiences (even) if antirealism were true, a metaphysician would then have good reason to assign a much higher number to the same conditional probability. Such a boost in conditional probability assignment could make a big difference in the posterior probabilities that reasonable metaphysicians would assign to the realist and anti-realist hypotheses respectively. Through the demonstration of illusions such as the Kanisza illusion (section 1), cognitive science has shown that the human brain is not only capable of, but even fairly prone to, creating non-veridical contours and other non-veridical effects. Thus, explanations of the occurrence of temporal passage experiences despite their non-veridicality is not at all far-fetched.

In short, by taking relevant cognitive science into account, a reasonable metaphysician would substantially revise the likelihood of the occurrence of passage experiences conditional on anti-realism. Letting E = experiences of passage, R = ontological realism about passage, and AR = ontological anti-realism about passage, we might expect the indicated types of evidence from cognitive science to boost the likelihood of E given AR from an initial value of, say, .001 (choosing a number out of a hat) to .40 (choosing another number out of the hat). This would make a very significant difference to the resulting posterior probability that a metaphysician informed by cognitive science (and utilizing Bayesian principles) would attach to anti-realism about passage.

Cognitive scientists would not be surprised by this sort of metaphysical move (although they might not like to describe it in the language of "metaphysics"). They routinely view the constructive activity of the brain as a massive factor in determining human experience. So, whether they would agree in detail on this particular example, the general drift of the analysis is completely congenial to their general perspective.

4. SECOND ILLUSTRATION: MORAL VALUE

Sharon Street (2006) formulates the defining claim of value realism as the claim that there are evaluative facts or truths that hold independently of all our evaluative attitudes, whereas anti-realism denies that there are such truths. However, as Street points out, there is a basic set of evaluative judgments that human beings tend to embrace across time and culture. These include the following judgments about reasons, which I shall call, collectively, EJ (for "evaluative judgments").

- The fact that something would promote one's survival is a reason in favor of it.
- The fact that something would promote the interests of a family member is a reason to do it.
- We have greater obligations to help our own children than we do to help complete strangers.
- The fact that someone has treated one well is a reason to treat that person well in return.
- The fact that someone is altruistic is a reason to admire, praise, and reward him or her. (Street 2006: 115)

Can a metaphysician (or meta-ethicist) choose between realism and anti-realism by reference to the likelihood of the widespread embrace of these value judgments given realism versus the likelihood of their widespread embrace given anti-realism? What is the likelihood that EJ would be widely embraced if there were independent moral truths and what is the likelihood of EJ being widely embraced if there were no such independent moral truths? How, in other words, should the following likelihoods be evaluated?

(1) $P_R(EJ) = ?$
(2) $P_{AR}(EJ) = ?$

Finally, can cognitive science present any helpful evidence in these matters?

Realists would say that these judgments could easily be widely accepted if realism were correct—that is, if there were independent moral truths—because of people's ability to "track" them. But could people track such truths? They might be able to do so if they had an (accurate) moral sense; but do they? Cognitive science can weigh in on this question. It certainly studies perceptual systems (also called "senses") and sometimes discovers new ones. Comparative cognitive science discovered echolocation in bats. Human cognitive neuroscience has discovered many types of *interoceptive* senses in the human brain, i.e. brain mechanisms for monitoring the positions and conditions of one's own bodily organs (see Craig, 2002; de Vignemont, 2011; Goldman, 2012).[9] There is no comparable discovery of any *moral* sense, whether an exteroceptive sense or an interoceptive sense.[10] This might be interpreted as evidence against the existence of any sense for tracking moral truths, which presumably militates against a high likelihood, under value realism, of broad convergence on moral judgments like EJ.

Is it any more likely that such a broad convergence on moral judgments would be made under the alternative hypothesis, i.e. the non-existence of independent moral truths? Street argues that such a broad convergence—especially convergence on the reasons listed in EJ—is substantially likely under anti-realism because evolution provides a very plausible avenue to this convergence via natural selection. Natural selection would select for mechanisms that tend to get organisms to act, feel, and believe in reproductively advantageous ways. Pro-attitudes toward the judgments in EJ would have precisely this property, because acting in the manners described by these judgments would have clear survival and reproductive advantages. Natural selection, she points out, often selects for mechanisms

---

[9] For an accessible treatment of Craig's research on the neuroanatomy of interoception—a sense that monitors the physiological condition of the body—see Craig (2010), though that article focuses specifically on the interoception of emotion.

[10] Admittedly, it is not clear how cognitive science could recognize a moral sense if it encountered one. Even if it could determine circumstances in which the brain represents an action, say, as right or wrong, how would it determine that such a representation is veridical or not? If it cannot make such a determination, how can it tell that a genuine moral *sense* is at work? However, by the same token, what evidence does the ordinary person or the armchair metaphysician have for thinking that we have anything like a moral sense, or any other method for recognizing good or bad reasons for favoring something?

that do just this, as in the case of the automatic reflex response that causes the hand to withdraw from a hot surface. She also points to "the striking continuity that we observe between our evaluative judgments and the more basic evaluative tendencies of other animals, especially those most closely related to us... [A]t some basic motivational level, chimpanzees seem to experience the fact that another chimpanzee has helped them, whether by sharing food, grooming them, or supporting their position within the group hierarchy, as 'counting in favor of' assisting that other individual in similar ways" (2006: 117). Since evolution seems to have favored our nearest animal relatives having similar traits, it would be "easy" for evolution to produce similar traits in a nearby species such as ours. For anybody not previously apprised of such facts, this is additional evidence that should boost the likelihood that EJ would be favored attitudes among humans as well. If we count evolutionary science as part of cognitive science (and the neuroscience branch of cognitive science certainly studies brain evolution), this would be another case in which evidence emerging from cognitive science is relevant to an epistemic choice between metaphysical alternatives.

Summing up, evidence from cognitive science can weigh in on both likelihoods (the one pertaining to realism and the one pertaining to anti-realism) in a substantial way. It can raise doubts about the existence of a moral sense, making it harder for a single body of moral judgments to become entrenched across time and culture. And it can make it clear how natural selection could promote the result that a single body of moral judgments, like EJ, would become entrenched across time and culture. Bayesian inference applied to changed likelihoods would give rise to changed posterior probabilities vis-à-vis the core hypotheses in question: value realism and value anti-realism.

5. THIRD ILLUSTRATION: NATURAL KINDS

An extremely influential idea in contemporary metaphysics, dating to the 1970s, is the idea that natural kinds have essences that are discovered by science and that such essences determine the extensions of our natural kind terms and concepts. Certain metaphysical necessities have also been inferred from this view. For example, if it is the essence of water to have the chemical composition H_2O, then it is necessarily the case that every sample of water has the chemical structure H_2O. Philosophical acceptance of kind essentialism also brought in its train (or was accompanied by) acceptance of certain *de re* necessities such as the necessity of origin. If woman Y was in fact my biological mother, then necessarily Y was my mother. No other person *could* have been my mother. All this is the product of work by Hilary Putnam (1975) and Saul Kripke (1980).

How could cognitive science challenge such metaphysical theses? Sarah-Jane Leslie (2013) mounts such a challenge as follows.[11] The rationale for the essentialist theory of natural kinds is, fundamentally, that people find it intuitively compelling to understand objects in the world in terms of this theory. This is part of their psychology, a thesis that Leslie labels *quintessentialism* (= psychological essentialism). Moreover, these intuitions are the outgrowth of an implicit set of beliefs, emerging early in preschooler development. In other words, Leslie points to an extensive body of literature by developmental psychologists according to which even young children are (psychological) essentialists. Their psychologies lead them to believe in essences for a wide variety of things they encounter. An essence is understood as something like a hidden inner structure. (Important contributions and reviews to this literature include Keil, 1989, and Gelman, 2003). Leslie provides illustrations of the supporting data for the presence of this idea in early childhood. From the philosophical perspective, her principal critical point is that the existence of psychological essentialism as a cognitive trait provides an *alternative* explanation of people's *intuitions* about kinds and essences. As Leslie puts it, "There are many explanations of why we may be fundamentally disposed to see the world in a particular way, only one of which is that *metaphysically or scientifically speaking, the world actually is that way*" (2013: 108; emphasis in the original). In other words, it is questionable whether the realist postulation of real-world essence is the best explanation of our essentialist intuitions. This is fully parallel to the issues raised in the first two examples of what is the (best) explanation of intuitions or attitudes

---

[11] I encountered Leslie's paper after most of the present paper was complete, including the three other illustrations analyzed in a Bayesian framework. As it happens, I had criticized Kripke's thesis of the necessity of origin in Goldman 1992. That treatment was extremely brief and under-developed, however.

that are admittedly highly prevalent or widespread. In effect, Leslie is advancing an anti-realist explanation of people's essentialist intuitions. Their prevalence is perfectly well explained by the independent existence of a certain (possibly innate) psychological trait; we don't need to postulate essentialist facts about physical objects.

Leslie does not rest content, however, with presenting the (anti-realist's) purely cognitivist explanation of essentialist intuitions. She argues independently, and at length, that physical science fails to support the essentialist views that Putnam and Kripke advance. For example, Putnam and Kripke advance the view that the necessary and sufficient condition of belonging to a natural kind is given by a hidden underlying structure found in its members. In the case of water the relevant structure (essence) is H_2O and in biological species the relevant structure is the genetic code. But this is false, Leslie argues, both with respect to chemical kinds and biological kinds. With respect to biological species, a member of one species may have more genetically in common with a member of another species than with a member of its own species. And with respect to chemistry, matters are much more complicated than the suggested essence acknowledges. She then concludes as follows:

> We can now pose the question: does science *actually* deliver such a privileged *same substance* relation, or do we simply have once again the quintessentialist intuition that science *must* do so? ... I shall argue that the relevant sciences deliver no such privileged *same substance* relation. (2013: 143)

Clearly, Leslie's argument is not confined to showing that cognitive science delivers relevant evidence. She also contends that physical science has a lot to offer. This part of her thesis, however, is simply independent of the part pursued here. It obviously does not challenge, but simply complements, the evidential relevance of the cognitive science, which she also supports for her selected domain.

Nonetheless, let us see how Leslie's materials both fit within the Bayesian framework used here. As with the first two illustrations, Leslie argues for the relevance of cognitive scientific evidence to the competing metaphysical hypotheses. If we focus only on the contribution of cognitive science to her analysis, it can play the same role in a Bayesian analysis as it did in our earlier examples. There is no analogue of the deployment of physical science evidence in the previous examples, but that constitutes no important disanalogy for present purposes. After all, it is not my purpose to deny an evidential role for physical science in these metaphysical controversies.

How would a Bayesian analysis proceed, then, for Leslie's case? The cognitive science portion of her evidence contributes to the probability of realism about physical essentialism by addressing the conditional probability that people would have essentialist intuitions on the assumption that essentialist realism is false. The idea is that given the fact of psychological essentialism—a built-in tendency to expect hidden essences—it would still be highly probable that children and grown-ups would have essentialist *intuitions* even if the physical world did not rampantly feature essences. This evidence should lead a metaphysician to raise her credence in the likelihood of the widespread incidence of essentialist intuitions (even) given the anti-realist hypothesis, and this change in likelihood will lower the posterior probability of essentialist realism.

Let us put some numbers in place to illustrate this point. Let $E =$ the regular occurrence of essentialist intuitions. Let $R =$ essentialist realism, the hypothesis that biological and chemical kinds (for example) actually have hidden-structural essences. Finally, let $AR =$ essentialist anti-realism, the hypothesis that biological and chemical kinds do not reveal hidden structural essences. Before Leslie brings psychological essentialism into play, how would a reasonable metaphysician evaluate the following two conditional probabilities (or likelihoods): the probability of E conditional on R and the probability of E conditional on AR? That is, what values might plausibly be assigned to $P_R(E)$ and to $P_{AR}(E)$? The former will presumably be relatively high, at least assuming that people are scientifically pretty competent. They will acquire essentialist intuitions if the world actually has hidden essences that can be uncovered. Grown-ups, at least, should acquire such intuitions. But the value of $P_{AR}(E)$ should be relatively low. If the real world has no hidden essences, why would people have essentialist intuitions? Enter now the fact that people (including preschoolers) have the cognitive trait of quintessentialism, which is acquired by normal maturation no matter what science is formally introduced in classrooms. Given this fact, which we assume to be contributed by cognitive science, $P_{AR}(E)$ must be adjusted upward.

Before we get the cognitive scientific evidence, it is plausible to substitute the following numbers into the Bayesian formula:

$$P_E(R) = \frac{P(R)P_R(E)}{P(R)P_R(E) + P(AR)P_{AR}(E)} = \frac{(.70)(.90)}{(.70)(.90) + (.30)(.20)}$$

$$= \frac{(.63)}{(.63) + (.06)} = 0.91$$

But once the cognitive scientific evidence is received, it might be plausible to raise $P_{AR}(E)$ to .90. Then the numbers will become:

$$\frac{(.70)(.90)}{(.70)(.90) + (.30)(.90)} = \frac{(.63)}{(.63) + (.27)} = 0.70.$$

Thus, an increase in the conditional probability of essentialist intuitions given anti-realism from .20 to .90 results in a decrease of the posterior probability of realism from 0.91 to 0.70. This is a non-negligible reduction in the probability of realism, due to the cognitive scientific evidence.

What about the contribution of the evidence from physical science? A perspicuous way of handling this is in terms of the prior probability of the truth of kind essentialism; or rather, the posterior probability of essentialism being true given the new evidence about biology and chemistry Leslie introduces. That too would reduce the probability of the truth of the realist hypothesis. Changing the prior probability (not here equated to the "Ur-probability") from .70 to .30, for example, yields the following final posterior probability for realism:

$$P_E(R) = \frac{(.30)(.9)}{(.30)(.90) + (.70)(.90)} = \frac{(.27)}{(.27) + (.63)} = .30$$

Now the posterior probability of realism is reduced all the way to .30. Clearly, a combination of both cognitive and physical scientific evidence can have a significant impact, as we would expect.

6. FOURTH ILLUSTRATION: THEISM

The existence of God is a central topic in metaphysics, spanning both the history of philosophy and contemporary philosophy. Traditionally, the positive arguments are predominantly deductive and a priori, the ontological and cosmological arguments being the most prominent examples. It is dubious, however, whether such arguments are terribly promising. Philosophers like them, of course, but it is questionable whether anybody else is blown away by them.

It is easy, of course, to produce a deductively valid argument for any specified conclusion. It is harder to produce a sound argument, and even harder yet to produce a sound argument for which the entire targeted audience believes the premises *justifiedly*. Genuine "proofs" of the existence of God, however, require some such justificational element. Historically, an influential empirical argument for God's existence in which the premises were regarded as justified (for almost anybody) is the argument from design. William Paley's version of this argument was highly persuasive in the early nineteenth century. However, the evolutionary theory developed by Darwin and his successors has greatly dampened the persuasiveness of this argument. Variation and natural selection seem eminently viable as the real origin of ostensibly designed features of the world.

I shall therefore focus on a distinct type of argument from an observable phenomenon, the extremely high incidence of theistic *belief* throughout known human history and culture. An ancient and widely invoked criterion of truth (at least in antiquity) was the *consensus gentiam* ("agreement of the people"), which states: "that which is universal among men carries the weight of truth". Aristotle appealed to this kind of criterion when invoking the opinion of the many. This idea might be re-used in the realm of theism. How could we express this approach in Bayesian terms?

The two hypotheses in the present case are "God exists" (G) and "God does not exist" ($\sim$G). Bayes' theorem implies that if we start with roughly equal prior probabilities for these hypotheses, the main driving force in determining a rational posterior credence will be the *likelihood ratio* (or fraction), that is, the likelihood of there being the evidence in question conditional on G divided by the likelihood of there being this same evidence conditional on $\sim$G. The evidence, once again, is the widespread incidence of belief in God (W). The two likelihoods are:

(1) $P_G(W)$ and
(2) $P_{\sim G}(W)$.

If $P_G(W)$ substantially exceeds $P_{\sim G}(W)$, then the likelihood quotient exceeds 1.0 and the occurrence or presence of W supports G. If $P_{\sim G}(W)$ exceeds $P_G(W)$, then the occurrence of W supports $\sim$G. One might initially be inclined to think that $P_{\sim G}(W)$ must be extremely small. Why would there be widespread belief in God if God didn't even exist? He would not be there to bestow favors on humankind, to answer prayers, to reveal himself to various prophets, etc. Given the small value of $P_{\sim G}$ (W) compared with $P_G(W)$, the fact that there *is* widespread belief should generate high credence in God's existence.

This is where possible psychological explanations of belief in God's existence become relevant, in straightforward analogy to the essentialism case. If there are strong psychological propensities toward theistic belief that would operate to produce such belief even in the absence of God's existence, then the value of $P_{\sim G}$ (W) might not be tiny at all. It might be quite substantial, perhaps even greater than the value of $P_G(W)$. As it happens, evidence for such strong propensities toward theistic belief are emerging from various psychological investigations.

Historically, Freud postulated a pathological need for a father figure to explain the prevalence of a God belief and Marx explained it in terms of indoctrination on the part of the powerful. Recently, books by various cognitive scientists, social scientists, and philosophers have pursued other potential explanatory themes (e.g. Atran, 2004; Boyer, 2001; Dennett, 2006). New evidence from cognitive science has also been accumulating. I will now review some of this evidence.

One theme floated by Boyer (2001) is called a "hypertrophy of social cognition": a willingness to attribute psychological states even when it is (evidentially) inappropriate to do so. The classic demonstration of this human tendency was the work of Heider and Simmel (1944). They made a film clip depicting geometrical shapes (circles, squares, triangles) moving about in systematic ways. People watching the film clip instinctively described these shapes as people—e.g. bullies, victims, heroes—who have various desires and goals. Young children also interpret such films in this fashion. Bloom and Veres (1999) show that similar results can be obtained even without bounded figures, simply with moving dots and groups of figures such as swarms of squares. In short, interpreting stimuli in terms of goals and purposes seems to be wired into our cognitive engine. That would explain our propensity to postulate unseen creatures like God, devils, sprites, etc. with purposes and designs, even in the absence of probative observational evidence. Similarly, Guthrie (1993) showed that people are inclined to attribute human characteristics to a wide variety of entities with scarcely any trace of humanity, for example, airplanes, automobiles, bags, bells, and even rocks. Babies have similar tendencies—ostensibly innate—to attribute intentional characteristics (Bloom, 2007).[12]

More generally, researchers on mindreading, or "theory of mind," have found substantial patterns of error, or "bias," in people's attribution of mental attitudes (mindreading). The best known general type of error is "egocentricity," in which people tend to project (or assign) their own current states to their targets, even when they have no reason to suppose that their targets are similarly situated. The best known bias of this kind goes by the label "curse of knowledge" because it involves people imputing their own knowledge or belief states to others when they have evidence to the contrary (Camerer et al., 1989). Similar tendencies have been demonstrated for egocentric projection of feelings and valuations.[13]

A new wrinkle in this territory, where both excess and misdirection of mentalization are found, led Ara Narenzayan et al. (2012) to conclude that theism is driven by normal people's excessive propensity to assign mental states. Narenzayan began with the well-documented finding that autism involves a deficit in "theory of mind," or mental state attribution. This deficit predicts that autistic individuals should be *less* inclined to imagine deities with mental states than normal people are, and hence they should have a diminished inclination to believe in such deities. This hypothesis was tested in a controlled study in which autistic adolescents were found to have less belief in God than did matched neuro-typical controls. Moreover, it was found that levels of mentalizing mediated this relationship. In other words, mentalizing *deficits* are a "pathway" to *dis*belief in God. This evidence lends interesting support to the

---

[12] How exactly is the statement to be defended that people attribute mental states of the indicated sorts *in the absence of probative evidence*? What kind of evidence would be probative? This can be answered in different ways. One answer would draw on a popular account of the nature of mental states, viz. the functional-role account. If being in a desire state or a goal state with a certain content is a matter of having dispositions to interact with environment inputs, behavior outputs, and also lawlike relations between a goal state and other kinds of internal states, then it appears that none of the attributions cited in the foregoing studies were based (even remotely) on solid evidence. They just seem (in many cases) to be based on lively movements and little else.

[13] See Goldman (2006: 164–73) for a review of the psychological literature on egocentric biases.

thesis that mentalizing "excesses" (in the population of normals) are heavily responsible for theistic belief, which takes hold in the absence of direct observational evidence.

Admittedly, this psychological evidence is less than overwhelming. It is an interesting and suggestive set of data points. But our purpose here is only to illustrate how cognitive scientific evidence—if and when it is sufficiently strong—can have an evidential bearing on the metaphysical issue. However, even if we grant for argument's sake that belief in God is (substantially) the product of runaway mentalizing, how would this affect the Bayesian calculus? As previously explained, it would affect the calculus by boosting $P_{\sim G}(W)$ to a level considerably higher than one might expect "a priori". This boost non-trivially affects the posterior credence that should be assigned to $\sim G$.

One doubt or question may occur to the reader concerning the argument presented to this point. A reader may feel that our argument—including all four examples—rests on little more than the observation that everything is potentially relevant to everything else. But haven't we known this since Duhem, and Quine's frequent reminders of the Duhemian thesis?[14] In light of this familiar fact, doesn't my push for the importance of cognitive science have to be buttressed by the demonstration of a special evidential role for cognitive science? Otherwise, why think that cognitive science deserves anything but an incidental and marginal role in the methodology of metaphysics? What is special about cognitive science that we should single it out as particularly important to metaphysics?

A partial answer—well-illustrated by the four examples above—is that metaphysicians often appeal to mental states as "data" for purposes of metaphysical theorizing. These mental states include beliefs, intuitions, experiences, and behavioral propensities. Within the class of behavioral propensities are verbal propensities to classify certain scenarios one way or another, e.g. as instances of causation or non-instances of causation. Cognitive science has much to say about all of these types of states and behaviors, including theories to explain and systematize them. Since such explanatory theories can either cohere or conflict with metaphysical theories (e.g. theories of causation), cognitive scientific perspectives have a distinctive

---

[14] Thanks to Jonathan Schaffer for expressing this worry.

bearing on metaphysical theory. This should have been especially clear in the examples of temporal flow and of theistic belief.

7. COGNITIVE-SYSTEMS RELATIONALISM: THE CASE OF COLOR

Thus far my illustrations of how cognitive science can contribute to metaphysics tend to favor anti-realist over realist metaphysical theories. How, one might wonder, is this compatible with my earlier espousal of a *realist* (as contrasted with conceptualist) approach to metaphysics? The problem here arises from the confusing terminology that has grown up in metaphysics (or metametaphysics). "Realism" is a notoriously elusive term to define, and different people use it in different ways. Without aspiring to completeness, let me say a few things about how I understand these terms and their relations to one another. The examples to be discussed in these final two sections will then fill out my picture via the theories I wind up endorsing (either fully or tentatively).

The sense of "realism" in which I have a high commitment is the sense in which it is roughly equivalent to "objectivism." Metaphysics should seek what is *really* or *objectively* true about the nature of things as opposed to what people may naïvely, commonsensically, or uncritically think about the nature of things. This does not, of course, imply that realism entails mind-independence in the sense that metaphysics should never be willing to characterize the nature of anything (including the nature of any property) in mentalistic or psychologistic terms. On the contrary, certain properties may be best characterized in precisely such ways. The property of color, for example, may be best spelled out in terms of relationships with kinds of mental states or kinds of cognitive systems. How does the taxonomical terminology of "realism" versus "anti-realism" relate to this point? Unfortunately, it is completely orthogonal to it. Anti-realism connotes a type of philosophical theory that is *revisionary*, at variance (in one or more ways) with naïve or commonsensical ways of thinking about the target phenomena. But this in no way implies a resistance to all matters mental, psychological, or cognitivistic. Also, anti-realist approaches do not reject all uses of the mental in the execution of metaphysics. Although anti-realists may be prepared to distance themselves from what is commonly thought, they need not deprive themselves of reliance on intuitions and experiences as prima facie evidence concerning the phenomena under investigation. How else can the theorist get started in picking out our quarry when we select color as the property (or relation) we mean to investigate? We must rely on our initial grasp of color phenomena, which includes the undergoing of color-perceptual experiences. This is compatible with the possibility that the fundamental nature of color, understood in a suitably "objective" and scientific fashion, is a complex phenomenon by no means exhausted by our initial familiarity with it. A child can recognize lightning by a characteristic visual experience. But the real (underlying) nature of lightning will radically outstrip what the child understands about it. Since the notion of realist metaphysics (as understood here) presupposes a convergence with scientific metaphysics, it should not be surprising that particular instances of metaphysics would invite cognitive scientific notions to play important roles. The final two sections of this paper illustrate this idea, using color and persistence over time as the metaphysical properties (or relations) of interest.

In this section I work my way toward a relationalist approach to the metaphysics of color. Relationalism—more specifically, *cognitive-systems relationalism* (C-relationalism)—is the second "template" I wish to advance in this paper as another type of example of what cognitive science can contribute to metaphysics. CS-relationalism claims that for certain properties or phenomena of metaphysical interest, the optimal ontological construal of their nature involves an added relatum that is not naïvely apprehended, the need for which is cognitive-scientifically well motivated. Moreover, the objects that are the potential values of this extra parameter (or "addicity") are themselves cognitive systems.

Relationalism about color was first formulated by E. W. Averill (1992) and considerably expanded more recently by Jonathan Cohen (2004, 2009). Cohen regards this view as a variety of realism (certainly as an alternative to irrealism). Let me expand a bit about what I mean by objectivism (which I equate with one construal of realism). It seeks to identify the objective features of the universe, where "objective" (in my terminology) connotes the truth about things as viewed from a *universal* or *cosmic* point of view, not merely a local or partial perspective. Realist or objectivist theories try to avoid anything that smacks of anthropocentrism, species chauvinism, or the like. This aim is shared by Cohen's relationalism about color, as we shall see.

A naïve theory of color is one that affirms and/or explicates our naïve understanding of color, and regards this as an adequate metaphysical understanding of the property itself. A good example of this is the conception of color Mark Johnston (1992) calls "revelation." This conception holds that the intrinsic nature of a color is fully revealed by a standard visual experience of it. Since the kind of visual experience tacitly referred to here is human experience, this implies that human color perception is fully revelatory of color's true nature. To the extent that relationalism aspires to a more objective, universal perspective on color, it seeks to avoid such species chauvinism. It especially seeks to avoid *unwitting* chauvinism, a recurrent danger in customary modes of doing metaphysics to the extent that it relies heavily on human intuitions and experiences.

Cohen (2004: 453–4) contrasts color relationalism and nonrelationalism as follows. Nonrelationalists typically understand color as a mind-independent or perceiver-independent phenomenon. A typical form of nonrelationalism holds that colors are a kind of physical property, e.g. a reflectance property of surfaces, a transmittance property of transparent surfaces and volumes, or an emittance property of luminous sources. By contrast, relationalism typically holds that colors are constituted in terms of relations between objects and perceivers (as well as values of other parameters such as viewing conditions). Color dispositionalism, for example, holds that colors are dispositions to cause certain sensations in certain kinds of minds.

Which kinds of minds? Red is commonly characterized as a disposition of object surfaces to reflect light in ways that cause *us*—i.e. normal human perceivers—to have a certain kind of visual experience. But can all color phenomena be specified in terms of relations between object surfaces, light, and *human* experience? What about distinctive color phenomena associated with what other species experience, especially species with different types of visual systems? As comparative color science shows, pigeon visual systems are tetrachromatic: they use four (functionally individuated) channels to encode color information. Therefore, an arbitrary color can be perceptually matched for a pigeon by a linear combination of four appropriately chosen primaries. In contrast, normal human visual systems are trichromatic: they use three (functionally individuated) channels to encode color information. An arbitrary color can be perceptually matched for a human being by a linear combination of three appropriately chosen primaries. As Cohen explains (2004: 462), because of this difference there are pairs of surfaces that are perceptual matches for human visual systems but are not matches for pigeon visual systems. The mantis shrimp has at least ten or twelve kinds of cones in its visual receptive system (Cronin and Marshall, 1989), so its color responsiveness is presumably many times more complicated and variegated than the human system.

Cohen proceeds to pose a dilemma for color science and metaphysics. The central question is: which of several alternative perceptual variants veridically represents the color of a given surface? He weighs the options as follows:

> The four choices in logical space are these: (i) confine our attention to human visual systems, declaring that how things look to pigeon (and other) visual systems is irrelevant to the colors of objects; (ii) defer to the pigeons, holding that the way things look to them determines the true colors of objects; (iii) declare that neither we nor the pigeons are the true arbiters of color, and instead select a different standard; (iv) adopt the ecumenical policy that both sorts of visual systems are right, and that one and the same object can have more than one color property. (Cohen, 2004: 462)

Alternative (iv) is relationalism, which can be explained as the relativizing of colors to types of visual systems. Of course, this is not the only bit of relativization needed for an adequate theory of color. Along with many other color philosophers and scientists, Cohen argues that the theorist needs multiple parameters, each of which can take many values, to provide enough relativization. However, relativization to types of visual systems is the most relevant kind for present purposes, so I highlight it in my presentation.

As Cohen expresses it, colors are constituted "in terms of relations to... kinds of visual systems... It is a consequence of this relational construal that one and the same object can be simultaneously green for your visual system and not green for the visual system of the pigeon on your window ledge" (2004: 463). I now add the obvious point that color science, including the cognitive part of color science, is what we need in order to supply the right values of visual-system parameters in order to obtain correctly relativized facts. Once suitable relativizations are in place, the facts in question would not be anthropocentric facts, or species-chauvinist facts. They would be cosmic facts, which hold from the "perspective" of the universe. This is the kind of fact sought by objectivism, or realism. Supplying such a fact—in detail, at any rate—hinges partly on cognitive science, because visual systems are proper parts of cognitive engines (which cognitive science studies).

Although the relationalist theory of color is (or aims to be) *realist* in the sense indicated above, it is also clearly *anti-realist* in the sense associated with the realism/anti-realism terminology. Ordinary people untutored in color science do not understand or represent the color red as a complex relational affair. It is more likely understood as a simple, monadic property of object surfaces. But color relationalism does not purport to be a theory about how red and other colors are commonsensically *understood*, or (mentally) *represented*. It is a theory about the *nature* of color (or colors). Thus, there is no inconsistency between calling relationalism a species of realism and yet also a kind of anti-realist theory.[15]

According to CS-relationalism there is no unique answer to the question of what color a given object or surface is; one must first relativize the question to a specified type of visual system (as well as viewing conditions, contrast conditions, etc). Then an answer is forthcoming (in principle).[16] Of course, ordinary thought and talk make no explicit mention of the parameters that relationalism invokes to constitute the colors. But such parameters, Cohen argues, are tacitly filled in by generalizing from our own case or the cases of organisms like us (2004: 471). When we say that x is green *simpliciter* we mean that x looks green to visual systems like our own and in viewing conditions like those we typically encounter. This is not an adequate general account of what color *is*, however, from a neutral and universal point of view. CS-relationalism provides a genuinely

---

[15] See Cohen (2009: 138–47) for broadly similar views, although we may not agree in every detail.

[16] In light of these facts, it is odd to find Sider (2011: 1–2) choosing a color example to support his insistence that proper metaphysical realism should carve nature at its joints. I don't necessarily disagree with Sider about the joint-carving goal of metaphysics, only with his assumption that unrelativized color classifications are a particularly clear example of successful joint-carving.

objective characterization of colors that holds independently of any particular species or visual system. The relational truths in question are truths "for" any cognizer capable of grasping them even if those cognizers do not themselves *instantiate* the relations in question. (They might be members of a species with no color-vision system at all.) In this sense, the theory does not "privilege" the position of one kind of visual system over others. This kind of story, of course, is attractive to science, the mission of which is to seek truths that can be appreciated by earthlings and aliens alike. Such truths are species-independent rather than anthropocentric or otherwise species-chauvinistic.

It is also a story to which science—including cognitive science—has contributed. This is no news to philosophers of color. They have been attuned to the deliverances of color science at least since the pathbreaking work of C. L. Hardin (1988).[17] But even though the relevance of cognitive science to color metaphysics is well known to philosophers of color, no analogous situation holds for other branches of metaphysics. The message of the present paper is therefore still timely. Section 8 moves to a different metaphysical terrain and argues (tentatively) for CS-relationalism in that branch of metaphysics, which has thus far featured rather little penetration by cognitive science (at least within the mainstream metaphysical literature[18]).

8. COGNITIVE-SYSTEMS RELATIONALISM: THE CASE OF PERSISTENCE

Assume that a metaphysician wishes to state the truth-conditions for the cross-temporal identity (or unity) of a pair of objects (or object-stages). The aim is to complete a schema of the following form:

---

[17] See Byrne and Hilbert (1997a, b).
[18] I make this qualification because there has been a substantial convergence of interests among both psychologists and philosophers on certain aspects of the metaphysics of persistence. Most of the direction of flow, however, has been from philosophy to psychology. Few philosopher-metaphysicians have made important use of psychological findings, especially in a metametaphysical vein. On the other hand, one can find a great deal of discussion of philosophers' debates about persistence (and other topics on physical-object ontology) by psychologists. Two particularly extensive and detailed treatments are Rips et al. (2006) and Scholl (2007).

Objects x and y at spatiotemporal locations L and L' respectively are numerically identical with one another (or bear the unity-relation to one another) if and only if—.[19]

Further assume that the metaphysician embraces the ubiquitous methodology of at least *beginning* from evidence of people's intuitive judgments about particular cases of identity through time. A theory that fails to conform substantially to this intuitional or judgmental evidence, or fares worse than its rivals, would face major obstacles. It would have a lot to "answer for" in the eyes of metaphysicians.

Does cognitive science have a contribution to make here? One possible contribution (rarely exploited) is to unearth evidence of persistence judgments that are not readily accessible to the subject himself or to casual observers. These judgments might be neither verbal nor explicit. But they might be detectable by inference from psychological experimentation. Such judgments might be extremely important components of a subject's wider thought and cognition. They might even lie at the foundation of other exercises of people's ability to track objects through time. Finally, establishing the existence and contents of such judgments, as well as how they are executed, might pose challenges to prevailing metaphysical theories about the persistence relation. Here is one such example.

A number of philosophers have held that sortals, or kind terms, play a pivotal role in judgments of identity over time. Indeed, some have held that identity over time is always *relative* identity, in the sense that such judgments must always be relativized to a sortal (Geach 1967; Griffin 1977). They must have the form "b is the *same F* as c" for some suitably chosen sortal F.

We can now report evidence from cognitive science that seems to cut against this sortal-based view of persistence, at least as a necessary component of persistence judgments. In particular, this evidence supports the notion that at a certain level of cognition an object's identity over time is computed without appeal (or only minimal appeal) to sortals. If this description is accurate, it is a case of cognitive-scientific findings having an evidential bearing on a metaphysical thesis about persistence. The evidence to which I

---

[19] I set aside here the issues concerning *how* things persist, e.g. via perdurance, endurance, and exdurance (cf. Lewis 1986). Debates over these alternative construals of persistence would take us far afield.

allude does not merely show that there are occasional or unusual judgments of the kind of question, but that they are made continually during waking life without awareness that one is doing so.

The beliefs or judgments in question are a feature of a sub-system of the visual system.[20] This sub-system is called the "*mid-level object-file system*," The term "mid-level" refers here to an intermediate level of cognition between low-level sensory processing and fully conceptual processing. An "object file"—a phrase introduced by Kahneman and Treisman (1984; cf. Kahneman et al., 1992)—is a visual representation that sticks to a moving object over time, storing and updating information about that object's surface features. In other words, it tracks or continually re-identifies an object even while the object's properties (e.g. color, size, shape, and kind) change. Here is how Flombaum, Scholl, and Santos (2009) explain the problem facing the visual system and how it appears to address the problem.

> The impoverished and rapidly changing stimulation on the retina looks very different from the stable world of discrete persisting objects that populate our visual experience. To get from the features on the retina to the objects that we experience, the visual system must solve several correspondence problems. One of these problems has to do with *sameness*: the visual system must decide whether each bit of stimulation reflects an object that has already been encountered (which might occasion the *updating* of an existing object representation) or a new one (which might occasion the *creation* of a new object representation)...The study of object persistence [has] converged on a core principle that guides the creation and maintenance of persisting object representations: the principle of *spatiotemporal priority*. When identifying objects as the same individuals over time, the visual system appears to rely on their spatiotemporal histories—that is, when, where and how they were encountered—to a greater extent than their visual surface features. (Flombaum et al., 2009: 135)

In this literature, researchers talk about "file folders" being created or destroyed and various information being added to the file folder, where a given file folder represents a single object persisting over time.

What is crucial about this "mid-level object-file" theory is that the system works (mainly) by attending to an object's spatiotemporal

---

[20] Although the research in question has focused mainly on the visual modality, the phenomena in question are not restricted to that modality. There are parallel findings for audition, for example.

properties, but not its *sortal* properties. The system tracks an object over time not by considering its shape, its color, or the kind of thing it appears to be, but what positions it occupies as it changes locations over time. Here I depart slightly from what is *actually* found in the research literature and consider what *might* be found (though it is very close to the actual findings). This is warranted by our interest in *possible* findings of cognitive science, not merely actual findings. (We are interested in what cognitive science is *capable* of contributing to metaphysics, not simply what we know at the present time it is prepared to contribute.) So suppose it were clearly stated (and this might indeed be the case, as suggested by later experiments to be reported) that the visual system continually makes persistence judgments that do not involve *sortals*, contrary to what the sortal-based theories of Geach and Griffin require.[21] This would be a clear refutation of a sortal-based philosophical theory, understood as an unqualified generalization about the mind's method of tracking identity over time. It would be especially significant because the mid-level object-file system is fully in place in infancy, by at least ten months of age (Xu and Carey, 1996; Spelke, Kestenbaum, Simons, and Wein, 1995). Here, then, would be cognitive scientific evidence with direct (and conclusive) bearing on a particular metaphysical thesis.

Complementary evidence for the properties just mentioned of the mid-level object-file system comes from a separately developed theory called "visual indexing," due to Zenon Pylyshyn (1989, 2004; Pylyshyn and Storm 1998). These investigators postulate a mechanism whereby object-based individuation, tracking, and access are realized. In an experimental paradigm for studying visual indexing called "multiple object tracking," or MOT, participants are shown a number of qualitatively identical objects on a screen. A few of these objects are flashed to indicate that they are the targets to which participants should attend. In the next phase of the session, all objects on the screen are set into random, unpredictable motion about the display, often changing their color, size, shape, and kind. When they stop moving, participants are asked to re-identify the objects originally shown as targets. This sounds like a difficult task,

---

[21] For a dissenting view about this interpretation, however, see one of the main investigators in the infancy research, Fei Xu (1997). She claims that "physical object" is itself a sortal. This is a very non-standard view, however, among psychologists (and probably philosophers as well).

but people are surprisingly adept at re-identifying members of the highlighted set (the targets) despite their continually crisscrossing one another *and* changing color, size, shape, and kind during motion. All this suggests that the system attends only to location, movement, and other such spatiotemporal properties while ignoring sortal properties. This is how the researchers interpret what transpires, and it is consistent with other evidence about the computational features of the mid-level object-file system.

Thus far, we have illustrated how cognitive scientific evidence proves relevant to past debates in the metaphysics of persistence. But this demonstration of evidential relevance is only of a piece with the first half of this paper. It does not address the theme presented in Section 7, concerning CS-relationalism. What do we say on this subject?

The next thing to be reported is a conclusion by relevant cognitive scientists that there is a second system for persistence judgments, independent of the mid-level object-file system, which *does* use sortals or kinds.[22] Apparently, this is the system people draw upon when deciding that a person ceases to exist when she dies, or that a car ceases to exist when it is crushed into a cube of metal at the junkyard, despite the fact that there is plenty of spatiotemporal continuity between the person's body and corpse in the first case and between the car and the metal cube in the second case.

Differences between the object-file system and the kind-based system can be illustrated with the help of Figure 8.2 below (from Carey and Xu, 2001). Each of the two systems can be launched into operation in connection with this figure. Suppose first that you examine Panel 1 but then lose perceptual contact with it and return five minutes later to view Panel 2. How would you describe what has happened? You would probably say that the rabbit has moved from above and to the left of the chair to below and to the right of it, while the bird has moved from the bottom left to the top right. In other words, you would re-identify the rabbit in Panel 1 with the rabbit in Panel 2, despite their difference in location. Numerical identity would be dictated by kind membership.

---

[22] My exposition of the two-systems persistence judgment literature draws extensively from the account of Carey (2009). Other summaries of roughly the same research can be found in Rosenberg and Carey (2009) and Scholl (2002).

Figure 8.2

Next imagine that a fixation point replaces the chair and Panels 1 and 2 are projected rapidly one after the other onto a screen you are viewing, while you maintain fixation on the common fixation point. (This is a kind of visual display that is well studied in the perception literature, so vision scientists know exactly how it will be seen by normal perceivers.) If the timing of the rapid change process supports what is called "apparent motion," what will your perception be? You will see two individuals each changing back and forth between a white bird-shaped object and a black rabbit-shaped object as they move side to side. The visual system so computes the numerical identity of the objects' undergoing apparent motion as to minimize the total quantity of movement. This system rarely takes sortal or kind information into account—only when spatiotemporal considerations are equated. Using evidence like this, Carey and Xu (2001) conclude that the kind-based object individuation system is *architecturally distinct* from the mid-level object-file system.

Suppose now that a metaphysician's aim is to formulate principles constitutive of object persistence, principles articulating standards for the correctness, or veridicality, of such judgments. The looming problem is how to get a consistent and unified set of principles that reflect the operational features of the two psychological systems. They seem to be in flat-out contradiction with one another. How can a single self-consistent set of principles be formulated for the *metaphysics* of persistence? Self-consistency is required for a satisfactory set of metaphysical principles, but how can this be attained if one has to honor the operations of both systems, which are quite different from one another? Adopting criteria that reflect the operations of both systems would seem, inevitably, to impose conflicting criteria. There seems to be no (consistent) way to merge the operational principles of both systems. So how could objective persistence *facts* be determined by two such conflicting sets of principles?

This raises the question whether, in light of the existence of two different identity-judgment systems, we can continue to assume that there are any objective *facts* of persistence at all, or that such facts can reflect (all of our) naïve judgments of persistence. If the two systems' basic operating principles are so different, can the metaphysician continue to rely on the reliability and evidential probity of their judgmental outputs? If not, which set of judgments should be deemed more reliable and trustworthy? How should we select the more trustworthy indicators of the metaphysical facts? A metaphysical and/or methodological conundrum seems to emerge here.

There are several ways that a metaphysician studying might respond. The first response I shall call the *two-families-of-propositions* response. According to this response, each psychological system endorses a distinct family of propositions. The canonical form of one of these families involves propositions that assert (or deny) numerical identity (or unity) relations between two objects with no third term for sortals. The canonical form of the second family involves propositions that assert or deny a ternary relation between pairs of objects plus a sortal. Call these propositions "two-place" and "three-place" propositions respectively. Evidently, even when a proposition in one family makes an assertion about the same pair of objects as the other does, they will convey different meanings, because the two relations in question must differ in meaning. In effect, the metaphysician is trying to diagnosis the original problem by saying that there is a "verbal dispute" between the sortalist and non-sortalist (cf. Hirsch, 2005). Sortal theorists and non-sortal theorists of persistence are simply using *words* differently. This approach does have the capacity to eliminate the original problem of inconsistency. But whether one is warranted in tracing the original problem to a *verbal dispute* is questionable. Certainly the mid-level object-file system is not a verbal system at all.

A second type of response is to insist that only one family of judgments is an "authoritative" family. Only judgments issued by the designated system are genuinely reliable indicators of the metaphysical facts of persistence. Call this the *privileged cognitive system* response.[23] What rationale might be offered for it, and what criteria for selecting the authoritative system should be used? The correct system, it might be argued, is the sortal-based system (supplemented, as it surely must be, by considerations of spatiotemporal continuity). The reason is that the two systems currently under discussion exemplify a well-known pattern described by so-called *dual-process* theorists (cf. Evans and Frankish, 2009). The mid-level object-file system is a paradigm case of a system-1 process in being evolutionarily old, unconscious, automatic, fast, etc. whereas the kind-based system is a paradigm case of a system-2 process in being evolutionarily recent, conscious, controlled, slow, etc. Reflecting on other dual-process pairs, it is noteworthy that system-1 members of the pair are typically more biased and inaccurate than their system-2 counterparts. System-1 processes may be viewed as mere *heuristics* for system-2 processes, and heuristics are known to be biased and error-prone.

A third type of response available to a persistence metaphysician is a version of CS-relationalism that mirrors CS-relationalism for color. Under this approach, no priority is assigned to either cognitive system as the determinant of truth conditions for persistence. Rather, we should craft truth conditions for re-identification that include relativity to cognitive systems, much as CS-relationalism for color includes a parameter for color-vision systems. Although

---

[23] I am indebted to Holly Smith for the formulation and endorsement of this response and for the gist of how it might be defended.

human beings have two systems for persistence judgments—according to the cognitive science literature summarized earlier—other creatures might have still different types of persistence systems. On what basis are human systems (or either one of the human systems) to be "privileged" over the systems of other creatures? An avoidance of arbitrariness is part of what drives Cohen toward relationalism about color, and it is one of my preoccupations here as well.

As explained in the previous section, I consider it an aim of metaphysics to characterize the world in "cosmic" terms. No prioritizing of "local" perspectives is allowed. Keeping the cosmic perspective in mind, can we really credit the notion that the human object-file system or the human kind-based system regularly generates the uniquely "correct" or "right" persistence judgments whereas other systems with even modest departures from these would go "wrong"? Would any different system inevitably fail to carve persistence at its joints? This is analogous to saying that only the human visual system represents color facts correctly, whereas pigeons, dogs, and mantis shrimp are fated to get the color facts systematically wrong. Such anthropocentrism is difficult to credit.

CS-relationalism can come to the rescue. It starts from the assumption that there are no unrelativized facts of the matter pertaining to object persistence. But it then finds facts of a sort by relativizing the truth conditions of persistence to this or that selected cognitive system, which could usefully be the user's own system (or one of these systems, in case there are two or more). By introducing this added parameter, CS-relationalism makes room for a new genre of persistence facts, which are perfectly objective in the sense we have emphasized: universal, cosmic, non-species chauvinistic. It would take the following form:

> (CSPERS)   Objects x and y (at spatiotemporal locations L and L' respectively) are object-unified *relative to cognitive system CS1* if and only if . . .

I shall not make a categorical choice between these alternative responses (although I do lean toward CS-relationalism). However, I now submit that here we find another prototype of a way in which cognitive science can contribute to metaphysics. By uncovering cognitive processes that are unavailable to introspection we get a much more nuanced understanding of the complex cognitive activities that go on "below the surface". These activities can pose puzzles or conundrums that confront the metaphysician with previously unimagined choices. The scientific revelations will not themselves be capable of resolving the newly posed metaphysical puzzles, but the metaphysics is bound to improve to the extent that it recognizes and grapples with the more complex array of choices. A scientifically improved understanding of color experience and persistence judgments presents a different kind of window on the generation and resolution of metaphysical problems that naturally go hand-in-hand with advances in cognitive science.[24]

Rutgers University

REFERENCES

Atran, S. (2004). *In Gods We Trust: The Evolutionary Landscape of Religion.* New York: Oxford University Press.
Averill, E. W. (1992). "The relational nature of color." *Philosophical Review* 101: 551–88.
Bloom, P. (2007). "Religion is natural." *Developmental Science* 10(1): 147–51.
Bloom, P., and C. Veres (1999). "The perceived intentionality of groups." *Cognition* 71: B1–B9.
Boyer, P. (2001). *Religion Explained.* New York: Basic Books.
Byrne, A., and D. R. Hilbert (eds) (1997a). *Readings on Color. Volume 1: The Philosophy of Color.* Cambridge, MA: MIT Press.
Byrne, A., and D. R. Hilbert (eds) (1997b). *Readings on Color, Volume 2: The Science of Color.* Cambridge, MA: MIT Press.
Cohen, J. (2004). "Color properties and color ascriptions: A relationalist manifesto." *Philosophical Review* 113(4): 451–506.
Cohen, J. (2009). *The Red and the Real.* Oxford: Oxford University Press.
Carey, S. (2009). *The Origin of Concepts.* Oxford: Oxford University Press.
Carey, S., and F. Xu (2001). "Beyond object files and object tracking: Infant representations of objects." *Cognition* 80: 179–213.
Chomsky, N. (1980). *Rules and Representations.* New York: Columbia University Press.

---

[24] Thanks to members of my spring 2013 metaphysics seminar at Rutgers University and members of a fall 2013 seminar at Princeton University as well as Jonathan Schaffer, Holly Smith, and Karen Bennett for valuable comments on various drafts of this paper.

Craig, A. D. (2002). "How do you feel? Interoception: The sense of the physiological condition of the body." *Nature Reviews Neuroscience* 3: 655–66.

Craig, A. D. (2010). "Interoception and emotion: A neuroanatomical perspective." In M. Lewis, J. M. Haviland-Jones, and L. Feldman Barrett (eds) *Handbook of Emotions*, 3rd edition (pp. 272–88). New York: Guilford Press.

Cronin, T. W., and N. J. Marshall (1989). "A retina with at least ten spectral types of photoreceptors in a mantis shrimp." *Nature* 339(6220): 137–40.

Dennett, D. C. (2006). *Breaking the Spell: Religion as a Natural Phenomenon*. New York: Viking.

Evans, J. S .B. T., and K. Frankish (eds) *In Two Minds: Dual Processes and Beyond*. Oxford: Oxford University Press.

Flombaum, J. I., B. J. Scholl, and L. R. Santos (2009). "Spatiotemporal priority as a fundamental principle of object persistence." In B. M. Hood and L. R. Santos (eds) *The Origins of Object Knowledge* (pp. 135–64). Oxford: Oxford University Press.

Geach, P. T. (1967). "Identity." *Review of Metaphysics* 21: 3–12.

Gelman, S. A. (2003). *The essential child: Origins of essentialism in everyday thought*. New York: Oxford University Press.

Goldman, A. I. (1987). "Cognitive science and metaphysics." *Journal of Philosophy* 84: 537–44.

Goldman, A. I. (1989). "Metaphysics, mind, and mental science." *Philosophical Topics* 17: 131–45.

Goldman, A. I. (1992). "Cognition and modal metaphysics." In Goldman, *Liaisons: Philosophy Meets the Cognitive and Social Sciences* (pp. 49–66). Cambridge, MA: MIT Press.

Goldman, A. I. (2007). "A program for 'naturalizing' metaphysics, with application to the ontology of events." *The Monist* 90(3): 457–79.

Goldman, A. I. (2012). "A moderate approach to embodied cognitive science." *Review of Philosophy and Psychology* 3(1): 71–88.

Gregory, R. L. (1966). *Eye and Brain*. London: Weidenfeld and Nicolson.

Griffin, N. (1977). *Relative Identity*. Oxford: Oxford University Press.

Guthrie, S. E. (1993). *Faces in the Clouds: A New Theory of Religion*. New York: Oxford University Press.

Hardin, C. L. (1988). *Color for Philosophers: Unweaving the Rainbow*. Indianapolis IN: Hackett.

Haslanger, S. (2003). "Persistence through time." In M. Loux and D. W. Zimmerman (eds), *The Oxford Handbook of Metaphysics* (pp. 315–54). Oxford: Oxford University Press.

Heider, F., and Simmel, M. (1944). "An experimental study of apparent behavior." *American Journal of Psychology* 57: 243–59.

Hirsch, E. (2005). "Physical-object ontology, verbal disputes, and common sense." *Philosophy and Phenomenological Research* 70(1): 67–97.

Johnston, M. (1992). "How to speak of the colors." *Philosophical Studies* 68: 221–63.

Joyce, R. (2006). *The Evolution of Morality.* Cambridge, MA: MIT Press.

Kahneman, D., and Treisman, A. (1984). "Changing views of attention and automaticity." In R. Parasuraman and D. R. Davies (eds) *Varieties of Attention* (pp. 29–61). New York: Academic Press.

Kahneman, D., A. Treisman, and B. Gibbs (1992). "The reviewing of object files: Object-specific integration of information." *Cognitive Psychology* 24: 175–19.

Keil, F. C. (1989). *Concepts, Kinds, and Cognitive Development.* Cambridge, MA: MIT Press.

Kripke, S. (1980). *Naming and Necessity.* Cambridge, MA: Harvard University Press.

Ladyman, J., and D. Ross (2007). *Every Thing Must Go: Metaphysics Naturalized.* Oxford: Oxford University Press.

Le Poidevin, R. (2007). *The Images of Time.* Oxford: Oxford University Press.

Leslie, S.-J. (2013). "Essence and natural kinds." In T. Gendler and J. Hawthorne (eds) *Oxford Studies in Epistemology, vol. 4* (pp. 108–66). Oxford: Oxford University Press.

Lewis, D. K. (1986). *On the Plurality of Worlds.* Oxford: Basil Blackwell.

Maudlin, T. (2007). *The Metaphysics within Physics.* Oxford: Oxford University Press.

McKay, D. (1958). "Perceptual stability for a stroboscopically lit visual field containing self-luminous objects." *Nature* 181: 507–8.

McTaggart, J. M. E. (1908). "The unreality of time." *Mind* 18: 457–84.

Narenzayan, A., W. M. Gervais, and K. H. Trzesniewski (2012). "Mentalizing deficits constrain belief in a personal god." *PLoS One* 7(5): 1–8.

Paul, L. A. (2010). "Temporal experience." *Journal of Philosophy* 107(7): 333–59.

Paul, L. A. (manuscript). "Experience and the Arrow."

Putnam, H. (1975). "The meaning of meaning." In H. Putnam, *Mind, Language and Reality* (pp. 215–71). Cambridge: Cambridge University Press.

Pylyshyn, Z. W. (2004). "Some puzzling findings in multiple object tracking MOT: I. Tracking without keeping track of object identities." *Visual Cognition* 11(7): 801–22.

Pylyshyn, Z. W., and R. W. Storm (1998). "Tracking multiple independent targets: Evidence for a parallel tracking mechanism." *Spatial Vision* 3: 179–97.

Rips, L. J., S. Blok and G. Newman (2006). "Tracing the identity of objects." *Psychological Review* 113(1): 1–30.

Schaffer, J. (2010a). "Monism: The priority of the whole." *Philosophical Review* 119(1): 31–76.
Schaffer, J. (2010b). "The internal relatedness of all things." *Mind* 119: 341–76.
Scholl, B. J., ed. (2002). *Objects and Attention*. Cambridge, MA: MIT Press.
Scholl, B. J. (2007). "Object persistence in philosophy and psychology." *Mind and Language* 22(5): 563–91.
Schuster, M. M. (1986). "Is the flow of time subjective?" *Review of Metaphysics* 39L: 695–714.
Sider, T. (2011). *Writing the Book of the World*. New York: Oxford University Press.
Spelke, E. S. (1990). "Principles of object perception." *Cognition Science* 14: 29–56.
Spelke, E. S., R. Kestenbaum, D. J. Simons, and D. Wein, (1995). "Spatiotemporal continuity, smoothness of motion, and object identity in infancy." *British Journal of Developmental Psychology* 13: 113–42.
Strawson, P. F. (1959). *Individuals: An Essay in Descriptive Metaphysics*. London: Methuen.
Street, S. (2006). "A Darwinian dilemma for realist theories of value." *Philosophical Studies* 27(1): 109–66.
Vignemont, F. (2011). "Bodily awareness." *Stanford Encyclopedia of Philosophy*.
White, R. (2010). "You just believe that because..." In J. Hawthorne and J. Turner (eds) *Philosophical Perspectives* 24: 573–615.
Xu, F. (1997). "From Lot's wife to a pillar of salt: evidence that physical object is a sortal concept." *Mind and Language* 12: 365–92.
Xu, F., and S. Carey (1996). "Infants' metaphysics: the case of numerical identity." *Cognitive Psychology* 30: 111–53.

GROUNDING, SUPERVENIENCE, AND CONSTITUTION

9. Multiple constitution

Nicholas K. Jones

1. INTRODUCTION

The problem of the many (henceforth **PM**) presents a serious threat to the coherence of our ordinary conceptual scheme: a contradiction follows from seemingly innocuous premises, all motivated from within that scheme. In this paper I outline a novel solution to **PM** according to which objects can be simultaneously constituted by many collections of particles. To support this proposal, I develop a conception of objects that implies it. On this view, objects are fundamentally subjects of change: the changes an object can survive are explanatorily prior to its constitution. From this perspective, **PM** arises and objects are multiply constituted because the changes that objects survive are too coarse-grained to distinguish between many different collections of particles in respect of their constituting the relevant object.*

§2 introduces the constitution relation that will be central to my discussion. §3 outlines **PM**, an adequacy condition on candidate solutions, and my proposed solution. §4 outlines my conception of objects and uses it to argue for my solution to **PM**. §5 develops the view further in response to some objections. §6 uses a discussion of mereology to offer a diagnosis of my solution's near-absence from the literature on **PM**. §7 concludes.

---

* Thanks to Mahrad Almotahari, Will Bynoe, Anil Gomes, Eleanor Knox, Jean-David LaFrance, Fraser MacBride, Rory Madden, Josh Parsons, Ian Rumfitt, and Al Wilson for discussion and comments. Versions of this material were presented to the YLWiP in London, the Serious Metaphysics Group in Cambridge, and the KCL departmental seminar; thanks to the audiences at all these events. This research was funded by an AHRC doctoral award, an RIP Jacobsen Fellowship, and a University of London Jacobsen Research Fellowship; thanks to all these organisations. I am especially grateful to my teacher, Dorothy Edgington, for her encouragement, advice, and detailed comments on many versions of this material.

2. CONSTITUTION

This section introduces the notion of constitution on which my discussion will focus.

Ordinary objects, the most familiar inhabitants of the macroscopic world,[1] are made out of other things. Statues are made out of clay, houses are made out of bricks, and humans are made out of organs, which are made out of tissue, which is made out of cells, which are made out of particles. My primary concern will be the sense in which one object is made out of many particles. Let us regiment this by saying that objects are *constituted* by (many) particles. And if x is one of the particles that constitute y, say that x *partially constitutes y*.

How do constitution and partial constitution differ from the more familiar notions of parthood and fusion? There are certainly similarities between these pairs of relations: constitution and fusion have a plural argument position and a singular argument position; partial constitution and parthood have two singular argument positions. (More on plurals shortly.) The difference is that fusion is defined in terms of parthood, whereas constitution is used to define partial constitution. That is, the difference concerns whether the plural-singular relation is defined from the singular-singular relation or conversely. I want to consider the sense in which individual objects are made from many particles in as theoretically neutral a setting as possible. The best approach is therefore to treat the plural-singular relation as primitive, rather than defined, without foreclosing the possibility of analysing it via a singular-singular relation later, as in standard mereology. Hence my focus on constitution. §6 discusses the connections between these relations in more detail.

Two questions arise. Firstly, are there any most fundamental particles, or might there be an infinite series of levels of increasingly fundamental particles, with the inhabitants of each level made out of those in the next? One can avoid taking a stand on this issue by selecting some level to serve as fundamental relative to the present discussion, and restricting one's quantifiers over particles to inhabitants of this level. Secondly, might material reality's ultimate

---

[1] Although this leaves the extension of 'ordinary object' imprecise, the idea is clear enough for present purposes. Throughout, 'object' is reserved for ordinary objects; 'entity', 'individual' etc. are used more inclusively, for any potential value of a nominal variable.

constituents not be individual particles but, say, regions of spacetime or non-individual stuff? One can avoid taking a stand here too. Even if particles are not ontologically basic, discourse about them is surely legitimate: not all meaningful discourse, or even all metaphysical disputes, need be conducted in absolutely fundamental terms.[2] So one can employ constitutional vocabulary whilst remaining neutral about whether one's discussion is couched at an ontologically basic level. Alternatively, subsequent talk about particles can be understood as a placeholder for talk about reality's ultimate material constituents, whatever they turn out to be; my discussion should be reformulable in terms of such basic entities without significant loss.

I am using 'constitution' to denote a binary relation between many particles and a single object. I therefore require the now standard apparatus of plural quantification and reference brought to prominence by George Boolos.[3] On this view, a plural term denotes not one plural individual, but one or more of those individuals over which our singular nominal quantifiers range. Likewise *mutatis mutandis* for plural variables. When α is a singular term/variable, $\ulcorner \alpha\alpha \urcorner$ and $\ulcorner$the αs$\urcorner$ will serve as plural terms/variables. I will also make liberal use of talk about collections; although syntactically singular, this should be understood as semantically plural talk about the elements of those collections.

Typically, some particles constitute an object without any one of them constituting that object. So the constitution relation is *collective* in its plural argument position. In this respect, constituting an object is akin to jointly writing a book or being arranged in a circle: in this collective sense, Russell did not write *Principia Mathematica* and neither did Whitehead, though Russell and Whitehead together wrote *Principia*; likewise, some chairs can be arranged in a circle without any one of those chairs being arranged in a circle.

---

[2] On one view, fundamentality is a property of entities. On this view, fundamental ontology concerns only some of what exists. On another view, fundamentality is a property of representations. On this view, fundamental ontology ignores topics not formulable using fundamental vocabulary. It is not obvious to me that ontologists should limit their interests in either of these ways.

[3] (Boolos, 1984). A useful overview is (Linnebo, 2010).

Objects are typically constituted by different particles at different times. So constitution should be relativized to a time. Temporal relativisation will, however, often be omitted for simplicity.

The constitution relation between particles and objects is less general than our ordinary notion of "being made out of" in at least three respects:

1. A jumper can be made out of (some) wool, or a statue can be made out of (some) clay. So a fully general constitution relation can hold between the denotation of a mass-noun and an object. Adequate treatment of this case requires more detailed investigation of the semantics and metaphysics of mass-nouns than is appropriate here. So I ignore it henceforth.
2. A jumper can be made out of a single woollen thread, or a statue out of a piece of clay. So a fully general constitution relation can hold between an object and another object. This case raises too many complexities and controversies to be considered here. Even the formal properties of object-object constitution—e.g. transitivity and asymmetry—are controversial.[4] So I ignore it henceforth.
3. A jumper can be made out of many woollen threads, or a statue made out of many pieces of clay. So a fully general constitution relation can hold between a collection of objects and a single object. Given the following plausible principle, I can harmlessly ignore this case in the sequel:

   For any objects xx and object y: xx constitute y iff y is constituted by the collection zz of all particles u such that: u partially constitutes something amongst xx.

My primary concern is not a fully general notion of "being made out of", but just the sense in which objects are made out of collections of particles. Some restriction in scope is needed to reduce complexity, simplify exposition, and permit detailed discussion within a single paper. The restrictions introduced here will hopefully not generate distortions later.

---

[4] Even if, say, the thread-jumper relation appears asymmetric (transitive), it may be a restriction (resp. the ancestral) of an underlying symmetric (resp. non-transitive) relation.

The logical and terminological preliminaries are now complete. Let us continue to **PM**.

3. THE PROBLEM OF THE MANY

Contemporary discussion of **PM** was initiated by Peter Unger.[5] I focus throughout on one representative instance of **PM** concerning Tibbles the cat. The problem is that the following are jointly inconsistent:

Solitude Tibbles is the one and only cat on his mat.
Abundance Many collections of particles on Tibbles' mat are equally good, and good enough, candidates to constitute cats.
Equality If many collections of particles are equally good, and good enough, candidates to constitute cats, then each of those collections constitutes a cat.
Unique Constitution (UC) Tibbles, like every other cat, is constituted by exactly one collection of particles.[6]

Abundance, **Equality** and **UC** jointly imply that many cats are on Tibbles' mat, contrary to **Solitude**.[7,8] Something has to give. But what?

Solitude seems innocuous: surely there often is just one cat on a given mat. The motivation for **Abundance** is that Tibbles' boundary, like that of any other typical cat, is indeterminate. Suppose one collection of particles is a better candidate to constitute a cat than

---

[5] (Unger, 1980).
[6] As stated, **UC** is false. Suppose some F-particles constitute Tibbles, and that each F-particle is made from two G-particles. Then surely Tibbles is also constituted by the G-particles from which the relevant F-particles are made, *contra* **UC**. So the particles relevant to **UC** should be restricted to either (i) absolutely fundamental particles (if such there be), or (ii) the elements of some relatively fundamental decomposition of reality into non-overlapping particles. These qualifications are left tacit in the sequel. See also §2.
[7] Note that since "a" candidate collection is not one plural individual but many particles, **PM** cannot be resolved by restricting constitution or fusion. **PM** does not presuppose a plenitudinous ontology.
[8] Does **PM** require the assumption that a cat is located where its constituent particles are located? No. Drop the restrictions to Tibbles' mat and suppose Tibbles is the only cat ever to exist. This affects neither the coming motivations for **Solitude**, **Abundance**, **Equality** and **UC**, nor their mutual inconsistency.

any other. Then that collection and no other does constitute a cat: the best candidate wins. So Tibbles' boundary is that of this privileged collection, and therefore not indeterminate. Since Tibbles' boundary is indeterminate, the supposition is false and **Abundance** is true. **Equality** seems justified because one way for the xs to be better candidates to constitute a cat than the ys is for the xs but not the ys to constitute a cat; for then the xs would be more cat-constituter-like than the ys. Finally, **UC** is a natural assumption about constitution: how could different collections of particles simultaneously constitute the same cat? Because these motivations turn on no peculiarity of Tibbles or of cats, the problem generalizes to all ordinary material objects, including ourselves. And because these motivations flow from our ordinary conception of cats, **PM** presents a serious threat to our ordinary conceptions of macroscopic reality and our own place within it. Something has gone badly wrong.[9]

Although several responses to **PM** already exist, none is entirely satisfactory.[10] Rather than evaluate these proposals in detail, I want to explore an unjustly neglected alternative. More options are needed, and my goal is to outline one such so that it can stand for evaluation alongside the competition. In doing so, I hope to reveal that the range of available positions is wider than is sometimes assumed, and to thereby help alleviate (or at least expose) a metaphysical myopia afflicting much contemporary thinking about objects and constitution. To take one example, symptomatic of this myopia, variants of my solution are absent from Brian Weatherson's helpful *Stanford Encyclopedia* survey article on **PM**.[11] This affliction is identified and discussed in §6.

The lesson I want to draw from **PM** is that we should reject **UC** and endorse:

---

[9] Unger originally accepted the incoherence of our ordinary conceptual scheme (Unger, 1980). His most recent discussion of **PM** concludes instead that we are not material objects, but simple immaterial souls for which **PM** cannot arise (Unger, 2006a, Ch. 7); see (Bynoe and Jones, 2012) for discussion.

[10] Perhaps the most popular solution to **PM** is (Lewis, 1993). Criticisms of Lewis have concerned: *de re* thought (McGee and McLaughlin, 2000); self-reference (Hawthorne, 2006a); freewill and our capacity to make genuine choices (Hudson, 2001) (Unger, 2006a, Ch. 7); quantified claims about indeterminacy (Sattig, 2010, §7.2). For alternative proposals, see (Quine, 1981b), (van Inwagen, 1990, Ch. 17), (Johnston, 1992), (Lowe, 1995), (Markosian, 1998), (Hudson, 2001), and (Sattig, 2010).

[11] (Weatherson, 2009).

Multiple Constitution (MC) Tibbles is constituted by many collections of particles.[12]

On this view, many different collections of particles can simultaneously constitute a single object. **Abundance** and **Equality** imply that many collections of particles on Tibbles' mat all constitute cats. So **Solitude** implies that these collections all constitute the same cat, namely Tibbles. This is consistent with (and implies) **MC** whereas it is inconsistent with **UC**.

To make things a little more concrete, suppose that a particular hair h is Tibbles' only borderline part. Let the T^+s be the particles that constitute Tibbles taken as including h; let the T^-s be the particles that constitute Tibbles taken as excluding h. Then **MC** amounts to:

The T^+s constitute Tibbles and the T^-s constitute Tibbles.

I will examine this response to **PM** in the remainder, leaving the simplifying supposition about h in force throughout.[13]

It is worth emphasizing an adequacy condition on solutions to **PM**: an adequate solution should comprise a theoretically unified whole. We should aspire to more than a mere technical fix or ad hoc collection of theses unified only by their role in blocking **PM**. Every solution will reject **Solitude**, **Abundance**, **Equality**, or **UC**. An adequate solution will explain why we should reject one principle rather than another. That explanation should emerge naturally from a background conception of objects and constitution. Compare the set-theoretic paradoxes: a consistent modification of naïve set-theory provides an adequate solution to the paradoxes only if motivated by a background conception of set, as ZF is motivated by stage-theory.[14] §4 outlines a conception of object and argues from it

---

[12] The qualifications in note 6 protect **MC** from being a near platitude.

[13] Distinguish my proposal from: Tibbles is constituted only by the plural union uu of the candidate collections. This view says that exactly one collection of particles constitutes Tibbles, whereas my proposal is that many do. Note that if only uu constitute Tibbles, the other collections are not equally good candidates, contrary to **Abundance**. My proposal does not even imply that uu do constitute Tibbles. This is a good thing; for there is no a priori guarantee that the union of all candidates to constitute an object is also a candidate to constitute that object. Although the union of the T^+s and the T^-s—i.e. the T^+s themselves—is a candidate, it is not guaranteed that the analogous claim holds in every case. The underlying logical point is that $R(xx, z) \wedge R(yy, z)$ does not imply $R(xx \cup yy, z)$.

[14] (Boolos, 1971).

to **MC**. My proposal therefore satisfies this adequacy condition and provides a theoretically unified solution to **PM**.

Neglect of this adequacy condition has led some astray. W. V. O. Quine connects realism with bivalence, and bivalence with determinacy, including determinacy in constitution. He concludes that realists must reject **Abundance**.[15] But since one can consistently retain bivalence and constitutional determinacy by rejecting **Solitude**, **Equality**, or **UC**, Quine's proposal does not satisfy this adequacy condition: realism about objects and constitution does not explain why we should reject one principle rather than another.

Ned Markosian also rejects **Abundance**.[16] He begins by denying that there is a finite non-trivial account of the conditions under which a collection has a fusion. Call this view brutalism. Brutalism is consistent with: exactly one collection of particles on Tibbles' mat has a fusion, and thereby a better claim to constitute a cat than any other such collection, though nothing informative can be said about why it's one collection rather than any other. So Markosian suggests endorsing that claim and rejecting **Abundance**. But brutalism is compatible with the negations of **Solitude**, **Equality**, and **UC**. So Markosian's proposal does not satisfy the adequacy condition: brutalism does not explain why we should reject one principle rather than any other.[17] Indeed, I know of no extant solution to **PM** that satisfies this adequacy condition.[18] This counts strongly in favour of my proposal.

The closest extant solutions to **MC** are due to E. J. Lowe and Mark Johnston.[19] I will focus on Lowe. Although Lowe explicitly rejects **MC**,[20] his view is difficult to interpret. And the best interpretation postulates equivocation on 'constitutes', with **UC** determinately true on one reading and **MC** determinately true on the other.

Following Lewis, Lowe invokes the apparatus of supervaluation, positing many sharpenings of the natural object-language in which

---

[15] (Quine, 1981b). Quine may also be interpreted as rejecting **Equality**. Likewise for Markosian below. Nothing above turns on this.

[16] (Markosian, 1998).

[17] Notice that I didn't motivate **Abundance** by appealing to the existence of a finite non-trivial account of when a collection has a fusion.

[18] A possible exception is (Lewis, 1993), when set against the backdrop of Lewis' wider linguistic and metaphysical views.

[19] (Lowe, 1995), (Johnston, 1992).

[20] (Lowe, 1995, pp. 180–1).

PM is couched.[21] Supertruth (superfalsity) is defined as truth (falsity) on each sharpening. Determinate truth (falsity) is identified with supertruth (superfalsity). Indeterminacy thus becomes lack of supertruth-value. Lowe then claims that one individual cn the mat is significantly more cat-like than any other: only this individual substance has, e.g. the history, persistence conditions, and modal profile of a cat; everything else on the mat is a particle or mere aggregate thereof. 'Tibbles' refers to this individual on each sharpening, though it is indeterminate which particles constitute it. This indeterminacy is accommodated by a sense of 'constitutes' on which its extension varies across sharpenings: on each sharpening, one candidate counts as constituting Tibbles, different candidates on different sharpenings. In this sense: (i) **Solitude** and **UC** are determinately true; (ii) either **Abundance**, or **Equality** is determinately false; (iii) it is indeterminate which particles constitute Tibbles. In another sense however, 'constitutes' marks only metaphysically significant distinctions between how collections of particles relate to an object. Because the differences between the candidates do not bear significantly on how they relate to Tibbles—their relations to Tibbles are of the same underlying kind—this delivers a sense in which each candidate counts as constituting Tibbles on each sharpening. So: (i) **UC** is determinately false and **MC** is determinately true; (ii) **Solitude**, **Abundance**, and **Equality** are all determinately true; (iii) there is no indeterminacy in Tibbles' constitution.[22]

Lowe's proposal fails the adequacy condition outlined above. His guiding claim is that a uniquely most cat-like individual is on Tibbles' mat. This is compatible with the negations of **Abundance**, **Equality**, and **UC**. So Lowe does not explain why we should reject one of those principles rather than another. Furthermore, Lowe simply builds **Solitude** into his guiding claim, rather than explaining why we should accept it. The next section develops a view that

---

[21] (Lewis, 1993).
[22] Why does Lowe need the second sense of 'constitutes'? Because as Lewis points out, stating the problem requires a sense in which the candidates are all equally good candidates to constitute cats (Lewis, 1993, pp. 173–4, 179–80). Couldn't Lowe invoke a metalinguistic (better: metasemantic) account of their equally good candidature? Not whilst recognizing that the differences between how the candidates relate to Tibbles are not metaphysically significant, and using 'constitute' to express the fundamental sense in which objects are made out of particles.

4. A CONCEPTION OF OBJECTS

My goal is a theoretically unified response to **PM**. This section proceeds by describing a conception of objects and constitution that justifies rejecting **UC** in favour of **MC**. The next section considers some objections.

4.1. The basic idea

My proposal is guided by the idea that objects are fundamentally subjects of change. Call the changes an object can survive its *characteristic changes*. The suggestion is that an object's fundamental nature or essence is given by its characteristic changes. An object is thus fundamentally a participant in the sort of event that results from the occurrence of its characteristic changes. This section elaborates this thesis.

One natural development of this suggestion invokes a *sui generis* four-place relation of ontological dependence: *x's having F ontologically depends upon y's having G*.[23] My suggestion is that an object *o*'s having a contingent intrinsic, temporal, or constitutional property *F* depends upon, or is grounded in, *o*'s having characteristic changes *G*.[24] Given an appropriate notion of essence, this goes hand-in-hand with the idea that an object's essence is its characteristic changes.[25]

One might doubt whether our grasp of essence, dependence, and grounding is robust enough to provide a secure theoretical foundation, regarding them merely as picturesque heuristics. I cannot fully alleviate these doubts here. But one way to approach these notions is via their methodological role and the constraints they place on those who employ them. Claims about grounding, essence, and dependence constrain the explanations available to the theorist.

---

[23] A close relative invokes a dyadic relation between states of affairs.
[24] This could be extended to modal, teleological, aesthetic... properties, but that goes beyond the scope of a response to **PM**.
[25] See (Fine, 1994) for more on essence, and (Fine, 1995) for the essence-dependence connection.

When one type of object, property, fact or whatever is said to depend upon another, the theorist making that claim is thereby committed to explaining all (or maybe just all the central) features of the dependent in terms of that on which it depends, and not to explain features of the latter in terms of the former. Similarly, attributing an essence to a thing brings an obligation to explain key aspects of the thing's behaviour in terms of its having that essence. That is the theoretical import of grounding, dependence, and essence.[26]

In these terms, my proposal requires that an object's intrinsic, temporal, and constitutional profiles be explained by its characteristic changes, and not conversely. The suggestion is not that characteristic changes are the sole explanatory factor; otherwise objects could have no contingent properties, assuming that essence, and hence characteristic change, is non-contingent. Rather, an object's characteristic changes combine with the contingent distribution of matter, property- and relation-instances, and events across space and time to explain why the object has the history (including constitutional history) that it does.[27] Whether or not this exhausts the content of the claims about dependence and essence with which this section began, it surely follows from them. Residual doubts about these notions may be alleviated by observing that any concept with these theoretical consequences could be invoked instead.

So, when an object o's putatively having an intrinsic, constitutional, or temporal property F cannot be explained in terms of o's characteristic changes (together with other contingent features of reality), o lacks F. When such an explanation can be given, o has F. Likewise *mutatis mutandis* for quantified claims about such properties. §4.3 argues that **MC** can be explained in this manner and **UC** cannot, and hence that **MC** is true and **UC** is false.

This is not a proposal about all material individuals, but only the paradigmatic sorts of ordinary object for which **PM** is problematic. The view is consistent with, e.g. portions of matter and aggregates of particles being subject to different orders of explanatory priority; in those cases, constitution plausibly explains characteristic

---

[26] (Stalnaker, 2012, pp. 113–15) defends a similar approach to views that allow quantifiers to range over things that do not exist. In brief: no high-level theoretical commitments without methodological consequences.

[27] This is a key theme from the neo-Aristotelian view in Wiggins (2001), esp. Chs. 2–4.

change. This might naturally be labelled a difference in ontological category.[28]

What exactly are the characteristic changes of, say, cats? §5.2 says a little more about this. But it may be helpful to distinguish two kinds of view now. On one view, characteristic changes are fundamentally macroscopic, in the sense of being changes in the object itself, rather than in its particulate parts. These are the changes a cat undergoes when it walks, pounces, digests etc. Although these kinds of behaviour have microphysical correlates, the first view says that changes involving the cat itself are what determine its history, rather than microphysical correlates thereof. On the second view, characteristic changes are fundamentally changes in particles; they are the microphysical correlates of macroscopic activity. Hybrid views are also possible. Luckily, I do not need to decide between these views here. What will matter to my argument is not the precise nature of characteristic changes, but their relative coarse-grainedness in the sense of being insensitive to distinctions between the candidates to constitute an object. However, this coarse-grainedness fits most naturally with the first, macroscopic view, and that is where my sympathies lie.

How does this help with **PM**? More detail follows, but an overview may be helpful. On my proposal, **PM** arises because Tibbles' characteristic changes are too coarse-grained to distinguish between the T^+s and the T^-s in respect of their constituting Tibbles: those collections are just too similar. Any explanation in terms of Tibbles' characteristic changes for why the T^+s constitute Tibbles also applies to the T^-s, yielding an explanation for why the T^-s constitute him. Likewise *mutatis mutandis* for an explanation of why the T^-s constitute Tibbles. At least one such explanation is correct: Tibbles is constituted by (at least) one of those collections of particles. But since Tibbles' characteristic changes cannot distinguish between

---

[28] Why is **PM** only problematic for ordinary objects? Because we're only entitled to the claims that generate **PM**, **Solitude** in particular, for reasonably familiar kinds of thing. It is not obvious that an abundance of, say, cat-like portions of matter on Tibbles' mat conflicts with our ordinary conception of reality or is otherwise objectionable. I claim that the things for which **PM** arises belong in a single category to which my proposal applies. But I remain neutral about how far beyond paradigmatic ordinary objects this category extends. Do such strange things as in-cars and out-cars belong in this category? (Hirsch, 1982, pp. 32–3) I am inclined to think so (at least, if in-cars exist), but nothing turns on it here.

these explanations, and it is in terms of those changes that Tibbles' constitution must be explained, it follows that both the T^+s and the T^-s do constitute Tibbles. So **UC** is false and **MC** is true. The next section elaborates the view further. §4.3 applies it to **PM** in more detail.

4.2. Kinds and paths

This section develops my proposal by discussing the connection between an object's characteristic changes and kind.

A useful notion is that of an object's path through space and time. Paths and characteristic changes go hand-in-hand: each path p corresponds to a class of (types of) characteristic changes, namely those changes an object o would have to survive in order for p to be o's path. Natural and non-arbitrary paths correspond to natural and non-arbitrary classes of changes. Gruesome and gerrymandered paths correspond to gruesome and gerrymandered classes of changes. Talk about paths and the features that characterize them thus provides an alternative way of describing characteristic changes.

Paths pass through regions at times. I will focus on the sense in which a path can pass through a region r at a time t without thereby passing through any proper subregion or superregion of r at t. In this sense, passing through is akin to exact occupation in the theory of location. Note however that an analogue of the following gloss on exact occupation is inappropriate here: x exactly occupies r at t iff x fills and fits within r at t. There are two reasons for this. The first is pragmatic: my solution to **PM** will require Tibbles' path to pass through several regions at a time, one for each candidate to constitute him at that time, and this appears to conflict with the gloss. The second reason is conceptual: my proposal requires that constraints on paths, including any that emerge from this gloss, be explicable via the characteristic changes of their occupants, and no such explanation has yet been provided.

An object's characteristic changes and path are not arbitrary; they depend on what kind or sort of thing it is.[29] The characteristic

---

[29] This is a second key theme from (Wiggins, 2001). See also note 27.

changes of a cat differ from those of, say, a squid or a pencil.[30] The relationship between kinds and characteristic changes can be understood in two ways. On one view, kind-classifications are notational variants on classifications by characteristic changes. On the other view, kind is a richer notion that determines an object's characteristic changes. The second view allows for kind-classifications more fine-grained than the first. Nothing that follows turns on which view is correct.

Each kind K privileges a class of paths appropriate to Ks; call these the *K-paths*. The individual Ks correspond one-one to K-paths: each K occupies exactly one K-path, and each K-path is occupied by exactly one K. What happens within an object's path at t determines its intrinsic properties and constitution at t. An object's path thus determines its history.

How do kinds privilege paths? Well, associated with each kind K is a cross-time relation R_K on regions: R_K holds from a region r at a time t to a region r' at a time t'. This relation picks up on the contingent distribution of matter, property- and relation-instances, and events across space and time to determine which paths are K-paths. Think of R_K as codifying the characteristic changes of Ks, and as thereby delineating the spatial and temporal boundaries of events of the sort that result from the occurrence of those changes.

How does R_K delineate the K-paths? A natural first suggestion is:

> For any regions r, r' and times t, t': some K-path passes through both r at t and r' at t' iff R_K holds from r at t to r' at t'.

Although this principle rules out many paths, it doesn't settle which paths are K-paths. Suppose that R_K holds (i) from r at t to r' at t', and (ii) from r' at t' to r^* at t^*. Then the principle implies that some path corresponds to (i) and some path corresponds to (ii). But the principle is silent about whether the same path corresponds to (i) and (ii), even if R_K also holds from r at t to r^* at t^*. More structure must be imposed on the relationship between R_K and K-paths.

---

[30] One might doubt that cats and squid have different characteristic changes. Maybe all living things have the same characteristic changes, with non-persistence features differentiating their paths. If so, then the relation I will shortly invoke to characterize paths should be understood to incorporate this non-persistence information.

We want to use the characteristic changes of cats, as codified by R_K, to select the K-paths from amongst the totality of paths. So let f_K be the (partial) two-place function from regions r and times t to paths such that:

- $f_K(r,t)$ is defined iff R_K holds from r at t to some r' at some t'.
- Path $f_K(r,t)$ passes through r at t.
- f_K satisfies:

$$(K=) \quad \forall r, r', t, t' [f_K(r,t) = f_K(r',t') \leftrightarrow R_K(r,t,r',t')]$$

Because R_K codifies the characteristic changes of Ks, the first bullet says that f_K maps r,t to a path iff the kinds of change that Ks survive are occurring in r at t; i.e. iff some K-path passes through r at t. So by the second bullet, f_K maps r,t to a path that passes through the same region (r) as a K-path at t. And (K=) says that f_K maps r,t and r',t' to the same path iff R_K holds from r at t to r' at t'; i.e. iff the characteristic changes of Ks are as they would have to be in order for a K in r at t to be in r' at t'. So I propose identifying the K-paths with the values of f_K. On this view, the structural relationships between R_K and K-paths are captured by f_K and (K=). Let p be a path that passes through r at t. Then p is a K-path iff, for any region r' and time t': p passes through r' at t' iff R_K holds from r at t to r' at t'. That is how R_K delineates the K-paths. Note finally an important consequence of this view: if cat-paths p and q pass through the same region at some time, they pass through exactly the same regions at all times; "they" are not two paths, but one. I will make use of this fact shortly.[31]

This proposal is silent about modal variation in K-paths. It is intended to apply only within a world w, to delineate w's K-paths on the basis of w's distribution of matter, property- and relation-instances, and events across space and time. But it is surely contingent which paths are K-paths. Tibbles could have continued sleeping this morning, rather than chasing a mouse. In that case, he would have occupied a different path than he actually does; this path would then have been a cat-path, even though it actually isn't. Moreover, if Tibbles had continued sleeping this morning, no cat would have

---

[31] K-paths can be modelled as classes of pairs $\langle r,t \rangle$ of regions r and times t. R_K can be modelled by a dyadic relation on such pairs. Then (K=) implies that R_K is an equivalence relation. On my proposal, K-paths are therefore modelled by equivalence classes under R_K of $\langle r,t \rangle$ pairs.

occupied his actual path, which would therefore not have been a cat-path. So the proposal must be enriched to accommodate modal variation in the K-paths.

The K-paths are determined by R_K and f_K. So contingency in the K-paths should result from contingency in R_K and f_K.[32] The extensions of contingent relations and the values of contingent functions (for given arguments) vary across worlds. My original proposal should now be modified so that f_K is a contingent two-place function from regions r and times t to paths such that:

- For any world w: $f_K(r, t)$ is defined at w iff R_K holds in w from r at t to some r' at some t'.
- For any world w: path $f_K(r, t)$ passes in w through r at t.
- f_K satisfies:

$$\forall w, r, r', t, t' (\text{At } w[f_K(r, t) = f_K(r', t')] \leftrightarrow \text{At } w[R_K(r, t, r', t')])$$

This last says that f_K maps r, t and r', t' to the same path in w iff R_K holds in w from r at t to r' at t'. The K-paths in w are exactly the values of f_K in w. Note that this is silent about when the same K occupies K-paths drawn from different worlds. It is also silent about whether worlds can differ only in respect of which Ks occupy which paths. My original proposal is obtained by fixing on a single target world w. To simplify discussion, however, I will largely ignore modal concerns in the sequel, and focus instead on applying the original proposal within a single world.

Four brief comments follow, by way of further clarification.

First comment: since each K occupies exactly one K-path, and each K-path is occupied by exactly one K, R_K captures the (intra-world) identity conditions for Ks. When R_K holds from r at t to r' at t', not only is some K in r at t and some K in r' at t'; one and the same K is in both r at t and r' at t'. And if one K is in both r at t and r' at t', then R_K holds from r at t to r' at t': a single K-path passes through those regions at those times. Relatedly, since Ks are located in space exactly when their paths pass through some region or other, R_K also captures the existence conditions of Ks.

---

[32] Since functions are just a type of relation, contingent functions are no more objectionable than contingent relations. Contingent relations can be modelled by functions from worlds to relations, and contingent functions by functions from worlds to functions. Thanks to Josh Parsons for discussion of contingent K-paths.

Second comment: despite being formally permissible, we should not identify Ks with either K-paths or classes of pairs of regions and times.[33] Ordinary objects are not abstracta, set theoretic constructions, or paths through space and time. Objects are the occupants of paths, the spatiotemporally located and causally efficacious loci of our interaction with concrete reality.[34]

Third comment: my proposal is independent of the epistemological and metaphysical picture associated with neo-Fregean foundations for mathematics.[35, 36] Principles like ($K=$) play a key role in such approaches, where they are called "abstraction principles". Within my proposal, a more appropriate label is Timothy Williamson's: ($K=$) is a two-level identity criterion.[37]

Fourth comment: the explanatory primacy of paths undermines the most powerful objection to coincident entities, namely the grounding problem.[38] The problem is that coincident objects are very similar—they are in the same place at the same time and constituted by the same particles—and yet not completely similar. A particularly pressing case arises when coincident objects have different futures. How is this possible, given their present similarity? Note first that the paths of different kinds of object are determined by different relations. There is no mystery about how relations can share some but not all relata. So there is no mystery about how a K-path and a K'-path can intersect and then later come apart. Since kinds and

---

[33] An alternative identifies Ks with pairs of K-paths and R_K. This allows distinct objects of different kinds to share a path. The remarks in the text apply to this proposal too. See also note 31.

[34] I thus reject the identification of objects with filled regions of spacetime. Maybe a variant proposal could accommodate that view. I will not attempt to develop one here.

[35] The classic neo-Fregean text is (Wright, 1983).

[36] This differentiates my proposal from a superficially similar one in (Simons, 2000), (Simons, 2008). Simons uses principles like ($K=$), in which the quantifiers range over occurrents, to capture the supposed ontological dependence of continuants on occurrents. My proposal is silent about this putative dependence and Simons does not discuss **PM**.

[37] (Williamson, 1990, Ch. 9).

[38] (Bennett, 2004) gives a nice overview of the problem. A variant is sometimes raised by asking how objects can coincide without "crowding each other out"; an example is (Sider, 2001, pp. 141, 154–5). I do not know whether my proposal addresses this because I do not understand the objection. One does not get a statue and lump of clay to coincide by pushing them together, but by making one from the other. Why should objects crowd each other out when one is made from the other?

paths are explanatorily prior to history and constitution, there is no mystery about how objects of different kinds can coincide and then later not do so. This strategy will not extend to coincidence between objects of the same kind, a phenomenon that even prominent defenders of coincidence like David Wiggins reject.[39] It does, however, seem likely that intensional differences between the characteristic changes of different kinds can explain modal differences between contingently permanently coincident members of those kinds. This may even extend to non-modal differences between necessarily permanently coincident objects of different kinds. However, the ultimate viability of these strategies turns upon broader issues in the metaphysics of modality that I cannot discuss properly here.

4.3. Constitution, solitude, and multiple constitution

This section puts the conception of objects developed in the preceding two sections to work resolving **PM**.

The motivating thought behind my proposal is that objects are fundamentally subjects of change, different kinds of change for different kinds of object. This manifests as the explanatory primacy of paths over constitution. How exactly does this explanation go? The natural suggestion is:

> **Path-Con** For any particles xx, object o and time t: xx constitute o at t iff, for some region r, (i) o's path passes through r at t, and (ii) xx occupy r at t.

Occupation here is exact occupation: xx exactly occupy r iff xx both fill and fit within r. Exact occupation is collective: xx can exactly occupy r without anything amongst xx exactly occupying r. The region that xx exactly occupy is the union of those regions occupied by things amongst xx (perhaps supplemented with a way of filling in any gaps).

Truths about constitution, including **UC** and **MC**, should be explicable via **Path-Con** and the characteristic changes of cats. I will exploit this to argue for **MC**.

---

[39] (Wiggins, 1968). (Fine, 2000) describes putative cases of extreme forms of same-kind coincidence.

Multiple constitution | 235

Let us apply the view described in the preceding section to cats. R_C is the relation that codifies the characteristic changes of cats. f_C is the (partial) function from regions r and times t to the cat-path (if any) that passes through r at t. R_C and f_C satisfy this instance of ($K=$):

(C=) $\forall r, r', t, t'[f_C(r,t) = f_C(r',t') \leftrightarrow R_C(r,t,r',t')]$

(C=) captures the structural relationships between R_C, cat-paths and f_C.

Let r^+ and r^- be the regions occupied now, at t_{now}, by the T^+s and the T^-s respectively, when hair h is a borderline part of Tibbles. I will argue that Tibbles' path now passes through both r^+ and r^-. Because the T^+s and the T^-s now occupy r^+ and r^- respectively, it then follows by **Path-Con** that both of those collections now constitute Tibbles.

Suppose Tibbles' path passes through only one region at any time prior to t_{now}: there was never more than one candidate to constitute Tibbles until now; i.e. **PM** did not arise before now. This unrealistic supposition will be dropped shortly. Let t_{early} be an earlier time, say, several months prior to t_{now}; let r_{early} be the region through which Tibbles' path passes at t_{early}. The question is this: how should Tibbles' path be extended from t_{early} to t_{now}, in order for the result to be a cat-path?[40] The T^+s and the T^-s are the only candidates to constitute Tibbles at t_{now}, and **PM** does not arise before t_{now}. So there are two ways of extending Tibbles' path to t_{now}. On one, Tibbles' path passes through r^+ at t_{now}. If that yields a cat-path, then the T^+s now constitute Tibbles. On the other, Tibbles' path passes through r^- at t_{now}. If that yields a cat-path, then the T^-s now constitute Tibbles. I will argue that both ways of extending Tibbles' path to t_{now} result in cat-paths, and hence that both the T^+s and the T^-s now constitute Tibbles.

Tibbles' path passes through r_{early} at t_{early}. It continues from then to pass through at least one of r^+ and r^- at t_{now}. That is, R_C holds from r_{early} at t_{early} to at least one of r^+ and r^- at t_{now}. Does R_C hold from r_{early} at t_{early} to only one of r^+ and r^- at t_{now}? It appears not. Surely the characteristic changes of cats cannot privilege one of

---

[40] If Tibbles persists beyond t_{now}, then extending Tibbles' path only as far as t_{now} will not yield a cat-path, but only a restriction of a cat-path. I ignore this complication henceforth.

r^+ and r^- over the other in respect of now containing a cat that was in r_{early} at t_{early}. What's now going on in those regions, the particles in them, and the paths connecting them to r_{early} at t_{early}, are so similar that the characteristic changes of cats cannot distinguish between them. So R_C holds from r_{early} at t_{early} to both or neither of r^+ and r^- at t_{now}. By hypothesis, R_C holds from r_{early} at t_{early} to at least one of those regions at t_{now}. So R_C holds from r_{early} at t_{early} to both of r^+ and r^- at t_{now}. So by (C=): f_K maps r_{early}, t_{early} to the same cat-path as both r^+, t_{now} and r^-, t_{now}; i.e. one single cat-path passes through r_{early} at t_{early} as well as through both r^+ and r^- at t_{now}. Since Tibbles' path passes through r_{early} at t_{early}, his path also passes through both r^+ and r^- at t_{now}. So by **Path-Con**: both the T^+s and the T^-s now constitute Tibbles. So **UC** is false and **MC** is true.

Furthermore, we may legitimately assume, the path of any cat on Tibbles' mat passes through at least one of r_{early}, r^+ and r^- at the relevant times: there are no other candidates. The last section pointed out that if cat-paths p and q pass through the same region at some time, then $p = q$. Since path-occupancy one-one correlates cats with cat-paths, it follows that exactly one cat is on Tibbles' mat: **Solitude** is true. **Abundance** holds because the T^+s and the T^-s do constitute cats. And (the relevant instantiation of) **Equality** holds because its consequent is true. So my conception of objects implies my solution to **PM**.

The preceding argument assumed that there is only one candidate to constitute Tibbles at t_{early}, and hence that his path then passes through only one region. Let us drop this unrealistic assumption. The argument was underwritten by the following thought: the T^+s and the T^-s are now too similar for the relatively coarse-grained characteristic changes of cats to distinguish between them. On my conception of objects, this amounts to: R_C cannot distinguish r^+ from r^- at t_{now}. So in particular, R_C cannot distinguish r^+ from r^- in respect of its holding from them at t_{now} to r_{early} at t_{early}. This motivating thought is indifferent as to whether some other region r^*_{early}, nearly coincident with r_{early}, is as good a candidate as r_{early} for having a cat-path—indeed, Tibbles' cat-path—pass through it at t_{early}. In other words: the argument is indifferent as to whether some particles in r^*_{early} at t_{early} are also candidates to constitute Tibbles at t_{early}. A parallel argument therefore concludes that R_C holds from

r^*_{early} at t_{early} to both r^+ and r^- at t_{now}. So by (C=): f_K maps r^*_{early}, t_{early} to the same cat-path as r^+, t_{now} and r^-, t_{now}. So by the argument two paragraphs ago and the transitivity of identity: f_K maps r^*_{early}, t_{early} to the same cat-path as r_{early}, t_{early}. So Tibbles' path passes through both r_{early} and r^*_{early} at t_{early}, as well as through r^+ and r^- at t_{now}. So by **Path-Con**: Tibbles is multiply constituted at t_{early}—by the particles then in r_{early} and also by those in r^*_{early}—as well as at t_{now}. Since cats correspond one-one with cat-paths, there is no threat here to Tibbles' being the only cat on his mat at t_{early}.

Let n be the smallest number of candidates there ever are to constitute Tibbles. One might object that (C=) is consistent with the existence of n cat-paths, and hence also n cats, on Tibbles' mat. Notice that this is no threat to **MC**, but only to **Solitude**; for whenever more than n candidates are on the mat, the objection implies that some of the n cats will be multiply constituted. The objection also relies on considering only the structural connections that (C=) imposes on cat-paths, f_C and R_C, neglecting the non-structural content of R_C itself. R_C codifies the characteristic changes of cats. In order for two cats to be on the mat at, say, t_{now}, one cat-path must then pass through r^+ and another through r^-. So R_C must now distinguish between r^+ and r^-. That is, the characteristic changes of cats must now distinguish between the T^+s and the T^-s. But that is simply not plausible given how similar those collections now are. How could the characteristic changes of cats privilege just one of those collections as the present constituter of a cat in r_{early} at t_{early}? **PM** only arises because the determiners of cat-locations cannot make such fine-grained distinctions; otherwise **Abundance** would fail. This undermines the objection. My proposal grants that the determiners of cat-locations are relatively coarse-grained, and that **Abundance** holds for that reason. This coarse-grainedness is then put to work bundling up the many candidates into one cat. The very phenomenon that generates **PM** thereby provides the key to resolving it.

We have seen that my conception of objects implies my solution to **PM**. My proposal therefore satisfies the adequacy condition described in §3: it is a unified whole. The next section develops the view further in response to some objections. §6 examines the relationship between constitution and mereology, given my solution to **PM**, and offers a speculative diagnosis of that solution's near-absence from the literature.

5. OBJECTIONS AND FURTHER DEVELOPMENTS

This section develops my proposal further in response to some objections.

5.1. Multiply located cats

On my proposal, Tibbles' path typically passes through many regions at a time, and path-occupancy provides the most basic way in which objects are in space. Doesn't it follow that Tibbles is multiply located, that he is in many places at a single time? And isn't that impossible?

There are two objections here. The first is linguistic: ordinary English sentences like 'Tibbles is in only one place at a time' should be true, and my proposal makes them false. To make it stick, this objection must be supplemented; my proposal about the metaphysics of objects must be connected with the semantics of ordinary locational discourse. Two such semantic analyses are available, one of which defuses the objection.

Let LOC be the property such that:

> For any region r and time t: r has LOC at t iff Tibbles' path passes through r at t.

Since Tibbles' path passes through many regions whenever he is multiply constituted, many regions have LOC at each such time. Let $LOC_1, LOC_2, \ldots$ be the properties obtainable by restricting the extension of LOC to a single region at each time. Regimenting English locational discourse using the two-place predicate 'x occupies r', the two rival semantic analyses of the one-place predicate 'Tibbles occupies r' are:

A1 At each time t, 'Tibbles occupies r' is coextensive with LOC.
A2 At each time t, 'Tibbles occupies r' is coextensive with LOC_n.

'Tibbles occupies no more than one region at a time' is false on **A1** and true on **A2**. The objection therefore succeeds if **A1** is true, and fails if **A2** is true. So, which view is correct?

On the one hand, LOC is more natural than any LOC$_i$.[41] In so far as assignments of natural semantic values provide better candidate interpretations than assignments of less natural values, **A1** is favourable to **A2**. On the other hand, **A1** makes many English sentences untrue that **A2** makes true. General principles like 'Nothing occupies more than one place at a time' provide one type of example. Another involves definite descriptions of locations: **A1** but not **A2** makes 'the place where Tibbles is sitting' improper, and hence any sentence featuring it untrue. In so far as assignments that make true more sentences that ordinary speakers by-and-large hold true provide better candidate interpretations than assignments that make true fewer such sentences, **A2** is favourable to **A1**.

These conflicting metasemantic pressures must be reconciled. We cannot settle this without more detail about meaning-determination. It does, however, seem reasonable to weight truth-maximization over naturalness here, and hence to favour **A2** over **A1**; in which case, the linguistic objection fails.

One might object to **A2** that selection of some LOC$_i$ over any other LOC$_j$ as the semantic value of 'Tibbles occupies r' would be arbitrary and unmotivated. This can be resisted in (at least) two ways. Firstly, the function from use to meaning is unknown, and possibly unknowable because we lack independent means to calibrate a method of testing hypotheses about it.[42] So it would be arbitrary and unmotivated to endorse an instantiation of **A2**. But it does not follow that instantiations of **A2** are arbitrary and unmotivated in any deeper sense incompatible with their truth, as opposed to their assertability or knowability. Secondly, we might accept that many different assignments of semantic value to 'occupies' fit our meaning-determining linguistic behaviour equally well, one such assignment for each LOC$_i$. The result will plausibly be indeterminacy in location-ascriptions; it will be indeterminate which instantiation

---

[41] Natural in the sense of (Lewis, 1983).
[42] (Williamson, 1994, pp. 205–9).

of **A2** is true.[43] Given **A2**, my proposal therefore entails indeterminacy in ordinary locational discourse.

The second version of this multiple-location objection is metaphysical: the *location* relation should hold between Tibbles and only one region at a time, whereas Tibbles' path passes through many regions at a time. The response to the linguistic objection weakens this metaphysical objection by accommodating the linguistic evidence for it. My proposal does, however, require some re-conceptualization of our intuitive picture of how objects are in space. Path-occupancy provides the primary sense in which objects are in space. Tibbles' path passes through many regions whenever **PM** arises. So my proposal delivers a strong sense in which Tibbles is multiply located whenever **PM** arises. The many regions in which Tibbles is located are, however, nearly coincident and differ by less than the contextually salient threshold for relevance to our ordinary practical and linguistic interests. That is why **Abundance** is not an unremarkable commonplace, but the source of a surprising puzzle. So this re-conceptualization is consistent with our ordinary experience of objects and their locations, the primary data of metaphysics.

5.2. What is R_C?

This section considers the following objection: I have not said enough about R_C to imbue my proposal with content. The objection might be strengthened by claiming that I cannot say anything detailed, informative, and true about R_C, and hence that I cannot make my proposal substantive.

The objection fails. §4.3 showed that the explanatory primacy of paths and characteristic changes has non-trivial consequences. Furthermore, (C=) and **Path-Con** together impose non-trivial structural constraints on the paths and constitution of cats. But this is not purely structural content; for R_C codifies the characteristic changes of cats. That is, R_C holds from r at t to r' at t' iff the characteristic changes of cats are as they would have to be in order for a cat in r at t to be in r' at t'. My proposal therefore has non-trivial structural and non-structural content.

---

[43] The logico-semantic upshot of this indeterminacy is a further issue I remain silent about here.

The objection might be nuanced in response. The nuanced complaint is not that my proposal lacks content, but that since I have given no specific details about R_C and the characteristic changes of cats, my proposal is overly unspecific and indefinite. This nuanced objection comes in two varieties.

The first variety requires a finite non-trivial explicit definition of R_C. But there is no reason to expect, and I have said nothing to suggest, that the vocabulary of English or any other natural language will be rich enough to provide this. This expressive deficit is no threat to regarding the bearing of R_C as a substantive and well-understood matter. This can be strengthened by invoking the fact that the cats form a natural kind. On broadly externalist views about the semantics of natural kind-terms, this undermines one key (and perhaps the only) motivation for believing an informative explicit definition of R_C to be possible; for on such views, no explicit definition is needed to fix an extension for 'cat'.[44] One might respond by denying that the cats form a natural kind. What motivates this response? Presumably, it's the absence of cats from fundamental physics. But that motivation is suspect: why should all natural kinds, or even all fundamental/basic kinds, appear within (or be definable in the language of) physics? We can (and in my view should) reject this impoverished form of physicalism and allow that the cats form a natural kind. Note also that rejecting this narrow physicalism does not bring commitment to immaterial substances: concreteness does not imply definability in the language of physics.

This externalist strategy will not extend to objects of non-natural kinds, such as artefact kinds. But I invoked externalism only as one way of motivating the claim that we have no right to expect an informative explicit definition of R_C. That claim does not require externalism, and other motivations for it may also cover non-natural kinds. One strategy begins by noting that our grasp of R_C is a largely practical matter, manifested in, e.g. our capacity to track cats through a diverse range of circumstances.[45] An argument from our grasping R_C to the possibility of our explicitly defining it therefore involves assimilating this practical capacity (knowledge-how) to

---

[44] (Wiggins, 2001, pp. 7–12, 77–86).

[45] Here is a third theme of (Wiggins, 2001, pp. 2, 3, 7, 18–20 and elsewhere). See notes 27, 29.

propositional knowledge-that. This intellectualist view is highly controversial.[46] But without it, our grasping R_C is neutral regarding the possibility of our informatively explicitly defining R_C. Absent an alternative reason to believe that such a definition is possible, this first version of the nuanced objection is unmotivated. I do not know what such a reason might be.

The second version of the nuanced objection does not require an explicit definition of R_C. Only some general guidance about the characteristic changes of cats is required. This is readily provided, e.g. cats survive through walking, pouncing, eating, sleeping, and purring; they do not survive through squashing, burning, starvation, and drowning. There is no threat here to regarding my gloss on R_C as substantive. So this objection also fails.

5.3. A problem of the many paths?

Does **PM** recur at the level of cat-paths? This section argues that it does not.

One type of reason to think that **PM** recurs at the level of paths invokes higher-order vagueness, the putative phenomenon of borderline cases to the borderline cases. I will, however, set higher-order vagueness aside and assume a well-defined and determinate range of candidates to constitute Tibbles. There are two reasons for this. Firstly, although §3 justified **Abundance** by appealing to indeterminacy in Tibbles' boundaries, it is controversial whether this is the only such justification, and Unger himself denies that it is.[47] It is an open question whether **PM** ultimately involves vagueness, or whether vagueness-specific phenomena like higher-order indeterminacy should be treated separately. Secondly, the existence and coherence of higher-order vagueness are both controversial.[48] Even setting worries about its coherence to one side, it is controversial whether higher-order vagueness can do the work of explaining seamless transition that motivates introducing it.[49] So even if higher-order vagueness is relevant to my discussion, serious work

---

[46] (Stanley and Williamson, 2001) defend this approach to knowledge-how; for discussion, see (Koethe, 2002), (Rumfitt, 2003), (Devitt, 2011).
[47] (Unger, 2006a, pp. 369–70, 394–6, 468–9).
[48] An excellent recent discussion is (Wright, 2010).
[49] (Graff-Fara, 2003).

is required before it can bear argumentative weight here. Let us therefore consider a different reason for thinking that a version of **PM** afflicts cat-paths.

Tibbles' path p_T passes through both r^+ and r^- at t_{now}. Let p be the path that differs from p_T only by not passing through r^+ at t_{now}. The similarity between the T^+s and the T^-s that generates **PM** might also seem to suggest that p is a cat-path, given that p_T is. Since each cat-path is occupied by exactly one cat, it would follow that two cats are on Tibbles' mat, and hence that my proposal does not solve **PM**, but merely relocates it. This section responds to this objection.

Luckily for me, p is not a cat-path. Cat-paths are the values of f_K. Because f_K satisfies (C=), cat-paths that pass through the same region at some time pass through exactly the same regions at all times; in which case, "they" are not two cat-paths, but one. Now, p and p_T both pass through r^- at t_{now}. But only p_T passes through r^+ at t_{now}. Since p_T is a cat-path—as was argued in §4.3—it follows that p is not a cat-path. So the objection fails. The structural conditions my proposal imposes on cat-paths preclude the possibility of overlapping cat-paths on Tibbles' mat.

A variant problem arises. p is a path, and very similar to p_T. Since p_T is a K-path for some kind K of object—i.e. *cat*—doesn't it follow that p is too, though for some other kind K'? Members of K' will be very similar to cats. Call them 'schmats'. Cats and schmats are so alike that motivations for **Solitude** should carry over to:

> **Schmolitude**   Tibbles is the one and only cat-or-schmat on his mat.

If schmats exist, then **PM** has only been relocated.

This variant problem is importantly different from the original one. This new problem concerns an abundance of hitherto unrecognized kinds of object, whereas **PM** concerns only an abundance of cats. **PM** arises because the T^+s and the T^-s are so similar that they are equally good candidates to constitute cats. Do these same similarities also make them equally good candidates to satisfy 'the xs constitute an object of some kind' when the two corresponding existential claims must be witnessed by different kinds? No: obviously. Factors relevant to the existence of kinds may differ from those relevant to the existence of cats; indeed, they probably will. Belief in the existence of Ks should align with the utility of Ks in systematizing, explaining, and predicting the behaviour of external reality. Cats are undeniably important to this project; schmats are not. No systematic, explanatory, or predictive utility comes from admitting a kind of object whose characteristic changes distinguish between the T^+s and the T^-s, but are otherwise just like those of a cat. The similarity between the T^+s and the T^-s that generates **PM** thus militates against regarding schmats as contributing to this theoretical project. **PM** therefore does not recur at the level of paths.

5.4. Inherited properties

Objects inherit many properties from their constituent particles. Intuitively, Tibbles has his particular mass and shape because he is constituted by some particles that (collectively) have that mass and shape. I will focus on mass as a representative example. There is a prima facie problem here for my proposal. Since the T^+s and the T^-s have different (collective) masses, it seems to follow from **MC** that Tibbles has different and incompatible masses, which is impossible. This section responds by outlining a suitable account of property-inheritance. This account also answers the following sceptical question: what is so special about Tibbles' path, in virtue of which it deserves that title? Wouldn't any permutation of cats across paths be equally acceptable? The answer is that Tibbles' path is uniquely privileged in determining what is true of him when.

5.4.1. Four kinds of property

This section narrows the scope of my account of inheritance. Four types of properties of objects will be distinguished on the basis of their inheritance from particles. Three will be excluded from my account. I do not claim that the four are exhaustive, or that there are only three exemptions. But they are some of the more obvious cases.

The first type of property are like mass-properties and shape-properties: Tibbles has a mass and shape because he is constituted by some particles with that very mass and shape. This is the simplest case, of what we might call *direct inheritance*.

The second type of property are not inherited. Modal and historical properties provide examples. Tibbles does not inherit his characteristic changes or properties like *being possibly squashed* and *having once been scattered* from his constituent particles. Such "hypothetical" properties that "look outside their instances" are hereby excluded from my discussion, so that it concerns only "categorical" properties.[50]

The third type of property correspond to large-scale properties of Tibbles' constituent particles. Examples include *purring* and *being hungry*. Other candidates involve functional, teleological, aesthetic, representational, and semantic properties.[51] Some (though maybe not all) of these properties are systematically connected in a law-like manner to properties of particles, though they are not possessed by particles themselves. These systematic connections create logical space for an analogue of the initial problem about mass. However, the problem does not arise because the connections are with large-scale properties of particles: the comparatively small-scale differences between Tibbles' candidate constituters cannot correspond to differences in whether he is, say, hungry or purring. Like the second type of property, I exclude such properties from the coming discussion.

The fourth type of property, like the third, is not directly inherited from Tibbles' constituent particles; they are, however, systematically connected to properties of particles in such a way that analogues of the initial problem about mass can arise. Examples may include colour-properties: although cats can be ginger, one might doubt whether their constituent particles can be (collectively) ginger. Suppose Tibbles' borderline hair h is his only non-ginger hair. Then whether Tibbles is ginger turns on whether the T^+s or the T^-s constitute him. On my proposal, both collections constitute him. It seems to follow that he is both wholly ginger and partly non-ginger, which is impossible. The simplest strategy is to provide a separate

---

[50] It is doubtful whether purely categorical properties exist. Even paradigmatic cases concern an object's behaviour across a range of counterfactual circumstances, and should therefore count as hypothetical. What matters for my purposes is only the exclusion of certain clearly non-inherited properties, rather than the metaphysical gloss by which it is effected.

[51] (Fine, 2003).

account of this indirect inheritance to parallel the account of direct inheritance below, though I cannot go into detail here.

5.4.2. Four options

Consider these inheritance principles:[52]

Naïve Tibbles has ϕ iff the particles that constitute him have ϕ.
Supervaluation Tibbles has ϕ iff every collection of particles that constitute him has ϕ.
Subvaluation Tibbles has ϕ iff some particles that constitute him have ϕ.
Relativization Tibbles has ϕ relative to the xs iff the xs both constitute him and have ϕ.

This section defends **Relativization**.

On my proposal, 'the particles that constitute Tibbles' is improper and instantiations of **Naïve** therefore untrue. An alternative is needed.

The T^+s and the T^-s have different masses. So **Supervaluation** implies that Tibbles does not have any particular mass. This makes it unclear in what sense Tibbles is really a material object. One might respond by applying **Supervaluation** to determinable properties alongside their determinates: since the T^+s and the T^-s are massive, Tibbles is also massive, despite lacking any particular mass. Three problems arise. Firstly, it is doubtful whether we should believe in both determinates and determinables; for what theoretical work is there for determinables that their determinates cannot do? Secondly, this damages our ordinary conception of the determinate/determinable contrast: what is having a determinable, if not having one of its determinates? Thirdly, this does not address the initial problem: the sense in which Tibbles is a material object remains obscure, given that he has no determinate mass-property. We should reject **Supervaluation**.

Subvaluation implies that Tibbles has the mass of the T^+s and also the mass of the T^-s, and hence that he has incompatible

---

[52] Alternatives are possible, though these are the most obvious and promising candidates.

masses. Since these are distinct determinates of the same determinable, this undermines our ordinary understanding of both the determinate/determinable contrast and property-incompatibility. Since no alternative understanding is available, we should reject **Subvaluation**.

Relativization modifies the logical form of Tibbles' possession of inherited properties, by relativizing instantiation to collections of particles that constitute him. Note that instantiation is relativized, not the property instantiated; for that would lead to an unattractive dualism of dyadic object-masses and monadic particle-masses. Let m^+ and m^- be the masses of the T^+s and the T^-s respectively. **Relativization** implies that Tibbles has m^+ relative to the T^+s and m^- relative to the T^-s. Since Tibbles does have m^+ (relative to the T^+s), this avoids the objection to **Supervaluation**. Since Tibbles does not have m^+ and m^- *simpliciter*, but only relative to the T^+s and T^-s respectively, this avoids the objection to **Subvaluation**. **Relativization** is therefore preferable to these rivals.

How should we understand relativized instantiation? There are two options. According to the first, the right-hand side of **Relativization** analyses its left-hand side: Tibbles' having ϕ relative to the xs is analysed as the xs constituting Tibbles and having ϕ. One might object that, like **Supervaluation**, this robs Tibbles of each determinate mass: Tibbles himself does not have a mass, but is merely related to some particles with that mass. Calling this relation 'constitution' does not help; for what is so special about constitution, as opposed to any other relation, that warrants ascribing m^+ to Tibbles on the basis of his being constituted by the T^+s? This certainly does not settle the issue. One might regard this not as a problem, but as a robust metaphysical basis for the thought that objects change their mass by changing the mass of their constitutents. But let us consider an alternative account of relativized instantiation instead.

This alternative denies that 'o has ϕ relative to the xs' is analysed by 'the xs both constitute o and have ϕ'. Instead, relativized instantiation is included in the primitive ideology—expressive resources— of the theory of instantiation. On this view, relativized instantiation is a *sui generis* mode of fact-formation, one that takes an object, property, and some particles to form a complex fact. **Relativization** expresses a(n instance of a) law governing this mode of fact-formation. I now consider two objections to this suggestion.

The first objection is that, given **Relativization**, Tibbles does not have any mass *simpliciter*, without relativization. The objection infers from this that Tibbles does not really have any mass. What does 'really' mean here? If 'really' means *simpliciter*—i.e. without relativisation—then the objection merely expresses the view. Instead, the claim must be that there is no sense at all in which Tibbles instantiates mass-properties, if he has them only relative to his constituters. Now, **Relativization** does imply a difference between the senses in which Tibbles has inherited and non-inherited properties. But is this difference objectionable? Does it follow that there is no sense in which Tibbles instantiates a mass? Lewis would have thought so. He complained that a similar proposal to time-index instantiation "alienates" objects from their properties.[53] This complaint was motivated by two thoughts:

(a) Instantiating a property is not analysable via the bearing of a relation—or any other "relation-like" entity—between property and bearer.
(b) Relativized instantiation is analysable via the bearing of a relation between property, bearer, and index.[54]

It follows that instantiation (*simpliciter*) and relativized instantiation are fundamentally different kinds of phenomena. Furthermore, on this view relativized instantiation is analysable via instantiation *simpliciter* (in the guise of relational bearing). But why should we grant (a) and (b)? Although Lewis invoked versions of Bradley's regress and Russell's paradox to justify (a), he gave no explicit argument for (b). An argument can, however, be extracted from Lewis' reduction of instantiation to set membership: membership is not relative to times or collections of particles; so relativized instantiation is not a variety of membership; relativized instantiation must therefore be understood in some other way, and the bearing of a relation is the only obvious candidate. The upshot is that rejecting Lewis' identification of instantiation with membership allows us to reject (b).

---

[53] (Lewis, 2002, pp. 5–7).
[54] For Lewis, the relevant index was a time. For us, the index is a collection of particles that constitute the property's bearer.

Having rejected (b), and having admitted one mode of fact-formation not analysable via the bearing of relations—i.e. instantiation *simpliciter*—there is no bar to admitting another. According to (a), instantiation *simpliciter* takes an object and monadic property to form a fact, without mediation by a relation.[55] So why not also treat relativized instantiation as taking an object, monadic property, and collection of particles to form a fact, without mediation by a relation? There remains a difference between the ways Tibbles has inherited and non-inherited properties. But to reject the proposal on that basis alone, without the backing of (b), is not to argue against it. Without an alternative argument for (b), there is no objection here to relativized instantiation of inherited properties.

The second objection begins with the difference in form between ordinary predications of inherited properties and the facts those predications report: ordinary predication is not explicitly relativized to constituters. Let F be a predicate ordinarily conceived as expressing an inherited property ϕ. What is F's semantic value? If objects weren't multiply constituted, F could express the property: *being an x that has ϕ relative to the particles that constitute x*. But multiple constitution creates problems: because 'the particles that constitute Tibbles' is improper, this proposal makes the predication 'F(Tibbles)' untrue. Since many attributions of inherited properties to Tibbles are true, a different approach is required.

A better suggestion mirrors **A2** from §5.1. Let f be a function that maps each object o to some particles that constitute o. Then F can express: *being an x that has ϕ relative to $f(x)$*. On this view, 'F(Tibbles)' is true iff Tibbles has ϕ relative to f(Tibbles). Since Tibbles is multiply constituted, many functions satisfy my initial description of f. Each delivers a different candidate semantic value for F. No candidate is more natural than any other, or privileged by the linguistic behaviour of ordinary speakers: they are equally good candidate values for F. Where many equally good candidate semantic values are available, vagueness arises. Borderline status is variation in truth-value under different assignments of these candidate values to the relevant expression(s).[56] So although **Relativization** generates

---

[55] Analogously, no set theoretically representable relation mediates the set-member connection, on pain of inconsistency. (Lewis, 2002, p. 8)
[56] See also note 43.

a mismatch between the surface form of ordinary predications and the facts they report, that mismatch also explains vagueness in ascriptions of inherited properties.

Note finally that **Relativization** can be motivated from within my proposal, or at least accords with its general spirit. On my proposal, the coarse-grainedness of Tibbles' characteristic changes causes his path to branch through many near-coincident regions whenever **PM** arises. What happens within Tibbles' path determines his history. So if Tibbles' path branches, as my proposal says, so should his history. In particular, that aspect of his history concerning his inherited properties whose possession is determined wholly by the particles within a branch of Tibbles' path, should branch. **Relativization** provides one way of implementing this, by relativizing Tibbles' possession of inherited properties at a time to the particles then in a branch of his path. **Relativization** thus provides a natural partner for my proposal.

5.5. Ghostly objects

Ordinary objects are material objects; they are spatiotemporally located, causally efficacious, massive, and made out of matter. This last clause creates tension with my proposal. Not all paths are occupied by objects. Indeed, many paths never pass through any region with material content. A natural view is that, as a matter of metaphysical necessity, such paths are unoccupied: ordinary objects must be constituted by particles whenever they exist. The tension arises because the explanatory primacy of paths over constitution makes it unclear how I can ensure that paths without material content are not occupied by objects, other than by brute stipulation. Say that a kind of object is *ghostly* if members of that kind can sometimes (or always) be constituted by no particles. The objection is that I cannot explain the impossibility of ghostly kinds, other than via the unedifying method of brute stipulation. Two responses are available.

The first response accepts that my proposal cannot rule out ghostly kinds, but takes this as a virtue rather than a vice. Belief in *K*s should go with the utility of *K*s in systematizing external reality.[57]

---

[57] See §5.3.

Ghostly kinds may in principle play a useful, or even essential, role in this theoretical project. For example, admitting an appropriate ghostly kind of object may allow us to systematize a particular variety of disturbance in a field, even if those disturbances occur only in regions devoid of particles. If this turns out to be the case, then we should believe in that ghostly kind. Since this cannot be ruled out a priori, it is a virtue of my proposal that it can allow for ghostly kinds.

The second response is less concessive; it seeks to show that my proposal can disbar ghostly kinds. Although I have been using the cross-time relation R_K on regions to codify the characteristic changes of Ks, this may not be the most ontologically perspicuous representation of characteristic changes. An alternative approach uses a cross-time relation S_K on collections of particles to codify the characteristic changes of Ks: S_K holds from particles xx at time t to particles yy at time t'. This approach treats the characteristic changes of Ks as primarily changes in their constituent particles. Let $r_{xx,t}$ be the region occupied by xx at t. Then S_K can be used to analyse R_K thus:

For any regions r, r' and times t, t': $R_K(r, t, r', t')$ iff, for some xx, yy: (i) $r = r_{xx,t}$, (ii) $r' = r_{yy,t'}$, and (iii) $S_K(xx, t, yy, t')$.

The K-paths are delineated by R_K, f_K and (K=) as before. This modified approach to characteristic changes implies that, for any kind K, K-paths only ever pass through regions occupied by particles. Together with **Path-Con**—the principle relating paths to constitution proposed in §4.3—this rules out ghostly kinds. The present objection therefore fails.

This strategy can be extended to respond to another style of objection, which draws on one that Theodore Sider and Dean Zimmerman have raised against Lynne Rudder-Baker.[58] I shall consider a version of Sider's objection. Let r be a red object constituted by red particles pp; let b be a blue object constituted by blue particles qq. Initially, r and b are separated. Later, pp and qq become intermingled, and maybe even interpenetrate. This intermingling does not destroy r or b, which continue to be constituted by pp and qq respectively. Whilst intermingled, pp and qq have the same

---

[58] (Zimmerman, 2002, pp. 603–6), (Sider, 2002, pp. 46–7), (Baker, 2000).

(collective) locations; so the paths of r and b then pass through just the same region. So **Path-Con** implies that r is then constituted by pp, by qq, and also by the plural union $pp \cup qq$ of all the particles, red and blue alike. But, the objector will claim, r should continue to be constituted by only the red particles pp; for the blue particles qq do not become parts of r, even though r and b spatially coincide.

One could respond by rejecting this last claim. This case is sufficiently unlike ordinary cases of constitution that theory can be allowed to adjudicate. But even granting that claim, **Path-Con** can be modified to avoid implying that qq or $pp \cup qq$ constitute r. The problem is that the right-hand side of **Path-Con** is too permissive. In order for some particles to constitute an object o of kind K, it is not enough that those particles occupy a region through which o's path passes; they must do so for the right reason. The right reason involves the characteristic changes of Ks: o's path should pass through the particle's location *because* those particles stand in S_K, the relation that codifies the characteristic changes of Ks. Since r, b belong to different kinds, their characteristic changes are codified by different relations S_r, S_b.[59] That pp and qq have the same (collective) locations does not imply that they possess exactly the same properties or stand in exactly the same relations. So intermingling pp with qq does not imply that qq or $pp \cup qq$ bear S_r to anything. So this modification of **Path-Con** does not imply that r is constituted by qq, or that it is constituted by $pp \cup qq$. So this version of Sider's objection does not undermine my proposal.[60]

6. MEREOLOGY

Two kinds of relation should feature in an account of the relations between objects and particles. One is a relation with two singular argument positions, one for particles and one for objects. This is the relation that Tibbles bears to this particle in his tail, to that particle in his heart, to this other particle in his skin, and so on. The

---

[59] If r, b belong to the same kind, then why deny that they are both constituted by $pp \cup qq$?

[60] A related worry concerns, e.g. neutrinos that pass through Tibbles' body without partially constituting him. This apparently commonplace occurrence is incompatible with the original version of **Path-Con**, but not with the modified version just described.

other relation has one plural argument position for a collection of particles and one singular argument position for an object. This is the relation between Tibbles and any collection of particles from which he is made. This section examines the relationship between these relations.

In §2, I took a plural-singular relation of constitution as basic and defined a singular-singular relation of partial constitution from it thus:

> x partially constitutes $y =_{df} x$ is one of some things that constitute y.

The goal was to enable us to focus on plural-singular constitution in as theoretically neutral a setting as possible. However, I also said that we shouldn't preclude the possibility of analysing this plural-singular relation via a singular-singular relation later. Standard presentations of mereology adopt that kind of approach.[61] Those presentations use a primitive singular-singular relation of parthood to define a plural-singular relation of fusion thus:

- x overlaps $y =_{df}$ something is part of both x and y.
- The xs are fused by $y =_{df}$ (i) each of the xs is part of y, and (ii) every part of y overlaps at least one of the xs.

Three kinds of view about the interaction between these two pairs of relations are possible. The first takes parthood as primitive, using it to analyse constitution and partial constitution. The second takes constitution as primitive, using it to analyse parthood and fusion. The third takes both parthood and constitution as primitive. My proposal requires the second approach.

6.1. Parthood as primitive

This section argues that my solution to **PM** is incompatible with the first approach, on which constitution is analysed as fusion. The incompatibility arises from this consequence of that approach:

> **Necessity of Fusion for Constitution (NFC)** For any particles xx and object o: if xx constitute o, then o fuses xx.

---

[61] The canonical discussion of mereology is Simons (1987).

Suppose my solution to **PM** is correct, so that (i) the T^+s constitute Tibbles, and (ii) the T^-s constitute Tibbles. By (i) and **NFC**: Tibbles fuses the T^+s. So by the definition of fusion: each of the T^+s is part of Tibbles. Since the T^+s include the particles that constitute Tibbles' borderline hair h, we have: (iii) the particles that constitute h are all parts of Tibbles. But by (ii) and **NFC**: Tibbles fuses the T^-s. So by the definition of fusion: each part of Tibbles overlaps at least one of the T^-s. Since none of the T^-s overlaps any of the particles that constitute h: none of the particles that constitute h is part of Tibbles. But that's inconsistent with (iii). So my solution to **PM** is incompatible with **NFC** and hence also with any mereological analysis of constitution that implies it.

The argument for the incompatibility between my proposal and **NFC** requires very little mereological structure. It does not require that fusion is unique or unrestricted, or even that parthood is transitive. And although parthood was not modally or temporally relativized in the argument, a variant could be run with those relativizations in place. My proposal's incompatibility with **NFC** is therefore independent of any particular theory of mereology; it arises from the mereological relations amongst the candidates to constitute Tibbles together with the formal structure of fusion itself.

What this shows is that the definition of fusion incorporates significant structure: approaching the object-particle relationship from a mereological perspective, with singular-singular parthood as sole primitive particle-object relation and hence fusion as sole plural-singular such relation, brings substantive commitments.[62] **MC** is not amongst the possibilities open to one who takes that approach. Standard mereology therefore does not provide a theoretically neutral setting for systematizing the relationships between reality's various organizational levels. §3 claimed that a metaphysical myopia afflicting much contemporary thought about objects and constitution is responsible for **MC**'s near-absence from the literature on **PM**. This myopia can now be diagnosed: (tacit) adherence to the order of analytic priority between the singular-singular and plural-singular exemplified by standard mereology. With that order of priority in place, **MC** is a non-starter.

---

[62] Fusion is not the only plural-singular relation definable within mereology. But it is, as far as I can see, the only plausible such relation with which to analyse constitution.

I envisage two kinds of response to these claims. The first modifies the definition of fusion to restore compatibility with **NFC**. This requires a relation R with the following features: (i) R is a plural-singular relation definable from parthood and logical vocabulary; (ii) interpreting 'fusion' as R makes **NFC** compatible with my proposal. Many relations have these features, though none is what 'fusion' normally means. This reinterpretation of **NFC** therefore does no better at making it compatible with my proposal than reinterpreting 'not' as synonymous with 'necessarily' makes 3 both odd and not odd. Moreover, it is unclear how the definition of fusion might be modified in accordance with (i) and (ii) whilst retaining a claim to capture anything like our ordinary notion of being made out of.

The second response denies that the incompatibility between my proposal and **NFC** is independent of mereological setting. In response to **PM**, Hud Hudson has suggested relativizing parthood to regions.[63] The definition of fusion is then modified accordingly:

- x overlaps y at $r =_{df}$ something is part of both x and y at r.
- The xs are fused by y at $r =_{df}$ (i) each of the xs is part of y at r, and (ii) every part of y at r overlaps at least one of the xs at r.

On Hudson's view, Tibbles fuses the T^+s at r^+ and the T^-s at r^-. Given the following account of constitution it follows that Tibbles is constituted by both the T^+s and the T^-s, as my proposal claims:

For any particles xx and object o: xx constitute o iff o fuses xx at some region.

So Hudson's relativization of parthood to regions allows for an analysis of constitution via fusion that's compatible with my solution to **PM**. Moreover, **NFC** comes out true on this approach.

This line of argument is broadly correct. Hudson's relativization of parthood to regions permits a mereological analysis of constitution that's compatible with my proposal. Indeed, Hudson's solution to **PM** proposal has much in common with my own. Both can be seen as implementations of the same basic idea: the same cat is made out of each candidate collection of particles. Hudson's implementation adds an argument position to the fundamental cat-particle relation,

---

[63] (Hudson, 2001, Chs. 1, 2).

in order to preserve the standard mereological analysis of the plural-singular relation using a singular-singular one. This does provide a way to make my proposal compatible with **NFC**. But does this strategy provide a good response to the argument for my proposal's incompatibility with **NFC**? That depends on whether the strategy is well-motivated. And that will be so only if one of the following is true. (a) There is independent reason to defend the standard mereological order of analytic priority. (b) There is independent reason to relativize parthood to regions. I know of no argument for (a) and this is not the place to explore (b). So let us tentatively set Hudson's proposal aside, and accept my proposal's incompatibility with **NFC**, and hence also with mereological analyses of constitution.

6.2. Constitution as primitive

Two kinds of view remain. One treats both parthood and constitution as primitive. Two points tell against this approach. Firstly, fewer primitives are *ceteris paribus* preferable to more; we should take both relations as primitive only if no alternatives remain. Secondly, if parthood and constitution are equifundamental, their extensions should be modally independent, which they surely are not. Although neither point is decisive, they motivate exploring the alternative.

The remaining view takes plural-singular constitution as sole primitive object-particle relation.[64] Singular-singular parthood is analysed thus:

> For any particle x and object o: x is part of o iff x is amongst some zs that constitute o.

On this view, parthood is partial constitution. It follows that Tibbles fuses the plural union of the collections of particles that constitute him.[65] So Tibbles fuses the T^+s and no other particles. The fact that Tibbles is multiply constituted thus combines with this analysis of parthood to uniquely privilege the T^+s in respect of Tibbles' fusing them.

---

[64] (Fine, 2010) defends this kind of view, though he doesn't consider multiple constitution.

[65] For any x: x is amongst the plural union of the collections that ϕ iff x is amongst some yy that ϕ.

This resolves an alternative version of **PM**. Rather than asking which particles constitute Tibbles, we could have asked which particles he fuses. A variant problem results from replacing constitution with fusion in **Equality, Abundance, Solitude,** and **UC**. The solution is that this variant on **Abundance** is false: there aren't many equally good candidates to be fused by a cat because my solution to the original, constitutional version of **PM** combines with my analysis of parthood to uniquely privilege the T^+s. However, a problem now arises: why not employ a similar response to the constitutional version of **PM**? Why not claim that Tibbles is constituted only by the union of all the candidate collections?

The answer is that fusion is a defined technical notion, whereas constitution is not. Both are plural-singular relations between particles and objects. But fusion is defined using singular-singular parthood. Constitution, however, is just the ordinary notion of being made out of; it cannot be assumed without argument that it, like fusion, is definable from any singular-singular relation. The motivation for **Abundance** is that many collections of particles are so similar that they seem to be equally good candidates for having a cat made out of them. This motivation must either be accommodated or explained away. One way to accommodate it is by having many equally good candidates to be fused by a cat. But this is not the only way. My proposal accommodates the motivation for **Abundance** by having two plural-singular relations—primitive constitution and derivative fusion—and many equally good candidates to be constituted by a cat. On this view, simply to claim that only the union of these candidates constitutes a cat is to reject the motivation for **Abundance** without explaining it away. Since fusion is not used to accommodate that motivation, we can reject the fusion-variant of **Abundance** without incurring a commitment to explain anything away. Since my analysis of parthood and solution to the constitutional version of **PM** imply that the fusion-variant of **Abundance** is false, we have good theoretical reasons to reject that principle.

On this view, fusion comes apart from being made out of in at least two ways:

- Objects can fuse particles from which they are not constituted. Suppose particles xx and yy are the candidates to constitute an object o. Then on my proposal, xx and yy both constitute o. But nothing guarantees that their plural union $xx \cup yy$ are also candidates to constitute o. So nothing guarantees that $xx \cup yy$ constitute o. Given my account of parthood, however, o does fuse $xx \cup yy$; for they include exactly the particles that partially constitute o.

- Objects can be constituted by particles they do not fuse. Tibbles, for example, is constituted by but does not fuse the T^-s.

The lesson is that a description of the object-particle relationship in terms of fusion alone omits important structure. The primary plural-singular relation of constitution is connected to fusion by a definitional chain that goes via singular-singular partial constitution/parthood. Information is lost by proceeding along the chain. As a result, we cannot capture using only fusion the sense in which the T^+s and the T^-s are evenly matched in their relationship to Tibbles. Capturing that fact requires the structure of multiple constitution that focusing on fusion omits.

7. CONCLUSION

The presentation and defence of my proposal are now complete. **PM** is resolved by allowing ordinary objects to be multiply constituted by many different collections of particles at a time (§3). Because this solution follows from my conception of objects (§4), the result is a unified theoretical package. The package departs from more orthodox conceptions of objects in at least two ways. Firstly, objects are not fundamentally complexes of particles, but things that survive through certain sorts of change. Secondly, the fundamental relation between particles and objects is not parthood, but a plural-singular constitution relation in terms of which parthood and fusion are analysed. Even if these proposals are ultimately unsuccessful, however, I hope to have shown that the prospects for an ontology that de-emphasizes constitution and mereology are better than one might otherwise have thought.

University of Birmingham

REFERENCES

Baker, L. R. (2000). *Persons and Bodies: A Constitution View*. Cambridge: Cambridge University Press.

Bennett, K. (2004). "Spatio-temporal coincidence and the grounding problem." *Philosophical Studies*, 118: 339–71.
Boolos, G. (1971). "The iterative conception of set." *The Journal of Philosophy*, 68: 215–32. Reprinted in (Boolos, 1998, pp. 12–39).
Boolos, G. (1984). "To be is to be the value of a variable (or some values of some variables)." *The Journal of Philosophy*, 81(3): 430–49. Reprinted in (Boolos, 1998, pp. 54–72).
Boolos, G. (1998). *Logic, Logic, and Logic*. Cambridge, MA: Harvard University Press.
Bynoe, W., and N. Jones (2012). "Solitude without souls: Why Peter Unger hasn't established substance dualism." *Philosophia*.
Devitt, M. (2011). "Methodology and the nature of knowing how." *Journal of Philosophy*, 108: 205–18.
Fine, K. (1994). "Essence and modality." *Philosophical Perspectives*, 8: 1–16.
Fine, K. (1995). "Ontological dependence." *Proceedings of the Aristotelian Society*, 95: 269–90.
Fine, K. (2000). "A counter-example to Locke's Thesis." *The Monist*, 83: 357–61.
Fine, K. (2003). "The non-identity of a material thing and its matter." *Mind*, 112: 195–234.
Fine, K. (2010). "Towards a theory of part." *Journal of Philosophy*, 107: 559–89.
Graff-Fara, D. (2003). "Gap principles, penumbral consequence, and infinitely higher-order vagueness." In Beall, J. C., editor, *Liars and Heaps: New Essays on Paradox*, Chapter 9. Oxford: Oxford University Press.
Hawthorne, J. (2006a). "Epistemicism and semantic plasticity." *Oxford Studies in Metaphysics*, 2: 289–324. Reprinted in (Hawthorne, 2006b, Ch. 9).
Hawthorne, J. (2006b). *Metaphysical Essays*. Oxford: Clarendon Press.
Hirsch, E. (1982). *The Concept of Identity*. Oxford: Oxford University Press.
Hudson, H. (2001). *A Materialist Metaphysics of the Human Person*. Ithaca, NY: Cornell University Press.
Johnston, M. (1992). "Constitution is not identity." *Mind*, 101: 89–105. Reprinted in (Rea, 1997, pp. 44–62).
Koethe, J. (2002). "Stanley and Williamson on knowing how," *Journal of Philosophy*, 99: 325–8.
Lewis, D. (1983). "New work for a theory of universals." *The Australasian Journal of Philosophy*, 61(4): 343–77. Reprinted in (Lewis, 1999, pp. 8–55).
Lewis, D. (1993). "Many, but almost one." In Bacon, J., Campbell, K., and Reinhardt, L., editors, *Ontology, Causality and Mind: Essays on the Philosophy of D. M. Armstrong*, pp. 23–37. Cambridge: Cambridge University Press. Reprinted in (Lewis, 1999, Ch. 9).

Lewis, D. (1999). *Papers in Metaphysics and Epistemology.* Cambridge: Cambridge University Press.
Lewis, D. (2002). "Tensing the copula." *Mind,* 111(441): 1–13.
Linnebo, Ø. (2010). "Plural Quantification." In Zalta, E. N., editor, *The Stanford Encyclopedia of Philosophy,* Winter 2010 edition. <http://plato.stanford.edu/entries/plural-quant/>.
Lowe, E. J. (1995). "The problem of the many and the vagueness of constitution." *Analysis,* 55(3): 179–82.
Markosian, N. (1998). "Brutal composition." *Philsophical Studies,* 92: 211–49.
McGee, V. and McLaughlin, B. (2000). "The lessons of the many." *Philosophical Topics,* 28: 129–51.
Quine, W. V. O. (1981a). *Theories and Things.* Cambridge, MA: Harvard University Press.
Quine, W. V. O. (1981b). "What price bivalence?" *Journal of Philosophy.* Reprinted with additions in Quine (1981a, Ch. 3).
Rea, M. C., editor (1997). *Material Constitution: A Reader.* Lanham, Boulder, New York, Oxford: Rowman & Lanham Publishers.
Rumfitt, I. (2003). "Savoir faire." *Journal of Philosophy,* 100: 158–66.
Sattig, T. (2010). "Many as one." In Zimmerman, D. W., editor, *Oxford Studies in Metaphysics: Volume 5,* Ch. 8. Oxford and New York: Oxford University Press.
Sider, T. (2001). *Four-Dimensionalism: An Ontology of Persistence and Time.* Oxford: Oxford University Press.
Sider, T. (2002). "Review of *Persons and Bodies: A Constitution View* by Lynne Rudder Baker." *The Journal of Philosophy,* 99: 45–8.
Simons, P. (1987). *Parts: A Study in Ontology.* Oxford: Oxford University Press.
Simons, P. (2000). "Continuants and occurrents." *Proceedings of the Aristotelian Society: Supplementary Volume,* 74: 59–75.
Simons, P. (2008). "The thread of persistence." In Kanzian, C., editor, *Persistence,* pp. 165–84. Ontos Verlag.
Stalnaker, R. (2012). *Mere Possibilities: Metaphysical Foundations of Modal Semantics.* Princeton, NJ: Princeton University Press.
Stanley, J., and Williamson, T. (2001). "Knowing how." *Journal of Philosophy,* 98: 411–44.
Unger, P. K. (1980). "The problem of the many." *Midwest Studies in Philosophy,* 5(V): 411–67. Reprinted in (Unger, 2006b, pp. 113–83).
Unger, P. K. (2006a). *All the Power in the World.* Oxford: Oxford University Press.
Unger, P. K. (2006b). *Philosophical Papers: Volume 2.* Oxford: Oxford University Press.

van Inwagen, P. (1990). *Material Beings*. Ithaca, NY and London: Cornell University Press.

Weatherson, B. (2009). "The problem of the many." In Zalta, E. N., editor, *The Stanford Encyclopedia of Philosophy*, Winter 2009 edition. <http://plato.stanford.edu/entries/problem-of-many/>.

Wiggins, D. (1968). "On being in the same place at the same time." *The Philosophical Review*, 77: 90–5. Reprinted in (Rea, 1997, Ch. 1).

Wiggins, D. (2001). *Sameness and Substance Renewed*. Cambridge: Cambridge University Press.

Williamson, T. (1990). *Identity and Discrimination*. Oxford: Basil Blackwell.

Williamson, T. (1994). *Vagueness*. London: Routledge.

Wright, C. (1983). *Frege's Conception of Numbers as Objects*. Aberdeen: Aberdeen University Press.

Wright, C. (2010). "The illusion of higher-order vagueness." In Dietz, R. and Moruzzi, S., editors, *Cuts and Clouds: Vagueness, its Nature and Logic*, Chapter 30. Oxford: Oxford University Press.

Zimmerman, D. (2002). "*Persons and Bodies*: Constitution without mereology?" *Philosophy and Phenomenological Research*, 64: 599–606.

10. Half-hearted Humeanism

Aaron Segal

> The Many, if once irrevocably defined as real, and as essentially independent, can never again be linked by external ties. They indeed thenceforth remain strangers.
>
> Josiah Royce, *The World and the Individual*

1. INTRODUCTION

There are many concrete things, or so I shall suppose: substances such as teacups, mountains, and dogs; events such as wars, birthday parties, and elections; and maybe other sorts as well. Now here's a vague but suggestive question: what is holding all the concrete things together? What makes them "line up" the way they do? One answer to this question is, "Nothing at all. There's nothing whatsoever holding the pieces together. It's just one thing and then another." A fair number of contemporary metaphysicians accept something like this answer. They subscribe to a package of theses—four, by my count—that are Humean in spirit. What's common to all the theses is that they are elaborations of Hume's claim that the contents of the world "are entirely loose and separate". What's distinctive about each thesis is the *way* in which the world's contents are said to be loose and separate.

The first, core, thesis is simply about the way things could have been, period. "There is no object, which implies the existence of any other if we consider these objects in themselves," says Hume.[1] More generally, no object places any constraint on the way anything *else* is. This gives us a patchwork principle for possibilities: for any number of things, any ways each could be intrinsically, and any spatiotemporal arrangement, there is no impossibility in their each being those ways, in that very arrangement.

---

[1] Hume (1978), 86.

Academic Books Marketing Department

Review Copy

OXFORD UNIVERSITY PRESS

With compliments

Title: Oxford Studies in Metaphysics, Volume 9
Author: Edited by Karen Bennett and Dean W. Zimmerman
Pub Date: March 2015
ISBN: 978-0-19-872925-9
Price: £22.00
Binding: Paperback
Website: http://www.oup.com/uk

Also available in Hardback | 978-0-19-872924-2 | £60.00

tel +44(0)1865 353250
fax +44(0)1865 353741
email reviewrequests.uk@oup.com
post Academic Marketing, Oxford University Press, Great Clarendon Street, Oxford OX2 6DP

The publisher requests that any review to: reviewrequests.uk@oup.com review.
Review copy enclosed. Please return a copy of the review to the Academic Marketing Department.
For further information about the book or its author please contact the Academic Marketing Department.

For example, I'm sitting here at my desk. But, claims the Humean, I, or at least some duplicate of me, could have been sitting here deskless and all alone, or at a desk of a different color or shape. There's nothing about me—other than my relational properties, like *being in front of a desk*—that absolutely guarantees that there be a desk here, or that the desk, if such there be, be a certain way. Or take two events, like my striking a match, followed by the match lighting. The Humean says that such a striking could have been followed by no lighting at all (even with the oxygen in the room as it actually was, etc.) or by a conflagration that consumed my house. Nothing with the force of logic makes them line up the way they do.

Of course, holding fixed the laws of nature as they are, some of those situations won't be possible. Presumably, given the laws of nature that are actually true—and the presence of oxygen in much the same quantity and distribution as was actually the case—my match striking had to cause a match lighting, in more or less the way it did. After noting this, we might be tempted to think that there are in fact *robust* causal or nomic connections "holding things together," even if there are no *absolutely* necessary connections. Indeed, causation and laws of nature are each alleged by some philosophers to genuinely hold the world's pieces together—at least those pieces that are events—much in the manner of glue. Enter the second Humean thesis, which denies that laws are glue-like, and the third Humean thesis, which denies that causation is glue-like.

The idea behind the glue imagery is this. To say that some law L is like glue is to say that for any sequence of events that instantiates L, it's *intrinsic* to that sequence *that* L is a law.[2] Consider the match striking and match lighting. There's probably no law that directly relates match strikings to match lightings, but pretend for the moment there is a law such as this: any match striking is followed by a match lighting. Call this law 'STRIKELIGHT'. Then my match striking and match lighting are related in the following way: they are such that STRIKELIGHT is a law. Of course, every other pair of things is also such that STRIKELIGHT is a law. But to say that STRIKELIGHT is like

---

[2] I am assuming that laws can have *instances*, and such instances are sequences of events. The idea is fairly intuitive, and I will not spend any time trying to make it more precise since my focus will be on the view that laws are *not* intrinsic to *any* events whatsoever.

glue implies that the pair, {my match striking, match lighting}, has the property, *being such that* STRIKELIGHT *is a law*, not in virtue of my match striking or match lighting's relations (or lack thereof) to anything *else*, but solely in virtue of what those two events are like and the intrinsic relations they bear to one another. God can *inspect just those events* and "see" that STRIKELIGHT is a law. Or so goes the 'nomic glue' idea.

Similarly, to say that causation is like glue is to say that causation is an intrinsic relation; it is intrinsic to any pair of events that instantiates it. Take the match striking and lighting again. The striking caused the lighting. *That* the striking caused the lighting is not true in virtue of their relations (or lack thereof) to anything *else*, but solely in virtue of what those two events are like and the intrinsic relations they bear to one another. God can *inspect just those events* and "see" that the one caused the other. Or so goes the 'causal glue' idea.

One can see that Hume himself denied both of these ideas. On Hume's view, every law is just a universal generalization. But whether a certain non-trivial universal generalization is a law, and hence true, depends on what's going on *with everything there is* and on that's being *all* that's going on. So its being a law can hardly be intrinsic to a sequence of events. And the same holds, *mutatis mutandis*, for causation, since (according to at least one of Hume's accounts) to say that a certain event caused another *just is to say*, at least in part, that a certain non-trivial universal generalization is a lawful truth. And even on contemporary Hume-inspired views of laws and causation, which differ in important ways from Hume's own views, the denial of intrinsicness is preserved.[3] Thus the second and third Humean theses.

Finally, adds the fourth thesis, there is no causal or nomic *straitjacket* to which the particular matters of fact must *conform*. Quite the opposite. The non-causal non-nomic truths wholly determine the causal and nomic truths, in at least this sense: the distribution of all properties and relations, causal and nomic ones included, globally supervenes on the distribution of non-causal, non-nomic properties and relations. So once God settles all the non-causal non-nomic questions, there's nothing more to settle.

---

[3] For qualifications of this claim, see §2.3.

These four theses constitute a tidy package. David Lewis (1986a, 1986b) was its foremost defender in recent years; others have followed suit in adopting it wholesale.[4] Indeed, there is a fairly natural chain of reasoning from the first, core, thesis, to the others. It goes like this[5]: if the first thesis is true, then there can't be any absolutely necessary connections between cause and effect or between whatever things are "connected" by a law of nature; that is, *causation* and *lawhood* can't be analyzed as a species of *entailment*. But then how are they to be reductively analyzed? At this point the philosopher thinks long and hard and sees no *local* facts in terms of which such analyses can be given; and as a matter of fact, it doesn't seem like widening her lens to encompass anything less than the whole of the concrete world is adequate to provide the materials for a reductive analysis of those concepts. But once she *does* widen her lens to that extent, the materials for a plausible analysis emerge: certain patterns in the particular matters of fact—perhaps the most simple and powerful ones—can serve as the laws, and then *causation* can be analyzed in terms of *lawhood*. And so it is that causation and laws are extrinsic; and since they are being *analyzed* in terms of the non-causal and non-nomic features of the world, they of course globally supervene on those features as well.

Despite how intuitive this chain of reasoning sounds, it contains several weak links; perhaps most importantly, it assumes without argument that *causation* and *lawhood* can be reductively analyzed in non-causal and non-nomic terms.[6] One could resist the whole chain of reasoning by simply denying that *there is* any reductive analysis

---

[4] See Hawthorne (2006a), pp. 126–7, for a summary of the Lewisian package; the package discussed by Hawthorne includes several more theses than I will consider here.

[5] Assuming Hume himself accepted something like the whole package—and there has been a recent flurry of scholarly activity surrounding the question of whether Hume in fact endorsed the third thesis (no causal glue) or anything like it (see Strawson (1989, 2002) and Broackes (1993))—his reasoning seems to at least have incorporated what follows in the text.

[6] Here is another place to balk: the version of the first thesis with which I will be working (see §2.2) is consistent with *causation* being a species of *entailment*, since the thesis requires only the possibility of an *intrinsic duplicate* of the cause not followed by an intrinsic duplicate of the effect; but it could very well be impossible—at least as far as the first thesis is concerned—for the cause itself (i.e. the event which is the cause) not to be followed by the effect (i.e. the event which is the effect).

of one, or both, of those concepts.[7] One who resists at that point would appear to be free to accept only some parts of the package. So, one might reasonably think, for instance, that there are no *absolutely necessary* connections between distinct things (no 'superglue' we might say), but that there are nevertheless weaker connections, causal or nomic, that are intrinsic to the event pairs whose members are so related. And, even if one goes along with the Humean in denying such *intrinsic* connections, one could still reasonably hold that causal and nomic facts are *further* facts that don't supervene on the non-causal non-nomic facts, and which perhaps constrain the way the non-causal non-nomic facts turn out.

Indeed, some philosophers have endorsed the first thesis, but rejected the others. David Armstrong is a good example. While he has been a prominent defender of the first (no 'superglue') Humean thesis (1989, 1997), here is what he has to say about the second and third (no 'glue') theses:

I now indicate briefly a consequence of combining the identification of singular causes with instantiations of a law (or laws) with my view, argued at length elsewhere, that laws are relations of universals...

Hence singular causation will be a completely intrinsic relation. The causal structure of a process will be determined solely by the intrinsic character of that process. This result was unsought, but I think it is a welcome consequence of my theory of laws. By contrast, any Hume-inspired theory of laws makes the lawlike nature of an instantiation of the law an extrinsic property of the instantiation. (2004)[8]

And, in much of his work (1985, 1989, 1997), he has denied the fourth, global supervenience thesis.[9] My impression is that he is far from being alone in his choosiness. The core Humean thesis commands a much more widespread allegiance among contemporary philosophers than the other Humean theses.[10]

---

[7] See Carroll (1994) and Maudlin (2007, Ch. 1) for a defense of primitivism about laws; Armstrong's (1985) view about laws is not, strictly speaking, primitivist, but his analysis of lawhood is in terms of the notion of *nomic necessitation*, which is surely a nomic concept. And see Tooley (1988) and Menzies (1999) for a defense of anti-reductionism about causation.

[8] See also Tooley (1988) and Menzies (1999) about causation.

[9] See also Tooley (1977) and Carroll (1994).

[10] Although heterodoxy about the core Humean claim has seen a recent upsurge, coming from the ranks of so-called "new essentialists"; see, e.g. Bird (2007, §8.1.1.1), Molnar (2007, §11.3), and Wilson (2010a, 2010b).

Let's call any position which, like Armstrong's, accepts the first thesis but denies at least one of the others, a 'Half-Hearted Humean' position. I will argue that, contrary to appearances, any Half-Hearted Humean position is inconsistent. The only viable options are Wholehearted Humeanism and a denial of the core Humean thesis. The arguments will follow shortly, but first I have to state the theses more precisely.

2. PRELIMINARIES

2.1. Intrinsicness

In expressing the first three theses, I have made use of notions such as *being intrinsic* and *being intrinsic to something*, so let me say a bit about what those amount to.

The intuitive idea is this: a property P is intrinsic to x if x has P solely in virtue of the way it is, and not (even partly) in virtue of its relations, or lack thereof, to things other than its parts. Otherwise, it is extrinsic to x. And P is an intrinsic property, *simpliciter*, if it is always intrinsic to anything that has it. Otherwise, it is an extrinsic property.

To fix ideas, I propose to take 'x is an intrinsic duplicate of y' as primitive and define both 'P is intrinsic to x' and 'P is intrinsic' in terms of it:[11]

(D1) '*P is intrinsic to x*' ('*x has P intrinsically*') $=_{df}$ Necessarily, for any z, if z is an intrinsic duplicate of x, then z has P (**all possible intrinsic duplicates of x have P**); otherwise, P is *extrinsic* to x (x has P *extrinsically*)

---

[11] As is probably evident, my proposed definitions are supposed to be adequate even if actualism is true; that is why they are more tortured than Lewis's (1983). The trouble is that they aren't really (thanks to David Johnson for impressing this upon me). For example, my definitions seem to deliver the wrong result that *coexisting with Charlie* is intrinsic to Charlie (since necessarily, something is an intrinsic duplicate of Charlie only if Charlie exists). In order to address this, an actualism-adequate set of definitions must work with a more complicated four-place primitive: 'x in w_1 is an exact replica of y in w_2'. (I omit the required modifications because they make the definitions even more tortured.) I think we understand this primitive well enough, although see Dorr and Hawthorne (2014, n. 27) for some skepticism about its intelligibility.

(D2) *'P is an intrinsic property'* $=_{df}$ Necessarily, for any z, if z has P, P is intrinsic to z (P is necessarily intrinsic to whatever has it) ≡ Necessarily, for any z, if z has P, then necessarily, for any z_1, if z_1 is an intrinsic duplicate of z, then z_1 has P (**no two possible intrinsic duplicates differ with respect to having P**)[12]; otherwise, P is *extrinsic*

The property *being spherical or one mile from a museum* is thus intrinsic to every sphere, since any duplicate of a sphere is also a sphere (let us suppose). But it is not intrinsic, period, since my car parked a mile from a museum is a duplicate of some other car that isn't (and surely isn't spherical).

And it will be helpful for precisely stating and discussing the first Humean thesis to have a way of talking about the *total way* a thing is intrinsically, or what we might call its 'intrinsic nature'. Conveniently, it is a straightforward matter to define 'P is an intrinsic nature of x' and 'P is an intrinsic nature' in terms of 'intrinsic duplicate':

(D3) *'P is an intrinsic nature of x'* $=_{df}$ Necessarily, for any z, z is an intrinsic duplicate of x iff z has P (**all and only possible intrinsic duplicates of x have P**)

(D4) *'P is an intrinsic nature'* $=_{df}$ Possibly there exists an x such that P is an intrinsic nature of x ≡ Possibly there exists an x such that necessarily, for any z, z is an intrinsic duplicate of x iff z has P (**all and only possible intrinsic duplicates of some possibile have P**)[13]

Now, in order to state the Humean theses, we will need to speak not only of monadic properties, but also of relations, such as *causation*, and take up the question whether they are intrinsic, or intrinsic to some things. The intuitive idea is the same as in the case of

---

[12] According to this definition, every impossible property is intrinsic. Henceforth, whenever I say 'intrinsic property' I should be understood to mean *'possible* intrinsic property'.

[13] Some useful facts follow from definitions (D1)–(D4): (1) The negation of an intrinsic property is intrinsic; (2) For any intrinsic nature Q and any intrinsic property P, Q entails P or $\neg P$; and (3) Necessarily for any x and any property Q that is an intrinsic nature of x, Q entails any property that is intrinsic to x. (Facts (1) and (2) follow assuming that *intrinsic duplication* is an equivalence relation.)

monadic properties. Thus, the relation *being an x and y such that x is a foot from y* is intrinsic to me and my briefcase, since it holds solely in virtue of the way the two of us are (or so we can suppose), on the other hand, the relation *being an x and y such that x and y are in the library* is extrinsic to us, since it holds partly in virtue of our relation to the library.[14]

Instead of changing the definitions I have given to accommodate this need, one should simply construe everything I apparently say about relations to be about monadic properties of multi-element sequences.[15] So, for example, contrary to appearances, I will not *really* be speaking about the relation, *being an x and y such that x caused y*, but about the monadic property, *being an x such that x is a sequence whose first element caused its second element*. But I will write as *though* I am referring to relations simply because it is less cumbersome and less distracting.[16] And I will indeed use the word 'relation'; you should just understand that to mean 'property of a multi-element sequence'. Given that I'm not really talking about relations, but about "relation-surrogates," I don't need to change the definitions of *intrinsic* or *intrinsic nature*. My definitions apply equally and without modification to the case of "relations"—and that's the last time I will put that word in scare quotes—since I was talking about them all along.[17]

That completes my brief remarks on *intrinsicness*. But I will add one final note to address a concern that some readers might have. I have not given a terribly informative *analysis* of '*P* is intrinsic (to *x*)' or '*P* is an intrinsic nature (of *x*)', as I have taken '*x* is an

---

[14] See Lewis (1986a).

[15] The reason I prefer this is not to avoid making the requisite change to the definitions, but to avoid speaking of polyadic relations altogether; and the reason I'd like to avoid *that* is that there appear to be deep and intractable problems with polyadic relations that are, as we might say, "permutation-sensitive". See Dorr (2004) and van Inwagen (2006). Those deep problems do not confront monadic properties of multi-element sequences. See van Inwagen (2006).

[16] In general, the locution 'being an $x_1 \ldots x_n$ such that $\ldots x_i \Phi x_j \ldots$' abbreviates 'being an *x* such that *x* is an n-termed sequence whose ... and whose *i*-th element Φ-d its *j*-th element and ...'.

[17] However, this discussion does serve as a reminder that my initial statement of the intuitive gloss on '*P* is intrinsic to *x*' should have taken sets and sequences into account; I should have said 'a property *P* is intrinsic to *x* if *x* has *P* solely in virtue of the way it is, and not (even partly) in virtue of its relations, or lack thereof, to things other than its parts *or parts of its members/elements*'.

intrinsic duplicate of y' as primitive. Indeed, giving a correct and informative analysis of 'intrinsic' is a formidable task, and I am unsure whether any such analysis *exists*.[18] But for the purposes of refuting any Half-Hearted Humean position, thankfully no such analysis is necessary. All that is needed is that (a) 'intrinsic' carries a consistent meaning throughout, and (b) our grasp of my primitive is firm enough so that whenever I make an assumption that involves the concept *intrinsicness*, we can understand it and see that it's true. I make only one such assumption and I will flag it explicitly; I trust it will be clear enough that my assumption is true. Now we can turn to the theses themselves.

2.2. Denial of necessary connections

Let's call the first thesis the 'DENIAL OF ABSOLUTELY NECESSARY CONNECTIONS', or 'DANC' for short. In my first pass at DANC, I offered this as a rough statement: "More generally, for any number of things, any ways each could be intrinsically, and any spatiotemporal arrangement, there is no impossibility in their each being those ways, in that very arrangement." The restriction to ways they could be *intrinsically* is needed for obvious reasons. There's no possible world in which one object has the property *coexisting with a dinosaur* and another object has the property *being such that there never was or ever will be a dinosaur*. The properties that an object has *extrinsically* place constraints on the way the rest of the world can be. The claim of the Humean is that none of those it has *intrinsically* do.

But the initial statement was a bit inaccurate in several respects. On the one hand, it was stronger than intended. To see why, consider a simple example: Bob and his mother Jane. Presumably, one way that Jane could be intrinsically is to have never produced any ova. But if Kripke (1980) is right about the necessity of one's origins, then there is no world in which Jane has never produced any ova and Bob *exists*, let alone be any which way intrinsically. Of course, Kripke might be wrong about the necessity of origins, but it is no

---

[18] For some attempts, see Lewis (1983), Langton and Lewis (1998), Lewis (2001), Weatherson (2001), Sider (1996, 2001). Lewis (1983) and Sider (1996) both analyze 'intrinsic property' in terms of 'intrinsic duplicate,' and then further analyze 'intrinsic duplicate' in terms of 'perfectly natural property'. I am unsure whether their further analysis succeeds.

part of DANC—that is, the thesis I've intended to discuss—to take issue with Kripke here. The intended thesis, applied to the case at hand, is that for each way_1 Bob could be intrinsically and each way_2 Jane could be intrinsically, there is a possible world in which there is $something_1$ that is way_1 together with $something_2$ that is way_2. So even if Bob couldn't co-exist with a Jane-who-produced-no-ova, someone very much like Bob—in fact, an intrinsic duplicate of Bob—could have co-existed with her (Lewis 1986a).

On the other hand, it was weaker than intended, in at least two respects: first, the thesis is not intended to be restricted to things in the actual world. In fact, it's not even supposed to be restricted to things in the *same* world, so merely prefixing the statement with a 'necessarily' operator won't be sufficient. A possibilist like Lewis has little trouble here; he can refer to and quantify over mere possibilia, and so he can just talk about duplicating and recombining *those*. For us actualists, things are a bit more complicated. What we want to say instead is this: if you take any total ways of being intrinsically, such that for each such way, possibly something is that way—here's where intrinsic natures come in handy—then there is no impossibility in *all* those ways being instantiated, and in any arrangement (and as many times for each way as you please).

Second, it is unduly restricted at least if 'thing' is understood, as it often is, to mean 'individual thing'. The thesis is not supposed to be restricted to the ways an *individual thing* can be intrinsically; remember, a *sequence of many things* instantiates an intrinsic nature— one that entails all the relations it instantiates intrinsically—and the thesis should allow for free recombination of those sorts of intrinsic natures.

Taking account of all this, here's a first pass at a more precise statement of the thesis.[19]

> DANC: For any sequence $\{Q_1, \ldots, Q_N\}$ of non-equivalent intrinsic natures, and any sequence of positive cardinals $\{a_1, \ldots, a_N\}$, and any disjoint spatiotemporal arrangement of a_1 instances of $Q_1 \ldots$ and a_N instances of Q_N, which fits those intrinsic natures, there is a possible world in which there are exactly

---

[19] See Darby and Watson (2010) for a very similar formulation.

a_1 instances of Q_1 ... and exactly a_N instances of Q_N in that very arrangement, and no objects other than their parts and any sums of those parts (size and shape of spacetime permitting).

Some of the jargon here could use an explanation. First, what exactly is a spatiotemporal arrangement? In the way I am using that term, it is a function from sequences of objects to sequences of regions—where an individual will be considered a single-element sequence by courtesy—which, intuitively, are the respective spatiotemporal locations of objects in the sequence.[20] And a certain sequence is *in* a certain arrangement iff every element in the sequence exactly occupies the region which that arrangement 'assigns' to it.[21]

Second, what is it for a spatiotemporal arrangement to *fit* certain intrinsic natures? It is easy to see what is meant by considering an example. Supposing that particular sizes, for example, are intrinsic properties, the principle shouldn't guarantee that an instance of an arbitrary intrinsic nature can exactly occupy *any which* spatiotemporal region: only those which are the same size as that entailed by the intrinsic nature. Now generalize: a spatiotemporal arrangement "fits intrinsic natures $Q_1 \ldots Q_N$" only if for any spatiotemporal property P that is *intrinsic*, and for any intrinsic natures among $Q_1 \ldots Q_N$ that entail P, it assigns to any instance of them a sequence of locations that has P.

Finally, what is a *disjoint* spatiotemporal arrangement? It is one that does not include overlapping spatiotemporal regions in two output sequences.

---

[20] I assume throughout that there are spatiotemporal regions; but this assumption could be dispensed with at the expense of some added complexity.

[21] Note well: a possible world in which there are "exactly a_1 instances of Q_1 ... and exactly a_N instances of Q_N *in that very arrangement*" need not be a world in which there are exactly a_1 instances of Q_1 ... and exactly a_N instances of Q_N, *period*. For instance, let Q_1 be the intrinsic nature of this chair and Q_2 be the intrinsic nature of an electron. There is obviously no possible world in which, say, there is exactly one instance of Q_1 and exactly one instance of Q_2; there are many more electrons in this chair than that! But there is some spatiotemporal arrangement of one instance of Q_1 and one instance of Q_2 such that there is a possible world in which there is exactly one instance of Q_1 and exactly one instance of Q_2 in that arrangement. Thus, the difficulties Efird and Stoneham (2008) raise about the use of 'exactly' do not arise, as far as I can tell, for the thesis I've formulated.

The restriction to disjoint spatiotemporal arrangements is seemingly needed for the following reason (the reason is of course more general, but I will illustrate it with an instance): there's probably no possible world in which a concrete object is red through-and-through and spatiotemporally overlaps a concrete object that is green through-and-through, because they can't mereologically overlap one another (there would have to be an entity that is both green through-and-through and red through-and-through), and it is probably not possible for two such concrete objects with no mereological overlap to spatiotemporally overlap. Since we don't want the principle to guarantee *that* possibility, it appears necessary to restrict the principle to disjoint arrangements.

But, as it turns out, restricting the principle in this way makes it too weak. For example, suppose I am identical to a human organism, *being conscious* is intrinsic to me, and my right arm is a duplicate of my left arm. Now, presumably the Humean would want to say this: there is a possible world in which there are two duplicates of me, and they spatiotemporally overlap in the region which one duplicate's left arm exactly occupies and the other duplicate's right arm exactly occupies. But that is not guaranteed by the thesis as I put it. Even assuming, as I do, that there are such things as my left arm, my right arm, and me-minus-both-arms, and hence intrinsic natures of each, the principle above still doesn't guarantee the possibility I mentioned. None of *those* body parts are conscious, and so none of them instantiates an intrinsic nature that entails *being conscious*. But the possibility I have described is one in which there are at least *two* things that are conscious.[22] Of course, we could "write in by hand" the truths about when some objects compose another one; maybe that wouldn't be so bad. But we'd also have to write in the conditions under which an object is conscious, and surely we'd prefer a very general principle over a hodge-podge amalgam of a general principle together with very specific "bridge principles".

---

[22] Nor would it help to point out that I could have lost my right arm, and so possibly, there is something that duplicates me-minus-right-arm *except that it's conscious*. Yes, that thing would have a certain intrinsic nature, and DANC would guarantee that it could be instantiated "next to" a duplicate of me, but that possible scenario is *still* not the one I have envisaged: *my* scenario involves two human beings who are both conscious *and two-armed*.

The solution is to remove the restriction to disjoint spatiotemporal arrangements and address the 'red and green all over problem' less drastically. We can simply put in a manual override, which says that there can be overlap only if the two intrinsic natures "say the same thing" about what's going on in the region of overlap. Here's a way to make the override precise: 'provided that for any objects x and y and region R such that x and y each exactly occupy R, x and y have the same intrinsic nature'.[23]

And we ought to ensure one more thing. Take the example of my two doppelgangers. The Humean will say not only that there is a possible world in which they *spatiotemporally* overlap, but one in which they *mereologically* overlap as well, i.e. they will both have as a part the very same arm. Some Humeans might think, as I suggested above, that *every* case of spatiotemporal overlap will involve mereological overlap. I am inclined to agree. But even if it's not always the case, the Humean will say that nothing *precludes* it.

So how should DANC be reformulated so as to guarantee the possibility of two duplicates of me sharing an arm? The answer is this: *no* reformulation is needed so long as we broaden a 'spatiotemporal arrangement' to include a specification of which of the arranged objects and their parts are identical to which others. (If one thinks that co-location or multi-location is impossible, one should add an additional proviso to that effect; otherwise they'd both be guaranteed.) Thus, one of the spatiotemporal arrangements that is guaranteed possible by DANC is one in which the left arm

---

[23] Two things to note: first, the thesis thus amended will do the trick only if DAUP, or something near enough, is true (see van Inwagen 1981); otherwise, this formulation will count certain obvious impossibilities as possible. If DAUP, and everything near enough, is false, the override will have to be put another way.

Second, the proviso is really short for this: 'provided that *if* those intrinsic natures *were* in that spatiotemporal arrangements, it *would* be the case that for any objects x and y...'; clearly enough, if there is some impossible scenario that this proviso is to rule out, then there need to be false counterpossibles. And some philosophers think there aren't any. Now, as Cian Dorr (2005, §4.1) notes, there are plenty of examples of what seem to be non-trivial true counterpossibles, and by analogy, there are plenty of examples of what seem to be false counterpossibles. If, however, you are not convinced by these examples—perhaps because of your semantics for counterfactuals—then, following Dorr, read the proviso as follows: 'provided that according to the fiction that those intrinsic natures are in that spatiotemporal arrangement, it is the case that for any objects x and y...'; *I assume* you think some according-to-an-impossible-fiction claims are false.

of one duplicate is not only colocated with, but also identical to, the right arm of the other duplicate.[24]

So here's the final version:

DANC: For any sequence $\{Q_1,\ldots,Q_N\}$ of non-equivalent intrinsic natures, and any sequence of positive cardinals $\{a_1,\ldots,a_N\}$, and *any* spatiotemporal arrangement of a_1 instances of $Q_1\ldots$ and a_N instances of Q_N, which fits those intrinsic natures, there is a possible world in which there are exactly a_1 instances of $Q_1\ldots$ and exactly a_N instances of Q_N in that very arrangement and no objects other than their parts and any sums of those parts (provided that (1) for any objects x and y and region R such that x and y each exactly occupy R, x and y have the same intrinsic nature and (2) size and shape of spacetime permits).

2.3. Delocalization of laws

Let's call the second thesis the 'DELOCALIZATION OF LAWS'. It says that no matter how wide a glance we cast, we won't be able to see, just by inspecting the intrinsic properties and relations that are instantiated, what the laws are. In the best case—when we glance at *all* the goings-on throughout spacetime—we would still have to see that there is nothing *else* going on. Put less imagistically, we can say this: necessarily, for any sequence of events E, and any proposition L, any relation which, (a) entails that L is a law and (b) is instantiated by E, is extrinsic to E (and a fortiori to the subsequence that is an instance of L).[25]

Truth be told, there might be some exceptions to the thesis in its full generality, even according to a Wholehearted Humean. Suppose, for example, there is a maximum possible size of spacetime, and consider a possible world W_1 in which spacetime has that size and is "filled to the brim". Suppose further a Humean view of laws, according to which laws are simply patterns in the phenomena. (Lewis's (1994) Best-System Analysis is a good example. On this

---

[24] I am assuming that there *is* such an object as my right arm. As I noted in n. 23, I have already made substantively the same assumption in formulating the manual override.

[25] Where *R entails proposition p* =$_{df}$ Necessarily, for any x, x has R only if p is true.

view a proposition is a law iff it is a theorem of the deductive system that strikes as good a balance as truth will allow between simplicity and strength.) It seems clear that any proposition L which is a law in W_1 is also a law in a world W_2 in which the global sequence of events in W_1 is duplicated; after all, there couldn't be anything else to "overturn" that law in W_2. So in W_1, any relation that for some L entails that L is a law and is instantiated by the global sequence of events, is intrinsic to that sequence.

But this case is, as we might say, "pathological": once you duplicate that sequence with respect to its *non-nomic* properties and relations, you've automatically duplicated it with respect to its *nomic* properties and relations as well. So the reason that sequence is intrinsically such that L is a law is not because law L is like "glue"; it's because the truth (and lawhood) of L happens to track the intrinsic *non*-nomic features of that sequence, no matter the environment in which it is embedded.

This suggests that we can isolate the exceptions to the DELO-CALIZATION OF LAWS in the following way. Say a *nomic property or relation* is one such that for some proposition L, it entails that L is a law. Every other property and relation is non-nomic. Then say that *x is a non-nomic duplicate of y* iff for any intrinsic non-nomic property or relation R, x has R iff y has R.[26] Finally, say that a sequence/relation pair is "nomologically innocent" iff necessarily, any non-nomic duplicate of that sequence instantiates that relation.

Here then is the official statement of the thesis:

DELOCALIZATION OF LAWS: Necessarily, for any sequence of events E and any nomic relation R it instantiates (where the pair $\{E, R\}$ is not nomologically innocent), E has R extrinsically.

2.4. Delocalization of causation

DELOCALIZATION OF CAUSATION, which is what I'll call the third thesis, is a natural counterpart of the DELOCALIZATION OF LAWS.

---

[26] Actually, for a reason I will discuss in §2.5, we need to be slightly more liberal about nomic duplication and restrict the required sharing to *perfectly natural* properties and relations (otherwise, pretty much every pair consisting of a sequence and a nomic relation it instantiates will come out nomologically innocent). So officially, *x is a non-nomic duplicate of y* iff for any intrinsic perfectly natural non-nomic property or relation R, x has R iff y has R.

It says that no matter how wide a glance we cast, we won't be able to see, just by inspecting the intrinsic properties and relations that are instantiated, whether there is any causation going on between the events.

In order to make this precise, let us say a relation

being an $x_1, \ldots, x_n$ such that $\Phi(x_1, \ldots, x_n)$,

is *causal* just in case it entails the relation,

being an $x_1, \ldots, x_n$ such that for some i and j ($1 \leq i, j \leq n$), a part of x_i caused a part of x_j

It's the sort of relation things bear to one another only if there is some causation involving only them and their parts.

Then a first pass at the thesis is this:

DELOCALIZATION OF CAUSATION: Necessarily, for any sequence of events E, and any causal relation CS it instantiates, E has CS extrinsically.

I will make two comments here. First, beware of confusion. In the philosophical literature on causation, one will find a thesis that goes by the name 'INTRINSICNESS'. That thesis is roughly this: any duplicate of a certain causal process (suitably qualified), *in a world with the same laws of nature*, will also be a causal process.[27] But the italicized phrase makes all the difference. One who endorses the DELOCALIZATION OF CAUSATION is not thereby committed to denying INTRINSICNESS, because the latter is consistent with the claim that for every causal process, there is *some* duplicate of it—in a world with different laws—that is not a causal process. Lewis, at least at one time, accepted the DELOCALIZATION OF CAUSATION *and* INTRINSICNESS.[28] This was not a logical blunder.

Second, just as with respect to the DELOCALIZATION OF LAWS, an exception ought to be allowed for, and for pretty much the same reason. Suppose again a Humean view of laws, according to which laws are simply patterns in the phenomena. And suppose further that INTRINSICNESS—the thesis I just mentioned—is true. Then the global sequence of events in the "maximal"

---

[27] See Hall (2004c).
[28] He came to reject INTRINSICNESS in his (2004) on independent grounds

world W_1 I considered above—together with any causal relation it instantiates—is a counterexample to the unrestricted version of DELOCALIZATION OF CAUSATION. After all, any world W_2 in which that sequence is duplicated is one in which all and only the laws of W_1 are true. So then by INTRINSICNESS, all the same causal facts hold of the duplicate. So any causal relation it instantiates is intrinsic to it.

But here again we can easily isolate the exceptions, and in an analogous fashion. Say *x is a non-causal duplicate of y* iff for any intrinsic non-causal relation R, x has R iff y has R.[29] Then say that a sequence/relation pair is "causally innocent" iff necessarily any non-causal duplicate of that sequence instantiates that relation. So the thesis is really this:

DELOCALIZATION OF CAUSATION: Necessarily, for any sequence of events E, and any causal relation CS it instantiates (where the pair $\{E, CS\}$ is not causally innocent), E has CS extrinsically.

2.5. Global supervenience

The second and third theses each give a *necessary* condition for determining whether a certain proposition is a law or that causation is happening between some events (respectively): inspect all the events there are and see *that* those are all the events. Any inspection less extensive than that will be inadequate to make those determinations.

But what, if anything, *is* adequate? The fourth thesis, which I shall call 'GLOBAL SUPERVENIENCE,' adds that it is sufficient to examine the "matters of fact" in order to make those determinations. As I put it earlier, the distribution of causal and nomic properties and relations globally supervenes on the distribution over all concreta of non-causal, non-nomic properties and relations.

This thesis is slightly different from the global supervenience thesis endorsed by Lewis (1986b, 1994). That thesis is that all the

---

[29] Again, as in n. 26, we actually need to be a bit more liberal about causal duplication (otherwise, pretty much every pair consisting of a sequence and a causal relation it instantiates will come out causally innocent). So officially, *x is a non-causal duplicate of y* iff for any intrinsic perfectly natural non-causal relation R, x has R iff y has R.

facts about a world globally supervene on the distribution of local intrinsic qualities and spatiotemporal relations.[30] Lewis intends his claim to be a 'contingent supervenience claim,' by which is meant that there is a restriction on the possible worlds for which the supervenience is alleged to hold. His is not a claim that for *any* two possible worlds, if they are alike with respect to X, they are alike with respect to Y. It's that for any two possible worlds *like ours in some specified respect*, if they are alike with respect to X, they are alike with respect to Y. Not so the thesis I am considering. Mine is an unrestricted quantification over possible worlds. Thus, GLOBAL SUPERVENIENCE is slightly stronger than Lewis's thesis. On the other hand, it is also weaker in that it broadens the subvening set to include all non-causal non-nomic properties and relations, rather than just local intrinsic qualities and spatiotemporal relations.

That being said, GLOBAL SUPERVENIENCE seems to best capture Lewis's central contention. After all, he concedes that physics might teach us that there are irreducible external relations beyond the spatiotemporal ones or emergent intrinsic qualities that aren't local.[31] What he *really* wants to resist, he says, are *philosophical* arguments for the falsity of his supervenience claim. In particular, he wants to resist the claim that certain "commonplace features of the world," such as causation and laws of nature, fail to so supervene. That's where he puts his philosophical foot down. Whatever else physics teaches us, causation and laws of nature won't be irreducible features of any world. And that's just GLOBAL SUPERVENIENCE.

But stating GLOBAL SUPERVENIENCE carefully presents something of a challenge. The difficulty does not lie in spelling out what 'globally supervenes' means. That's been hashed out already a great deal, and I will simply follow others in defining it thus: where A is a set of properties and relations, let an *A-isomorphism* be a function f that is one-to-one and for any property or relation R in A, and any sequence X_1 of objects in f's domain, X_1 instantiates

---

[30] Where a local quality is one that needs nothing bigger than a point at which to be instantiated.
[31] Some philosophers have indeed claimed that quantum-theoretic "nonseparability" teaches us just that. See Maudlin (2007, Ch. 2). Frank Arntzerius (2012, Ch. 2) claims that even classical physics teaches us the same.

R iff the sequence of images (under f) of the elements of X_1 instantiates R.[32]

Then,

'a set A of properties and relations globally supervenes on a set B of properties and relations' $=_{df}$ for any worlds w_1 and w_2, every B-isomorphism from w_1's domain onto w_2's domain is an A-isomorphism. (In our case, there will be a restriction to the *concrete* domain of the two worlds.)[33]

The difficulty, rather, lies in distinguishing between causal and non-causal relations and nomic and non-nomic relations.[34] My discussion of the Delocalization theses suggests a straightforward way to distinguish between them: say (as I have already done) that a *causal relation* is one that is causation-entailing, and otherwise it's non-causal; and a *nomic relation* is one such that for some proposition L, it entails that L is a law; otherwise it's non-nomic. But defining those terms that way and leaving GLOBAL SUPERVENIENCE as is would have the distinct disadvantage of trivializing the thesis. If you take any causation-entailing relation and disjoin it with a relation that is not a causation-entailing relation or law-entailing relation, like *being temporally prior to*, the resulting disjunctive relation is not a causation-entailing relation or a law-entailing relation. But then it is far too easy to see that the causation-entailing relations (and the same with the law-entailing relations) globally supervene on the distribution of relations that are neither causation-entailing nor law-entailing. Here's a simple recipe for cooking up, in any world, just a few non-causation-entailing non-law-entailing relations that will settle all the causal facts: take a maximally specific causation-entailing relation—one that specifies, down to the last detail, all the causation that is happening between events in that world—and disjoin it with some relation, **DECOY**, such that neither it nor

---

[32] Where a sequence X_2 is 'a sequence of images of the elements of X_1' only if it is isomorphic to X_1 with respect to order in the sequence; that is, for any a and b, if a comes before b in X_1, then $f(a)$ comes before $f(b)$ in X_2.

[33] This is equivalent to what Sider (1999) calls 'strong global supervenience'; see his n. 10.

[34] See Earman and Roberts (2005) for a survey of past attempts to address the difficulty—and analogous difficulties with related formulations—along with their own attempt. I address it differently from each of the ways they discuss.

its negation is causation-entailing or law-entailing, and which the events in that world do *not* instantiate. Then the resulting disjunctive relation and the negation of **DECOY** (which the events *do* instantiate) are non-causation-entailing and non-law-entailing relations instantiated by the events in that world, which will jointly settle the causal facts that obtain in the world. And it is fairly easy to see that for any world there will be such instantiated relations that are neither causation-entailing nor law-entailing and which trivially suffice to settle the causal and nomic facts.

But we can accept the suggested definition and skirt the problem, I think, if we stick closer to Lewis's own formulation of the supervenience thesis. Lewis, as is well known, distinguishes between relations which are *perfectly natural* and those which aren't.[35] The ones that are perfectly natural are ones that "carve the beast of nature at its joints." They make for genuine similarity between any two pairs (or sequences more generally) that instantiate them. And his global supervenience thesis is *really* a thesis about the supervenience of all properties and relations on *perfectly natural ones*: perfectly natural local intrinsic qualities and spatiotemporal relations (which are themselves perfectly natural).

So by adopting an analogous modification to GLOBAL SUPERVENIENCE, we can indeed define 'causal relation' and 'nomic relation' as I have suggested. GLOBAL SUPERVENIENCE, then, is the following thesis: the distribution of all properties and relations globally supervenes on the distribution of perfectly natural non-causal non-nomic properties and relations over all concreta. This is a non-trivial thesis; or at least it cannot be shown trivial in virtue of including the "tricky disjunctions" in the supervenience base. Those disjunctions are surely not perfectly natural if there is anything to the natural/non-natural distinction at all.

3. FROM DENIAL TO DELOCALIZATION

3.1. *From denial to delocalization of laws*

Now we are set to begin the arguments. The argument for the entailment from DANC to the DELOCALIZATION OF LAWS will be

[35] See, inter alia, Lewis (1983).

fairly simple: the guiding idea is that if laws are intrinsic, then there are intrinsic natures which entail propositions inconsistent with one another. But then DANC allows us to "patch" together those intrinsic natures, and thus entails that there is a possible world in which a contradiction is true.

Here's a more careful version. Suppose, for reductio, the following claim, a claim which is entailed by the denial of the DELOCALIZA-TION OF LAWS: possibly there is some sequence of events E_1, some proposition L_1, and some relation R which entails that L_1 is a law, such that R is intrinsic to E_1. For example, suppose that in the actual world, the relation, *being such that it is a law that all point masses attract with a force proportional to the product of their masses and inversely proportional to the square of the distance between them*, is intrinsic to some sequence of events.

Now I assume the following: necessarily, for any sequence of events E and proposition L, such that a relation which entails that L is a law is intrinsic to E, possibly there is a sequence of events E_2 and a proposition L_2 which is *inconsistent* with L, such that there is some relation which entails that L_2 is a law and is intrinsic to E_2. My assumption is only *slightly* stronger than the assumption that the laws of nature are contingent. It adds to that a parity assumption about the intrinsicality of conflicting laws: necessarily, if one law is intrinsic to some events, then possibly there is a law inconsistent with the first one which is *also* intrinsic to some events.[36] So long as laws are contingent, that surely seems right. To continue with

---

[36] One might object to this on grounds that have nothing to do with intrinsicality: given an Armstrongian account of laws, if some proposition p is a law, then nothing inconsistent with p could be a *law* (and, a fortiori, nothing inconsistent with p could be such that *its being a law* is intrinsic to some sequence) even if some such thing could be *true* (and hence p is indeed contingent). For laws express "necessitating relations" between universals and univerals are freely recombinable. If N(F,G) is a law, then how could there be a *law* inconsistent with that one unless there is a universal ¬G, or, more generally, some universal incompatible with G?

But this is a problem not so much for my claim as for Armstrong. He has to recognize the actual truth, and a fortiori the possible truth, of "exclusion laws," like Pauli's Exclusion Principle. He has several accounts of such laws (1997: 233), but whatever account he gives, he has to concede there could be such things. And, if there can be a law that universal F nomically excludes universal G, then it will be inconsistent with the possible law that universal F nomically necessitates universal G.

Moreover, he grants that *nomic necessitation* is a determinable with determinates, corresponding to different degrees of probabilifying. So there could be inconsistent possible laws in this way: one law is that univeral F probabilifies universal G with

my example, if the Law of Universal Gravitation really is intrinsic in the way I have supposed, then it ought to be possible that the relation, *being such that it is a law that all point masses attract with a force proportional to the product of their masses and inversely proportional to the **cube** of the distance between them*, is intrinsic to some sequence of events. It would be peculiar, to put it mildly, if only the Law of Universal Gravitation had a special capability of being intrinsic that no possible law inconsistent with it possessed.

Returning to the general point, it follows from my assumption, together with our supposition, that possibly, there is some sequence of events E_1, some proposition L_1, and some relation R which entails that L_1 is a law, such that R is intrinsic to E_1, and possibly there is a sequence of events E_2 and a proposition L_2 which is *inconsistent* with L_1, such that there is some relation which entails that L_2 is a law and is intrinsic to E_2.[37] So there are two propositions, L_1 and L_2, which are inconsistent with one another, and (a) possibly there is some sequence of events, E_1, and some relation R that entails that L_1 is a law is intrinsic to E_1, and (b) possibly there is some sequence of events, E_2, and some relation R that entails that L_2 is a law is intrinsic

---

probability .46, and the other law is that it does so with probability .78. It can't very well be both!

Finally, laws involving magnitudes—whatever account he gives of them—will be ripe for incompatibilities.

[37] Technically, what follows without any special assumptions about iterated modalities is the proposition expressed by this sentence where the second occurence of 'possibly' is understood to occur within the scope of the first occurence. But I further assume that whatever is possibly possible is just plain possible (the axiom characteristic of **S4**, interpreted in the usual way). So we can go on to infer the claim expressed by the sentence that follows in the text. (Alternatively, one can avoid recourse to **S4** if one assumes (a) the validity of the inference of (the de re) "There is a proposition L_1 such that possibly there is some sequence of events E_1 and some relation R which entails that L_1 is a law, such that R is intrinsic to E_1" from (the de dicto) "Possibly there is some sequence of events E_1, some proposition L_1 and some relation R that entails that L_1 is a law, such that R is intrinsic to E_1," together with the following version of the Parity Premise: (b) For any proposition L_1, if possibly there is some sequence of events E_1 and some relation R which entails that L_1 is a law, such that R is intrinsic to E_1, then there is some proposition L_2 which is inconsistent with L_1 such that possibly there is some sequence of events E_2 and some relation R which entails that L_2 is a law, such that R is intrinsic to E_2. One could then infer from our supposition the claim expressed by the sentence that follows in the text without relying on **S4**.)

to E_2. So then there are two intrinsic natures, Q_1 and Q_2, each of which entails that some proposition is a law, and those propositions are inconsistent with one another.[38]

Then assume DANC for conditonal proof. DANC allows us to patch together Q_1 and Q_2 into a single possible world—so long as size and shape permits—and so entails that there is a possible world in which two inconsistent propositions are both laws, and hence both true. And of course there is no such possible world. So by reductio, we can conclude that our initial supposition is false. That is, it's not possible that there is some sequence of events, E_1, some proposition L_1, and some relation R that entails that L_1 is a law, such that R is intrinsic to E_1. But since every relation that is instantiated by something is instantiated by it either intrinsically or extrinsically, it follows that necessarily, for any sequence of events E, and any proposition L, any relation that (a) entails that L is a law, and (b) is instantiated by E, is extrinsic to E. Then by conditional proof, conclude that DANC entails that necessary truth.

The careful reader will note that I have "overshot," since that necessary truth is stronger than the DELOCALIZATION OF LAWS, which allows an exception for nomologically innocent pairs, and is thus too strong even for the Wholehearted Humean. And there's at least one simple reason I overshot: my argument had to assume the satisfaction of the "size and shape permitting" proviso at the final step of the argument, and that *might not* always be satisfied. Whether it is depends of course on the "size and shape" of the two sequences that instantiate intrinsic natures Q_1 and Q_2. To address this, my argument ought to be modified slightly so that it proceeds in two stages: first, restrict our quantification over sequences to *manageable* sequences, where a sequence is manageable, let's say, if two duplicates of it could fit comfortably in a spacetime of maximal size; the conclusion of the first stage is that no nomic relation is ever intrinsic to a *manageable* sequence.[39] Second, generalize. Infer from the conclusion of the first stage that a proposition's being a law is

---

[38] This follows assuming that (1) necessarily, everything has an intrinsic nature, and (2) necessarily for any x and any property Q that is an intrinsic nature of x, Q entails any property that is intrinsic to x. See n. 13.

[39] The argument does require a slightly different version of the 'Parity Premise', but it seems as obviously true as the original version.

a *wholly extrinsic matter*, which is to say this: a difference between two sequences with respect to whether some proposition is a law (or some propositions are laws) doesn't, all by itself, make for an intrinsic difference. Thus, any two sequences that are non-nomic duplicates are intrinsic duplicates, period.[40]

From which we can conclude this: necessarily, for any sequence of events E and any nomic relation R it instantiates (where the pair $\{E, R\}$ is not nomologically innocent), E has R extrinsically.[41] (For necessarily, for any sequence of events E and any nomic relation R it instantiates, if the pair $\{E, R\}$ is not nomologically innocent, then R differs between non-nomic duplicates of E; and hence it differs between intrinsic duplicates of E; and hence it is extrinsic to E.) As should be apparent, the conclusion just is the DELOCALIZATION OF LAWS. By conditional proof, we can conclude that DANC entails the DELOCALIZATION OF LAWS.

3.1.1. Reply

I can see only one remotely plausible reply on the Half-Hearted Humean's behalf: deny that the laws are contingent.[42] This is a high price for anyone to pay. But the pricetag is much higher for the Half-Hearted Humean, at least with regard to non-probabilistic laws. She will be committed to the claim that all the properties that figure into those laws—such as *having a rest mass of XYZ* and *having a charge*

---

[40] I am assuming here that the *perfectly natural* intrinsic non-nomic properties and relations settle *all* the intrinsic non-nomic properties and relations; this assumption is needed because 'non-nomic duplication' is defined in terms of the sharing of perfectly natural properties and relations (see n. 26).

[41] Of course, a Humean—one who accepts DANC—can't be too liberal about what pairs she holds are nomologically innocent, since in many cases my argument immediately establishes that a certain nomic relation is not intrinsic to a certain sequence. Thankfully for the Humean, the case of a maximal-sized spacetime filled to the brim (see. §2.3) is immune to such a direct argument, because the "size and shape" proviso cannot be satisfied, and hence my argument falters at the stage at which it employs DANC.

[42] The Half-Hearted Humean can distinguish between different laws if she wants: some laws, she'll say, are extrinsic and contingent, other laws are intrinsic and necessary. No laws are both contingent and intrinsic. If that's what she says, then simpy restrict the criticism that follows to whichever laws she claims are intrinsic, and hence necessary.

of XYZ—are extrinsic to their bearers. If she assumes otherwise, then since those laws are necessary and non-probabilistic, there would surely be absolutely necessary connections between intrinsic natures.

For example, take the Law of Conservation of Linear Momentum. If that law is necessary, and, moreover, rest mass is intrinsic, then DANC is false. There would be no possible world in which, say, some lonely particle has a certain rest mass at t_1, it follows a trajectory in spacetime such that its velocity remains constant until t_2, but its rest mass is *different* at t_2. And that's a 'violation' of DANC.[43] So the proponent of DANC who concedes that the Law of Conservation of Linear Momentum is necessary would be forced to conclude that *having a rest mass of XYZ* is not intrinsic. That's not a happy thing to say.[44]

And it's not just the properties that figure directly into the laws. Pretty much all properties would have to be extrinsic to their bearers. Any proposition entailed by a necessary truth is necessary. So the proposition that bread always nourishes would be necessary. But then the property *being bread* and the property *being nourished* couldn't be intrinsic properties, since we would then have a violation of DANC: there would be no possible world in which I ingest bread and fail to be nourished. This is clearly an extremely hefty price.

3.2. From denial to delocalization of causation

Turning now to the DELOCALIZATION OF CAUSATION, the guiding idea is a bit different. I will give two arguments for the conclusion that DANC entails the DELOCALIZATION OF CAUSATION: they both rely only on some formal property or properties of causation; and they both exploit the fact that DANC guarantees the possibility of *any* spatiotemporal arrangement (of instances of any intrinsic

---

[43] That it's a violation of DANC follows straightforwardly assuming a perdurantist or stage-theoretic reading of the previous sentence. Assuming an endurantist reading, that it's a violation follows assuming there could be a *non*-lonely particle that met that description; and of course there could be.

[44] Although, see Field (1980) and the defense of a 'Comparativist' view about mass in Dasgupta (2014). For some critiques of Field, see Hawthorne (2006b).

natures), including ones in which the instances overlap (so long as the overlap is between things with the same intrinsic nature).

3.2.1. Argument from Causal Loops: first version

My first argument—or at least the first version of it—relies only on the premise that there cannot be a "causal loop": that is, it is not possible for there to be a sequence of events, such that each event causes the next event in the sequence, and some event appears twice in the sequence. I will argue that the conjunction of DANC and the denial of the DELOCALIZATION OF CAUSATION entails that such things *are* possible. So that conjunction has to go; and so if we keep DANC, we have to accept the DELOCALIZATION OF CAUSATION.

Here's the argument in greater detail. Assume DANC is true. Now, it is surely possible for an event to cause a duplicate of itself. Just think of an idealized case of falling dominoes. Consider such a possible pair of events, (E_1, E_2), and call the intrinsic nature each one instantiates, '**Falling Domino**'. Since E_1 caused E_2, naturally enough the pair instantiates the causal relation,

being an x and y such that x caused y,

otherwise known as *causation*. And now suppose, for reductio, that the pair instantiates *causation* intrinsically. Then (E_1, E_2) has an intrinsic nature—call it '**Domino Pair**'—which entails the following relation:

*being an x and y such that x's intrinsic nature is **Falling Domino** and y's intrinsic nature is **Falling Domino** and x caused y*

But DANC allows us to 'take' as many instances of an intrinsic nature as we wish, and 'put them' in any spatiotemporal arrangement, so long any spatiotemporal coincidence happens between things that have the same intrinsic nature. So we can 'take' two instances of **Domino Pair** and arrange them so that the event that is the effect in the one pair *is the very same event* as the cause in the other pair. After all, those 'two' events have the same intrinsic nature, i.e. **Falling Domino**. And we need not stop there: we can 'string along' such instances until we have a sequence of events, each with intrinsic nature **Falling Domino**, each of which causes the next member of the sequence, and such that the sequence *eventually cycles back on* *itself*.[45] Putting the conclusion less picturesquely, if DANC is true, then *there is some possible world in which* there is a sequence of events, each with intrinsic nature **Falling Domino**, each of which causes the next element of the sequence, and such that some element appears twice in the sequence. But there can't be any such causal loops. By reductio, we can conclude that the pair (E_1, E_2) instantiates causation extrinsically.

Of course, there was nothing special about the pair (E_1, E_2) beyond their being duplicates of one another; any such pair would do. As a matter of fact, I didn't really need to 'start' with such a pair. For example, consider the following three possible pairs of (non-duplicate) events: (E_1, E_2), (E_3, E_4), and (E_5, E_6), where E_1 caused E_2, E_3 caused E_4, and E_5 caused E_6, and where E_2 and E_3 are duplicates, E_4 and E_5 are duplicates, and E_6 and E_1 are duplicates.

Then assume DANC. By an analogous argument (assume causation is intrinsic to all of them, string them along until the sequence cycles, invoke premise that there are no causal loops) I can show that it's not the case that causation is intrinsic to *all three* pairs. And there's nothing *at all special* about those pairs.

Moreover, we need not confine our attention to causal relations of *pairs* of events. You can take a vast sequence of events, which are perhaps intricately and systematically interconnected. So long as two of them are duplicates—one of which causes the other—and the whole lot can be duplicated and arranged in spacetime so that the duplicating events overlap in such a way as to cycle, an analogous argument to the one I just gave will show that the vast sequence

---

[45] Here's a more formal argument. It follows from DANC that if {**Domino Pair**} is a sequence of intrinsic natures, {3} is a sequence of positive cardinals, and ϕ is a spatiotemporal arrangement that maps one instance of **Domino Pair** to the sequence of regions {R_1, R_2}, another instance to the sequence {R_2, R_3}, and a third instance to the sequence {R_3, R_1} (where that arrangement "fits"), and the element in the first instance, which was mapped to R_2, is identical to that element of the second instance which was mapped to R_2, etc. then there is a possible world in which there are exactly three instances of **Domino Pair** in that arrangement—provided that for any objects x and y and region R such that x and y each exactly occupy R, x and y have the same intrinsic nature (and size and shape permit). Let 'ϕ' name the arrangement described. The antecedent seems to be true and the proviso is met, so it follows that there is a possible world in which there are exactly three instances of **Domino Pair** in ϕ. From which it follows that there *is* a possible world in which an event E that exactly occupies R_1 caused an event that exactly occupies R_2 which caused an event that exactly occupies R_3, which in turn caused E.

of events will have certain causal relations extrinsically. And again, it's not really necessary to 'start' with two duplicates related by causation.

So this argument immediately establishes that certain sequences instantiate some causal relations extrinsically (if at all). But there are certain sequence/relation pairs such that my argument cannot immediately establish that the relation is instantiated by the sequence extrinsically (if at all), at the very least because of the "size and shape" proviso in DANC. However, as with the argument from DANC to the DELOCALIZATION OF LAWS, the second stage is to generalize. Infer from the conclusion of the first stage that the instantiation of any causal relation is a *wholly extrinsic matter*, which is to say this: a difference between two sequences with respect to whether there is any causation going on between (the parts of) the elements of the sequence doesn't, all by itself, make for an intrinsic difference. Thus, any two sequences that are non-causal duplicates are intrinsic duplicates period.[46]

From which we can conclude this: necessarily, for any sequence of events E, and any causal relation CS it instantiates (where the pair $\{E, CS\}$ is not causally innocent), E has CS extrinsically. (For necessarily, for any sequence of events E, and any causal relation CS it instantiates, if the pair $\{E, CS\}$ is not causally innocent, then CS differs between non-causal duplicates of E; and hence it differs between intrinsic duplicates of E; and hence it is extrinsic to E.) As should be apparent, the conclusion just is the DELOCALIZATION OF CAUSATION. By conditional proof, we can conclude that DANC entails the DELOCALIZATION OF CAUSATION.

The only premise of my argument—aside from the "generalizing maneuver"—is that causal loops are impossible. I assume that causal loops are impossible because I think they are conceptually impossible. But I recognize that not everyone will agree with me on the latter point.[47] Perhaps some of those who disagree have been persuaded that such things are conceptually possible by reading apparently coherent science fiction stories, such as Robert Heinlein's

---

[46] As in n. 40, I am assuming that the *perfectly natural* intrinsic non-causal properties and relations settle *all* the intrinsic non-causal properties and relations; this assumption is needed because 'non-causal duplication' is defined in terms of the sharing of perfectly natural properties and relations (see n. 29).

[47] See, e.g. Lewis (1986b, Ch. 18) and Hanley (2004).

"All You Zombies" or Robert Silverberg's "Absolutely Inflexible," which seem to involve just such things. I am persuaded by these stories of the conceptual possibility of causal loops to about the same extent that I am persuaded by Jorge Luis Borges' "Aleph" of the conceptual possibility of proper parthood loops (see Sanford 1993); which is to say, not at all.[48] Whatever appearance of conceptual possibility there is in such cases seems to derive from the fact that we don't grasp the whole situation "all at once".[49] But that's just a piece of psychological autobiography. And in any case, others may simply not see any conceptual impossibility in causal loops to begin with. So I will offer a justification for the claim that a certain *sort* of causal loop is indeed impossible, and then point out that a version of my Argument from Causal Loops relies only on that weaker premise.

3.2.2. Argument from Causal Loops: second version

It is a conceptual truth, I take it, that causation is irreflexive. Nothing can cause itself. So *if* it were a conceptual truth that causation is transitive, then it would be a conceptual truth that there are no causal loops. And indeed, some philosophers think it a conceptual truth that causation is transitive. As Ned Hall (2004a) puts it, "That causation is, necessarily, a transitive relation on events seems to many a bedrock datum, one of the few indisputable a priori insights we have into the workings of the concept." But as Hall goes on to say, that position has come under attack from philosophers armed with a variety of counterexamples.[50] Here is such an example (from Hartry Field): John doesn't like Joe, so he puts a bomb in front of his house (he *really* doesn't like him). Joe smells the fuse burning and so runs and defuses it, and so survives. So John's placing the bomb caused Joe to smell the bomb; and Joe's smelling of the bomb caused the bomb to be defused; and the bomb's defusal caused Joe's

---

[48] Here is one of the things Borges wrote: "I saw the Aleph from every point and angle, and in the Aleph I saw the earth and in the earth the Aleph and in the Aleph the earth." This too is, in some sense, *apparently* coherent, especially if you take frequent breaks when reading it.

[49] See also van Inwagen (1993).

[50] See also McDermott (1995) and Ehring (1997).

survival. But it doesn't *seem* like John's placing the bomb caused Joe's survival.[51]

There are philosophers who have dug in their heels and insisted that even in such putative counterexamples, transitivity holds; although we would not usually *say* "John's placing the bomb caused Joe's survival," it is nonetheless strictly speaking true.[52] And I think they're *right*. But I need not insist on that here. The reason is that my argument only needs the assumption that a *certain sort* of causal loop is impossible. And that can be justified in turn by the assumption that causation is transitive in *certain cases*. One can capture such restricted versions of transitivity with any instance of the following schema (where 'Φ' is replaced by a predicate that involves no causal vocabulary and is "wholly qualitative"): necessarily, for any events E_1, E_2, and E_3, if E_1 caused E_2, E_2 caused E_3, and $\Phi(\{E_1, E_2, E_3\})$, then E_1 caused E_3. And any such instance (so long as what is substituted for 'Φ' isn't trivially satisfied) may of course be consistent with there being counterexamples to the claim that causation is transitive *everywhere and always*. Importantly, the cases in which transitivity seems to fail are *unusual* in some way: as a matter of fact, many of them are unusual in the very same way.[53]

Now, I do not claim that I know what to substitue for 'Φ'. But I do claim that the existence of counterexamples to a fully general claim of transitivity shouldn't shake our confidence that causation is *usually* transitive, that transitivity holds in general *provided* that a highly unusual condition (which is perhaps very difficult to specify) does not obtain. And, moreover, that in many cases we can simply see that the condition does not obtain.

To take the simple example with which my argument began, if we know that domino$_1$ fell, causing (duplicate) domino$_2$ to fall in just the same way, which in turn caused (duplicate) domino$_3$ to fall in just the same way, then it seems we can validly infer that

---

[51] Cited in, among others, Lewis (2004).
[52] See Lewis (2004, §2.3) and Hall (2004a, 2004b).
[53] See Lewis (2004, §2.3). Here's how we might characterize the structure of most of the counterexamples: some event threatens to do something, but also does something that contributes to the undoing of that very threat. (It is put roughly this way by Collins, Hall, and Paul (2004), p. 40.) Thus, the placement of the bomb threatens to kill Joe, but it also alerts Joe to the threat and thus contributes to the undoing of that threat.

domino₁'s falling caused domino₃'s falling. No failure of transitivity seems in the offing once we fix the intrinsic natures of the events in the sequence in that way.[54] But the fact that the transitivity of causation holds in any such case, together with the assumption that causation is irreflexive, implies that causal loops consisting solely of such falling dominoes are impossible.

And of course, it's not the case that causation is transitive only when it comes to duplicate falling-domino-events. As I've suggested, it's transitive in a large class of cases. And that fact, together with the assumption that causation is irreflexive, implies more generally that many sorts of causal loops are impossible.[55] So to anyone who is sceptical of the premise that *every sort* of causal loop is impossible, I can offer a version of the Argument from Causal Loops that relies not on that fully general premise, but only on instances of it. Of course, the relevant instances are the sorts of causal loops which are (a) guaranteed possible by the conjunction of DANC and the claim that causation (or some causal relation) is intrinsic, and (b) demonstrably impossible, assuming certain true restricted transitivity claims.[56]

3.2.3. Argument from Transitivity Violation

Alas, almost nothing is uncontroversial in philosophy: not only are there philosophers who deny that causal loops are all impossible,

---

[54] If you think that other *external* conditions need to be satisfied for transitivity to hold—like there being nothing *else* going on in the vicinity other than falling dominoes—that will present no special difficulty for my argument; after all, DANC guarantees the possibility of the causal loop of falling dominoes *and nothing else*.

[55] Where to say that a particular sort of causal loop is impossible is to assert some instance of the following schema: necessarily, there is no sequence of events $\{E_1, \ldots, E_N\}$, such that (1) each event causes the succeeding event in the sequence, (2) some event appears twice in the sequence, and (3) $\Phi(\{E_1, \ldots, E_N\})$. Any such instance could be derived from a restricted claim of transitivity (together with the assumption of irreflexivity) if the fact that $\{E_1, \ldots, E_N\}$ satisfies the predicate that substitutes for Φ implies that any three-membered subsequence of $\{E_1, \ldots, E_N\}$ satisfies a condition sufficent for transitivity.

[56] I should note that this version of the argument requires a bit more generalizing at the second stage of the argument—to cover the cases in which the transitivity of causation fails—but that seems to make the generalizing maneuver no less plausible.

Half-hearted Humeanism | 293

there are also those who deny that causation is irreflexive.[57] To those philosophers I offer another argument, which exploits the point I made in the previous section about a true restricted transitivity claim, and relies neither on the premise that causation is irreflexive nor on the premise that causal loops are impossible. The basic idea of this argument is simple: the conjunction of DANC and the assumption that causation is intrinsic entails the possibility of violations of transitivity in the sorts of cases in which causation is necessarily transitive. So DANC entails that causation is not intrinsic. Then another application of the "generalizing maneuver" delivers the result that DANC entails the DELOCALIZATION OF CAUSATION.[58]

The details are as follows: consider again a possible pair of domino-falling events, (E_1, E_2), where E_1 caused E_2. Again, call the intrinsic nature of each event, '**Falling Domino**'. Now suppose, for reductio, that causation is intrinsic. Then (E_1, E_2) has an intrinsic nature—again, call it '**Domino Pair**'—which entails the following relation:

*being an x and y such that x's intrinsic nature is **Falling Domino** and y's intrinsic nature is **Falling Domino** and x caused y*

And it surely seems that there is another possible pair of domino-falling events, (E_3, E_4), where that pair is a duplicate of (E_1, E_2) but for the fact that it *does not instantiate causation* (or any causal relation).[59] But since (as we have supposed) causation is intrinsic, then so is its negation.[60] So then (E_3, E_4) has an intrinsic nature—call it '**Domino Pair**$_{NoCause}$'—which entails the following relation:

*being an x and y such that x's intrinsic nature is **Falling Domino** and y's intrinsic nature is **Falling Domino** and x does not cause y*

DANC then allows us to patch together two instances of **Domino Pair** and one instance of **Domino Pair**$_{NoCause}$, in such a way that—

---

[57] Lewis (1986b) denies it (Postscripts to "Causation," §F); he does concede that causal dependence is irreflexive, but that is of no use for the argument in the previous section.

[58] Thanks to John Hawthorne for suggesting this alternative argument.

[59] To put this in terms of the jargon I used to formulate the DELOCALIZATION OF CAUSATION, my assumption amounts to the claim that the sequence/relation pair {(E_1, E_2)/*causation*} is not causally innocent.

[60] See n. 13.

assuming a restricted transitivity claim for which I argued in the previous section—there are two events, x and y, where it's both the case that x caused y and it's *not the case* that x caused y.[61] And there can be no such thing. So by reductio, we can conclude that DANC entails that causation is extrinsic.

The second stage of the argument is the same as in the previous argument: infer from the conclusion of the first stage that the instantiation of any causal relation is a *wholly extrinsic matter*...which entails the DELOCALIZATION OF CAUSATION. By conditional proof, we can conclude that DANC entails the DELOCALIZATION OF CAUSATION.

3.2.4. Objection: Temporal direction is intrinsic

Objection: The central objection I anticipate is directed at my Argument from Causal Loops and rests on two assumptions:

1. *Temporal direction is an intrinsic relation.*
   So if my match striking came before its lighting, then it is *intrinsic* to the pair (my match striking, the match lighting) that the match striking *is earlier than* the match lighting.
2. *One event can cause another only if the one occurs before the other.*
   Thus, backward and simultaneous causation are both impossible.

[61] Here's a more formal argument. It follows from DANC that if {**Domino Pair**, **Domino Pair**$_{NoCause}$} is a sequence of intrinsic natures, {2,1} is a sequence of positive cardinals, and ϕ is a spatiotemporal arrangement that maps one instance of **Domino Pair** to the sequence of regions {R_1, R_2}, another instance to the sequence {R_2, R_3}, an instance of **Domino Pair**$_{NoCause}$ to the sequence {R_1, R_3} (where that arrangement "fits"), and the element in the first instance, which was mapped to R_2, is identical to that element of the second instance which was mapped to R_2, etc. then there is a possible world in which there are exactly two instances of **Domino Pair** and one instance of **Domino Pair**$_{NoCause}$ in that arrangement—provided that for any objects x and y and region R such that x and y each exactly occupy R, x and y have the same intrinsic nature (and size and shape permit). Let 'ϕ' name the arrangement described. The antecedent seems true and the proviso is met, so it follows that there *is* a possible world in which there are exactly two instances of **Domino Pair** and one instance of **Domino Pair**$_{NoCause}$ in ϕ. From which it follows that there *is* a possible world in which an event x that exactly occupies R_1 caused an event y that exactly occupies R_2 which caused an event z that exactly occupies R_3—and, I am assuming, the triple {x, y, z} satisfies a condition sufficient for causal transitivity, so x caused z—but where x did *not* cause z. Impossible!

If both of these assumptions are true, then none of the problematic situations which I claimed are guaranteed possible—assuming DANC is true and causation is intrinsic to certain sequences—are really guaranteed possible. For instance, consider the simple example involving the intrinsic nature **Domino Pair**. That intrinsic nature entails the relation:

*being an x and y such that x's intrinsic nature is **Falling Domino** and y's intrinsic nature is **Falling Domino** and x caused y*

Then assumption (2) implies that it also entails the relation:

being an x and y such that x is earlier than y

But then since that relation is intrinsic (per assumption (1)), there is no spatiotemporal arrangement of three instances of **Domino Pair** that satisfies the description I gave in my argument (in §3.2.1) *and* which *fits*. The spatiotemporal arrangement I considered assigns one instance of the intrinsic nature to $\{R_1, R_2\}$, another to $\{R_2, R_3\}$, and a third one to $\{R_3, R_1\}$.[62] That's how we get a causal loop But then it doesn't *fit* **Domino Pair**, an intrinsic nature every one of whose instances instantiates the *earlier than* relation. In order to fit, it would have to be the case that R_1 is earlier than R_2, and R_2 is earlier than R_3, and R_3 is earlier than R_1. And there is no such set of spacetime regions. (The objection assumes that there can't be "*earlier than* loops".)

Reply: Before I get to my main reply, I will note two things. First, the objection is only directed at my Argument from Causal Loops; even if its two assumptions are true, no part of my Argument from Transitivity Violation is affected. That's not a reply to the objection, of course, as much as a reminder that even if my reply is unsuccessful, the Half-Hearted Humean is not out of the woods. Second, the assumptions upon which the objection rests are hefty and far from obvious. Perhaps (2) is a natural companion to the assumption (of my argument) that causal loops are impossible, in that they both reflect a conservative view about when causation can occur.[63] But (1) involves a hefty add-on, and one that seems very

---

[62] See n. 45.
[63] Thanks to an anonymous referee here.

unHumean at that.[64] Of course, my argument is directed against a Half-Hearted Humean, and she might be *very* faint-hearted about her Humeanism. But it is still noteworthy that she has to take on a seemingly independent hefty commitment.

Now for my main reply: she *can't* take on that hefty commitment, not so long as she is commited to DANC. The reason is that a very natural extension of DANC—one which I don't think any proponent of DANC could reasonably deny—makes precisely the same sort of trouble for the view that temporal direction is intrinsic as DANC makes for the view that causation is intrinsic. In essence, the objection has merely shifted the problem from one allegedly intrinsic relation to another.

The natural extension of DANC I have in mind, which we can call 'DANC*', is something of an abstraction from DANC. DANC* doesn't guarantee the possibility of *spatiotemporal* arrangements at all, or at least not directly. Rather, it guarantees the possibility of any mereological arrangement of instances of any intrinsic natures, where a mereological arrangement is a specification of which objects overlap (in the mereological sense of 'overlap') which others, and on what parts; such an arrangement remains silent on the spatiotemporal locations of objects. Of course, an analogous proviso to the one in DANC applies here as well: the mereological arrangement can specify overlap only between parts that share the same intrinsic nature. It couldn't very well be the case that you and I overlap on my head and your arm.

Now, it's a fairly straightforward matter to show that DANC* entails that temporal direction is not intrinsic. All we need is the possibility of a pair of duplicate events—like two beats of a metronome—one of which occured before the other. (Our falling dominoes would do, but I'll leave them aside so that issues involving *causation* don't confuse the reader.) Let us call each beat's intrinsic nature "**Metro Beat**," and the pair's "**Beat Pair**". Suppose temporal direction is intrinsic; then **Beat Pair** entails the following relation:

---

[64] Note that if a proponent of DANC accepts (2) but denies (1), then there is yet a third—and even quicker—argument that she is committed to the DELOCALIZATION OF CAUSATION. If (1) is false, then DANC guarantees the possibility of, for example, two instances of **Domino Pair** that are temporal inverts of one another; and that's clearly impossible if causation is intrinsic, (2) is true, and no pair can instantiate both *earlier than* and *later than*.

*being an x and y such that x's intrinsic nature is **Metro Beat** and y's intrinsic nature is **Metro Beat** and x is earlier than y*

But then there are two arguments—perfectly analogous to the Argument from Causal Loops and the Argument from Transitivity Violation—which show that DANC* entails the possibility of an impossible situation. (And remember, the objection requires the assumption that there can't be "earlier than" loops; and so I can safely assume that as well in replying.) By reductio, conclude that temporal direction is not intrinsic.

I suppose the Half-Heared Humean might endorse DANC but not DANC*. That would leave her in an unenviable position, and perhaps an unstable one as well. DANC* seems to be nothing but a more abstract version of DANC, and the central motivation for DANC—that any "violation" of it would constitute a deeply mysterious necessary connection—seems equally a motivation for DANC*.

3.3. From denial to joint delocalization

That concludes my argument for the claim that DANC entails both Delocalization theses. I'd *like* to argue straightaway that DANC entails GLOBAL SUPERVENIENCE by arguing that the conjunction of the Delocalization theses entails GLOBAL SUPERVENIENCE. And I could do so if those theses didn't make an exception for "nomologically/causally innocent pairs". But because they *do* make such an exception, matters aren't as straightforward. (I'll presently explain why they make matters less straightforward.) Instead, I have to first argue that DANC entails *another* thesis—which I shall call 'JOINT DELOCALIZATION'—a thesis that is, at least on the face of it, slightly stronger than the conjunction of the two Delocalization theses, and which *does* straightforwardly entail GLOBAL SUPERVENIENCE.

In the course of arguing for the DELOCALIZATION OF LAWS, I arrived at the (interim) conclusion that,

> (1) A difference between two sequences with respect to whether some proposition is a law (or some propositions are laws) doesn't, all by itself, make for an intrinsic difference. So any two sequences that are non-nomic duplicates are intrinsic duplicates, period.

And in the course of both arguments for the DELOCALIZATION OF CAUSATION, I arrived at the (interim) conclusion that,

> (2) A difference between two sequences with respect to whether there is any causation going on between (the parts of) the elements of the sequence doesn't, all by itself, make for an intrinsic difference. So any two sequences that are non-causal duplicates are intrinsic duplicates, period.

But what I need in order to argue for GLOBAL SUPERVENIENCE is this thesis:

> JOINT DELOCALIZATION: A difference between two sequences with respect to both whether some proposition is a law (or some propositions are laws) *and* whether there is any causation going on between (the parts of) the elements of the sequence doesn't, all by itself, make for an intrinsic difference. **So any two sequences that are non-causal, non-nomic duplicates are intrinsic duplicates, period.**[65]

And JOINT DELOCALIZATION doesn't *straightforwardly follow* from the conjunction of (1) and (2): perhaps a departure in just the nomic facts makes no intrinsic difference, and a departure in just the causal facts makes no intrinsic difference, but a departure in *both* respects does make for an intrinsic difference. Call this suggestion 'Hairsplit' (not to be tendentious). Now, I'm not sure Hairsplit is a genuine epistemic possibility; and I am unaware of any account of causation and laws which would have it as a result. But so as not to leave room for such accounts, I will show that the Argument from Causal Loops can be extended to deliver the result that DANC entails JOINT DELOCALIZATION.[66] (Note that if the Delocalization theses didn't make an exception for "nomologically/causally innocent pairs," then they would imply that all causal and all nomic properties are, without exception, extrinsic; which would then imply that any non-causal, non-nomic duplicates are intrinsic duplicates, since they share all intrinsic properties and relations.[67])

---

[65] Where *x is a non-causal, non-nomic duplicate of y* iff for any intrinsic perfectly natural non-causal, non-nomic relation *R*, *x* has *R* iff *y* has *R*.

[66] One could likewise extend the Argument from Transitivity Violation to deliver the same result.

[67] I am assuming that the perfectly natural (non-causal, non-nomic) properties and relations settle all the less-than-perfectly natural (non-causal, non-nomic) ones.

Assume DANC is true. Now, consider again, if you are not too tired of them, a possible pair of duplicate domino-falling events, (E_1, E_2), which are such that E_1 caused E_2 *and* the Law of Universal Gravitation is a law. Call its intrinsic nature '**Domino Pair$_{+\text{Gravity}}$**'. Now, according to Hairsplit, the relation,

> being an x and y such that x caused y or the Law of Universal Gravitation is a law,

is intrinsic to (E_1, E_2). After all, any pair that lacked that relation would fail to be an intrinsic duplicate of (E_1, E_2). So that relation is entailed by **Domino Pair$_{+\text{Gravity}}$**.

And there is, presumably, another possible pair of duplicate domino-falling events, (E_3, E_4), which are such that E_3 caused E_4 *and* the Law of Universal Schmavitation is a law. (Where the Law of Universal Schmavitation is some proposition inconsistent with the Law of Universal Gravitation.) Call its intrinsic nature '**Domino Pair$_{+\text{Schmavity}}$**'. Then, according to Hairsplit, the relation,

> being an x and y such that x caused y or the Law of Universal Schmavitation is a law,

is intrinsic to (E_3, E_4). After all, any pair that lacked that relation would fail to be an intrinsic duplicate of (E_3, E_4). So that relation is entailed by **Domino Pair$_{+\text{Schmavity}}$**.

Now, DANC guarantees that it is possible that there are *two* event loops—a million miles apart, say—one of which is "constructed" solely from instances of **Domino Pair$_{+\text{Gravity}}$** and the other of which is "constructed" solely from instances of **Domino Pair$_{+\text{Schmavity}}$**. But that's not in fact possible, since it would involve *either* an impossible sort of causal loop or the truth of two inconsistent propositions. So Hairsplit is false. By conditional proof, conclude that DANC entails that Hairsplit is false. And since DANC entails (1) and (2), it entails JOINT DELOCALIZATION.

4. FROM DELOCALIZATION TO GLOBAL SUPERVENIENCE

Now I can move to GLOBAL SUPERVENIENCE, the final thesis in the Wholehearted Humean's package. There are several extant arguments for GLOBAL SUPERVENIENCE; none of them seems compelling to me.[68] But granting the core Humean idea that there are no absolutely necessary connections between distinct things, there is indeed a refreshing and compelling argument for GLOBAL SUPERVENIENCE. Its first premise is that DANC entails JOINT DELOCALIZATION. Its second premise is that JOINT DELOCALIZATION in turn entails GLOBAL SUPERVENIENCE. As is hopefully clear, I have argued for the first premise in §3.3; now I will argue for the second premise.

4.1. The argument

The argument is quite simple. Its only "moving part" is this assumption:

INTRINSIC SETTLES ALL: Any two possible sequences of concreta which are intrinsic duplicates, and such that each one *exhausts* the concreta—that is, each sequence instantiates the relation *being all the concreta there are*—instantiate all the same qualitative properties/relations, period.

Think of a simple case: I tell you that in W_1 there is a monkey, and nothing else concrete (other than its parts); and in W_2 there is a monkey, and nothing else concrete (other than its parts); and I further tell you that the monkeys are intrinsic duplicates. Isn't it obvious that the monkeys don't differ at all, except perhaps in a nonqualitative way? To use my initial and intuitive characterization of intrinsicality as a guide, if you know how a certain monkey is in itself, and you know that it is not related to *any other* mereologically disjoint concrete object (since you know there is no other), don't you know everything you need to know to determine the properties it has *ex*trinsically, i.e. the properties it has in virtue of the way it is (intrinsically) and the relations it stands or fails to stand in to other things? It would certainly seem so. (I told you I'd flag where it is that I am leaning on our grasp of the concept *intrinsicness*. Here it is. And as I said, I trust it is clear enough that my assumption is true.) Now extend the thought to multi-element sequences of concreta: it still seems just as obviously true.

---

[68] See Schaffer (2007) for a survey of the arguments; he and I differ, it seems, with respect to the force of his so-called arguments from *methodology* and *science*.

Now assume JOINT DELOCALIZATION for conditional proof. Then any two possible sequences of concreta that are non-causal, non-nomic duplicates are intrinsic duplicates, period. But then, assuming INTRINSIC SETTLES ALL, any two possible sequences of concreta that are non-causal, non-nomic duplicates, and such that each one exhausts the concreta, instantiate all the same qualitative properties/relations, period. And that implies GLOBAL SUPERVENIENCE.[69] Thus, JOINT DELOCALIZATION entails GLOBAL SUPERVENIENCE. And as I argued in §3.3, DANC entails JOINT DELOCALIZATION. So DANC entails GLOBAL SUPERVENIENCE.

5. CONCLUSION

I have argued that DANC quite plausibly entails three other Humean theses. The final turn of the screw is to note that it is extremely unattractive, if not demonstrably inconsistent, to hold GLOBAL SUPERVENIENCE together with a governing conception of either *causation* or *lawhood*.[70] If causal facts or laws really *do* govern or

---

[69] I assume that necessarily, if there are concreta, then there is a sequence of all concreta. (I also assume that *being all the concreta* is a perfectly natural, non-causal, non-nomic relation; but that plays no substantive role. If you think that relation is not perfectly natural, then simply reformulate GLOBAL SUPERVENIENCE to accommodate that.) Let B be the set of all perfectly natural non-causal, non-nomic properties/relations, and let A be the set of all qualitative properties/relations. For any worlds w_1 and w_2, any function f that is a B-isomorphism from the concrete domain of w_1 to the concrete domain of w_2 is such that for any sequence X_1 of all the concreta in w_1, the sequence X_2 of images (under f) of the elements of X_1 instantiates the relation *being all the concreta there are*, and for any (other) perfectly natural non-causal, non-nomic property/relation R, X_1 instantiates R iff X_2 instantiates R; and so they instantiate all the same qualitiative properties/relations. But since I assume that necessarily, if there are concreta, then there is a sequence of all concreta, it follows that for any worlds w_1 and w_2, such that there are concreta in w_1, any function f that is a B-isomorphism from the concrete domain of w_1 to the concrete domain of w_2 is such that *there is* some sequence X_1 of all the concreta in w_1, and the sequence X_2 of images (under f) of the elements of X_1 instantiates all the same qualitative properties/relations as X_1; and hence is such that for any qualitative property/relation R, and *any* sequence of concreta in w_1, that sequence instantiates R iff the sequence of images (under f) of the elements of that sequence instantiates R; that is, it is an A-isomorphism. (And for any worlds w_1 and w_2, such that there are *no* concreta in w_1, it is trivial that any B-isomorphism from the concrete domain of w_1 to the concrete domain of w_2 is an A-isomorphism.)

[70] On the distinction between governing and non-governing conceptions of *lawhood*, see Beebee (2000).

constrain the particular matters of fact, then why couldn't the particular matters of fact underdetermine the causal or nomic facts? Why couldn't different causal or nomic facts underlie the same patterns in the phenomena? Those questions are especially pressing given what *appear* to be distinct scenarios that exhibit that very sort of underdetermination (see Tooley (1988) and Carroll (1994)). Someone with a Humean account of laws and causation can, in a principled way, drive a wedge between appearance and reality. They have an *explanation* of the fact, if it is a fact, that those scenarios are not really distinct after all.[71] But, absent such an account, it would seem that no such explanation could be given. GLOBAL SUPERVENIENCE would be an inexplicable constriction of what appears to be modal space.

The upshot then is that we face a stark choice: either there are *absolutely* necessary connections between distinct existents or it really is "just one damn thing after another." If she accepts my arguments, the Half-Hearted Humean could of course do one of two things: accept the whole Humean package or reject DANC and give up Humeanism entirely. My arguments are silent on which course to take. But either way she goes, she needs to get off the fence.[72]

Yeshiva University

REFERENCES

Armstrong, D. (1985). *What Is a Law of Nature?* Cambridge: Cambridge University Press.
Armstrong, D. (1989). *A Combinatorial Theory of Possibility*. Cambridge: Cambridge University Press.
Armstrong, D. (1997). *A World of States of Affairs*. Cambridge: Cambridge University Press.
Armstrong, D. (2004). "Going Through the Open Door Again: Counterfactual versus Singularist Theories of Causation." In Collins, Hall, and Paul (2004).

---

[71] They do owe an explanation of why we *think* they are. See §5 in Collins, Hall, and Paul (2004, Ch. 1).

[72] Many thanks to Karen Bennett, Kenneth Boyce, John Hawthorne, Amelia Hicks, David Johnson, Alvin Plantinga, Bradley Rettler, Peter van Inwagen, Dean Zimmerman, and anonymous referees from *Oxford Studies in Metaphysics* for extensive feedback on earlier drafts. Thank you as well to the audience at my talk at the Israeli Philosophical Association's 2012 meeting, and to the Institute for Scholarship in the Liberal Arts at the University of Notre Dame for a travel grant.

Arntzenius, F. (2012). *Space, Time, and Stuff*. Oxford: Oxford University Press.

Beebee, H. (2000). "The Non-Governing Conception of Laws of Nature." *Philosophy and Phenomenological Research*, 61:3.

Bird, A. (2007). *Nature's Metaphysics: Laws and Properties*. Oxford: Oxford University Press.

Broackes, J. (1993). "Did Hume Hold a Regularity Theory of Causation." *British Journal for the History of Philosophy*, v. 1.

Carroll, J. (1994). *Laws of Nature*. Cambridge: Cambridge University Press.

Collins, J., N. Hall, and L. A. Paul (2004). *Causation and Counterfactuals*. Cambridge, MA: MIT Press.

Darby, G., and D. Watson (2010). "Lewis's Principle of Recombination: Reply to Efird and Stoneham." *Dialectica*, 64:3.

Dasgupta, S. (2014). "Absolutism vs. Comparativism about Quantity." In *Oxford Studies in Metaphysics*, viii, Oxford: Oxford University Press.

Dorr, C. (2004). "Non-Symmetric Relations." In *Oxford Studies in Metaphysics*, vol. 1, Oxford: Oxford University Press.

Dorr, C. (2005). "What We Disagree about When We Disagree about Ontology." In *Fictionalist Approaches to Metaphysics*, ed. Mark Kalderon, Oxford: Oxford University Press.

Dorr, C., and J. Hawthorne (2014). "Naturalness." In *Oxford Studies in Metaphysics*, viii, Oxford: Oxford University Press.

Earman, J., and J. Roberts (2005). "Contact with the Nomic: A Challenge for Deniers of Humean Supervenience about Laws of Nature Part I: Humean Supervenience." *Philosophy and Phenomenological Research*, 71:1.

Efird, D., and T. Stoneham (2008). "What Is the Principle of Recombination?" *Dialectica*, 62:4.

Ehring, D. (1997). *Causation and Persistence*. Oxford: Oxford University Press.

Field, H. (1980). *Science without Numbers*. Princeton, NJ: Princeton University Press.

Hall, N. (2004a). "Causation and the Price of Transitivity." In Collins, Hall, and Paul (2004).

Hall, N. (2004b). "Two Concepts of Causation." In Collins, Hall, and Paul.

Hall, N. (2004c). "The Intrinsic Character of Causation." In *Oxford Studies in Metaphysics*, vol. 1, Oxford: Oxford University Press.

Hanley, R. (2004). "No End in Sight: Causal Loops in Philosophy, Physics, and Fiction." *Synthese*, 141:1.

Hawthorne, J. (2006a). "Motion and Plenitude." In *Metaphysical Essays*, Oxford: Oxford University Press.

Hawthorne, J. (2006b). "Quantity in Lewisian Metaphysics." In *Metaphysical Essays*, Oxford: Oxford University Press.

Hume, D. (1978). *A Treatise of Humean Nature*, ed. P. H. Nidditch, 2nd edn. Oxford: Oxford University Press.

Kripke, S. (1980). *Naming and Necessity*. Cambridge: Harvard University Press.

Langton, R., and D. Lewis (1998). "Defining 'Intrinsic'." *Philosophy and Phenomenological Research*, 58:2.

Lewis, D. (1983). "New Work for a Theory of Universals." *Australasian Journal of Philosophy*, 61: 343–77.

Lewis, D. (1986a). *On the Plurality of Worlds*. Oxford: Blackwell.

Lewis, D. (1986b). *Philosophical Papers*, ii. Oxford: Oxford University Press.

Lewis, D. (1994). "Humean Supervenience Debugged." *Mind*, 103 (412).

Lewis, D. (2001). "Redefining 'Intrinsic'." *Philosophy and Phenomenological Research*, 63:2.

Lewis, D. (2004). "Causation as Influence." In Collins, Hall, and Paul (2004).

Maudlin, T. (2007). *The Metaphysics within Physics*. Oxford: Oxford University Press.

McDermott, M. (1995). "Redundant Causation." *British Journal for the Philosophy of Science*, 46: 523–44.

Menzies, P. (1999). "Intrinsic vs. Extrinsic Conceptions of Causation." In Sankey, H. (ed.), *Causation and Laws of Nature*. Dordrecht: Kluwer.

Molnar, G. (2007). *Powers: A Study in Metaphysics*. Oxford: Oxford University Press.

Sanford, D. H. (1993). "The Problem of the Many, Many Composition Questions, and Naive Mereology." *Noûs*, 27:2.

Schaffer, J. (2007). "Causation and Laws of Nature: Reductionism." In *Contemporary Debates in Metaphysics*, eds. Hawthorne, J., T. Sider, and D. Zimmerman. Oxford: Blackwell.

Sider, T. (1996). "Intrinsic Properties." *Philosophical Studies*, 83.

Sider, T. (1999). "Global Supervenience and Identity across Times and Worlds." *Philosophy and Phenomenological Research*, 59.

Sider, T. (2001). "Maximality and Intrinsic Properties." *Philosophy and Phenomenological Research*, 63:2.

Strawson, G. (1989). *The Secret Connexion*. Oxford: Oxford University Press.

Strawson, G. (2002). "David Hume: Objects and Power." In *Reading Hume on Human Understanding*, Millican, P. (ed.), Oxford: Oxford University Press.

Tooley, M. (1977). "The Nature of Laws." *Canadian Journal of Philosophy*, 7.

Tooley, M. (1988). *Causation: A Realist Approach*. Oxford: Oxford University Press.

van Inwagen, P. (1981). "The Doctrine of Arbitrary Undetached Parts." *Pacific Philosophical Quarterly* 62:2.

van Inwagen, P. (1993). "Naive Mereology, Admissible Valuations, and Other Matters." *Noûs*, 27:2.
van Inwagen, P. (2006). "Names for Relations." *Philosophical Perspectives*, 20.
Weatherson, B. (2001). "Intrinsic Properties and Combinatorial Principles." *Philosophy and Phenomenological Research*, 63:2.
Wilson, J. (2010a). "From Constitutional Necessities to Causal Necessities." In *The Semantics and Metaphysics of Natural Kinds*, London: Routledge.
Wilson, Jessica M. (2010b). "What Is Hume's Dictum and Why Believe It?" *Philosophy and Phenomenological Research*, 80:3.

11. The coarse-grainedness of grounding

Kathrin Koslicki

1. INTRODUCTION

After many years of enduring the drought and famine of Quinean ontology and Carnapian meta-ontology, the notion of ground, with its distinctively philosophical flavor, finally promises to give metaphysicians something they can believe in again and around which they can rally: their very own metaphysical explanatory connection which apparently cannot be reduced to, or analyzed in terms of, other familiar idioms such as identity, modality, parthood, supervenience, realization, causation, or counterfactual dependence.[1] The notion of ground is typically intended to indicate relative ontological fundamentality: what is grounded in something else is thought to be less ontologically fundamental than that in which it is grounded; grounds are in turn taken to be more ontologically fundamental than what is grounded in them. It may also be possible to define a notion of absolute ontological fundamentality in terms of grounding: the absolutely ontologically fundamental would then be that which is itself completely ungrounded, but which serves as ground for other things. Many, though not all, grounding theorists think of grounding as a connection between propositions, facts, states of affairs, or whatever it is that is expressed by declarative sentences. Many, though not all, take grounding to be factive, referentially transparent, well-founded, irreflexive, asymmetric, transitive, non-monotonic, and metaphysically necessary. (More on the alleged characteristics of grounding below.) Often, phenomena such as the following are cited as putative examples of grounding connections:

(1) a. Systematic connections between entire realms of facts (mental/physical; moral/natural; etc.).

---

[1] See for example Audi (2012a), (2012b); Bennett (2011a), (2011b), (forth.); Correia and Schnieder (2012); Fine (2001), (2012); Jenkins (2011); Raven (2012); Rosen (2010); Schaffer (2009), (2010); Schnieder, Hoeltje, and Steinberg (2013); Trogdon (2013).

    b. Truthmaking.
    c. Logical cases (e.g. the connection between conjunctive facts or disjunctive facts and their constituent facts).
    d. The determinate/determinable relation.

Supposing that these four types of phenomena in fact exhibit grounding connections, we can illustrate them by means of the following more specific examples:

(2) a. <u>Moral/Natural</u>: The fact that an act is a telling of a lie grounds the fact that the act is morally wrong.
    b. <u>Truthmaking</u>: The truth of the proposition that snow is white is grounded in the existence of the state of affairs, snow's being white.
    c. <u>Logical Cases</u>: The fact that the ball is red grounds the fact that the ball is red or round.
    d. <u>Determinate/Determinable</u>: The fact that the ball is crimson grounds the fact that the ball is red.

One may legitimately wonder whether much of anything has been accomplished by subsuming the four types of phenomena cited above, and perhaps others as well which I have not listed, under a single general rubric of grounding. My own view, which will emerge in the course of this paper, is that classifying all of these phenomena as exhibiting grounding connections does not achieve much in the way of illumination. There are important and fairly obvious differences between these cases which have been obscured by creating the illusion that they are all connected via the single relation or operation of grounding. The important work of giving a positive account of the nature of the connections at issue still remains to be done, even after classifying all of these phenomena as exhibiting grounding connections; and we have not made much progress in that direction by applying a single label to what are evidently quite distinct phenomena. In fact, by treating a collection of phenomena which is in fact heterogeneous as though it were homogeneous, we have, if anything, taken a dialectical step backward.[2]

---

[2] Similar sentiments are also expressed in Wilson (2014). Although Wilson and I both reach the same conclusion, viz. that grounding is too coarse-grained to perform the metaphysical work for which it is intended, we arrive at this conclusion in different ways and I do not share all of the substantive commitments she makes along the way. In particular, I diverge from Wilson in the following three main respects. First, I do

For several decades, it was widely believed that at least some of the explanatory asymmetries cited above, e.g. systematic connections between entire realms of phenomena such as the moral and the natural in (2.a), could be analyzed by means of the notion of supervenience, viz. the idea that any difference with respect to one type of phenomenon (e.g. the moral) entails a difference with respect to another (e.g. the natural). However, after a period of lively interest in supervenience, even its most committed champions were forced to conclude that this notion is not strong enough and lacks the right formal profile to yield a relation of genuine and asymmetric dependence (cf. Kim (1993)). For one thing, supervenience is not in and of itself an asymmetric relation. Secondly, supervenience serves to mark merely a relation of necessary covariance between its relata. But any such purely modal relation is too explanatorily coarse-grained to capture and illuminate the nature of the connections at issue. The coarse-grainedness of supervenience can be illustrated, for example, by considering two philosophers who occupy radically different positions concerning the moral/natural connection (e.g. an ethical naturalist and an ethical non-naturalist), but who are nevertheless able to endorse the very same supervenience claim

---

not follow Wilson in taking the relations she calls "small 'g' grounding relations" (e.g. parthood, composition, realization, constitution) themselves to be relations of metaphysical dependence. Rather, my own position is that these relations *induce* different varieties of metaphysical dependence in different circumstances and in different respects. Thus, in certain cases and in certain respects, the parts composing a whole may depend on the whole in question; and in certain cases and in certain respects, a whole may also depend on its parts. But we lose the ability to make these distinctions if we simply identify parthood itself as a relation of metaphysical dependence. Secondly, and relatedly, I depart from Wilson's position that absolute fundamentality together with her "small 'g' grounding relations" give us the apparatus sufficient to capture the *directionality* of relative fundamentality. Even if we assume an absolutely fundamental level as fixed, such relations as parthood can still induce metaphysical dependence relations going in both directions, both towards the absolutely fundamental and away from the absolutely fundamental. In order to capture the directionality of relative fundamentality, it is thus necessary to make room for the different varieties of metaphysical dependence, in addition to Wilson's "small 'g' grounding relations". Thirdly, I am not convinced that it is legitimate, from the perspective of a metaphysician, to assume an absolutely fundamental level as fixed. Like Rosen, I want to leave it open whether relative fundamentality turns out to be a well-founded relation. Wilson's and my own resistance towards the recent wave of enthusiasm about grounding should also be kept separate from the skeptical stance of others who object to the idioms of grounding, metaphysical priority, or metaphysical dependence on the grounds that they find these notions to be confused, unintelligible, incoherent, or redundant (e.g. Daly (2012), Hofweber (2009)).

concerning the moral and the natural, e.g. that the moral strongly supervenes on the natural. Given that such a scenario is possible (and, in fact, actual), we may conclude that supervenience does not yield a sufficiently fine-grained characterization of the nature of the connection at issue, i.e. one which would allow us to draw a meaningful distinction between two radically different philosophical positions.

At least with respect to its formal properties, then, grounding does appear to hold more promise than supervenience for the purposes of developing an approach to relative fundamentality, if only because grounding is commonly stipulated to be asymmetric and not definable in modal terms. However, as we will discover below, grounding nevertheless suffers from some of same deficiencies as supervenience: most prominently, grounding also fails to be sufficiently fine-grained to do its intended explanatory work. In addition, there is doubt as to whether the phenomena collected together under the rubric of grounding are really unified by the presence of a single relation. And, finally, grounding turns out not to be particularly helpful in capturing and illuminating what is philosophically important about the traditional substance/non-substance distinction. In the end, we will find that, although grounding performs better than supervenience in some ways, it does not solve all of the problems to which a supervenience-based approach to relative fundamentality falls prey.

2. THE HETEROGENEITY OF GROUNDING

What are we supposed to learn from being told that the phenomena in (2) are all to be subsumed under the single general rubric of grounding? The details of how this question is to be answered of course depend on the particular account under consideration. For the sake of concreteness, I will indicate how several different grounding enthusiasts would respond to the question just posed.

2.1. Grounding as a well-founded partial order

In Schaffer (2009), we are told that the usefulness of the grounding idiom derives, at least in part, from the fact that we can put this notion to work in defining or providing informative equivalences for a whole host of other important metaphysical concepts (viz. the "grounding family"), such as "(absolutely) fundamental", "derivative", "exists", "integrated whole", "mere aggregate" or "interdependence" (pp. 373–4). When it comes to characterizing grounding itself, Schaffer remarks that this notion is best conceived of as a two-place predicate which can take arguments denoting entities from arbitrary ontological categories, e.g. not only facts, propositions, states of affairs (or whatever entities are to be paired up with declarative sentences), but also concrete particular objects, abstract objects, properties, or what have you (p. 375). Thus, in addition to the phenomena cited above, Schaffer also counts the following as clear cases of grounding:

(2) e. Sets/Members: The singleton set containing Socrates is grounded in its sole member, Socrates.
f. Holes/Hosts: The holes in a piece of Swiss cheese are grounded in the piece of Swiss cheese in which they reside.
g. Abundant/Sparse Properties: The abundant property, *grueness*, is grounded in some combination of sparse properties.

Schaffer furthermore assumes that grounding induces a partial ordering over the entities it relates (i.e. that grounding is irreflexive, asymmetric, and transitive) and that it is well-founded (i.e. that it bottoms out in minimal elements which ground everything else but are themselves ungrounded).

Applying Schaffer's definitions and equivalences to the cases at hand, we can deduce that the grounded entities mentioned in (2.a)–(2.g) are all derivative, since in Schaffer's view everything that is grounded is derivative. (It is left open whether the entities that are doing the grounding are absolutely fundamental, since (2.a)–(2.g) do not reveal whether these entities are themselves grounded in further entities.) Thus, an act's being morally wrong, for example, is classified by Schaffer's account as derivative, because, by (2.a), this fact is grounded in the fact that the act is a telling of a lie; similarly, for the other grounded entities that are appealed to in (2.b)–(2.g). Schaffer's approach also allows us to infer that the grounded entities appealed to in (2.a)–(2.g) as well as their grounds exist (on the assumption that these statements are true), since the entities in question are either absolutely fundamental or derivative and whatever is either absolutely fundamental or derivative, in Schaffer's view, exists. Schaffer's other definitions of "integrated whole", "mere aggregate", and "interdependence" are not obviously applicable to the cases at hand: these definitions concern the relations between parts and wholes, which appear not to be immediately relevant to the cases in (2).

Those who were hoping to achieve some clarification in their understanding of what fundamentality and derivativeness come to by being directed towards the alleged interconnections between the members of the grounding family may walk away from Schaffer's account with some measure of disappointment. His account, after all, tells us merely that "grounds" is a primitive two-place predicate with the formal characteristics of a partial ordering that is defined over a domain with minimal elements. Thus, to learn that, say, a certain physical fact is absolutely fundamental is to learn only that this entity functions as a minimal element in a domain over which a certain well-founded partial order is defined; and to learn that, say, a certain mental fact is derivative is to learn only that this entity bears the relation in question, directly or indirectly, to the minimal elements in the domain. But the same of course can be said, for example, of a domain consisting of letters belonging to a certain alphabet, the strings constructed out of these letters in accordance with certain rules, and the partial ordering, *is a substring of*. Moreover, the mere fact that the letters function as minimal elements relative to this domain, in the sense of not being further divisible into anything that itself counts as a string of the alphabet in question, while strings that are constructed out of one or more letters are classified as complex, does not necessarily capture what the physicalist has in mind when he recommends that we consider certain physical facts as absolutely fundamental and mental facts as derivative. For the physicalist may well acknowledge that the absolutely fundamental physical facts in question exhibit the same degree of complexity as the derivative mental facts: such a possibility could arise for example if facts in general (whether physical or mental) are taken to be complex across the board, i.e. constructed out of further constituents (e.g. objects, properties, relations) via some construction operation. The notions of grounding, absolute fundamentality and derivativeness that are at issue in characterizing these versions of physicalism, in that case, could not be those of construction, simplicity, and complexity, since such notions would not succeed in drawing a meaningful distinction between mental and physical facts.[3] Based on what Schaffer has so far told us, then, it seems that we cannot yet distinguish between grounding and other well-founded partial orderings and the notions of absolute fundamentality and derivativeness which might be defined in terms of these idioms. I suspect, however, that, whatever exactly our expectations might have been to begin with, they would not be satisfied by an account which presents us with such an unconstrained conception of grounding, absolute fundamentality, and derivativeness.[4]

2.2. Grounding as a generic kind

We find a somewhat more restrictive, and hence more informative, characterization of grounding and related concepts in Rosen (2010). Unlike Schaffer, Rosen conceives of grounding as a relation among facts, and hence imposes some constraints on the types of entities which may figure as the relata of the grounding relation. Facts, for Rosen, are structured entities individuated by their constituents (e.g. objects, properties, relations) and their manner of composition (e.g. the order in which a certain relation applies to its relata). Like Schaffer, Rosen takes grounding to be asymmetric, irreflexive, and transitive, i.e. to impose a partial order on its domain. Unlike Schaffer, however, Rosen wants to leave open whether grounding turns

---

[3] Here I diverge from the approach to relative fundamentality taken by Bennett (2011a), (2011b), and (forth.), who considers construction, or what she calls "building operations", to be the primary vehicle that takes us from the more fundamental to the less fundamental.

[4] In addition to the formal properties cited above, Schaffer would also appeal to what he considers to be paradigm cases of grounding, in order to differentiate grounding from other well-founded partial orderings which are numerically distinct from the grounding relation. However, given that I am not convinced that the alleged grounding connections are unified under a single relation, I am also unsure of what exactly would constitute a paradigm case of grounding. Since the alleged cases of grounding strike me as a heterogeneous collection, I cannot consider all of these phenomena equally to be paradigm cases exhibiting a single relation. Which then are we to accept as paradigm cases, which do we discard, and on the basis of what considerations?

out to be well-founded.[5] In addition, Rosen assumes that grounding is non-monotonic: for example, if a fact, [p], grounds a fact, [q], then there is no guarantee that this grounding connection is preserved by expanding the grounds with some arbitrary fact, [r], since [r] may be completely irrelevant to whether and why [q] obtains. To illustrate, even though it may be plausible to think that the ball's being crimson grounds the ball's being red, we may wish to deny that the ball's being crimson *and round* also grounds the ball's being red, since the ball's shape does not seem to contribute anything to an explanation of why the ball has the color that it does. In this respect, grounding is taken to be similar to other explanatory concepts like causation and different from logical entailment, which is preserved under arbitrary expansion of the premise set. Finally, Rosen considers grounding connections to be metaphysically necessary, i.e. to be governed by the following Entailment Principle: if the fact, [p], grounds the fact, [q], then it is metaphysically necessary that p entails q. Thus, if the ball's being crimson grounds the ball's being red, then the following conditional holds with metaphysical necessity: if the ball is crimson, then the ball is red.

Despite the fact that Rosen's account imposes various substantive requirements on the notion of grounding which go beyond those posited by Schaffer's account, we may nevertheless wonder whether our initial question has been adequately addressed, even in the face of these additional constraints. Supposing that all the cases cited in (2) present us with what Rosen would regard as genuine grounding connections, we may ask again: what exactly has been established by subsuming this plurality under the single rubric of grounding?[6] We might at this point be tempted to entertain the

---

[5] Thus, some constraints on grounding (viz. well-foundedness) are also removed by Rosen, so that his notion of grounding does not end up being more restrictive than Schaffer's in every respect.

[6] Since Rosen takes the relata of the grounding relation to be facts, (2.e)–(2.g), in their present form, do not obviously conform to Rosen's apparatus. For now, I will simply assume that we can view statements like that in (2.e), "The singleton set containing Socrates is grounded in its sole member, Socrates", as in some way elliptical for something which does fit with Rosen's factual approach to grounding, e.g. "The fact that the singleton set containing Socrates *exists* is grounded in the fact that its sole member, Socrates, *exists*". The issue of whether such existential paraphrases really do justice to what is going on in cases like (2.e)–(2.g), however, will take on some prominence below.

following response to this question: by collecting the data together in this way, we have learned at least that what might at first strike us as a quite disparate collection of correlations in reality presents us with a *unified* phenomenon. Rosen in fact takes on board the assumption that grounding presents us with a unified phenomenon as a working hypothesis:

> I begin with the working hypothesis that there is *a single salient form of metaphysical dependence* to which the idioms we have been invoking all refer. The plan is to begin to lay out the principles that govern this relation and its interaction with other important philosophical notions. If the notion is confused or incoherent, we should get some inkling of this as we proceed. On the other hand, if all goes smoothly, we will have neutralized the main grounds for resistance, in which case there can be no principled objection to admitting the notion as intelligible, to be used in raising and answering philosophical questions insofar as this proves fruitful. [Rosen (2010), p. 114; my italics][7]

Schaffer also assumes the unity of grounding and considers the burden of demonstrating the falsity of this hypothesis to rest with those who oppose it:

> Whereas Aristotle claimed that there were many notions of priority, singling out priority in nature as foremost among them [...], this objector goes further, holding that priority in nature is *itself* 'said in many ways.' By way of reply, I see no more reason to consider this a case of mere homonymy, than to consider various cases of identity as merely homonymous. In both cases, there is a common term, and the same formal structure. This is some

---

[7] I want to be clear that I am currently only interested in the question of whether grounding presents us with a unified phenomenon. This question concerning the unity of grounding should be kept separate from some of the other qualms Rosen mentions in the passage quoted above which one might have about grounding, e.g. whether the notion is confused, incoherent, or unintelligible. I am happy to grant that some varieties of metaphysical priority or dependence are at issue in (2.a)–(2.g) and that such notions are coherent and intelligible, despite the fact that they are not reducible to modality, existence, counterfactual dependence, supervenience, realization, causation, identity, and the like. The question I am currently asking is whether all of the cases in (2), and whatever else grounding enthusiasts would subsume under the same rubric, present us with *a single unified* phenomenon. To be fair, Rosen's main focus in his paper is, I think, on putting to rest worries concerning the coherence and intelligibility of grounding and he is therefore less explicitly concerned with establishing the unity of grounding. After all, if one thought that the idiom of grounding was not even coherent or intelligible, then of course the question of whether alleged grounding connections present us with a unified phenomenon would not even arise.

evidence of real unity. At the very least, I would think it incumbent on the objector to provide further reason for thinking that the general term 'grounding' denotes no unified notion. [Schaffer (2009), pp. 376–7, his italics]

The hypothesis that grounding is a unified phenomenon, as it is presented by Schaffer and Rosen, is open to several different interpretations. In its strongest form (the "single-relation" interpretation), the unity hypothesis states that there is only a single grounding relation and it is exemplified by all cases which allegedly present us with grounding connections. A somewhat weaker version of the unity hypothesis (the "single-genus" interpretation) allows for distinct specific grounding relations, but posits that these distinct specific grounding relations fall under a single generic kind, viz. grounding. A yet weaker reading of the unity hypothesis (the "mere resemblance" interpretation) requires only that the distinct relations which go under the name "grounding" exhibit various objective similarities. Whatever interpretation Schaffer and Rosen were hoping to support, their respective accounts provide direct and positive evidence only for the weakest of the three readings of the unity hypothesis, viz. the mere-resemblance interpretation.[8] The most we can say concerning the single-genus interpretation is that Rosen's and Schaffer's approaches to grounding are neutral with respect to it: nothing they say is, strictly speaking, incompatible with this reading of the unity hypothesis; but we are also not given any positive reasons in favor of embracing it. In contrast, the strongest reading of the unity hypothesis, viz. the single-relation interpretation, is explicitly discouraged by the information we are given.

In Schaffer's case, we have already seen that his grounding relation is formally indistinguishable from other well-founded partial orderings which are presumably not numerically identical with the grounding relation, such as the relation, *is a substring of*, when applied to a domain consisting of letters belonging to a certain alphabet and the strings that can be constructed out of them.[9] But

---

[8] Schaffer has since informed me (personal communication) that, from among the three interpretations listed above, he feels most drawn to the single-genus interpretation.

[9] As I indicated in an earlier note, since I take it to be itself a controversial matter what constitutes a paradigm case of grounding, an appeal to alleged paradigm cases

even Rosen's account pushes us in the direction of positing several distinct specific grounding relations which objectively resemble each other in various respects. Whether we are also licensed to infer that these various objectively similar relations belong to a single generic kind is simply underdetermined by the evidence Rosen provides.

To see why, within Rosen's framework, we are driven away from the single-relation interpretation of the unity hypothesis, consider first the contrast between the determinable/determinate relation, at issue in (2.d), and the genus/species relation, illustrated in (2.h):

(2) h. <u>Genus/Species</u>: The fact that this geometrical figure is a square is grounded in the fact that this geometrical figure is an equilateral rectangle.

(2.h) follows the Aristotelian way of thinking of the genus/species relation, which Rosen adopts, according to which a geometrical figure for example has the more specific property of being a square at least in part in virtue of its having the more general property of being a rectangle. By contrast, as illustrated in (2.d), the relation between determinable facts (e.g. the ball's being red) and determinate facts (e.g. the ball's being crimson) is supposed to be exactly reversed: the ball is said to instantiate the more general determinable property, red, in virtue of its instantiating the less general determinate property, crimson. In addition, while (2.h), in Rosen's view, is an example of a reductive relationship which can be expressed in the form of a real definition (viz. "To be a square is to be an equilateral rectangle"), he urges us not to think of the relationship in (2.d) in this way: the essence of the determinate property, crimson, for Rosen, is not expressible in the form of a real definition which mentions the determinable property, red, together with some differentiating feature. If we go along with the details of Rosen's diagnosis, then the appropriate reaction to these two cases would seem to be to posit at least two distinct specific grounding relations, e.g. the genus/species relation and the determinable/determinate relation. Whether these two alleged specific grounding relations fall under

---

does not yet help me in singling out even a unique generic notion among the possible contenders which satisfy the formal properties of a well-founded partial ordering.

a single more generic kind, viz. grounding, is left open by the information with which we are provided.

There are other striking differences between the connectiors cited in (2). For example, in the logical cases, which are illustrated in (2.c) by the relationship between a disjunctive fact (e.g. the ball's being red or round) and its constituent facts (e.g. the ball's being red; the ball's being round), overdetermination of the grounded fact by its alleged grounds is permissible. A disjunctive fact of the form, [p v q], may obtain in virtue of [p]'s obtaining, or it may obtain in virtue of [q]'s obtaining, or it may obtain in virtue of the fact that both [p] and [q] obtain. The truthmaking cases, illustrated in (2.b), behave in this way as well, since a single true proposition may be made true by a number of different states of affairs: for example, the proposition that someone is a philosopher can be made true by Socrates' being a philosopher, Plato's being a philosopher, and so on. There is no incompatibility which arises from the idea that distinct truthmakers act as alleged grounds for the truth of a single proposition.

But now consider the determinable/determinate relation: in this case, notoriously, the determinate facts which are invoked as the alleged grounds for a given determinable fact rule out that some other determinate fact also obtains which involves the attribution of a different determinate property to the same entity. For example, if the ball's being red (all over) is grounded in the ball's being crimson (all over), then that same determinable fact cannot also at the same time be grounded in the ball's being maroon (all over), since a ball cannot simultaneously be both crimson (all over) and maroon (all over). Similarly, in the genus/species case, assuming that Rosen is correct in thinking that something's belonging to a certain species is at least in part grounded in its belonging to a certain genus, there is no leeway here in how a given specific fact may be grounded, as long as we stay at the same level of generality: the specific fact that a certain geometrical figure is a square can only be partially grounded in the generic fact that the figure is a rectangle; it cannot also simultaneously be partially grounded in its being a triangle, since being a triangle and being a rectangle are incompatible.

Thirdly, as has been noted by several writers (e.g. Fine (2012), pp. 43–6), truthmaking has the following unique feature which distinguishes it from all the other alleged grounding connections. When we consider the relation between the truth of a proposition and a state of affairs which is supposed to make it true, one of the relata of the alleged grounding connection in this case is a representational entity, viz. a proposition or some appropriate item which is capable of being true or false. This truthbearing entity represents the world as being a certain way and it is fairly closely connected to some associated linguistic entities, e.g. sentences which express the proposition in question. The other relatum of the truthmaking relation, in contrast, is a worldly entity of some sort (e.g. a state of affairs) whose existence is supposed to explain the truth of the proposition in question. In this respect, truthmaking differs from all the other alleged grounding connections, since the remaining cases are supposed to draw both of their relata from a purely worldly domain.

In fact, each of the relations that is instantiated in (2) can be differentiated from each of the other relations, either on the basis of the differences to which we have already pointed or on the basis of some other distinguishing mark which will emerge below. The fact that the relations instantiated in (2) exhibit different characteristics, by Leibniz's Law, entails that the relations in question are themselves distinct as well, thereby discounting the strongest, single-relation interpretation of the unity hypothesis. Nevertheless, despite these clear differences between the relations at issue, the data in (2) might still be taken to be at least compatible with the next weaker reading of the unity hypothesis, viz. the single-genus interpretation, according to which grounding imposes on its alleged instances at least the unity of a generic kind. But even this weaker interpretation of the unity hypothesis would have to be supported by explicit arguments: it cannot be inferred merely from the presence of objective similarities that are shared by various distinct specific alleged grounding relations.

Rosen's account only draws attention to the various ways in which the phenomena which he thinks exhibit "a single salient form of metaphysical dependence" resemble each other, thereby providing direct support only for the weakest of the three readings of the unity hypothesis, viz. the mere-resemblance interpretation. But not all objective similarities are in fact indicative of the presence of a single genus. If such an inference were licensed, then we would be justified for example in assigning all instances of jade to a single kind of mineral, since they are after all objectively similar in various respects, when in fact we have learned that such a classification would be incorrect, since instances of what is commonly called "jade" exhibit sufficiently different chemical compositions to warrant a distinction between two different kinds of minerals, jadeite and nephrite. Thus, to establish that, for example, the genus/species relation and the determinable/determinate relation are correctly classified as two species which fall under a single genus, viz. grounding, it is not enough to show merely that these relations resemble each other in various objective respects, e.g. by being irreflexive, asymmetric, transitive, non-monotonic and metaphysically necessary. If the genus/species relation and the determinable/determinate relation were indeed two species which belong to a single genus, then, given Rosen's conception of real definitions, we should expect to be able to state the essence of these two specific relations in the form of a real definition which mentions the genus to which they belong (viz. grounding) together with some differentiating feature which distinguishes the two specific relations from each other. It is not clear, however, what more Rosen could say at this point to convince those of us who are skeptical even of the weaker, single-genus interpretation of the unity hypothesis, given that he (like Schaffer) takes grounding to be a primitive relation, i.e. irreducible and indefinable. For a primitivist like Rosen or Schaffer, the most we can do is to elucidate the notion of grounding by bringing out some of its characteristics, e.g. the formal properties that govern grounding. But this strategy by itself does not distinguish between the mere-resemblance and the single-genus interpretation of the unity hypothesis.

Given the considerations adduced so far, then, grounding theorists cannot take themselves to have established anything stronger than the mere-resemblance interpretation of the unity hypothesis, according to which alleged grounding connections resemble each other in various objective respects. Whether these distinct but similar relations which go under the name "grounding" also fall under a single genus at this point has been neither confirmed nor disconfirmed by the evidence we have been given. Considering the great hype that surrounds the notion of ground, one might be excused for being somewhat underwhelmed by this result. A philosopher who is interested in the problems surrounding personal identity, for example, would not feel that great progress has been made by being informed that the relation of numerical identity either falls under the same genus as, or is at least objectively similar to, the relation of being the same height as, since both of them are equivalence relations and hence exhibit some objective formal similarities. And yet that is roughly the dialectical situation in which we find ourselves when we are referred to the notion of ground as a promising tool in terms of which to develop an illuminating approach to relative fundamentality.[10]

2.3. Grounding as essential connectedness

Audi (2012b) goes to greater lengths than most grounding theorists in attempting to provide explicit support for the hypothesis that grounding presents us with a unified phenomenon. Moreover, he is quite explicit in endorsing the strongest, single-relation interpretation of the unity hypothesis:

Even the view that there is only a generic similarity, that there is a different species of noncausal determination at work in each case, strikes me as under-motivated. What differentiates the species? If it is only that one concerns normative properties, another determinables, still another dispositions, this does not yet give us a reason to think that *how the determination works* differs in each case, simply because it relates different kinds of fact. So I take the burden of proof to be on those who think there are different relations at work to show why, to show in what way the determination differs in the different cases. I will proceed, then, on the assumption that there is just one noncausal determination relation at work in the relevant examples. [Audi (2012), p. 689; Audi's italics]

In order to increase the plausibility of the unity hypothesis under its strongest single-relation reading, Audi has to place fairly severe restrictions on the collection of phenomena which he would recognize as genuine instances of grounding. For example, from among the eight examples cited in (2.a)–(2.h), Audi would classify only

---

[10] I suppose it is still left open by what has just been said that grounding might be a determinable relation (on analogy with the property of being red) of which the genus/species relation is a determinate (on analogy with the property of being crimson). I suspect, however, that Rosen would find this idea unattractive, since grounding would then turn out to be a less fundamental phenomenon than its determinate manifestations, e.g. the genus/species relation, just as he would regard something's being red as a less fundamental fact than its being crimson, given that the determinable fact is supposed to be grounded in the determinate fact.

three as involving genuine grounding connections: the relation between the instantiation of moral and natural properties in (2.a); the relation between the instantiation of semantic and non-semantic properties in (2.b); and the relation between the instantiation of determinable and determinate properties in (2.d). Given Audi's approach to grounding, we should not expect the other cases to conform to the same pattern as those which he regards as being indicative of a genuine grounding connection, despite the intuitions to the contrary cited by Schaffer, Rosen, and other grounding enthusiasts. (I will come back to the question of how Audi would treat the relation between sets and their members, in (2.e), as well as that between holes and their hosts, in (2.f).) In general, Audi takes grounding to be a non-causal determination relation which underwrites the correctness of non-causal explanations and which obtains in cases in which a certain genuine property or relation (e.g. semantic, moral, aesthetic) cannot be instantiated brutely, but rather is instantiated only in virtue of the instantiation of some other type of property or relation (e.g. a natural one).[11]

Given the limitations Audi sets on which types of connections are to be considered to be genuine cases of grounding, the scope of his unification thesis, if successful, of course also decreases in ambitiousness. But we might think that this price is worth paying, as long as the chances of singling out a genuinely unified phenomenon have been improved by cutting down on the range of cases that are supposed to be unified by means of this strategy. But even with respect to Audi's restricted class of phenomena there are nevertheless reasons to be skeptical as to whether a single non-causal determination relation, in all of these cases, underwrites the correctness of the corresponding non-causal explanations.

---

[11] Since the scope of Audi's grounding relation is narrower than that of Rosen's, Audi can also accept certain additional constraints on grounding which would be incompatible with Rosen's framework. In particular, because Audi does not recognize the logical cases, e.g. (2.c), as exhibiting genuine grounding connections, he is able to accept a constraint he calls "Minimality", according to which the grounds for some fact must be jointly, but not individually, sufficient to bring about the fact in question. Minimality would be violated by a disjunctive fact, [p v q], which obtains in virtue of both of its constituent facts, [p] and [q], obtaining, since [p] individually and [q] individually are already sufficient to make it the case that the disjunctive fact, [p v q], obtains.

The best hope for unification, within Audi's framework, lies with an additional constraint he imposes on the grounding relation called *"Essential Connectedness"*. According to this principle, when the instantiation of a certain property or relation grounds the instantiation of some other property or relation, then it lies in the nature of the properties or relations appealed to in a given grounding claim that their instances should be connected in this way:[12]

> For example, when a given instance of maroonness grounds a coincident instance of redness, this fact manifests the natures of the relevant properties. It is part of their essence to behave in this way when instantiated. This is not to give an explanation of *why* the relevant facts stand in a grounding relation, and indeed there may not be an explanation, properly so called. The point of this characterization is simply to chart an important relation between the essences of properties and the grounding relations that obtain among their instances. [Audi (2012), p. 695]

Can Essential Connectedness be used to establish the single-relation interpretation of the unity hypothesis? Recall, first, that we have already drawn a distinction above between the alleged grounding relations that are instantiated in two out of the three cases Audi recognizes as genuine cases of grounding: the semantic/non-semantic case in (2.b) and the determinable/determinate case in (2.d). In the semantic/non-semantic case, we observed that the relation in question imposes unique type constraints which are not found in the other alleged cases of grounding: truthmaking, for example, takes as its relata a pair consisting of a representational and a non-representational entity. In addition, overdetermination of what is grounded by its alleged grounds is permitted in the semantic/non-semantic case, but disallowed in the determinable/determinate case. These considerations provide evidence in favor of positing two distinct specific relations in two of out of the three cases just cited.

It remains to distinguish the third case, viz. the moral/natural connection, from the other two. In this instance as well, we come

---

[12] Like Schaffer and Rosen, Audi also takes grounding to be a primitive, and hence indefinable, relation. Thus, Essential Connectedness is not supposed to contribute to a definition of grounding, but merely to help elucidate grounding by pointing to one of its characteristics. Audi also denies that all cases of grounding are themselves grounded; that is, one cannot always expect to be able to ground a grounding claim by appealing to Essential Connectedness.

across unique features which do not generalize to the other cases in which Audi discerns genuine grounding connections. Consider the contrast between (2.d), in which a determinable property is said to be instantiated in virtue of its being the case that a determinate property is instantiated, and (2.a), according to which a moral property is instantiated in virtue of its being the case that a natural property is instantiated. Essential Connectedness states that both grounding connections hold in virtue of the natures of the properties at issue. Thus, applying Essential Connectedness to (2.d), we learn that it lies in the natures of the properties, red and crimson, that instantiations of crimson ground instantiations of red. Applying Essential Connectnedness to the case of (2.a), we would similarly expect it to be the case that it lies in the nature of the properties, moral wrongness and lie-telling, that an instantiation of lie-telling by an act grounds an instantiation of wrongness by that same act. But at this point an interesting and systematic difference emerges between the moral/natural case and the determinable/determinate case: in the moral/natural case, at least for a non-Kantian, the connection between the properties or relations in question appears to be defeasible in a way in which the connection between determinable and determinate properties or relations is not. To illustrate, in a particular case, an act may be an instance of lie-telling and nevertheless fail to be morally wrong, if, for example, the lie in question is being told to save someone's life. In contrast, the relationship between crimson and red is not similarly susceptible to extenuating circumstances: instantiations of crimson always and in every circumstance give rise to simultaneous instantiations of red by the same object. One might suspect that this contrast can be traced to a difference in the varieties of necessity that are operative in these two cases, viz. metaphysical necessity in the determinable/determinate case and normative necessity in the moral/natural case. But such a divergence with respect to the modal force of the connection at issue again underwrites the suspicion that the relations in question themselves are distinct.[13]

---

[13] It should be noted that Audi is aware of this objection to his account and addresses it in Section IV.5 of his paper. In his response, Audi attempts to make a case for thinking that the difference just pointed to originates from a difference in the relata in question, and not from a difference in the relations. In his view, the fact that a lie was told is a full ground only of the act's prima facie wrongness and merely

Thus, the evidence we have examined up to this point, contrary to what is suggested by prominent grounding theorists, calls into question the strongest version of the unity hypothesis, according to which all alleged cases of grounding are unified under a single relation. Whether the distinct relations which obtain in these cases at least fall under a single genus has been neither confirmed nor disconfirmed by the data in question. The most to which grounding theorists are at this point entitled therefore is the relatively weak objective-similarity reading of the unity hypothesis. To appreciate just how weak this reading of the unity hypothesis is, however, we should keep in mind that the phenomena in question are equally compatible with the following interpretation, which we might call the "objective-difference" reading of the corresponding "heterogeneity of grounding" hypothesis. According to this reading, we should interpret the phenomena in question as presenting us with a heterogeneous collection, since the distinct relations that are instantiated in alleged cases of grounding exhibit objective differences. Given that we have observed both objective similarities and objective differences between the alleged grounding connections, the unity of grounding hypothesis under the objective-similarity reading is no more supported by the evidence than the heterogeneity of grounding hypothesis under the objective-difference reading. As working hypotheses, then, the unity of grounding and the heterogeneity of grounding stand roughly on equal footing.

3. GROUNDING AND THE SUBSTANCE/ NON-SUBSTANCE DISTINCTION

So far, my main goal has been to argue for the coarse-grainedness of grounding by emphasizing the lack of unity inherent in the collection of phenomena that are identified as alleged cases of

---

a partial ground of the act's all-things-considered wrongness (Audi 2012b, p. 703). However, the very fact that such a maneuver is required in the moral/natural case, but not in the determinable/determinate case, strikes me as further evidence that there is a difference in "how the determination works", and not just a difference in the nature of the relata. If this is right, then we would have encountered one more reason in favor of positing distinct relations in the different alleged cases of grounding. But there is obviously more to be said about the details of the moral/natural case and I do not take these very complex issues to have been settled by my very brief remarks.

grounding. At this point, I want to shift my attention to a different way in which the coarse-grainedness of grounding manifests itself, namely through the failure of the grounding idiom to capture and illuminate what is philosophically interesting and important about the traditional substance/non-substance distinction.[14] For the purposes of this argument, we may grant the grounding theorist the strongest reading of his working hypothesis, according to which all genuine cases of grounding are unified under a single relation. The question now before us is, rather, whether the application of this allegedly unified and unifying relation manages to accomplish much significant philosophical work when it is applied to those connections between the fundamental and the derivative to which the traditional substance/non-substance distinction is intended to give voice. I argue in what follows that we will again walk away with disappointment if we expect much illumination from the application of the grounding idiom to this domain.

3.1. Candidate fundamental and derivative entities

The candidates listed in (3) below have been thought by some philosophers to possess the relatively *high* degree of fundamentality characteristic of those entities within a given ontology which deserve to be included among the substances (assuming of course that there are such things). We can leave open for present purposes the question of whether these entities are (or ought to be) classified as absolutely fundamental as well, since my present focus is on the notion of relative fundamentality which is meant to go along with the grounding idiom:

(3) a. Entities which belong to the inventory of fundamental physics (e.g. fields or fundamental particles).
 b. God.
 c. Cartesian minds.
 d. Positions in spacetime (according to an absolute conception of spacetime).
 e. Unified natural wholes.
 f. Simples.

---

[14] See for example Simons (1998) for helpful discussion of the substance/non-substance distinction, and an interestingly skeptical attitude towards it.

g. Platonic universals.
h. Haecceities.
i. Aristotelian forms.

In contrast, the following candidates have been thought by some philosophers to possess the relatively *low* degree of fundamentality characteristic of those entities within a given ontology which deserve to be excluded from the category of substances (assuming again that the entities in question exist):[15]

(4) a. Boundaries.
  b. Holes.
  c. Tropes (moments, modes).[16]
  d. Aristotelian universals.
  e. Heaps.
  f. Mereological sums (fusions, aggregates).
  g. Collections (e.g. non-empty sets, committees, ...).
  h. Artifacts.
  i. Artworks.
  j. Intentional objects (e.g. fictional characters, the golden mountain).

My intention at present is not to endorse any of the classifications that are cited in (3) and (4). Rather, I am interested in examining whether philosophers who are sympathetic to at least some of these classifications might avail themselves of the idiom of grounding, and its associated notions of relative fundamentality and derivativeness, as a suitable vehicle to express the contrasts they have in mind when they assign some entities to the category of substances and others to a non-substantial category of some sort.

---

[15] We have already encountered (4.b) and (4.g) in the form of (2.e) and (2.f), in connection with Schaffer's category-neutral grounding relation.

[16] I am thinking here of non-reductive trope theorists in the Aristotelian tradition (e.g. Edmund Husserl, Roman Ingarden, Jonathan Lowe), who take tropes (moments, modes) to be less fundamental than the concrete particular objects which are their bearers. In contrast, reductive trope-theorists in the nominalist, empiricist, Humean tradition (such as Keith Campbell, C. B. Martin, and D. C. Williams) take tropes to be more fundamental than the concrete particular objects which are their bearers; these philosophers would want to place tropes in (3), rather than (4). For more on this dispute, see Koslicki (forth. b).

3.2. Degrees of substancehood

I mentioned just now that, for the purposes of the present discussion, I want to view the cases listed in (3) and (4) through the lens of relative fundamentality, leaving open whether any of the entities cited in (3) are properly classified as fundamental in some absolute sense. In this vein, it would be possible to say, for example, that tropes (otherwise known as "moments" or "modes") are less fundamental than the concrete particular objects which are their bearers, while leaving open whether the concrete particular objects which act as the bearers of tropes are themselves absolutely fundamental. In fact, there may very well be good reasons for thinking that at least some of these concrete particular objects ought not to be classified as absolutely fundamental (e.g. because they are composite). Given this approach, together with the assumption that (3) and (4) present us with the sorts of cases to which the traditional substance/non-substance distinction is intended to apply, it follows that the relevant notion of substancehood currently at issue should also be understood as a comparative one which comes in degrees. Thus, when substancehood is understood as an indicator of relative fundamentality, as opposed to absolute fundamentality, then the notion of substancehood at issue must itself be one which would permit us to classify an entity, or type of entity, as *more of a substance than*, or as more deserving of substance status than, some other entity, or type of entity. (Aristotle seems to have had something roughly of this sort in mind when he introduced the distinction between the "primary" and the "secondary" substances: I take it that the primary substances, in his mind, are even more deserving of substance status than the secondary substances, even though both types of entities count as substances.) All the while, we should leave it open, for present purposes, whether, in addition to this comparative notion of substancehood, an entity which is classified as relatively more fundamental than another (i.e. as more deserving of substance status than another) is also fundamental absolutely (i.e. a substance *simpliciter* or in some absolute sense). Certainly, some of the items listed in (3) would strike those who are committed to them as rather natural candidates to be regarded as absolutely fundamental; but there is no need to settle this question now, given that we are currently engaged in an investigation into the nature of relative fundamentality. (In what follows, when I speak of fundamentality, I continue to have in mind relative fundamentality, unless otherwise indicated.)

3.3. *The existential paraphrase strategy*

Since the items listed in (3) and (4), to which the traditional substance/non-substance distinction is meant to apply, at least on the face of it appear to be non-propositional, non-factual entities which cannot in any obvious way be paired with declarative sentences, it is also not immediately obvious how the idiom of grounding, with its associated connectives (e.g. "grounds", "is grounded in", "because", "because of", "in virtue of", "is nothing over and above", or "is explained by") will be of much help to us in capturing the philosophically relevant differences between the candidate entities with relatively high degrees of fundamentality listed in (3) and those with relatively low degrees of fundamentality listed in (4).

As it stands, a declarative sentence of the form "___ because God" or "___ in virtue of Platonic universals" is not even grammatical in English, when "___" is filled in with another noun-phrase, since connectives, such as "because" or "in virtue of", which are supposed to be indicative of grounding connections, cannot take simple noun-phrases as their complements. And while sentences of the form "God grounds ___", "A heap is grounded in ___", or "___ is explained by God" are at least grammatical in English, when "___" is filled in with another noun-phrase, the constructions in question still leave us with crucial unanswered questions. For example, if confronted with a sentence of the form, "A heap is grounded in ____", where "____" is filled in by another noun-phrase, the natural response is: "But *what is it about* the heap that is supposed to be grounded in *something-or-other* about ____?" and "*What is it about* ____ that is supposed to ground *something-or-other* about the heap?" If grounding is to be understood as a relation which connects propositions, facts, states of affairs, or whatever goes naturally with declarative sentences (as Rosen, Audi, and others assume), then constructions like "God grounds ___", "A heap is grounded in ___", or "___ is explained by God" must be understood as elliptical; and there is nothing we can immediately glean from these grounding constructions which gives us explicit guidance on how to fill in the ellipsis in question.[17]

When grounding theorists are confronted with the question of how the ellipsis under consideration is to be filled in, a popular move seems to be to supply "exists" or "existence" in order to turn the noun-phrases which apparently denote non-propositional, non-factual entities into ones which conform to the propositional, factual format that is presupposed by many grounding theorists for sentences expressing grounding connections:[18]

(5) a. <u>Boundaries</u>: Boundaries *exist* because the concrete particular objects whose boundaries they are *exist*.
b. <u>Holes</u>: The *existence* of holes is grounded in the *existence* of the concrete particular objects whose holes they are.
c. <u>Tropes</u>: Tropes *exist* in virtue of the concrete particular objects which are their bearers *existing*.
d. <u>Aristotelian universals</u>: The *existence* of an Aristotelian universal is explained by the *existence* of the concrete particular objects which exemplify it. And so on.

But there are two basic problems with this strategy. First, the existential paraphrase strategy illustrated in (5) creates the illusion that the contrasts relevant to the cases listed in (3) and (4) are all purely existential, i.e. that there is some single difference with respect to the conditions of existence which obtains between entities with a higher and entities with a lower degree of fundamentality, namely that the latter exist because the former exist. But many of us have come to believe that there is more going on in the contrasts illustrated in

---

[17] Since Schaffer's grounding relation is category-neutral, his account does not require us to understand the noun-phrases flanking "grounds" as elliptical for something that could be expressed by means of a declarative sentence. However, for reasons noted above, Schaffer's account is, if anything, even more liable than Rosen's or Audi's to leave us feeling perplexed as to what exactly we are supposed to have been told about the relationship between a grounded entity and its ground.

[18] Audi, for one, would not want to sign on to the existential paraphrase strategy, since he denies that existence is a genuine property. Thus, a statement like "Boundaries exist", in Audi's view, fails to denote a fact, since it does not attribute a genuine property to an object or objects. But Audi's resistance to the existential paraphrase strategy puts him in the minority among grounding enthusiasts. In the next section, I turn to an alternative strategy for how grounding theorists might deal with non-factual cases such as those in (3) and (4) which is more amenable to Audi's approach to grounding.

(3) and (4) than what could be captured in terms of some single asymmetry concerning the conditions of existence governing the entities in question. For example, with respect to (5.c), if tropes can be essential to their bearers, then it seems equally plausible to think that a concrete particular object exists because those tropes which are essential to it exist. But it would constitute a violation of the alleged asymmetry of grounding to say both that the existence of an essential trope is grounded in the existence of its bearer and that the existence of the concrete particular object which is the bearer of the essential trope in question is also grounded in the existence of its essential trope. In addition, even if such situations of mutual grounding were to be admitted, it would still be desirable to have the resources required to express the idea that there is an interesting and philosophically important categorical difference between tropes and their bearers, namely that tropes are the kinds of things which need bearers, while concrete particular objects are the kinds of things which can act as the bearers of tropes, but which themselves do not and cannot have bearers. But the existential paraphrases in (5) do not seem to supply the apparatus necessary to capture such a categorical distinction. And while this particular point may not generalize in exactly this form to the other cases canvassed above, it nevertheless helps to bring out that the existential paraphrases in (5) do not fully get to the heart of the contrasts illustrated in (3) and (4).[19,20]

Secondly, and relatedly, even if the sentential reformulations in (5) did do justice to the intended contrasts conveyed by (3) and (4), the existential idiom is nevertheless too coarse-grained to bring out the interesting ontological differences between entities with a higher

---

[19] The possibility just described should be regarded as more than a purely hypothetical scenario for those who are sympathetic both to trope-theory and to essentialism. For from the perspective of a trope theorist, a predication of the form "a is essentially F" would have to be analyzed as involving an F-ness trope whose presence in its bearer (viz. the object, a, in question) is essential to that bearer. Suppose for example the property of being human is essential to Socrates; then, according to a trope-theoretic framework, a particular humanity trope inheres in Socrates and, by hypothesis, it does so essentially. Now consider the following two grounding claims: "Socrates' existence is grounded in the existence of his humanity trope" and "The existence of Socrates' humanity trope is grounded in Socrates' existence". If the grounding theorist wishes to accept only the latter but not the former of these statements, nothing that has been said up to this point concerning the idiom of grounding explains this preference.

[20] See also Koslicki (2013a) for arguments against existential construals of ontological dependence which apply to the existential paraphrases in (5) as well.

degree of fundamentality, such as those in (3), and entities with a lower degree of fundamentality, such as those in (4). Arguably, the candidate derivative entities cited in (3), if they exist and if in fact they are correctly classified as possessing a relatively low degree of fundamentality, do not all have their derivative status for the same reasons. If there are such things as boundaries, Aristotelian universals, heaps, artifacts, and the like, and if they are in fact derivative in some sense compared to the entities listed in (4) under the rubric, "candidate fundamental entities", then ideally our approach to relative fundamentality should be sufficiently fine-grained to allow us to distinguish between the different factors that are at play in accounting for the derivative status of these entities. Thus, our ontological and meta-ontological apparatus should be nuanced enough to capture the relevant respects in which, for example, a boundary is different from an Aristotelian universal, a heap or an artifact, even though they are all in some sense derivative compared to entities which belong in the inventory of fundamental physics, God, Cartesian minds, unified natural wholes, simples, Platonic universals and the like (if in fact there are such things). In order to explain the derivative status of artworks and fictional characters, it would be natural to appeal at least in part to the fact that creative acts of intentional agents are required to bring these entities into existence and imbue them with the qualities they come to exhibit; but this line of reasoning may be completely irrelevant to a general explanation of the derivative status of boundaries, holes, and tropes. Similarly, in order to explain the derivative status of heaps, we may wish to appeal to their non-unified character; but lack of unity may again be out of place in an account of the derivative status of tropes. All these more fine-grained explanatory factors which indicate that entities in (3) and (4) have their fundamental or derivative status for different reasons are simply glossed over in the purely existential reformulations of the intended contrasts given in (5).

3.4. Alternative grounding strategies

Although Rosen is primarily focused on those alleged grounding connections whose relata are straightforwardly compatible with his factual approach to grounding, he does briefly address the question of how one might approach cases which apparently involve non-propositional, non-factual entities from the perspective of a grounding theorist:

> Some philosophers believe that the aim of ontology is not simply to say what there is, but rather to say what *really* exists, or what exists in the most fundamental sense.... Such philosophers may say: Of course the lectern exists; it's a thing; it's real. But it is not an *ultimate* constituent of reality; it is not *ontologically real*. What could this mean? Here is one possibility. Say that a fact is fundamental (or brute) if it does not obtain in virtue of other facts, and that a *thing* is fundamental if it is a constituent of a fundamental fact. Then we might say that fundamental ontology seeks a catalog of the fundamental things. When the fundamental ontologist says that the lectern is not 'ultimately real', all he means is that the various facts concerning the [lectern]—including the fact that it exists—ultimately obtain in virtue of facts about (say) the physical particles in the vicinity, facts that do not contain the [lectern] itself as a constituent. [Rosen (2010), p. 112]

Rosen's suggestion is that we can derive a fundamental/non-fundamental distinction for non-factual entities, such as lecterns, from a corresponding fundamental/non-fundamental distinction for facts in roughly the following way, where the operative notion of fundamentality appears to be an absolute one:

Absolute Fundamentality/Non-Fundamentality for Facts:
A fact, [p], is *absolutely fundamental* if [p] does not obtain in virtue of any other facts, i.e. if [p] is ungrounded; otherwise, [p] is *not absolutely fundamental*.

Absolute Fundamentality/Non-Fundamentality for Non-Factual Entities:
A non-factual entity, a, is *absolutely fundamental* if it figures as a constituent in a fundamental fact; otherwise, a is *not absolutely fundamental*.

To illustrate, a fact concerning physical particles might be classified as a fundamental fact, according to this scheme, if it does not obtain in virtue of some further fact. Correspondingly, the physical particles themselves, which figure as constituents in such fundamental facts, would be designated as fundamental entities. In contrast, a lectern presumably would not figure as a constituent in fundamental facts; rather, we would expect facts about lecterns (including, but not limited to, facts about their existence) to obtain in virtue of, i.e. to be grounded in, other facts. Hence lecterns, following Rosen's proposal, would be classified as not absolutely fundamental.

It is easy to see that this idea, as it stands, does not do justice to the intended contrasts listed in (3) and (4), since it was explicitly left open whether the entities cited in (3) are correctly classified as absolutely fundamental. To illustrate, suppose a trope is merely less fundamental than the concrete particular object which is its bearer, without the bearer itself being absolutely fundamental. In its current form, Rosen's proposal would lump together both the trope and its bearer as not absolutely fundamental, since presumably facts about both of them obtain in virtue of other facts, without giving us the ability to distinguish between the different degrees of non-fundamentality we want to assign to tropes and their bearers. But perhaps Rosen's proposal can be adapted to reflect a difference in the degree of relative fundamentality or non-fundamentality adhering to entities of different types:

Relative Fundamentality/Non-Fundamentality for Facts:
A fact, [p], is *less fundamental than* a fact, [q], if [p] is grounded in [q], where [q] may or may not be absolutely fundamental.

Relative Fundamentality/Non-Fundamentality for Non-Factual Entities:
A non-factual entity, a, is *less fundamental than* a non-factual entity, b, if facts about a are grounded in facts about b, where facts about b may or may not be absolutely fundamental.[21]

To prevent this proposal concerning relative fundamentality and non-fundamentality from simply collapsing into the existential paraphrase strategy, which we have already considered and disposed of earlier, the alleged grounding connections in question cannot be purely existential, i.e. they cannot simply be of the form:

---

[21] In addition to the weaknesses I point to below, this proposed definition of relative fundamentality for non-factual entities in terms of relative fundamentality for facts may also be problematic for other reasons. For example, it might be possible that certain facts about a are grounded in certain facts about b, while nevertheless certain facts about b are grounded in certain facts about a. A scenario of this sort would lead to a situation in which a is classified both as more fundamental and as less fundamental than b, according to a single notion of relative fundamentality. (Thanks to Jonathan Schaffer for raising this point.)

(6) a. [The redness trope exists] is grounded in [The rose exists].

For (6.a) is of course simply an instance of the more general existential claim in (5.c). Rather, if the proposal currently under consideration is to present us with a new idea about how to derive a notion of relative fundamentality and non-fundamentality for non-factual entities from one that is defined in the first instance for facts, at least one of the relata of the alleged grounding relation in question has to be non-existential, e.g.

(6) b. [The redness trope exists] is grounded in [The rose is red].

Presumably, in order for the proposed schema to work in its intended fashion, the allegedly grounded fact, [The redness trope exists], should not tacitly contain the rose as a constituent; and the alleged ground, [The rose is red], similarly should not implicitly contain the redness trope as a constituent. After all, the redness trope is supposed to be classified as a less fundamental entity than the rose, because facts about the redness trope (i.e. facts in which the redness trope figures as a constituent) are said to be grounded in facts about the rose (i.e. facts in which the rose figures as a constituent). I assume therefore that the facts under consideration cannot be hybrid facts, i.e. facts which contain as constituents both the allegedly more fundamental entity and the allegedly less fundamental entity in question.

Suppose, then, that the occurrence of "red", in the statement, "The rose is red", which is used to pick out the ground in question, is analyzed as denoting something other than the rose's redness trope: it might, for example, be analyzed instead as denoting the universal, viz. redness, with the predicational tie, "is", indicating a relation such as that of characterization, exemplification or instantiation. In that case, the alleged ground, [The rose is red], has as constituents the rose (a concrete particular object), redness (a universal) and characterization (a relation which obtains between them). We can then read the alleged grounding claim in (6.b) as asserting that the existence of the redness trope in question is grounded in the rose's being characterized by the universal, redness. More generally, according to the proposal currently under consideration, tropes would be classified as less fundamental than their bearers, because facts in which tropes figure as constituents (e.g. facts concerning the existence of tropes) are grounded in facts in which their bearers together with other entities figure as constituents (e.g. facts about the characterizing relation obtaining between a concrete particular object and a universal).[22]

Whatever the merits of this proposal are for the particular case at hand, it does not straightforwardly generalize in its present form to the other cases listed in (3) and (4). For facts about the characterizing relations which obtain between concrete particular objects and the universals they exemplify do not help us understand, for example, the derivative status of heaps, mereological sums, sets, artifacts or artworks, or the fundamental status of God, Cartesian minds, or positions in spacetime. In each case, in order to arrive at a suitable grounding claim that is tailored to the particular case at hand, the facts which are related by the alleged grounding claim in question in effect have to reflect the reason why the entities in question have the relatively fundamental or non-fundamental status they do. In the case of artworks, for example, it might be appropriate to bring out their relatively low degree of relative fundamentality through alleged grounding connections between facts about artworks and facts about the artists who created them. Thus, perhaps the existence of Michelangelo's *David* is grounded in facts about the shape Michelangelo imposed on a certain block of marble with certain representational intentions in mind. But, again, the relationship between the properties of an artwork and the intentional acts of the artist who created it is peculiar to this particular case and does not yield a general characterization of derivativeness that is applicable to non-factual entities across the board.

At this point, we can also see why the alternative grounding strategy we have been considering is not particularly helpful in capturing or illuminating what is important about the traditional

---

[22] A suggestion along these lines is also roughly what Audi seems to have in mind, when he proposes that we apply his approach to grounding to cases involving constitution or composition by noting for example that a fact like [x is a statue] might be grounded in [x is clay of a certain shape] or [the ys are arranged in a certain way] (cf. Audi (2012b, p. 701). Since Audi does not believe in existential facts at all, however, both relata of the alleged grounding connections in question would have to be non-existential facts.

substance/non-substance distinction. For whatever useful information we can glean from an alleged grounding claim such as (6.b) concerning the relationship between more fundamental and less fundamental entities must be extracted from the facts themselves which figure as the relata of the alleged grounding claim at issue, and not from the additional consideration that these facts are related by means of an alleged grounding relation. In the case of (6.b), once it is clear what constituents figure in the relevant facts in question and how these constituents are related, then the philosophical work required in elucidating the derivative status of tropes relative to the concrete particular objects that are their bearers and the universals they instantiate has been accomplished. And while expressing this relationship in the form of a grounding claim does encapsulate the idea that some asymmetric explanatory relationship obtains between the allegedly more fundamental facts or entities and the allegedly less fundamental facts or entities, nothing that is specifically tailored to the particular cases that are listed in (3) and (4) follows from thinking of this asymmetric explanatory relationship in terms of grounding. Upon learning that a fact, [p], grounds a fact, [q], we cannot deduce for example that the constituents that figure in [q] are the results of creative acts involving intentional agents or that the constituents that figure in [p] include concrete particular objects which stand in characterizing relations to universals. But this is exactly the kind of illuminating work we should be able to expect from a relation which is supposed to capture what is philosophically interesting and important about the traditional substance/non-substance distinction.

3.5. The multiple dimensions of non-fundamentality

I have argued in other work (cf. Koslicki (2012a), (2013a), (2013b), (forth. c)) that, in order to draw sufficiently fine-grained distinctions among the candidate derivative entities such as those listed in (3) and (4) above, it is necessary to recognize multiple dimensions of non-fundamentality, among them the following:

(i) *Abstraction*. An entity, x, may be non-fundamental in a particular way relative to an entity, y, numerically distinct from x, if it is essential to x that it is in some way "abstracted" from y;

x is a feature of y; y is x's bearer. In this case, y is more complex than x; by focusing on x, we gain a partial, but not complete, perspective on y.[23]

(ii) *Construction*. An entity, x, may be non-fundamental in a second way relative to an entity, y, numerically distinct from x, if it is essential to x that it is in some way "constructed" out of y, together with other entities. In that case, y is an essential constituent of x; x is more complex than y; by focusing on y, we gain a partial, but not complete, perspective on x.[24]

But even (i) and (ii) do not yet encompass all the distinctions necessary to do justice to the full range of data we encounter in (3) and (4). In addition to (i) and (ii), at least the following additional factors are relevant to an adequate characterization of relative non-fundamentality:

(iii) *Artificiality*. An entity, x, may be non-fundamental in a third way relative to some entity, y, numerically distinct from x, if x is essentially the result of a creative act involving an intentional agent, y.[25, 26]

---

[23] Although the language of "focusing", or "gaining a partial or complete perspective on something" sounds epistemic, I intend (i) and (ii) to be understood as aiming at the metaphysical conditions underlying these epistemic contrasts.

[24] Bennett (2011a), (2011b), (forth.), in her account of relative fundamentality, focuses exclusively on what she calls "building relations". And while it might seem as though Bennett's "building relations" only include what falls under my rubric of construction, her approach might in fact be sufficiently broad to encompass some of my other dimensions of non-fundamentality, in particular abstraction and possibly even artificiality. As I indicate in the text, I do take construction operations to induce a certain kind of non-fundamentality, but these operations point to only one, among several, important dimensions of non-fundamentality. We would not have succeeded in painting a complete picture of non-fundamentality, if we restricted ourselves solely to the idea that some entities are constructed out of others by means of some construction operation.

[25] Some theists hold that everything other than God is created by God, an intentional agent, and hence that everything other than God counts as artificial by the lights of (iii). I have in mind a notion of artificiality which would allow for example for a contrast between a tree (a natural organism) and a computer (an artifact created by human intentional agents), even though for the theist both the tree and the computer would count as being part of the created world.

[26] There are extensive bodies of literature (too extensive to cite here) relevant to the distinction between what is natural and what is artificial, i.e. the result of acts of creation involving intentional agents. The nature of intentional objects (e.g. the Gorgon that Perseus seeks) has been one of the main topics of interest since the early

(iv) *Disunity*. An entity, x, may be non-fundamental in a fourth way relative to some entity, y, numerically distinct from x, if x exhibits a lower degree of unity than y.

In my view, we need to recognize at least these four dimensions of relative non-fundamentality, and their correlative versions of relative fundamentality, in order to capture the metaphysically significant distinctions that are present among the candidate derivative and fundamental entities listed in (3) and (4). (And I am in principle open to recognizing further dimensions of non-fundamentality, if a plausible argument can be mounted to the effect that (i)–(iv) still do not supply us with the necessary apparatus to capture all the ontologically relevant facts that need to be accounted for in order to characterize an entity's derivative or fundamental status.)

The four dimensions of non-fundamentality cited above may also interact in various complex ways. To illustrate, tropes, holes, boundaries, or Aristotelian universals are sometimes taken to be abstracted from, and hence derivative in one particular way of, the concrete particular objects that are their bearers. And yet, despite their abstracted status, these entities may nevertheless be regarded as exhibiting a high degree of unity, e.g. perhaps because they are regarded as simple in the sense of not being constructed out of constituents, and hence count as unified by default. Moreover, their abstracted status also leaves open whether the entities in question are the results of creative acts involving intentional agents (e.g. a boundary around a particular piece of land) or natural (e.g. an Aristotelian universal or a naturally formed hole in a rock formation). Heaps, mereological sums, collections, artifacts, artworks, and natural unified wholes, in contrast, may be taken to be in some sense constructed out of their parts or constituents; but whether they are unified or disunified, artificial or natural, is not immediately settled by their status as constructed entities. And while artifacts, artworks, and intentional objects are arguably the results of certain kinds of creative acts involving intentional agents, some of them may be

---

days of analytic philosophy. An entire subfield of philosophy (aesthetics) is devoted to the study of artworks. Artifacts have perhaps not received as much attention from philosophers as they deserve, at least in the last hundred years or so; but see, for example, Evnine (2014); Ingarden (1960), (1965); Margolis and Laurence (2007); Thomasson (2003), (2009).

classified as abstracted (e.g. an afterimage); others as constructed (e.g. a sculpture). In addition, some of them may have a relatively high degree of unity (e.g. certain artifacts whose constituents work together to fulfil a certain function), whereas others may exhibit a relatively low degree of unity (e.g. an artwork consisting of components that are scattered across multiple geographical locations). Finally, heaps, mereological sums, and collections, which may be taken to be constructed entities, also appear to exhibit a relatively low degree of unity compared to other more unified entities (e.g. natural unified wholes, tropes, simples, Platonic universals).[27]

4. CONCLUSION

My main purpose in this paper has been to bring out why the grounding idiom does not perform as well as one might think, and as well as we have been led to believe based on the recent flurry of enthusiasm surrounding the notion of grounding, in providing a plausible approach to relative fundamentality. Given our observations above, we may conclude that a ground-theoretic approach to relative fundamentality performs poorly in at least the following two respects. Firstly, the idiom of grounding does not capture and illuminate what is philosophically interesting and important about the traditional substance/non-substance distinction, and is therefore ill-suited for the formulation of a criterion of substancehood. Secondly, the grounding idiom is not sufficiently fine-grained to shed much light on the nature of the connections that are at play in putative cases of grounding.

---

[27] The notion of ontological dependence might strike us as more helpful than that of grounding in capturing the sorts of distinctions between the more fundamental and the less fundamental, or the absolutely fundamental and the non-fundamental, to which the traditional substance/non-substance distinction is intended to give voice. For example, Kit Fine and Jonathan Lowe both define notions of ontological dependence which they take to be adequate for the purposes of formulating a criterion of substancehood (see Fine (1995); Lowe (1994), (2005), (2012), (2013)). I discuss these definitions of ontological dependence and the attempt to formulate a criterion of substancehood in terms of them in more detail in other work (see especially Koslicki (2012a), (2013a), (2013b)). I argue that these definitions of ontological dependence are also still too coarse-grained to do justice to the full range of phenomena illustrated in (3) and (4), since they do not take into account the different dimensions along which an entity can be classified as relatively fundamental or derivative.

Upon learning that a fact, [p], grounds a fact, [q], the approaches to grounding we considered above do allow us to draw several inferences. For example, on the basis of a grounding claim of the form, "[p] grounds [q]", we are licensed to conclude that [p] and [q] both exist; that [p] is more fundamental than [q] and that [q] is more derivative than [p], according to a sense of "(relatively) fundamental" and "derivative" that is defined directly in terms of grounding. In addition, we may infer from the grounding claim in question that the relation between [p] and [q] is similar to, but not identical to, causal determination, though the specific features that are attributed to grounding differ from account to account.

At the same time, when presented with a grounding claim of the form, "[p] grounds [q]", we are left in the dark with respect to many other questions which ideally should be resolved by a sufficiently fine-grained approach to relative fundamentality. For example, we cannot infer from the grounding claim in question whether [q] can also be simultaneously grounded by some other fact, [r], of the same level of generality as [p], without resulting in an incompatibility. The grounding claim in question furthermore leaves open the following questions: whether [p] figures in a real definition for [q]; whether [q] is reducible to [p]; whether [p] is more or less general than [q]; whether [p] and [q] are a pair consisting of a non-representational and a representational entity of some sort; whether p entails q with logical necessity, with metaphysical necessity, or only with normative necessity; and whether there is some determinate mereological or set-theoretic relationship between the constituents of [p] and the constituents of [q]. In addition, the grounding claim in question does not settle for us whether [p] has as a constituent an entity which should be classified as more deserving of substance status than the entities which figure as constituents in [q] and, if so, to what specific explanatory factor such a difference in ontological status might be traced.

This evidence suggests that the grounding idiom lacks the requisite unity to tie together the collection of data which allegedly exhibit grounding connections under a single relation. Rather, we are led to believe that a variety of distinct specific relations are at work in these alleged cases of grounding, such as the genus/species relation, the determinable/determinate relation, truthmaking, and so on. These distinct specific relations and their relata all have different philosophically interesting characteristics and hence should be studied separately. The grounding idiom also runs into trouble when we try to apply it to apparently non-factual, non-propositional cases, in particular those connections between the fundamental and the derivative to which the traditional substance/non-substance distinction is intended to give voice.

In order to arrive at a sufficiently fine-grained approach to relative fundamentality, I suggested above that we must instead recognize several distinct dimensions along which an entity, or a type of entity, may be classified as more or less deserving of substance status. According to such an approach, when we ask in a particular case whether some entity, or type of entity, is more or less fundamental than another, we must always specify the particular respect in which something is to be categorized as more or less derivative than something else to which it is being compared. Currently available idioms of grounding do not reflect the various gradations of relative fundamentality and non-fundamentality I have distinguished: (i) whether an entity is essentially abstracted from something more complex; (ii) whether an entity is essentially constructed out of other entities; (iii) whether an entity is essentially the result of a creative act involving an intentional agent; or (iv) whether an entity exhibits a high or low degree of unity. Just as one and the same thing can be both good in some respects (e.g. dancing) and bad in others (e.g. playing basketball), one and the same entity, according to this multi-dimensional conception, can be both more fundamental than another in certain respects (e.g. its degree of unity) and less fundamental than another in others (e.g. its naturalness). It is only when we make room for multiple dimensions of fundamentality and non-fundamentality that we can do justice to the data that presents itself to the ontologist and meta-ontologist.[28]

University of Alberta

---

[28] Some of the research for this paper was conducted while I held the 2012–2013 Alvin Plantinga Fellowship at University of Notre Dame's Center for Philosophy of Religion. I am very grateful to the Center's co-directors, Mike Rea and Sam Newlands, for providing me with the opportunity to spend a year in this stimulating environment, and to the Templeton Foundation for its financial support. The Center for Philosophy of Religion as well as the Notre Dame philosophical community at large proved to be an excellent sounding board for my developing ideas on grounding, ontological dependence, fundamentality, and substancehood. This paper was presented at the University of Oklahoma in the Fall of 2013 and at an Invited

REFERENCES

Audi, Paul (2012a). "A Clarification and Defense of the Notion of Grounding". In Correia and Schnieder (eds), pp. 101–21.

Audi, Paul (2012b). "Grounding: Toward a Theory of the *In-Virtue-Of* Relation". *Journal of Philosophy*, Vol. CIX, No. 12 (December 2012), pp. 685–711.

Bennett, Karen (2011a). "Construction Area: No Hard Hat Required". *Philosophical Studies*, Vol. 154, pp. 79–104.

Bennett, Karen (2011b). "By Our Bootstraps". *Philosophical Perspectives*, Vol. 25, No. 1, pp. 27–41.

Bennett, Karen (forth.). *Making Things Up*. Forthcoming with Oxford University Press.

Blatti, Stephan, and Sandra Lapointe (eds) (2013). *Ontology After Carnap*. To appear with Oxford University Press.

Chalmers, David, David Manley, and Ryan Wasserman (eds) (2009). *Metametaphysics: New Essays on the Foundations of Ontology*. Oxford: Clarendon Press.

Correia, Fabrice, and Benjamin Schnieder (eds) (2012). *Metaphysical Grounding: Understanding the Structure of Reality*. Cambridge: Cambridge University Press.

Daly, Chris (2012). "Skepticism about Grounding". In Correia and Schnieder (eds), pp. 81–100.

Dumitru, Mircea (ed.) (2013). *Metaphysics, Meaning, and Modality: Themes from Kit Fine*. To appear with Oxford University Press.

Evnine, Simon (2009). "Constitution and Qua Objects in the Ontology of Music". *British Journal of Aesthetics*, Vol. 49, pp. 203–17.

Evnine, Simon (2014). *Making Objects and Events: A Hylomorphic Ontology*. In progress.

Feser, Edward (ed.) (2013). *Aristotle on Method and Metaphysics*. Basingstoke: Palgrave Macmillan.

Fine, Kit (1995). "Ontological Dependence". *Proceedings of the Aristotelian Society*, Vol. 95, pp. 269–90.

Symposium on Grounding, held at the American Philosophical Association Central Division meeting in Chicago in February 2014. I would like to thank members of the audience at both places for their interesting feedback and especially my co-symposiasts, Jonathan Schaffer and Kelly Trogdon, for a very engaging discussion. While working on this paper, I received excellent detailed comments from both Jonathan Schaffer and Paul Audi, which helped me understand their views much better than I otherwise would have. Finally, I benefited greatly from discussing this material with the members of the 2013 Metaphysics Summer Reading Group held in Boulder, especially Rebecca Chan, Michaela McSweeney, and Noel Saenz.

Fine, Kit (2001). "The Question of Realism". *Philosophers' Imprint*, Vol. 1 (No. 1), available at <www.philosophersimprint.org/001001/>.
Fine, Kit (2012). "A Guide to Ground". In Correia and Schnieder (eds), pp. 37–80.
Hale, Bob, and Aviv Hoffman (eds) (2010). *Modality: Metaphysics, Logic, and Epistemology*. Oxford: Oxford University Press.
Hofweber, Thomas (2009). "Ambitious, Yet Modest, Metaphysics". In Chalmers, Manley, and Wasserman (eds), pp. 260–89.
Husserl, Edmund (1900–01). *Logische Untersuchungen*. Halle, Germany: M. Niemeyer.
Ingarden, Roman (1960). *Das Literarische Kunstwerk*, mit einem Anhang (*Von den Funktionen der Sprache im Theaterschauspiel*), 2nd edn. Tübingen, Germany: Max Niemeyer Verlag.
Ingarden, Roman (1965). *Der Streit um die Existenz der Welt*, Vols. I–II. Tübingen, Germany: Max Niemeyer Verlag.
Jenkins, Carrie (2011). "Is Metaphysical Dependence Irreflexive?" *The Monist*, Vol. 94, No. 2, pp. 267–76.
Kim, Jaegwon (1993). *Supervenience and Mind: Selected Philosophical Essays*. Cambridge Studies in Philosophy. New York: Cambridge University Press.
Koslicki, Kathrin (2008). *The Structure of Objects*. Oxford: Oxford University Press.
Koslicki, Kathrin (2012a). "Varieties of Ontological Dependence". In Correia and Schnieder (eds), pp. 186–213.
Koslicki, Kathrin (2012b). "Essence, Necessity and Explanation". In Tahko (ed.), pp. 187–206.
Koslicki, Kathrin (2013a). "Ontological Dependence: An Opinionated Survey". In Schnieder, Hoeltje, and Steinberg (eds), pp. 31–64.
Koslicki, Kathrin (2013b). "Substance, Independence and Unity". In Feser (ed.), pp. 169–95.
Koslicki, Kathrin (forth. a). "Essence and Identity". To appear in Dumitru (ed.).
Koslicki, Kathrin (forth. b). "Questions of Ontology". To appear in Blatti and Lapointe (eds).
Koslicki, Kathrin (forth. c). "The Unity of Integrated Wholes". To appear in Madden and Toner (eds).
LePoidevin, Robin, Peter Simons, Andrew McGonigal, and Ross Cameron (eds) (2009). *Routledge Companion to Metaphysics*. London: Routledge.
Linsky, Bernard, and Edward Zalta (1996). "In Defense of the Contingently Nonconcrete". *Philosophical Studies* (Special Issue: Possibilism and Actualism), Vol. 84, No. 2–3, pp. 283–94.
Lowe, E. J. (1994). "Ontological Dependency". *Philosophical Papers*, Vol. XXIII, No. 1, pp. 31–48.

Lowe, E. J. (2005). "Ontological Dependence", *Stanford Encyclodedia of Philosophy* <http://plato.stanford.edu/entries/dependence-ontological/>; last revised in 2009.

Lowe, E. J. (2012). "Asymmetrical Dependence in Individuation". In Correia and Schnieder (eds), pp. 214–33.

Lowe, E. J. (2013). "Some Varieties of Metaphysical Dependence". In Schnieder, Hoeltje, and Steinberg (eds), pp. 193–210.

Madden, James, and Patrick Toner (eds) (2013). *Recent Hylomorphism*. To appear with Oxford University Press.

Margolis, Eric, and Stephen Laurence (eds) (2007). *Creations of the Mind: Theories of Artifacts and Their Representation*. New York: Oxford University Press.

Raven, Michael (2012). "In Defence of Ground". *Australasian Journal of Philosophy*, Vol. 90, No. 4, pp. 687–701.

Rosen, Gideon (2010). "Metaphysical Dependence: Grounding and Reduction". In Hale and Hoffman (eds), pp. 109–36.

Schaffer, Jonathan (2009). "On What Grounds What". In Chalmers, Manley, and Wasserman (eds), pp. 347–83.

Schaffer, Jonathan (2010). "Monism: The Priority of the Whole", *Philosophical Review*, Vol.119, No.1, pp. 31–76.

Schnieder, Benjamin, Miguel Hoeltje, and Alexander Steinberg (eds) (2013). *Varieties of Dependence (Basic Philosophical Concepts)*. Munich, Germany: Philosophia Verlag.

Simons, Peter (1998). "Farewell to Substance: A Differentiated Leave-Taking". *Ratio (New Series)*, Vol. 11, No. 3, pp. 235–52.

Tahko, Tuomas (ed.) (2012). *Contemporary Aristotelian Metaphysics*. Cambridge: Cambridge University Press.

Thomasson, Amie (2003). "Foundations for a Social Ontology". *Protosociology*, Vol. 18–19: *Understanding The Social II: Philosophy of Sociality*, pp. 269–90.

Thomasson, Amie (2009). "Social Entities". In Le Poidevin, Simons, McGonigal and Cameron (eds), pp. 545–54.

Trogdon, Kelly (2013). "An Introduction to Grounding". In Schnieder, Hoeltje, and Steinberg (eds), pp. 97–122.

Wilson, Jessica (2014). "No work for a theory of grounding". *Inquiry* 57.5–6, 535–79.

12. A universe of explanations

Ghislain Guigon

> Metaphysical considerations suggest that to be a serious candidate for describing actuality, a spacetime should be maximal. For example, for the Creative Force to actualize a proper subpart of a larger spacetime would seem to be a violation of Leibniz's principles of sufficient reason and plenitude. If one adopts the image of spacetime as being generated or built up as time passes then the dynamical version of the principle of sufficient reason would ask why the Creative Force would stop building if it is possible to continue.... Some readers may be shocked by the introduction of metaphysical considerations in the hardest of the "hard sciences." But in fact leading workers in relativistic gravitation, though they don't invoke the name of Leibniz, are motivated by such principles (see, for example, Geroch 1970, p. 262; Penrose 1969, p. 253).
>
> John Earman[1]

1. INTRODUCTION

We can distinguish between two fundamental questions about explanation. The first one, "What is explanation?", may be called the General Explanation Question. The second one, "Under what circumstances do truths have an explanation?", may be called the Special Explanation Question. An answer to the General Explanation Question may take two forms. It may take the form of an analysis of the notion of explanation or it may consist in an axiomatic theory that articulates the most general principles about explanation. On the other hand, the Special Explanation Question is the demand for necessary and jointly sufficient conditions any truth must satisfy in order for it to be the case that it has an explanation. Within the past few years, there has been a growing body of philosophical literature concerning the General Explanation Question. By contrast, I think that it is fair to say that the Special Explanation Question, with which this paper is concerned, has received less attention.

[1] In Earman 1995, pp. 32–3.

The distinction between the General and the Special Explanation Questions should be reminiscent of Peter van Inwagen's (1990) famous distinction between the General Composition Question (What is composition?) and the Special Composition Question (When does composition occur?). The analogy is intended to suggest that there are three general answers to the Special Explanation Question: always, never, and sometimes. I call *explanatory universalism* the first of these answers. According to explanatory universalism, truths have an explanation under every circumstance. In other words, explanatory universalism is the view that the early modern rationalist principle of sufficient reason (hereafter, PSR) is true:

PSR: For any proposition x, if x is true then there is a proposition y such that y explains x.[2]

The second answer to the Special Explanation Question may be called *explanatory nihilism*. It is the view that every truth is *brute*, i.e. unexplained. According to the third answer to the Special Explanation Question, explanation is restricted to a certain class of truths, which means that some truths have an explanation while others are brute.

I believe that answers to the Special Explanation Question deserve the attention of philosophers. First, these theses have consequences on answers to what we may call *applied explanation questions*. Roughly, an applied explanation question is a question of the form "What explains what?"—or "What is more fundamental than what?" Applied explanation questions play central roles in various fields of inquiry. Some have recently argued that one of the most central questions of metaphysics is "What *metaphysically* explains what?" or "What grounds what?"[3] On the other hand, a fundamental question of physics is arguably "What physically explains

---

[2] Here I follow other authors in interpreting PSR as a principle about explanation; see, e.g. Della Rocca 2010, p. 1, Meyer 2012, and Graham Oppy 2006, pp. 275–90. Della Rocca (2010) uses the label *"rationalism"* to refer to the view that PSR is true. But the label "explanatory universalism" is a better mnemonic device for distinguishing this from other answers to the Special Explanation Question. Moreover, "rationalism" connotes philosophical theses about innate ideas and a priori knowledge that are independent of PSR. Using the label "explanatory universalism" avoids confusion.

[3] See, e.g. Schaffer 2009 and Paul 2012.

what?"[4] The Special Explanation Question can rightly be regarded as *meta*metaphysical in the sense that answers to this question have methodological implications about the way we answer applied explanation questions. For instance, it seems that one must believe that explanatory nihilism is false in order to be justified in maintaining that there is a non-vacuous answer to applied explanation questions. Furthermore, it has become a common practice in philosophy to claim that some specific phenomenon is brute or unexplained— e.g. truth, composition, resemblance, naturalness. Brutalist strategies seem to rely on the assumption that admitting that some truths have no explanation is permitted in some circumstances. Yet one may wonder whether there are such circumstances and what they are. But this means engaging with the Special Explanation Question.[5]

Second, answers to the Special Explanation Question may appear to conflict with general principles about explanation, as the following discussion shall illustrate. Yet if some of our beliefs about the correct answer to the Special Explanation Question conflict with some of our beliefs about general principles about explanation, some of these beliefs have to be revised. I believe that there is no good ground to assume a priori that our beliefs about which general principles about explanation are true are more immune to

---

[4] Although this question is, in practice, often subsumed under the question: Which model or theory is best to explain the *phenomena*? For instance, big bang theory has been judged superior to the steady state theory because it provides an explanation for the cosmic microwave background radiation.

[5] Notice that if we assume that there are several *species* of explanation, e.g. metaphysical, physical, and biological explanations, then we can distinguish between *species* of the Special Explanation Question: In which circumstances does metaphysical explanation arise? In which circumstances does physical explanation arise? And so on. Different answers to these questions are compatible. For instance, one may endorse explanatory universalism about physical explanation—each truth that represents a state of the universe has a physical explanation—and explanatory nihilism about metaphysical explanation—metaphysical explanation never takes place. In this paper, I shall not commit myself to any particular view about *species* of explanation because my focus is on the *genus*: explanation. But notice that sometimes it seems wrong to interpret a brutalist claim as the claim that some truth has no explanation *tout court*. Sometimes such claims are better interpreted as meaning that some facts lack a certain *species* of explanation. For instance, a nominalist who takes the resemblance of red particulars as being brute only intends to claim that this fact has no further *metaphysical* explanation. Her intention, however, is not to claim that there is no *physical* explanation of the resemblance of red particulars.

revision than our beliefs about answers to the Special Explanation Question.[6] Thus investigating possible conflicts between answers to the General and the Special Explanation Questions seems to be a good place to start developing a reasoned picture of the explanatory structure of the world.

This article is a modest contribution to this programme as its focus is on explanatory universalism. Explanatory universalism corresponds to the traditional doctrine according to which PSR is true, a doctrine that has been held by philosophers like Aquinas, Spinoza, and Leibniz among others. Despite its impressive intellectual pedigree, PSR is routinely dismissed as an unsupported metaphysical dogma. However, I share the early modern rationalists' warm feelings towards PSR. For explanatory universalism is an intuitive and elegant doctrine. When asked to answer a meaningful why-question, our natural attitude is always to think that this question is *in principle* answerable, even if it may be impossible for us to *know* its answer. Of course, why-questions are sometimes vexing, and frustration may lead us to entertain the possibility of the question being unanswerable. But if the question truly makes sense, and if there really is a fact of the matter about the truth of the *explanandum*, then it seems to me very difficult to admit that such a truth just emerged out of nothing. Michael Della Rocca (2010) has recently argued that proponents of the restricted answer to the Special Explanation Question must provide a principled account of why inexplicability is sometimes acceptable while in most cases it isn't. Like him, I think that in the absence of such an account the division between explained and brute truths appears somewhat arbitrary. For the absence of such an account means that proponents of a restricted answer to the Special Explanation Question fail to provide necessary and jointly sufficient conditions any truth must satisfy in order for it to be the case that it has an explanation. By contrast, explanatory universalism provides a unified picture of the explanatory structure

---

[6] Taking the analogy with the debate about composition seriously here may be instructive. Extensional mereology may rightly be conceived of as an answer to the General Composition Question. Considering the debate on the Special Composition Question, it is noticeable that some philosophers take agreement with extensional mereology as a virtue, whereas other philosophers have claimed to be warranted in endorsing an answer to the Special Composition Question that appears to conflict with extensional mereology.

of the universe. Moreover, it seems that science, throughout its history, has developed under the fruitful working hypothesis that what happens in the world must be explicable. And as the opening quotation from John Earman (1995) suggests, PSR may play an important role in discriminating cosmological models that are good candidates for describing reality.[7]

This paper is going to defend explanatory universalism from a simple and direct valid argument according to which PSR has the consequence that there is a truth that explains every truth, namely an *omni-explainer*. I shall describe this argument in section 2. I have no doubt that opponents to PSR would agree that this argument challenges explanatory universalism. For the claim that there is an omni-explainer is counterintuitive on its face. But I suspect that several explanatory universalists may be willing to endorse the conclusion that, if PSR is true, then there is an omni-explainer. My purpose in section 3 is to explain why explanatory universalists should not endorse the strategy that consists in biting the bullet in favour of the existence of an omni-explainer. The reason why biting the bullet in favour of an omni-explainer is wrong is that the existence of an omni-explainer conflicts with the principle that explanation is irreflexive. Section 3 is thus a defence of the principle that explanation is irreflexive that consists of two steps. First, on the assumption that PSR yields that there is an omni-explainer, the most natural and plausible way to relax the principle of irreflexivity of explanation yields a counterintuitive doctrine, namely *necessitarianism*. Second, general considerations on explanation support the view that no further way of relaxing the ban on self-explanations is warranted. So, in light of my defence of the irreflexivity of explanation, the argument according to which PSR implies that some truth explains all truths constitutes a powerful argument against explanatory universalism. But, in section 4, I shall argue that explanatory universalists can resist this argument. For it relies on an assumption that explanatory universalists can legitimately reject, namely the assumption

---

[7] I say that PSR seems to play an *important* role here, not that it plays an *essential* role. As a referee has remarked correctly, the full strength of PSR may not be required to motivate the space-time maximality principle Earman is talking about. Non-arbitrariness about the "theatre of dynamics" may be enough. But Earman's point is that PSR seems to be the underlying metaphysical assumption behind the view that the "theatre of dynamics" is non-arbitrary.

that explanation distributes over conjunction. In the final section, I consider a plausible revision of this assumption. I argue there that, given the revised assumption, explanatory universalism seems to yield a striking picture of the explanatory structure of the universe. I shall indicate why the resulting model does not appear utterly implausible to me.

2. EXPLAINING ALL TRUTHS

Explanatory universalists maintain that whatever is the case has a sufficient reason for its being the case, hence that PSR is true. Early modern rationalists have suspected that we can derive from this principle that there is a sufficient reason for whatever is the case. Given my understanding of PSR in terms of explanation, the claim that there is a sufficient reason for whatever is the case amounts to the thesis that there is an *omni-explainer*:

> *Omni-explainer:* there is a true proposition x such that, for any proposition y, if y is true, then x explains y.

One may expect an argument from PSR to the thesis that there is an omni-explainer to involve a quantifier shift fallacy or some strong assumptions about the explanatory structure of the universe. But no, there is a simple and direct valid argument from PSR to the thesis that some truth explains every truth that only appeals to the assumption that explanation is *dissective*:

> *Dissection:* For any propositions x, y, and z, if z is an explanation for $(x \& y)$, then z is an explanation for x and z is an explanation for y.

Dissection is a corollary of the claim that explanation is monotonic, i.e. the claim that any *explanans* explains all the logical consequences of what it explains.[8] There are powerful reasons to deny monotonicity that are independent of whether *Dissection* is true, however (see section 4). But my appeal to the claim that explanation is dissective

---

[8] Cf. Humberstone 1985, pp. 401–2. In general, an operator O is monotonic if and only if, for any propositions x and y, if y is a logical consequence of x, then Oy is a logical consequence of Ox.

here is motivated by the fact that most authors in the contemporary literature about PSR appear to endorse this claim.[9]

An interesting variation on the notion of an omni-explainer is that of *collective omni-explainers*: for any propositions $x_1, \ldots, x_n \ldots, x_1, \ldots, x_n \ldots$ are collective omni-explainers when whatever is the case is explained to be the case by one or the other of $x_1, \ldots, x_n \ldots$. The notion of collective omni-explainers is worthy of attention because the claim that there are collective omni-explainers directly follows from PSR: if every truth has an explanation, then there are true propositions $x_1, \ldots, x_n \ldots$ such that whatever is the case is explained to be the case by one or the other of them. The logical link between PSR and the thesis that there are collective omni-explainers is the ground for the argument called to attention here.[10]

Roughly, the argument runs as follows. If we assume for *reductio* that there are collective omni-explainers but no omni-explainer *tout court*, then we can map each of the collective omni-explainers onto a true proposition that it does not explain. Then if we form the conjunction of these mapped-to propositions, it follows from the claim that some truths collectively explain all truths that some of the collective omni-explainers, call it O, explains this conjunction. However, given *Dissection*, if O explains the conjunction of mapped-to propositions, O explains each of its conjuncts too. But this leads straight to a contradiction. For given the assumption that there is no omni-explainer *tout court*, there has to be a truth that O does not explain, and this truth has to be a conjunct of the conjunction of mapped-to propositions. But, given *Dissection*, O explains each of the conjuncts of this conjunction. So by *reductio* if explanation is assumed to be dissective, the claim that there are collective omni-explainers yields the conclusion that there is an omni-explainer *tout court*. Since PSR entails that there are collective omni-explainers we can conclude that PSR entails that there is an omni-explainer *tout court*.

---

[9] These authors include van Inwagen (1983), Bennett (1984), Hudson (1997), Pruss (2006), Oppy (2006), Della Rocca (2010), and Meyer (2012).

[10] This argument is an adaptation of Humberstone's (1985) derivation of omniscience *tout court* from *collective* omniscience.

Here is a more precise statement of the argument. For expository purposes, I make the over-simplified assumption that the set of collective omni-explainers contains only two propositions: r and s.[11] So on the assumption that r and s are collective omni-explainers, every truth is either explained by r or by s. Suppose for *reductio* that neither r nor s is an omni-explainer *tout court*. Then to each of our collective omni-explainers there corresponds some true proposition that it does not explain. So using the indexed modal operator 'E_r' to mean 'r explains', for some proposition p, it is the case that

(1) $p \,\&\, \neg E_r p$

read as "p is true and r does not explain p". Likewise, using the indexed modal operator 'E_s' to mean 's explains', for some proposition q, it is the case that

(2) $q \,\&\, \neg E_s q$

read as "q is true and s does not explain q". Then forming the conjunction of the first conjunct of (1) with the first conjunct of (2) we obtain the antecedent of (3)

(3) $(p \,\&\, q) \to (E_r(p \,\&\, q) \lor E_s(p \,\&\, q))$,

which is an instance of the claim that r and s collectively explain all truths: if the conjunction of p and q is true, then either r or s explains it as they collectively explain all truths. The antecedent of (3), namely ($p \,\&\, q$), follows from (1) and (2). So by *modus ponens* we are entitled to derive the consequent of (3). However, given *Dissection*, the consequent of (3) is inconsistent with the conjunction of (1) and (2). For by *Dissection* the first disjunct of the consequent of (3) entails that r explains p, which contradicts (1), and its second disjunct entails that s explains q, which contradicts (2). So by *reductio* either r explains every truth or s does.

This argument can be reconstructed in a bimodal logic of the two operators 'E_r' and 'E_s' as a derivation of '$(p \to E_r p) \lor (q \to E_s q)$' from (3):

[11] The argument generalizes in a straightforward way to any finite number n ≥ 2 of collective omni-explainers, as the previous informal sketch of the argument shows, since we can form conjunctions with n terms for all finite n ≥ 2. Whether the argument still works when an infinite set of collective omni-explainers is assumed is the topic of the appendix.

(3) $(p \,\&\, q) \to (\mathrm{E}_r(p \,\&\, q) \lor \mathrm{E}_s(p \,\&\, q))$
(4) $\mathrm{E}_r(p \,\&\, q) \to \mathrm{E}_r p$ by *Dissection* applied to $(p \,\&\, q)$
(5) $\mathrm{E}_s(p \,\&\, q) \to \mathrm{E}_s q$ by *Dissection* applied to $(p \,\&\, q)$
(6) $(p \,\&\, q) \to (\mathrm{E}_r p \lor \mathrm{E}_s q)$ a truth-functional consequence of (3), (4), and (5)
(7) $(p \to \mathrm{E}_r p) \lor (q \to \mathrm{E}_s q)$ a truth-functional equivalence of (6).

Since (7) entails that either (1) or (2) is false, its import is that either r explains every truth or s does, hence that there is an omni-explainer *tout court*. I should emphasize that none of the disjuncts of (7) can be deduced from (3). Letting 'O' name an omni-explainer *tout court*, we do not know whether $\mathrm{O} = r$ or $\mathrm{O} = s$. In general, each of the collective omni-explainers is an equally good candidate to be an omni-explainer *tout court*, and there may be several of them.

So, given *Dissection*, PSR entails that there is an omni-explainer. Explanatory universalists endorse PSR. So, if *Dissection* is true, explanatory universalists are committed to the existence of an omni-explainer, namely a truth that explains every truth. I have no doubt that opponents of PSR would regard this argument as a weighty objection to explanatory universalism. For the claim that there is an omni-explainer is counterintuitive. But I am less certain that every proponent of PSR will appreciate the strength of this argument. For, as I emphasized at the beginning of this section, the thesis that there is a sufficient reason for whatever is the case is a thesis classical explanatory universalists intended to demonstrate and defend. So the purpose of the next section is to explain why I think that explanatory universalists should not welcome the result that PSR entails that there is an omni-explainer. The reason why they should not welcome this result is that the existence of an omni-explainer conflicts with the principle that explanation is irreflexive, which I shall defend. Some philosophers, both among opponents and proponents of PSR, have thought that some specific failures of this principle are admissible. My task in the next section is to argue that these philosophers are wrong. If I am right, there is no refuge for explanatory universalists in allowing for failures of the principle that explanation is irreflexive. So while the conclusion of the present section is that explanatory universalism has a counter-intuitive consequence—namely, that there is an omni-explainer—if *Dissection* is true, the conclusion of the next section shall be that explanatory universalists are in serious trouble if *Dissection* is true. This is the reason why *Dissection* will be the focus of section 4.

3. PSR AND THE BAN ON SELF-EXPLANATIONS

I believe that the strongest reason to resist the claim that there is an omni-explainer is that this claim contradicts the seemingly undeniable principle that explanation is *irreflexive*:

Irreflexivity: For any propositions x and y, if x is an explanation for y, then $x \neq y$.

The claim that explanation is irreflexive is inconsistent with the claim that there is an omni-explainer because an omni-explainer explains *every* truth including itself. So if PSR entails that there is an omni-explainer, it also entails that explanation is not irreflexive. The deduction of an omni-explainer from PSR exhibits an apparent conflict between PSR and the principle that explanation is irreflexive.

Several authors of the tradition have suspected that PSR yields a commitment to the view that something is its own sufficient reason, hence that PSR conflicts with *Irreflexivity*. But what they have failed to notice is that whether the conflict is genuine or not depends on how explanation interacts with *truth functions*, and in particular with conjunction. For the outcome of the previous section is that PSR entails that there is an omni-explainer—and so conflicts with *Irreflexivity*—provided we assume that *Dissection* is true. In my view, this result puts much dialectical pressure on *Dissection*—which I shall examine in the next section—as *Dissection* seems to be the root of the explanatory universalist's troubles.

But as I suspect that some explanatory universalists may welcome the result that PSR yields that there is an omni-explainer, I suspect that some explanatory universalists may be tempted to commit themselves to the rejection of *Irreflexivity*. For, undeniably, the claim that there is a certain being whose existence is self-explanatory is a traditional thesis that classical explanatory universalists embraced and aimed to demonstrate. My purpose in this section is to explain why I believe that this reaction to the deduction of an omni-explainer from PSR is misguided. For I shall argue that explanatory universalists should not allow for violations of

Irreflexivity. If I am right, then my defence of *Irreflexivity* justifies the view that explanatory universalists should not welcome a commitment to the existence of an omni-explainer. For if PSR entails that there is an omni-explainer, *Irreflexivity* leads to the conclusion that PSR is false.

My argument for *Irreflexivity* consists of two steps. In section 3.1, I shall argue that, on the assumption that PSR yields that there is an omni-explainer, the most natural and plausible way to relax the principle of irreflexivity of explanation yields the counterintuitive view that *necessitarianism* is true. In section 3.2, I shall offer a general argument in favour of the view that there is no legitimate way of relaxing the ban on self-explanations. In light of my defence of *Irreflexivity*, the existence of an omni-explainer is inadmissible. So the present section is aimed to strengthen the argument according to which PSR yields that there is an omni-explainer. Nevertheless, this argument is not irresistible, or so I shall argue in section 4.

3.1. Necessitarianism

The view that we can relax the ban on self-explanations seems to be shared by Peter van Inwagen who writes:

Secondly, no *contingent* state of affairs may be its own sufficient reason. This would seem to be an essential feature of the concept of a sufficient reason. (I introduce the qualification 'contingent' in order to accommodate those who hold that a necessary state of affairs is its own sufficient reason. Whether or not this is so will make no difference to our argument.) (van Inwagen 1983, p. 203)

According to van Inwagen's suggestion, adequate answers to the General Explanation Question should not assume *Irreflexivity* among their axioms or theorems. Instead what they should assume is the following qualified version of this principle:

Contingent Irreflexivity: For any contingent propositions x and y, if x is an explanation for y, then $x \neq y$.

The thought seems to be that while, given *Irreflexivity*, no proposition whatsoever is its own explanation, *Contingent Irreflexivity* leaves open the possibility that some necessary proposition explains itself, a possibility some theists take seriously. Van Inwagen's suggestion appears to me as the most plausible and natural restriction of the principle that explanation is irreflexive. It is worthy of interest here because *Contingent Irreflexivity* also leaves open the possibility that, if there is an omni-explainer, this proposition is a necessary truth that explains itself.

But the problem with van Inwagen's suggestion is that, given the deduction of an omni-explainer from PSR, if *Contingent Irreflexivity* is assumed, PSR yields *Necessitarianism*:

> *Necessitarianism:* For any proposition x, if x is true then x is necessarily true.

This thesis should be associated with the seventeenth-century Dutch rationalist Spinoza (1985, pp. 433–9), who defended the thesis that nothing in nature is contingent, but all things are of necessity.

Suppose that there is an omni-explainer O. Then, given *Contingent Irreflexivity*, O cannot be a contingent truth. So O must be a necessary truth. But if so, on the further assumption that any *explanans* strictly implies its *explananda*, every truth is necessary. Hence, if PSR is assumed to yield the conclusion that there is an omni-explainer, the further assumption that *Contingent Irreflexivity* is true (and *Irreflexivity* is false) leads to the conclusion that PSR entails *Necessitarianism*.

Philosophers are familiar with the belief that PSR entails *Necessitarianism* because of a famous argument proposed by van Inwagen and others.[12] The main difference between my deduction of *Necessitarianism* from PSR and van Inwagen's argument is that the latter relies on the assumption that the conjunction of all contingent truths can be formed, while mine doesn't rely on such an assumption.[13]

---

[12] See also Hill (1982) and Bennett (1984, p. 115). Van Inwagen's argument runs as follows. Assume that PSR is true and *Necessitarianism* is false. *Necessitarianism* being false there are contingent truths. Form the conjunction of all contingent truths as c. Conjunctions of contingent truths are contingent and true; hence c is a contingent truth. By PSR there is an explanation, say e, for c. Since explanation is *factive*, e is true. If so, e is either necessarily or contingently true. If e is necessarily true, then, on the further assumption that any *explanans* strictly implies its *explananda*, so are c and its conjuncts. But this result conflicts with our assumption that there are contingent truths of which c is the conjunction. So e must be contingent. But if e is a contingent truth, e is a conjunct of c. By *Dissection* we can derive that e explains itself, contrary to the assumption that no contingent proposition is self-explanatory. So e must be a necessary truth. Yet we have already seen that this result conflicts with the assumption that *Necessitarianism* is false. Therefore, if PSR is true so is *Necessitarianism*.

[13] The deduction of an omni-explainer from PSR only appeals to an arbitrary conjunction x such that to each of the collective omni-explainers y there corresponds a

This difference is important because one can resist the assumption that the conjunction of all contingent truths can be formed (Oppy 2006, p. 281).

Another advantage of my derivation of *Necessitarianism* from PSR compared to van Inwagen's original argument is that it allows me to emphasize that restricting the principle of irreflexivity of explanation to contingent truths is essential in order to deduce *Necessitarianism* from PSR. For a crucial step in the derivation of *Necessitarianism* from PSR is the deduction of the claim that there is an omni-explainer. Yet if *Irreflexivity* holds unrestrictedly, no truth whatsoever is an omni-explainer and so *Necessitarianism* cannot be deduced.[14]

So, prima facie, the strategy that consists in biting the bullet in favour of the existence of an omni-explainer and in admitting that there may be a self-explanatory necessary truth (and no self-explanatory contingent truth) is *wildly* unappealing. For this strategy yields the counterintuitive conclusion that *Necessitarianism* is true. If a commitment to PSR requires us to endorse both the claim that there is an omni-explainer and the claim that *Necessitarianism* is true, then I think that we might well wonder whether the game is worth the candle. For the belief that things may be different than they are is both deeply entrenched into our system of beliefs and well-motivated.

But I should emphasize that Michael Della Rocca (2010), who defends PSR, thinks that the game is worth the candle even if PSR yields *Necessitarianism*. Della Rocca writes:

Precisely because necessitarianism is an implication of the PSR, the intuitive pressure leading to the PSR is intuitive pressure leading to necessitarianism.

conjunct of *x* that *y* does not explain. That there is such a conjunction follows from PSR and the claim that no proposition is an omni-explainer *tout court*, which we assumed for *reductio*.

[14] That *Necessitarianism* does not follow from PSR if *Irreflexivity* is assumed to hold unrestrictedly is true of van Inwagen's original argument too. For suppose for *reductio* that *Necessitarianism* and PSR are both true. Then let us assume that we can form the conjunction of all (necessary) truths. By PSR this conjunction has an explanation. By *Necessitarianism* this explanation is a necessary truth. But if so the explanation of the conjunction of all (necessary) truths is a conjunct of this conjunction. Given *Dissection*, the explanation of the conjunction of all necessary truths explains itself, which contradicts *Irreflexivity*. Therefore, if *Irreflexivity* holds unrestrictedly and *Dissection* is true, then PSR is *incompatible* with *Necessitarianism*.

A clear-headed proponent of the PSR can be expected to embrace necessitarianism for precisely this reason. (Spinoza certainly did.) "Oh, that necessitarianism stuff is something I knew about all along," the rationalist might say. (Della Rocca 2010, p. 9)

According to Della Rocca, the deduction of *Necessitarianism* from PSR merely confirms what he knew all along, namely that *Necessitarianism* is part of the explanatory universalist doctrine. Then since he thinks that PSR is intuitive he concludes that *Necessitarianism* is intuitive too. This is provocative. But whatever one's views about the plausibility of *Necessitarianism*, I believe that Della Rocca's "clear-headed proponent of PSR" is getting confused. For, as I have explained, the view that PSR implies *Necessitarianism* is false if no proposition whatsoever explains itself. Yet, on Della Rocca's own lights, there are strong reasons to stand firm on the ban on self-explanations. I shall discuss these reasons to maintain *Irreflexivity* in section 3.2. My argument will allow me to reject further restrictions of the principle that explanation is irreflexive that have been defended by Hud Hudson (1997) and Alexander Pruss (2006).

3.2. Standing firm on the ban on self-explanations

Several explanatory universalists have committed themselves to failures of *Irreflexivity*. First, Della Rocca has endorsed the view that *Necessitarianism* follows from PSR. Yet since *Necessitarianism* follows from PSR *only if* we admit a self-explanatory necessary truth, Della Rocca's position is coherent only if he denies that *Irreflexivity* holds unrestrictedly. Other explanatory universalists have thought that they can *avoid* the conclusion that *Necessitarianism* follows from PSR by admitting some further violations of *Irreflexivity*. Hudson (1997) has proposed to admit *true necessary falsehoods* in order to avoid a commitment to *Necessitarianism*. He argues that the existence of true necessary falsehoods appears justified if we endorse David Lewis's (1986a) genuine modal realism and the doctrine of unrestricted composition.[15] Then if we assume that the omni-explainer is neither a contingent nor a necessary truth but a true necessary falsehood, *Necessitarianism* does not follow from the claim that there is an omni-

---

[15] See Feit 1998 for a reply to Hudson's argument regarding the link between genuine modal realism and the thesis that there are true necessary falsehoods.

explainer. Yet if the omni-explainer is a true necessary falsehood, then there is a *self-explanatory* true necessary falsehood. Finally, Alexander Pruss has maintained that there is a good candidate for a self-explanatory *contingent* truth (2006, pp. 97–125). Pruss's candidate is a proposition that represents a libertarian free action of creation (2006, p. 124). The situation Pruss has in mind involves a necessarily existing and essentially good God who, when deciding what kind of a universe to create, finds that no world is the best of all; and so God chooses to create one of the best worlds freely (2006, pp. 116–17). Thus Pruss's cosmological scenario implies the rejection of *Contingent Irreflexivity*.[16]

I believe that the general strategy of these explanatory universalists is misguided because I contend that we are justified in maintaining that *Irreflexivity* is true. So here I shall offer a general argument for *Irreflexivity* following which *no* violation of *Irreflexivity* should be allowed.

Several writers have emphasized that explanation and cognate notions are fundamentally irreflexive. For instance, Oppy writes:

If one asks "Why S?", one can never be satisfied with the alleged explanation "Because S!".... It is true that in colloquial language it is common for people to say that something or other is "self-explanatory"; but what they mean when they say this is usually that the thing in question is obvious, not that

---

[16] If pressed to explain why I am not convinced by Pruss's particular alleged counterexample to *Contingent Irreflexivity*, I should say that the reason why, in his scenario, God acted *indifferently* is that no world is the best overall. Since the proposition that there is no best world overall is undoubtedly distinct from that representing God's action, I don't see why we should admit a violation of *Irreflexivity* here. Some may reply that the proposition that no candidate for creation is the best universe overall does not suffice to fully explain why it is this world, instead of another one, that has been created. I could not agree more. But if so, the right conclusion is that Pruss's scenario is a counterexample to PSR.
Modern explanatory universalists would have agreed with me on this conclusion. Spinoza himself denied that God has free will on the basis of PSR. But he also denied that the world is created. Leibniz, on the other hand, maintained that PSR entails that some world is better than any other world. Otherwise, God would have no reason to act: "And to say that the mind will act when it has reasons to act, even if the ways of acting are absolutely indifferent—this is to speak again very superficially and quite indefensibly. For you don't have a sufficient reason to act unless you have a sufficient reason to act in precisely such-and-such a way... So when there's a sufficient reason to do any particular thing, there's also a sufficient reason to do it in a certain particular way, which means that the various alternative ways of doing it are not indifferent." (Alexander 1956, Leibniz's 5th paper).

it literally provides its own explanation.... As intimated above, "A because A" is always an explanatory solecism; hence "A explains A" can never be true. (Oppy 2006, pp. 277–8)

If "p because p" is a mistake of the grammar of explanation, then *Irreflexivity* must be a formal truth that holds of any proposition. In a similar vein, Benjamin Schnieder (2011, p. 454) claims that "$\neg(p$ because $p)$" is a theorem of his logic for 'because'. Last but not least, Kit Fine (2012, p. 5) assumes as a constitutive rule of inference of his pure logic of ground that strict ground operators are non-circular, i.e. that nothing strictly grounds itself. The notion of a strict ground is firmly connected to that of an explanation. As Fine writes

We might think of the strict grounds as moving us down in the explanatory hierarchy. They always take us to a lower level of explanation and, for this reason, a truth can never be a strict ground for itself. (Fine 2012, p. 3)

Here Fine appears to justify the non-circularity of the strict ground operator in terms of the irreflexivity of explanation. So, contra these explanatory universalists that I mentioned at the beginning of this section, there seems to be a wide consensus in contemporary metaphysics in favour of the view that explanation and cognate notions are irreducibly irreflexive. If this consensus is justified, we should not relax the ban on self-explanations

But is it justified? I think so. Consider Della Rocca's account of the rejection of explanations by means of Aristotelian forms by early modern philosophers:

Such forms were introduced—or so the caricature goes—to explain changes in the world. A pan becomes hot, for example, because it acquires the form of heat. Such explanation came to be seen and is still seen by most as bankrupt. To explain something's becoming hot in terms of its acquisition of the form of heat is trivial: in order to explain why the pan becomes hot, we need to appeal to features *not so closely tied*—as the form of heat is—to the phenomenon to be explained. If explanation of a certain phenomenon by means of such forms were the whole explanation, then this phenomenon would remain inexplicable. (Della Rocca 2010, p. 3; my emphasis)

Della Rocca's account seems correct to me. But why is it that, if explaining p in terms of q is trivial, p remains unexplained? This is so because a plausible requirement on explanations is that, in order for q to be an explanation for p, q must be informative about p.[17] Given that by definition an alleged explanation that is trivial is not informative, no genuine explanation is trivial. But why are alleged explanations by Aristotelian forms trivial? Della Rocca thinks that they are so because he maintains the following:

> *Distance:* for any x and y, if x and y are *too closely tied*, then x is neither an explanation for y nor is y an explanation for x.

What 'closely tied' means here is vague. Still there is a clear connection between the notion of an alleged explanation that is insufficiently informative and that of an alleged *explanans* that is too closely tied to its *explanandum*. If the transmission of information is a necessary requirement on explanations, so is *Distance*. *Distance* entails, however, that no proposition whatsoever can be its own explanation. This is because, for every proposition x, no proposition is more closely tied to x than x itself. So here is one way of justifying *Irreflexivity*: the requirement of transmission of information justifies *Distance*, which itself justifies *Irreflexivity*. I believe that this way of reasoning is correct. Therefore, I contend that we should stand firm on the ban on self-explanations.

But if so, Della Rocca seems to be hoist by his own petard. Given his commitment to *Distance*, he must commit himself to *Irreflexivity*. But then his open-minded attitude towards *Necessitarianism* is irrelevant. For given *Irreflexivity*, if the derivation of an omni-explainer is sound, PSR does not entail *Necessitarianism* (see section 3.1). Since I agree with Della Rocca that *Distance* is true, biting the bullet in favour of *Necessitarianism* as he does is not a strategy that I can recommend to any "clear-headed" proponent of PSR.

Moreover and more importantly, since I maintain *Irreflexivity*, I contend that explanatory universalists cannot endorse the claim that there is an omni-explainer. For, given *Irreflexivity*, explanatory universalism is refuted if PSR implies that there is an omni-explainer. According to me then, there is only one adequate way explanatory universalists can evade this problem: they must *solve* it by showing that PSR does not imply that there is an omni-explainer. But the

---

[17] An instance of this principle is Lewis's (1986b, pp. 217–18) claim that a causal explanation must be informative about the *causal history* of the *explanandum*.

claim that there is an omni-explainer follows from PSR by *Dissection*. This means that explanatory universalism is false if *Dissection* is true. Fortunately, *Dissection* is not true, or so I shall argue in the next section.

4. CONJUNCTION AND EXPLANATION

I do not believe that the deduction of an omni-explainer from PSR is cogent because this deduction essentially relies on *Dissection*, namely the claim that for any propositions x, y, and z, if z is an explanation for $(x \ \& \ y)$, then z is an explanation for x and z is an explanation for y. Yet explanatory universalists can legitimately deny *Dissection*, or so I shall argue.

Whether *Dissection* is true depends on how the explanation operator interacts with truth functions, and in particular with conjunction. So let us assume that there is a consequence operator $\Rightarrow^*$ such that, necessarily, for any propositions x and y, x explains y iff x is true, $x \neq y$, and $x \Rightarrow^* y$. Then whether *Dissection* is true depends on the strength of $\Rightarrow^*$. Of course, *Dissection* is true if $\Rightarrow^*$ is assumed to be as strong as material implication or classical entailment. But there is a powerful reason to think that $\Rightarrow^*$ must be stronger than both classical material implication and classical entailment. This reason has to do with *relevance*. Intuitively, for a proposition to explain another, the former must contribute to the obtaining of the latter. In other words, the *explanans* must be relevant to the *explanandum*. However, if $\Rightarrow^*$ is as weak as classical material implication or classical entailment, then a true proposition may turn out to have a fully irrelevant *explanans*. If $\Rightarrow^*$ is understood in terms of classical material implication, then the fact that François Hollande is the actual president of France explains why the Earth rotates towards the east. If $\Rightarrow^*$ is understood in terms of classical entailment and there are both contingent and necessary truths, then every necessary truth, and a fortiori every logical necessity, turns out to be explained by every contingent truth. It is for such reasons that the claim that explanation is classically monotonic, i.e. the claim that any *explanans* explains all the (classical) logical consequences of what it explains, appears implausible. For this claim generates fully irrelevant explanations. So the claim that explanation is classically monotonic does not constitute a legitimate reason to assume that *Dissection* is true.

A natural thought, then, is to conceive of $\Rightarrow^*$ in terms of relevant implication. The suggestion is that, for any distinct and true propositions x and y, x is a sufficient reason or full explanation for y if and only if x is a true relevant sufficient condition for y, and $x \neq y$. This suggestion entails that *Dissection* is true. For, for any x, y, and z, if z relevantly implies $(x \& y)$, z relevantly implies x and relevantly implies y by suffixing and &-elimination.[18] However, I shall argue that there are good reasons to maintain that explanation is stronger than relevant implication. These reasons imply that *Dissection* is false.

Consider the following quotation from the famous explanatory universalist Leibniz:

Now, by that single principle, viz. that there ought to be a sufficient reason why things should be so, *and not otherwise,* one may demonstrate the being of a God, and all the other parts of metaphysics or natural theology; and even, in some measure, those principles of natural philosophy, that are independent upon mathematics: I mean the dynamical principles, or the principles of force. (Alexander 1956, 2nd paper, §1; my emphasis)

According to Leibniz, a sufficient reason or full explanation for a proposition must tell us why things are so *and not otherwise*. This means that, for Leibniz, a genuine explanation for a proposition must be *discriminatory*: it must discriminate the actual situation from counterfactual ones.[19] Such an account of explanation requires that,

---

[18] The suffixing axiom of relevant logic states that, for any x and y, if x relevantly implies y, then, for any z, if y relevantly implies z then x relevantly implies z. The &-elimination axiom states that, for any x and y, $(x \& y)$ relevantly implies x and relevantly implies y.

[19] On the discriminatory feature of explanation see also the quote from Leibniz in note 16 above. Let me emphasize that Leibniz maintained that there are necessary truths. So if his principle of sufficient reason is meant to apply to these truths as well, as it certainly is, then his requirement that explanations tell us why things are so, *and not otherwise,* implies us to have a look at *impossible* counterfactual situations. These situations may correspond to the *non-normal* worlds, or "logic fictions", of the semantics for relevance logic; see Priest 2008. As a matter of fact, Leibniz does consider a world that is, according to him, such a logic fiction when he replies to Clarke. He calls such worlds merely "abstractly possible" and maintains that there are some abstract possibilities that fail to be genuine metaphysical possibilities because they violate PSR: "This supposition of two indiscernibles—e.g. two pieces of matter that are perfectly alike—does indeed seem to be abstractly possible, but it isn't consistent with the order of things, or with God's wisdom, which doesn't allow anything without reason. Ordinary lay-people fancy such things because they rest content with incomplete

in order for a proposition to explain another, the former proposition must be relevant to the latter. However, requiring that the *explanans* contains *some* chunk of relevant information about the *explanandum* is not enough if what we want is to *fully* explain why things are so *and not otherwise*. For let us suppose that p relevantly implies q while r is irrelevant to q (where p, q, and r are three distinct truths). Then (p & r) is a true proposition that contains some relevant piece of information about q. Yet if one attempts to explain why q is the case by merely appealing to (p & r), one fails to say whether q would be true or false if p were false and r were true or whether q would be true if p were true and r were false, despite the fact that these questions have a determinate answer. Merely explaining q in terms of (p & r) does not suffice to discriminate the actual state of the universe from counterfactual states of the universe because it does not tell us on what, within (p & r), q genuinely depends. This is the reason why (p & r) is not a sufficient reason, or genuine explanation, for q on Leibniz's account of a sufficient reason. But if so, the Leibnizian account of explanation is incompatible with *Dissection*. For *Dissection* typically generates alleged explanations that contain chunks of information that are irrelevant to the *explanandum*.

Let me assume that the following is a satisfactory explanation of why a is black: a is black because a is a raven and genetic mechanisms X occur within all ravens that are responsible for biochemical reactions Y which produce their distinctive black pigmentation. And let me assume for the sake of the argument that the fact that I placed a mug on my desk explains that there is a mug on my desk. On these assumptions, the following appears to be a plausible explanation of why a is black and there is a mug on my desk: a is black and there is a mug on my desk because a is a raven, genetic mechanisms X occur in all ravens which are responsible for biochemical reactions Y which produce their distinctive black pigmentation, and I placed a mug on my desk. So by *Dissection* we can derive that a is black because a is a raven, genetic mechanisms X occur in all ravens which are responsible for biochemical reactions Y which produce their distinctive black pigmentation, and I placed a mug on my desk. But

---

notions, thus regarding something as outright possible on the grounds that it is abstractly possible." Alexander 1956, Leibniz's 5th reply.

it seems that *a* would still be black in a counterfactual situation in which I had placed no mug on my desk. That I placed a mug on my desk is irrelevant to explain why *a* is black. Indeed, knowing that I placed a mug on my desk does not increase our understanding of why *a* is black. This information seems parasitic on what explains that *a* is black instead of being part of a genuine explanation of why *a* is black. So it is counterintuitive to think that the proposition that I placed a mug on my desk can take place in a genuine explanation of why *a* is black. I believe that the Leibnizian account of explanation is motivated by such intuitions.

In the previous example, *Dissection* yields an alleged explanation of why *a* is black that does not tell us whether *a* would be black in a situation in which I placed no mug on my desk, although this question has a determinate answer. In general, the point is that for any propositions *w*, *x*, *y*, and *z* such that *w* explains *x* and *y* explains *z*, if we assume that (*w* & *y*) explains (*x* & *z*), then *Dissection* entails that (*w* & *y*) explains both *x* and *z* despite the fact that *y* may be irrelevant to *x* and *w* to *z*. In such a case, explaining *x* in terms of (*w* & *y*) does not tell us whether *x* would be true if *w* were true and *y* were false, and it does not tell us whether *x* would be true if *w* were false and *y* were true, although these questions have a determinate answer. So *Dissection* generates alleged explanations that do not tell us how the *explanandum* is connected with the alleged *explanans* because they contain *too much* information. According to the Leibnizian account of explanation, such alleged explanations are mere *pseudo* explanations. For they fail to explain why things are so, *and not otherwise*. So *Dissection* is incompatible with the Leibnizian account of explanation that I favour.

But is the Leibnizian account of explanation plausible? James Woodward has argued that a successful scientific explanation should not merely provide a nomologically sufficient condition for the *explanandum*, but should be such that it "could be used to answer a set of what-if-things-had-been-different questions" that "insure that the *explanans* will perspicuously identify those conditions which are relevant to the *explanandum* being what it is" (Woodward 1979, p. 55) (see also Woodward 2003). The claim is that a successful act of explanation should not only tell us that the *explanandum* derives from the alleged *explanans* but should tell us *how* the *explanandum* depends on the alleged *explanans* (Hitchcock 2005, p. 112). Of course, what Woodward and Hitchcock are talking about here are *linguistic acts* of explanation rather than the ontological and objective notion of explanation that is relevant to the purpose of this paper and is independent of any such act. But linguistic acts of explanation are intended to grasp, or to make intelligible, the explanatory connections that take place in the world. So it is reasonable to think that, if Woodward and Hitchcock are right about the fact that acts of explanation are successful only if they tell us how the *explanandum* depends on the alleged *explanans*, then this can only be because something like the Leibnizian fine-grained account of explanatory connections in the world is true.[20]

In this section, I have argued that the great explanatory universalist Leibniz is committed to the view that a proposition is not merely another true proposition that relevantly implies the latter. Then I have argued that the Leibnizian fine-grained view about explanation is incompatible with *Dissection*. The view is that a genuine explanation must only contain those true sufficient conditions that are relevant to the obtaining of the *explanandum* in order to discriminate why things are so *and not otherwise*. Since *Dissection* typically generates alleged explanations that contain superfluous information, it is false on the Leibnizian view. Finally, I have emphasized that the Leibnizian view on explanation that I favor is supported by recent considerations concerning the nature of scientific explanations. Therefore, explanatory universalists need not be, and I say are not, committed to *Dissection*. Since the deduction of an omni-explainer from PSR essentially relies on *Dissection*, I conclude that explanatory universalism is not refuted by this argument.

---

[20] Gideon Rosen (2010, pp. 116–17) also seems to share the view that *Dissection* is false. Rosen does not discuss *Dissection* but the related principle that, for any truths *x* and *y*, if *x* explains *y*, then, for any *z*, (*x* & *z*) explains *y*, which I shall call *Strengthening* (Rosen calls it "monotonicity", but I prefer to reserve the label "monotonicity" to describe another principle). But Rosen's reasons to deny *Strengthening* appear to me as close, if not identical, to my reasons to deny *Dissection*. Moreover, the rejection of *Strengthening* appears to imply the rejection of *Dissection*. See also Guigon 2011 for another argument against *Dissection* understood as a principle about causal explanation.

5. CODA

I would like to conclude this article by considering a weaker version of *Dissection* that is not challenged by the argument of the previous section and which seems plausible to me:

> *W-Dissection:* For any propositions x, y, and z, if z is an explanation for $(x \,\&\, y)$, then if z is a conjunction, then either z is an explanation for x and z is an explanation for y, or some conjunct of z explains x and some conjunct of z explains y; if z is not a conjunction, z is an explanation for x and z is an explanation for y.[21]

I am not going to argue for *W-Dissection* here. The reason why I find this principle congenial is that I cannot think of any good reason to reject it. Notice also that the argument of the previous section would justify a general account of the interaction of explanation with truth functions that does not restrict itself to propositions that exhibit a particular syntactic structure (viz. conjunctions).[22] But for reasons of space, I shall not pursue this line of inquiry here. The issue I shall focus on is whether PSR still yields an omni-explainer if we substitute *W-Dissection* for *Dissection*. I shall argue that it doesn't.

When casting the deduction of an omni-explainer from the assumption that there are collective omni-explainers, I assumed that there are only two collective omni-explainers: r and s. Now suppose that r is a conjunctive truth having exactly two conjuncts: u and v. And suppose that s is not a conjunctive truth. Then if we substitute *W-Dissection* for *Dissection*, step (4) of the argument must be replaced by

(4′) $\quad E_r(p \,\&\, q) \to (E_r p \lor E_u p \lor E_v p)$

But (7)—the claim that either r or s is an omni-explainer *tout court*—does not follow from (4′) and the assumption that s is not conjunctive. Instead what follows from (4′) is

(7′) $\quad (p \to (E_r p \lor E_u p \lor E_v p)) \lor (q \to E_s q)$

---

[21] I am greatly thankful to Natalja Deng for having suggested this weaker version of *Dissection* to me.
[22] I am grateful to an anonymous referee for stressing this point.

Since the first disjunct of (7′) is compatible with (1)—the claim that p is true but not explained by r—it does not follow from (7′) that there is an omni-explainer *tout court*. This means that, if we substitute *W-Dissection* for *Dissection* in the deduction of an omni-explainer from PSR, the conclusion that there is an omni-explainer does not follow, and PSR no more conflicts with the principle that explanation is irreflexive.

Still there is something important about the interaction of PSR, *Irreflexivity*, and *W-Dissection* that this argument reveals. If (7′) is true and (7) is false, then by *W-Dissection* it follows that (p & q) is not explained by s; otherwise, since s is not a conjunctive truth, the second conjunct of (7′) would be true contrary to (2), namely the assumption that s does not explain q. So (p & q) is explained by r. Since there is no omni-explainer *tout court*, let me assume, this means that at least one proposition, either p or q, is neither explained by r nor by s but by a *further* proposition: a conjunct of r that is neither identical to r nor to s. But if so, it is not the case that r and s collectively explain *all* truths. There are more collective omni-explainers than we started with. Isn't this puzzling?

Yes and no. In fact, I would not be surprised if it could be shown that, for any number n, if we assume as a working hypothesis that there are n collective omni-explainers, then PSR, *Irreflexivity*, and *W-Dissection* together entail that there are more than n collective omni-explainers. If this could be shown, then this would mean that the limit of the set of collective omni-explainers is not attainable, or that this set can never be fulfilled. Such a result should not surprise us too much because we are familiar with the idea that the conjunction of PSR and *Irreflexivity* entails that there is no actual ultimate level of explanation. More astonishing, I suggest, is the result that our assumptions about how explanation combines with *conjunction* play a determining role in whether PSR and *Irreflexivity* together entail that there is no actual ultimate level of explanation. Now it is true that philosophers tend to repudiate the claim that there is no actual fundamental level of explanation.[23] But, looking at physical cosmology and causal explanation, I wonder if the demand for an actual fundamental level of explanation is not just another dogma of metaphysics.

[23] See, e.g. Cameron 2008.

Standard or Friedmann-Robertson-Walker (FRW) big bang models imply that for every time t there is a time t' that is prior to t and is such that the state of the universe at t' is a cause of the state of the universe at t. In this way, "the principle *Every event has a cause*... is satisfied in the FRW big bang models" (Earman 1995, p. 209). If every event has a cause, every proposition that represents the occurrence of an event has a causal explanation. So PSR, understood as a principle about *causal* explanation, is true within standard big bang models. In these models, the structure of time is continuous and open.[24] This entails that no state of the universe is a cause of itself and that no proposition is its own causal explanation. So *Irreflexivity*, understood as a principle about causal explanation, is also true in standard big bang models. Accordingly, there is no actual fundamental cause, no actual first state of the universe, and so no actual fundamental level of causal explanation in FRW models. But what of the big bang itself then? Well, the whole point is that, in FRW models, the big bang singularity at $t = 0$ is excluded from the class of actual moments of time. The big bang singularity is an *ideal* rather than an actual limit of time. Physicists interpret this claim as meaning that, according to FRW big bang models, the cosmic time interval is *open* in the past. But this does not mean that time is infinite in FRW big bang models. For the duration of the past interval is still *finite*, around fifteen billion years. In a similar vein, a chain of explanations can be open without being infinite, and, strictly speaking, the combination of PSR and *Irreflexivity* merely commit us to such an open chain of explanations.[25] Since the past interval is finite, it is impossible to travel infinitely in a *regular* way into the past. Still, in some sense, there are infinitely descending causal chains, and so infinitely descending chains of causal explanation, in FRW big bang models. For the causal chain asymptotically approaches the big bang singularity without attaining it. The closer we are to the big bang, the smaller is the temporal extension of the state of the universe. In this way, as we are approaching the big bang singularity we are approaching the limit

---

[24] Cf. Meyer 2012 on the interaction between closed models of time and the principle of sufficient reason. In his article, Meyer rejects PSR on the misleading grounds that PSR entails *Necessitarianism*.

[25] A chain of explanations is open if for any point x in this chain, there is a real number $r > 0$ such that the interval $(x + r, x - r)$ is contained in the chain.

of the set of collective causal omni-explainers, and so getting closer to fulfilling this set. But it can never be fulfilled as the limit of the set, the big bang singularity, is not attainable. Therefore, standard big bang models are plausible models of the universe that provide us with an acceptable understanding of what a world without an actual ultimate level of (causal) explanation looks like.

In closing, in this article I have defended explanatory universalism, the view that PSR is true, against an argument that purports to show that PSR entails that some truth explains every truth. This argument constitutes a challenge to explanatory universalism because it implies that PSR conflicts with the principle that explanation is irreflexive, which I have maintained against other proponents of PSR. I have argued that the derivation of an omni-explainer from PSR does not refute explanatory universalism because this argument essentially appeals to *Dissection* which explanatory universalists can legitimately deny. According to me, explanatory universalists should maintain that a genuine explanation of a fact must contain no information that does not contribute to the explanation of this fact. If this is correct, then *W-Dissection*, from which it does not follow that PSR entails that there is an omni-explainer, appears more plausible than *Dissection*.

Naturally, if my defence of explanatory universalism commits me to the claim that there is no actual ultimate level of explanation, I do not expect it to gain large popularity among philosophers. This is a venerable *trilemma*: the principle of sufficient reason, the unrestricted ban on self-explanations, and the claim that there is an actual fundamental level of explanation cannot all be true together. The tradition from Aquinas to Leibniz contends that PSR is true and that there is an actual *self-explanatory* level of explanation, thereby rejecting that explanation is necessarily irreflexive. On the other hand, many contemporary metaphysicians maintain that there is an actual fundamental level of explanation and that nothing is its own explanation, thereby rejecting PSR. But in this domain the metaphysician can learn from physical cosmology. And if standard big bang models are plausible representations of physical reality, then we must acknowledge that a theory that commits us to PSR, to the ban on self-explanations, and to the denial of an actual fundamental level of explanation is not implausible. In any case, such a theory is not refuted by the argument according to which PSR entails that there is an omni-explainer.

APPENDIX

When stating the derivation of an omni-explainer from the claim that there are collective omni-explainers and *Dissection* in section 2, I have assumed for ease of exposition that the set of collective omni-explainers is finite. But since, given the content of section 5, it does not seem implausible that explanatory universalists are committed to infinitely many collective omni-explainers, one may legitimately wonder whether the claim that there is an omni-explainer still follows from PSR and *Dissection* when an infinite set of collective omni-explainers is assumed.

An objector may think that it doesn't on the grounds that we can only form conjunctions of a *finite* number of propositions. Yet since our argument proceeds by mapping each of the collective omni-explainers onto a true proposition that it does not explain and in forming the conjunction of these mapped-to propositions, if there are infinitely many collective omni-explainers, this conjunction may have an *infinite* number of conjuncts.

Here is a model to illustrate this problem. Let 'G' stand for the set of collective omni-explainers and suppose that G = {..., o_3, o_2, o_1}, which is a backward infinite series and where 'o_1', 'o_2', 'o_3', etc. are names for collective omni-explainers. Suppose that propositions have truth-functional structure, and that each member of S is atomic. Now suppose that each o_i in the series explains each later member in the series. For instance, o_2 explains o_1, o_3 explains o_2 and o_1, and so on. Suppose also that there is another proposition p outside the series that is explained by o_1 but which does not explain anything. In this model, for any collective omni-explainer o_i, the propositions that o_i does not explain always come lower in the series. So we can map each of the collective omni-explainers onto its immediate ancestor for the need of the proof: o_1 can be mapped onto o_2, o_2 can be mapped onto o_3 and, in general, we can map any o_i onto o_{i-1}. Now the problem is that for the purpose of the argument we would need to be able to form the conjunction of these mapped-to propositions. But since the set of collective omni-explainers is infinite, the set of mapped-to propositions—which is simply the set of immediate ancestors of every collective omni-explainer here—is itself infinite. So if, as my objector thinks, we cannot form infinite conjunctions, we cannot form the conjunction of mapped-to propositions. If so, the deduction of an omni-explainer from PSR is blocked.[26]

Several things can be said in response to this objection. First, I must admit that I do not think that metaphysicians should worry about infinite conjunctions. As readers familiar with the literature on the metaphysics of modality should know, the hypothesis that we can form such infinite conjunctions is essential to recent linguistic ersatzist projects.[27] If infinite conjunctions are acceptable in that context, as I think they are, then I see no reason to think that they are unacceptable in the context of my argument.

If we allow for infinite conjunctions, then the argument of section 2 will run as follows. We will have an infinite series of propositions of the following form:

p_1 & $\neg E_{o1} p_1$
p_2 & $\neg E_{o2} p_2$
....
P_n & $\neg E_{on} p_n$
etc.

Then we should consider the following instance of the claim that there are collective omni-explainers:

$(\exists_\omega)(p_1 \& p_2 \& \ldots \& p_n \ldots) \rightarrow (E_{o1}(p_1 \& p_2 \& \ldots \& p_n \ldots) \lor E_{o2}(p_1 \& p_2 \& \ldots \& p_n \ldots) \lor \ldots \lor E_{on}(p_1 \& p_2 \& \ldots \& p_n \ldots) \ldots)$.

Then if the syntactical rules that we used in the derivation of (7) from (3) are assumed to apply to infinitary contexts, the conclusion that there is an omni-explainer *tout court* can still be derived if there are infinitely many collective omni-explainers.

But if my objector insists that we cannot form infinite conjunctions, then I suggest that we use a truth predicate in this particular context in order to represent such infinite conjunctions. The thought

---

[26] This model was brought to my attention by an anonymous referee to whom I am grateful.
[27] See Melia 2001, p. 20 and Sider 2002, p. 287.

that the main purpose of the truth predicate is to represent such infinite conjunctions is traditional among deflationists about truth.[28] In this case, the idea is to replace *Dissection* by:

Dissection#: $\forall S \, \forall z (E_z(\text{the proposition that all the members of S are true}) \rightarrow \forall x \in S \, E_z x)$;

where *Dissection#* reads "for any set S of propositions and any proposition z, if z explains the proposition that all the members of S are true, then z explains all the members of S". On the assumption that we can use the truth predicate to represent infinite conjunctions, *Dissection#* should be as plausible as *Dissection*.

The argument then goes as follows. Let, again, G be a backward infinite series of collective omni-explainers. Suppose for *reductio* that none of the members of G is an omni-explainer *tout court*. Then to each o_i in G we can associate a true proposition $f(o_i)$ that o_i does not explain. Take U the set of all $f(o_i)$s such that o_i is in G. By *Dissection#*, we get:

(#): $\forall o_i \in G \, (E_{o_i}(\text{the proposition that all the members of U are true}) \rightarrow \forall x \in U \, E_{o_i} x)$.

Now since the members of G are collective omni-explainers, there is a member o_j of G such that o_j explains the proposition that all the members of U are true. By (#) it follows that, for all $x \in U$, o_j explains x. But since $f(o_j)$ is in U, we get the conclusion: o_j explains $f(o_j)$. Yet by assumption $f(o_j)$ is not explained by o_j. Contradiction. Hence, given *Dissection#*, some member of G is an omni-explainer *tout court*. Q.E.D.[29]

University of Geneva

---

[28] See, for instance, Quine 1970, p. 12: "We may affirm the single sentence by just uttering it, unaided by quotation or by the truth predicate; but if we want to affirm some infinite lot of sentences, then the truth predicate has its use." See also Halbach 1999.

[29] This paper has benefited greatly from discussions with members of eidos, the Swiss Centre in Metaphysics. I thank them all. I am especially thankful to Natalja Deng, Fabrice Correia, Alexander Skiles, and Alexander Bown. I am also greatly indebted to Karen Bennett, Baptiste Le Bihan, Stephan Leuenberger, Clare Mac Cumhaill, Ulrich Meyer, Graham Peebles, Johannes Stern, and Cain Todd and to anonymous referees for OSM.

REFERENCES

Alexander, H. G. (ed.) (1956) *The Leibniz-Clarke Correspondence* (New York, NY: Barnes and Noble).
Anderson, A. R. and N. D. Belnap (1975) *Entailment: The Logic of Relevance and Necessity*, i (Princeton, NJ: Princeton University).
Bennett, J. (1984) *A Study of Spinoza's Ethics* (Indianapolis, IN: Hackett).
Cameron, R. P. (2008) "Turtles All the Way Down: Regress, Priority, and Fundamentality", *Philosophical Quarterly* 58: 1–14.
Della Rocca, M. (2010) "PSR", *Philosophers' Imprint* 10/7: 1–13.
Earman, J. (1995) *Bangs, Crunches, Whimpers, and Shrieks: Singularities and Acausalities in Relativistic Spacetimes* (New York, Oxford: Oxford University Press).
Feit, N. (1998) "More on Brute Facts", *Australasian Journal of Philosophy* 76: 625–30.
Fine, K. (2012) "The Pure Logic of Ground", *Review of Symbolic Logic* 5: 1–25.
Geroch, R. P. (1970) "Singularities", in M. Carmeli, S. I. Fickler, and L. Witten (eds.), *Relativity* (New York, NY: Plenum Press), 259–91.
Guigon, G. (2011) "Merely Possible Explanation", *Religious Studies* 47: 359–70.
Halbach, V. (1999) "Disquotationalism and Infinite Conjunctions", *Mind* 108: 1–22.
Hill, C. (1982) "On a revised version of the principle of sufficient reason", *Pacific Philosophical Quarterly* 63: 236–42.
Hitchcock, C. (2005) "... And Away from a Theory of Explanation Itself', *Synthese* 143: 109–24.
Hudson, H. (1997) "Brute Facts", *Australasian Journal of Philosophy* 75: 77–82.
Humberstone, I. L. (1985) "The Formalities of Collective Omniscience", *Philosophical Studies* 48: 401–23.
Lewis, D. K. (1986a) *On the Plurality of Worlds* (Oxford, Malden: Blackwell).
Lewis, D. K. (1986b) "Causal Explanation", in *Philosophical Papers*, ii (Oxford, New York: Oxford University Press), 214–40.
Melia, J. (2001) "Reducing Possibilities to Language", *Analysis* 61: 19–29.
Meyer, U. (2012) "Explaining Causal Loops", *Analysis* 72: 259–64.
Oppy, G. (2006) *Philosophical Perspectives on Infinity* (Cambridge, New York: Cambridge University Press).
Paul, L. A. (2012) "Metaphysics as Modeling: The Handmaiden's Tale", *Philosophical Studies* 160: 1–29.
Penrose, R. (1969) "Gravitational Collapse: The Role of General Relativity", *Revista del Nuovo Cimento*, Serie I, 1, Numero Speciale: 252–76.

Priest, G. (2008) *An Introduction to Non-Classical Logic: From If to Is* (Cambridge: Cambridge University Press).
Pruss, A. R. (2006) *Sufficient Reason: A Reassessment* (Cambridge, New York: Cambridge University Press).
Quine, Willard V. O. (1970) *Philosophy of Logic* (Cambridge, MA: Harvard University Press).
Rosen, G. (2010) "Metaphysical Dependence: Grounding and Reduction", in B. Hale and A. Hoffmann (eds.), *Modality: Metaphysics, Logic and Epistemology* (Oxford: Oxford University Press), 109–36.
Russell, B. and A. N. Whitehead (1927) *Principia Mathematica*, 2nd edition, vol. 1, (Cambridge: Cambridge University Press).
Schaffer, J. (2009) "On What Grounds What", in D. Chalmers, D. Manley, and R. Wasserman (eds.), *Metametaphysics* (Oxford: Oxford University Press), 347–83.
Schnieder, B. (2011) "A Logic for 'Because'", *Review of Symbolic Logic* 4: 445–65.
Sider, T. (2002) "The Ersatz Pluriverse", *Journal of Philosophy* 99: 279–315.
Spinoza, B. (1985) *The Collected Works of Spinoza*, i, ed. E. Curley (Princeton, NJ: Princeton University Press).
van Inwagen, P. (1983) *An Essay on Free Will* (Oxford: Clarendon Press).
van Inwagen, P. (1990) *Material Beings* (Ithaca: Cornell University Press).
Woodward, J. (1979) "Scientific Explanation", in *British Journal for the Philosophy of Science* 30: 41–67.
Woodward, J. (2003) *Making Things Happen* (Oxford: Oxford University Press).

13. Return of the living dead: reply to Braddon-Mitchell

Fabrice Correia and Sven Rosenkranz

In the last volume, we resurrected the Growing Block Theory (GBT) from its grave, devising a coherent formulation of it and arguing that its burial was premature (Correia and Rosenkranz 2013). In particular, we aimed to show that properly construed, GBT has the wherewithal to explain how we might easily come to know that we are living on the edge of reality which it posits—contrary to what, in their respective ways, Bourne (2002), Braddon-Mitchell (2004), and Merricks (2006) had argued. Braddon-Mitchell remains unconvinced. In his reply, he instead sets out 'to put a stake through the lumbering zombie of the growing block theory' (Braddon-Mitchell 2013: 351).

We had thought we had gained firm ground. But here we are back in the mire, facing Van Helsing's rotten stake. The mire is deep, and the attempt not to lose our foothold sees us ignoring subtle distinctions that ultimately do not matter for survival. As long as we stand firm, the creature will not crumble. It is the rotten stake that will.

1.

To set the record straight Braddon-Mitchell first contends that he did not make the mistake we charged him with, i.e. to have misconstrued GBT as working with a tenseless, rather than tensed, notion of what fundamentally THERE IS.[1] He is quite content, he says, with

---

[1] Just as in our original paper, we here use capital letters for the quantifiers and the existence-predicate, ranging exclusively over things in time, whenever they are meant to express the metaphysically fundamental notions of whose nature GBT, presentism, and eternalism give competing accounts. By contrast, when used in normal font, the present-tensed existence-predicate expresses the notion of being present, the past-tensed existence-predicate expresses the notion of having been present, and the

conceding that according to GBT, what THERE IS changes as what used to be present is receding into the ever more distant past and new layers, or hyperplanes, are being added to the block (Braddon-Mitchell 2013: 352). And yet, later on Braddon-Mitchell (2013: 358) writes:

What distinguishes my version of the GBT from presentism is the genuine existence, from the perspective of each time, of multiple hyperplanes that timelessly and tenselessly exist in the way that presentists can't countenance.

This is certainly not the best way to defuse the charge. For, if at present, the hyperplane of the present time EXISTS timelessy and tenselessly, then surely in the past it is likewise among the things that then EXISTED. What else could 'timeless and tenseless existence' mean? According to GBT, however, the hyperplane of the present time is *not* among the things that EXISTED in the past. What distinguishes GBT from presentism is rather that according to the former but not the latter, some things presently EXIST that are no longer present.

The passage just quoted notwithstanding, Braddon-Mitchell acknowledges that according to the view under scrutiny, at each time we have a differently sized block, composed of more layers or hyperplanes than any of its predecessors at any earlier such moment (Braddon-Mitchell 2013: 352). For each such time, at that time, THERE IS a unique block extending into the past of that time. It is the present EXISTENCE of such a back-block, rather than its being subject to growth as time goes by, that Braddon-Mitchell thinks does all the harm (Braddon-Mitchell 2013: 352).

According to GBT, each past hyperplane and its contents still EXIST; and so we may legitimately ask, as we look back, what was going on on such a hyperplane, *now* that we are sitting on the edge of reality in the future of it. Thus, to use one of Braddon-Mitchell's own examples, consider the hyperplane about 56 years into the past of 2014, when Arthur Prior was writing the last lines of 'The Syntax of Time-Distinctions'. According to GBT, that earlier hyperplane still EXISTS, and so does Arthur Prior, and, if we allow

future-tensed existence-predicate expresses the notion of going to be present. See Section 4 for further clarification of the notion of being present at work.

ourselves an ontology of events, so does the event of Prior's writing the last lines of 'The Syntax of Time-Distinctions'.[2] So far so good. However, or so Braddon-Mitchell's thought continues, it would now seem that the proponent of GBT is bound to admit that, lo and behold, there is Arthur Prior, still pottering about in his study on that past hyperplane, writing the last lines of 'The Syntax of Time-Distinctions', with a pot of steaming coffee right beside him, judging that his latest thoughts are cutting-edge, while in fact but unbeknownst to him, the bleeding edge of reality lies 56 years ahead (see Braddon-Mitchell 2013: 353, 355).

This narrative is nothing that proponents of GBT should be willing to accept—and for principled reasons that we thought we had made plain. Even if Braddon-Mitchell never ignored that GBT works with a tensed notion of what THERE IS—contrary to what we diagnosed and what the quoted passage after all suggests—it now at least seems clear that he gets the nature of this notion wrong. If this is any consolation, he is not alone in doing so (see Bourne 2002: 364; Merricks 2006: 105; cf. also Blake 1925: 427).

To claim that, at the present time, Arthur Prior still EXISTS commits the proponent of GBT to the thought that Arthur Prior either presently exists (is about) or existed in the past (was about). Since Arthur Prior does not presently exist (is not about), he accordingly existed in the past (was about). Similarly, *modulo* GBT, that the event of Prior's writing the last lines of 'The Syntax of Time-Distinctions' still EXISTS implies that this event either is presently unfolding or was unfolding in the past. As we already know, it is not presently unfolding and so must have unfolded in the past: since no one can be writing any line without being alive, neither Arthur Prior nor any of his temporal parts is presently writing the last lines of 'The Syntax of Time-Distinctions', any more than he is presently judging his thoughts to be cutting-edge. And the coffee, too, has long gone cold.[3]

---

[2] On the particular version of GBT which we presented in our original paper, and to which we will return in Section 4, EVERYTHING is instantaneous—just as Braddon-Mitchell's preferred salami metaphor suggests. Even so, Braddon-Mitchell's examples concern ordinary people like Arthur Prior and Julius Caesar rather than mere time-slices of them. Until Section 4, we will follow Braddon-Mitchell in this, since until then nothing much hinges on the matter.

[3] The coffee matters, as it is a reminder that GBT has no need for Forrest's 'highly controversial thesis' that the 'Past is Dead' according to which 'the hyperplane that is the objective present is the only one that contains consciousness' because 'consciousness is some by-product of the causal frisson that takes place on the borders

2.

Does the failure to see this have anything to do with the fact that Braddon-Mitchell prefers to think of GBT as a 'hybrid' (Braddon-Mitchell 2013: 352)? Yes and no.

Yes, if by 'hybrid' he means a view that combines a conception of the back-block as being composed of *tensed* facts with an eternalist conception of facts as both *immutable* and *ceaselessly obtaining*, in such a way that if in 1958, THERE WAS the present-tensed fact that Prior is writing the last lines of 'The Syntax of Time-Distinctions', then presently, THERE IS the present-tensed fact that Prior is writing the last lines of 'The Syntax of Time-Distinctions' which continues to obtain. However, proponents of GBT—if they acquiesce in fact-talk at all, which they need not do—will either systematically distinguish between the continued EXISTENCE of tensed facts and their continued obtaining—in such a way that even if, presently, THERE IS the fact that Prior is writing the last lines of 'The Syntax of Time-Distinctions', this fact no longer obtains. Or else, they will insist that such facts change over time in that the same fact that in 1958 was the fact that Prior *is* writing the last lines of 'The Syntax of Time-Distinctions', now is the fact that, 56 years ago, Prior *was* writing the last lines of 'The Syntax of Time-Distinctions', and as such still obtains. We have explored these two conceptions of tensed facts in some detail elsewhere (Correia and Rosenkranz 2011 and 2012). However, our earlier presentation of GBT made no play with facts at all, which is why we will not expand on these issues here

No, if by 'hybrid' Braddon-Mitchell means a view that agrees with eternalism on the correct tensed description of what it is that happened 56 years ago. For, even the eternalist will deny that by

---

of being and non-being' (Forrest 2004: 359; Forrest 2006: 162; Braddon-Mitchell 2004: 201). The coffee still EXISTS, and so does the event of its cooling down, but neither is the coffee still about nor is it still cooling down nor is, therefore, the event of its cooling down still in the process of unfolding. That difference has evidently nothing to do with the correct observation that the coffee and other sundries from 1958 are not, at present, alive or sentient or conscious: they never were. The equally correct observation that Arthur Prior, though he still EXISTS, is no longer conscious or sentient or alive has no more relevance in the current context than the observation that his weight is no longer indenting the cushion of his office chair. There is nothing 'highly controversial' about any of *this*, not even for the eternalist. It is unclear what further work Forrest's hypothesis is meant to do.

claiming the event of Prior's writing to EXIST eternally, and a fortiori to EXIST at present, she is bound to hold that it is presently unfolding. The event is unfolding in 1958, for sure, and so it is presently the case that, in 1958, it was unfolding. But it is not, at present, unfolding—its present EXISTENCE notwithstanding. To recall the Priorian thought we already quoted in our original paper, one ought to distinguish—and in ordinary thought does distinguish—'between the history that an event *has*, and the bit of history that it *is*' (Prior 2003: 10). Not even eternalists will be prone to conflating the two.[4]

Past hyperplanes and their contents are *past* even if they still EXIST, and so are importantly different from the lower storeys of an apartment-block and their contents. The look back from the edge of reality on to the back-block is not like Jimmy Stewart's look out of Hitchcock's *Rear Window*. Where t_0 is the present time, the truth that the past hyperplanes are presently earlier than t_0 does not make them any less past, it rather reaffirms their pastness: a hyperplane h is earlier than t_0 iff at some time, t_0 is present while h is past (Broad 1923: 58; McTaggart 1927: § 610; Prior 1967: 4; Correia and Rosenkranz 2011: 22). Now is that time.

If a given hyperplane is past, so is ANYTHING instantaneous populating it, including, if such there be, snapshot ways for matters to stand.[5] However, Braddon-Mitchell seeks to forge a distinction between talk about what is the case at a given past *time*, on the one hand, and talk about what is the case at a past *location*, or *on* a past hyperplane, on the other (Braddon-Mitchell 2013: 354–6; cf. also 357 where he speaks instead of what is the case *in* a time as opposed to what is the case *at* that time). If 'On a past hyperplane' is meant to function like a tense-operator that shifts the circumstances of evaluation to an earlier position in the A-series, it is unclear what is gained, for plausibly, 'On h, p' will then be equivalent to 'At the time at which h is located, p'. It would rather seem that, at least for the dialectical purpose for which Braddon-Mitchell introduces the distinction, 'On h, p' must be taken in a

---

[4] Blake (1925: 427) may be an exception to the rule when he writes that since 'the very nature of an event is to be an occurrence, a happening', 'it is impossible for me to understand how an event can actually exist at a time when it is *not* happening' (emphasis in the original).

[5] See footnote 8.

sense in which if *h* is past, WHATEVER, on *h*, was going on, still is going on, provided that despite its being located in the past, it still EXISTS—and this would indeed make 'On *h*' quite unlike the tense-operator 'At *t*' (see Braddon-Mitchell 2013: 354–5, where the unembedded present tense is used in order to describe what Prior did on a past hyperplane; cf. also Bourne 2002: 364; Merricks 2006: 105). However, it is very doubtful whether there is such a coherent sense that would not make all but the most boring truths of this form come out false, since it seems as plain as day that not EVERYTHING that was going on still is going on.[6]

3.

In our original paper, we claimed that proponents of GBT will inevitably understand the invitation to consider what was going on *at* an earlier time, or hyperplane, as the invitation to consider what was going on when the block of reality had grown as far as, but no further than, that time or hyperplane (Correia and Rosenkranz 2013: 336). Although this claim still strikes us as correct, it needs qualification.

We surely can, while keeping the domain of what THERE IS at present fixed, look back at what was going on at an earlier time, or on the hyperplane that corresponds to that time, and describe what we see *in terms of the quantificational resources we presently have*. The manoeuvre is familiar from the philosophy of modality. We can say, consistently, that there is a possible world in which the emperor

[6] If the '*p*' in 'On *h, p*' is itself tenseless, then it would trivially follow from the truth of 'On *h, p*' that it is still the case that *p* – but then the same holds *mutatis mutandis* for 'At *t, p*', and the distinction between 'On *h, p*' and 'At the time at which *h* is located, *p*' collapses. It is anyway hard to see how anything troublesome would follow from tenseless truths of the form 'Believes{Prior, ⟨Prior is on the edge of reality⟩, *t*}', where *t* is some time in 1958, for the belief that they ascribe will still be true iff, at *t*, Prior is on the edge of reality, his being presently dead notwithstanding. We do not evaluate the belief Prior held some time in 1958 as now being false just because the tensed proposition then believed is not now true, in as much as we do not evaluate the belief in the proposition ⟨Dean is here⟩ that Dean holds in New York as being false in Barcelona just because Dean is not in Barcelona. If the belief-ascription 'Believes{Prior, ⟨Prior is on the edge⟩, *t*}' was true, where *t* is some time in 2014, then it would indeed follow that Prior was believing falsely. But for such a *t* this belief-ascription is false, if for no other reason than that Prior died in 1969. We will return to this matter in Section 4.

Li Zhu does not exist, and so in which nothing is identical to Li Zhu, without thereby saying, inconsistently, that there is a possible world in which there is something, i.e. Li Zhu, such that nothing is identical to it. Similarly, in the temporal case. In agreement with common usage, let 'now' be a temporally rigid designator of the present time, just as 'Li Zhu' is a modally rigid designator of Li Zhu.[7] Then we can say that, in 1958, the event of Prior's writing the last lines of 'The Syntax of Time-Distinctions' was unfolding while now did not EXIST for another 56 years—and also say that for all times t (or hyperplanes h) later than 1958, in 1958, the event of Prior's writing the last lines of 'The Syntax of Time-Distinctions' was unfolding while t (or h) did not yet EXIST—where all this is perfectly consistent with GBT's further claim that, in 1958, THERE WAS no time, or hyperplane, such that the event of Prior's writing unfolded before it. And just as we can say that there is a possible world in which the Tang dynasty ends with Li Ye and not Li Zhu—something we could not have truly said about that world had it been actual—we can say that, in 1958, it is the year 1958, and not now, that is on the edge of reality—something which GBT implies we could not have truly said about 1958 back in 1958.

Acknowledging this latter implication, Braddon-Mitchell (2013: 360) writes that, according to GBT as thus conceived,

it's possible for things to exist from the perspective of one part of being—2013—where from the perspective of some of those existing things, from their own perspective 2013 does not exist. Of course the idea that there might be two such events such that at one of them they both exist, but at the other only one of them does can be made technically coherent with the appropriate handling of accessibility relations in a logic.

That basically sums it up. But then Braddon-Mitchell (2013: 360) goes on to file a complaint:

But understanding the metaphysics so described is another matter. Those asymmetries of existence are not just odd. They take out the block from the growing block—we have gone far from the idea of trying to add dynamism to a block universe. It's a strange volume of spacetime that has locations at which other locations exist, but at those locations the first location doesn't! The thought would be that there is at each A-time a block universe of

---

[7] This is Braddon-Mitchell's 'indexical conception of 'now'—NOW$_{index}$' (Braddon-Mitchell 2013: 351). See footnote 9 for further elucidation.

different sizes, where each of these whole blocks exists only from the perspective of its last slice. It's true of the blocks that exist at every A-time that from the perspective of almost all of its parts the entire block doesn't exist. That's a strange mereology indeed: strange enough to suggest that this is not a view which really has block universes in it at all.

This complaint is of questionable force. On the one hand, the fact that tensed theories of time are in at least prima facie tension with parts of current physical theory is no news; and if this was the worry, the explicit focus on GBT, as opposed to presentism, would be misleading at best. On the other hand, to 'add dynamism to a block universe' was never GBT's game—at least as long as 'block universe' is here understood to denote a universe EVERY two slices of which EXIST at each other. This is, no doubt, part of the eternalist's preferred reading of 'block universe'. But talk about block universes may well have an alternative interpretation on which GBT does not, in any objectionable way, 'take out the block from the growing block'—an alternative interpretation which denies that, FOR EVERY pair of distinct hyperplanes h and h', at h, h' EXISTS. As C. D. Broad, the founding father of GBT, aptly put it, 'when an event, which was present, becomes past, it does not change or lose any of the relations which it had before; it simply acquires in addition new relations *which it could not have before, because the terms to which it now has these relations were then simply non-entities*' (Broad 1923: 67; emphasis added). Van Helsing is obviously trying to stake the wrong man's creature.[8]

---

[8] The most relevant of the relations that Broad has in mind is that of precedence (or being earlier than), which, in Braddon-Mitchell's terms, he regards as a tensed 'quasi-B-relation' (Braddon-Mitchell 2013: 352, 357). Since we endorsed Broad's position in our original paper, just as we are doing now, it becomes clear that from the very onset we were defending what Braddon-Mitchell decides to call 'PTGB' (Braddon-Mitchell 2013: 357). In continuation of the passage quoted Broad goes on to say that 'nothing has happened to the present by becoming past except that fresh slices of existence have been added to the total history of the world'. Some commentators have, quite uncharitably in our view, interpreted this last sentence as implying that nothing ever loses any of its properties, tensed or untensed, by becoming past (Zimmerman 2011). But if it is sufficient in order for Émilien's birth to have ceased to be present, and to have become past instead, that new slices have been added to the block, then surely such an addition should likewise be sufficient in order for Émilien no longer to be being born but to have been born in the past. Does this train of thought ultimately lead to the conclusion that presently dead people like Prior are no people but mere 'ghosts' and that past events, like the one that unfolded when Émilien was born, are no events but mere 'shadows', as both Braddon-Mitchell (2013: 358) and Zimmerman (2011)

4.

Nothing of the foregoing controverts our claim that, given knowledge of GBT, we can always easily come to know that we, or rather our present time-slices and the hyperplane to which they belong, are on the edge of reality. Since, in his reply, Braddon-Mitchell nonetheless contends that his 'epistemic objection still survives', we will give it another go (Braddon-Mitchell 2013: 360).

There is a sense of 'present' according to which, uncontroversially, always, FOR ALL times t, at t, t and ALL and ONLY things located at t are present. In that same sense, always, FOR ALL times t, at t, 'now' refers to the present time (i.e. t). By contrast, it only holds at the present time, that 'now' refers to now, since 'now'—like the complex demonstrative 'this hyperplane'—is an indexical that is temporally rigid.[9]

---

suggest? Although Williamson (2013), for one, endorses some such conclusion, it is by no means forced upon us. It all depends on whether a convincing case can be made that the categories of persons, events etc. not only require that ALL persons sometimes metabolize, and ALL events sometimes unfold, but moreover that they always do. Our ordinary ways of classifying things into persons, events etc. do not univocally suggest that this stronger requirement is in place: we still call certain past events 'births' (and so 'events') and certain dead people 'philosophers' (and so 'persons').

[9] It is this anodyne sense of 'the present time'—in which always, FOR EVERY time, at that time, that time is the present time—which plays a central role in the formulation of GBT. Understood in this way, 'the present time' does not function like an indexical (even if there might be another use of the term in English according to which it does). It would at places seem that GBT's critics take 'the present time' to function like an indexical, and so to function just like 'now', without noticing that this is not the sense intended in the formulation of the view they criticize (Merricks 2006: 103, 106; Braddon-Mitchell 2004: 199). Indeed, the distinction between the temporally rigid 'now' and the temporally flexible 'the present time' might easily be missed, because always, at ALL times, the two expressions co-refer. Thus both of the following hold:

(i) Always, FOR ALL times t, at t, 'now' refers to t.
(ii) Always, FOR ALL times t, at t, 'the present time' refers to t.

Nevertheless, these expressions are not semantically equivalent, and this is seen once we embed them in tense-logical contexts. Thus, while (1) is true, (2) is false, and while (3) is false, (4) is true:

(1) Always, FOR ALL times t, at t, t satisfies 'one day hence, now = ...'.
(2) Always, FOR ALL times t, at t, t satisfies 'one day hence, the present time = ...'.
(3) Always, FOR ALL times t, at t, t satisfies 'one day hence, now is later than ...'.
(4) Always, FOR ALL times t, at t, t satisfies 'one day hence, the present time is later than ...'.

Braddon-Mitchell's epistemic objection challenges GBT's ability ever to afford us knowledge that what is present, in this anodyne sense of 'present', is on the edge of reality. Accordingly, if we can show that GBT affords such knowledge, the challenge is met. Here it should be observed that the charge is that GBT invites scepticism—that its truth would make the sought-after knowledge hard if not impossible to attain—and not that we can have no knowledge of its own truth (Braddon-Mitchell 2013: 351–2). It is therefore perfectly legitimate for proponents of GBT to address the challenge by assuming their own theory as known.

According to presentism, always, EVERYTHING is present. Once we assume, with Broad (1923: 56), that 'EVERYTHING' and 'SOMETHING' exclusively range over things in time that are instantaneous, such as hyperplanes or time-instants, presentism accordingly implies that always, NOTHING was or will be present. According to GBT, by contrast, always, EVERYTHING either is or was present, where indeed SOMETHING is present and SOMETHING was present. GBT further implies that always, EVERYTHING that is present will always in the future be SOMETHING: the block never shrinks. Under the same ontological assumption as before, GBT accordingly implies that always, NOTHING will be present, and that always, EVERYTHING that is present always in the past was NOTHING—in stark contrast with eternalism. The latter claim captures the idea that EVERYTHING that is present belongs to the latest addition to the block. Consequently, GBT clearly differs from both presentism and eternalism.[10]

Similar considerations apply to individual token-utterances. Thus, although (5) and (6) are both true, (7) is true but (8) is false:

(5) Always, FOR ALL times t, at t, if 'a' refers to t, any utterance of 'Now = a' made at t is true.

(6) Always, FOR ALL times t, at t, if 'a' refers to t, any utterance of 'The present time = a' made at t is true.

(7) Always, FOR ALL times t, at t, if 'a' rigidly refers to t, any utterance of 'One day hence, now = a' made at t is true.

(8) Always, FOR ALL times t, at t, if 'a' rigidly refers to t, any utterance of 'One day hence, the present time = a' made at t is true.

[10] Braddon-Mitchell at some point argues that GBT might after all turn out to be no more than a notational variant of presentism. His argument would seem to assume that presentists can avail themselves of quantification over things that no longer exist (i.e. are no longer present). However, while both presentists and proponents of GBT

Provided that always, EVERYTHING in time is instantaneous, always, FOR EVERY x and EVERY y, x is later than y iff sometimes, y is present while x will be present. Given the same proviso, it follows that, according to GBT, always, EVERYTHING that is present is such that NOTHING is later than it (see Broad 1923: 66). But for x to be on the edge of reality just is for x to be such that NOTHING is later than it.[11] Accordingly, if one knows GBT and what it implies, and also knows that always EVERYTHING is instantaneous, then provided that one knows in addition that x is present, one is in a position to know by competent deduction that x is on the edge of reality. So all that remains to be shown is that we are in a position to know that *this* hyperplane, i.e. the hyperplane on which we are considering the matter, is present. But this is rather easily shown.

Always, FOR ALL times t, at t, 'This hyperplane is F' is true iff the hyperplane located at t satisfies 'F'. Always, FOR ALL times t, at t, FOR ALL x, x satisfies 'is present' iff x is identical to or located at t. Therefore, always, FOR ALL times t, at t, 'This hyperplane is present' is true iff the hyperplane located at t either is identical to t or located at t. Granted that always, at EVERY time, THERE IS a unique hyperplane located at that time, the right-hand side of this equivalence must hold always and FOR ALL times t. Consequently we arrive at the claim that, always, FOR ALL times t, at t, 'This hyperplane is present' is true. Note that the latter will hold on any of the competing views, i.e. presentism, eternalism, and GBT alike. In particular then, on anyone's count, at present 'This hyperplane is present' is true; and since at present 'This hyperplane' refers to *this* hyperplane, we can conclude that *this* hyperplane is present—and so, by the foregoing, that it is on the edge of reality. By analogous reasoning, we can establish that now is the present time and so on

---

accept that, in the past, SOMETHING was present which is not now present, the latter but not the former accept that SOMETHING is such that, in the past, it was present although it is not now present. In the light of this structural difference, it becomes unclear how plausible it is to contend, as Braddon-Mitchell does, that 'the striking isomorphisms between [GBT] and presentism make them a very likely candidate for [...] treatment [as a case of quantifier variance] if anything ever was' (Braddon-Mitchell 2013: 358–9).

[11] This is Braddon-Mitchell's 'objective' conception of 'now' which he labels 'NOW$_{ls}$', where the subscript stands for 'last slice' (Braddon-Mitchell 2013: 351).

the edge of reality. It accordingly seems that the epistemic challenge has been met head-on.

However, Braddon-Mitchell keeps asking: 'How do we know that here in spacetime the events are present?', where 'here in spacetime' is equivalent to 'on this hyperplane on which we are when asking this question' and 'present' is here intended to mean 'on the edge of reality' (Braddon-Mitchell 2013: 356). The foregoing considerations, that basically summarize the argument given in our original paper, show how we can know this. And in this respect, Caesar would not have been any worse off when, back in 60BC, he had asked himself whether his very thinking was on the edge of reality.

Yet, undeterred by such considerations, Braddon-Mitchell (2013: 358) writes:

But I'm allowed to say that he [i.e. Caesar] EXISTS$_{2013}$ in 60BC. So why can't I ask whether he BELIEVES$_{2013}$ that he is PRESENT$_{2013}$ in 60BC? That would be a false belief. To deny that, at 2013, Caesar BELIEVES$_{2013}$ anything treats existence very differently from other attributions when we look back at the past: at 2013 Caesar EXISTS$_{2013}$ in 60BC, but Caesar does not BELIEVE$_{2013}$ that he is PRESENT$_{2013}$ at 2013.

Presumably, what is here meant by 'Caesar EXISTS$_{2013}$ in 60BC' is that, in 2013 when Braddon-Mitchell was writing, Caesar EXISTED by virtue of having been present 2,073 years earlier; and what is meant by saying that 'Caesar BELIEVES$_{2013}$' a given thing is that, in 2013, Caesar either was believing that thing or had been believing that thing in the past. Similarly, for Caesar to presently BELIEVE a given thing is for Caesar either to be presently believing that thing or to have believed that thing in the past. And yes indeed, Caesar did believe something when 60BC was present, without believing anything at present (or in the year 2013, for that matter). For, again, no one can be believing anything without being alive; and if we know anything about history, we know that Caesar is not presently alive (nor alive in 2013, for that matter).

What was that thing that Caesar believed back in 60BC? Was it the present-tensed proposition that the time of his believing is *now*? This is a singular proposition about now, and given that *ex hypothesi*, in 60BC, now did not yet EXIST, Caesar could not have believed this proposition back in 60BC. Unlike 'now', the description 'the edge of reality' is not a temporally rigid term. So back in 60BC, Caesar did not think of now by thinking about the edge of reality.

Neither did Caesar believe, of now, that the time of his believing is *it*, in virtue of having believed the present-tensed proposition that the time of his believing is on the edge of reality. Provided that Caesar had the concept of being on the edge of reality at all, in 60BC he at most believed—knowledgeably if the aforementioned considerations are correct—the present-tensed proposition that the time of his believing is on the edge of reality, without believing anything at all about now.

Braddon-Mitchell uses terms such as 'PRESENT$_{2014}$' rather than temporally rigid designators like 'now'. It is unclear what reading of terms such as 'PRESENT$_{2014}$' he has in mind. Let us suppose, on his behalf, that 'PRESENT$_{2014}$' involves no singular reference to now, but is rather equivalent to 'on some hyperplane 2,074 years in the future of t', where 't' names 60BC. Might Caesar have believed, back in 60BC, the present-tensed proposition that his believing is PRESENT$_{2014}$, in this sense of 'PRESENT$_{2014}$'? Perhaps. For Caesar might not have known what time it was, i.e. that back then, t was present; or he might not have accepted GBT which, back in 60BC, would have informed him that no hyperplane 2,074 years in the future of t EXISTED then. But none of this poses any problem for GBT. It is certainly no part of GBT's job description to ensure that people, or their temporal parts, always know what time it is, or that they have the knowledge that knowledge of the theory affords. In any case, in 60BC, Caesar did not believe the present-tensed proposition that his believing is PRESENT$_{2014}$ by believing the present-tensed proposition that his believing is on the edge of reality: while the first was false 2,074 years ago, the second was true 2,074 years ago. So although Braddon-Mitchell's question makes perfect sense, and Caesar would indeed have believed falsely if, implausibly, in 60BC he had believed to be PRESENT$_{2014}$, in the aforementioned sense of 'PRESENT$_{2014}$', this shows nothing of interest.

CONCLUSION

One may have qualms about the ontology of things in time as instantaneous that our version of GBT accepts. One may also wonder how GBT, and its postulation of a present edge of reality, might survive in the light of what certain parts of current physics suggest—a worry that equally afflicts presentism. All this would be fair comment. However, if what we have argued is correct, as we submit it is, the suggestion that even if known to be true, GBT cannot account for our knowledge that we are presently on the edge of reality turns out to be nothing more than a sophism. As such it is powerless to send GBT back to its grave. And so ultimately we hold our ground, the creature prevails, and it is Van Helsing's rotten stake that turns to ash.

University of Neuchâtel ICREA and University of Barcelona

REFERENCES

Blake, R. M. (1925). 'On Mr. Broad's Theory of Time'. *Mind* 34: 418–35.
Bourne, C. (2002). 'When am I? A tense time for some tense theorists?' *Australasian Journal of Philosophy* 80: 359–71.
Braddon-Mitchell, D. (2004). 'How do we know that it is now now?' *Analysis* 64: 199–203.
Braddon-Mitchell, D. (2013). 'Fighting the Zombie of the Growing Salami'. *Oxford Studies in Metaphysics* 8: 351–61.
Broad, C. D. (1923). *Scientific Thought*. London: Routledge.
Correia, F., and S. Rosenkranz (2011). *As Time Goes By: Eternal Facts in an Ageing Universe*. Mentis: Paderborn.
Correia, F., and S. Rosenkranz (2012). 'Eternal Facts in an Ageing Universe'. *Australasian Journal of Philosophy* 90: 307–20.
Correia, F., and S. Rosenkranz (2013). 'Living on the Brink, or Welcome Back, Growing Block!' *Oxford Studies in Metaphysics* 8: 333–50
Forrest, P. (2004). 'The real but dead past: a reply to Braddon-Mitchell'. *Analysis* 64: 358–62.
Forrest, P. (2006). 'Uniform grounding of truth and the Growing Block theory: a reply to Heathwood'. *Analysis* 66: 161–3.
McTaggart, J. M. E. (1927). *The Nature of Existence*, Vol. II. Cambridge: Cambridge University Press.
Merricks, T. (2006). 'Goodbye Growing Block'. *Oxford Studies in Metaphysics* 2: 103–10.
Prior, A. N. (1967). *Past, Present and Future*. Oxford: Clarendon Press.
Prior, A. N. (2003). *Papers on Time and Tense*, new edition. Oxford: Oxford University Press.
Williamson, T. (2013). *Modal Logic as Metaphysics*. Oxford: Oxford University Press.
Zimmerman, D. (2011). 'Presentism and the Space-Time Manifold'. In: C. Callender (ed.), *The Oxford Handbook of Time*, Oxford: Oxford University Press, 163–244.

AUTHOR INDEX

Abelard 75
Aczel, P. 23, 31
Alexander of Aphrodisias 65, 66, 67, 87
Alston, W. 53, 57, 90, 124
Aristotle 30, 61, 62, 63, 64, 65, 66, 67, 68, 69, 70, 71, 72, 73, 74, 75, 84, 85, 86, 87, 88, 192, 314, 327, 342
Armstrong, D. 46, 57, 87, 94, 95, 121, 124, 259, 266, 267, 282, 302
Arntzenius, F. 279, 303
Atran, S. 193, 210
Audi, P. 306, 320, 321, 322, 323, 324, 328, 329, 335, 342
Averill, E. W. 197, 210

Bach, K. 96, 99, 124
Baker, A. 74, 88
Balaguer, M. 53, 57
Beebee, H. 301, 303
Belnap, N. 141, 146, 168, 374
Bennett, K. 57, 131, 168, 306, 312, 337, 342
Beuno, O. 77, 88
Bird, A. 266, 303
Blake, R. 378, 380, 389
Bloom, P. 193, 194, 210
Boghossian, P. 133, 135, 141, 145, 157, 169
Boolos, G. 17, 19, 20, 21, 31, 209, 223, 259
Bourne, C. 376, 378, 381, 389
Boyer, P. 193, 210
Braddon-Mitchell, D. 376, 377, 378, 379, 380, 381, 382, 383, 384, 385, 386, 387, 388, 389
Bradley, F. H. 172, 248

Braun, D. 110, 124
Broackes, J. 265, 303
Burali-Forti, C. 23, 26, 31
Burge, T. 102, 124
Burgess, J. 90, 91, 92, 124, 125
Bynoe, W. 222, 259
Byrne, A. 191, 210

Cameron, R. 121, 124, 154, 169, 368, 374
Campbell, K. 259, 326
Cantor, G. 3, 4, 5, 6, 7, 8, 9, 10, 11, 12, 13, 15, 16, 17, 18, 19, 20, 21, 22, 23, 25, 26, 27, 28, 29, 30, 31, 33, 34, 35, 36, 37, 38, 39, 40, 41, 42, 47, 52
Cappelen, H. 96, 124
Carey, S. 204, 205, 206, 210, 213
Carroll, J. 266, 302, 303
Chalmers, D. 143, 169
Chomsky, N. 116, 117, 121, 125, 177, 210
Church, A. 17
Cohen, J. 197, 198, 199, 200, 209, 210
Collins, J. 291, 302, 303, 304
Colyvan, M. 72, 74, 87, 88
Correia, F. 306, 332, 379, 381, 389
Cortens, A. 121, 145
Craig, A. 186, 211
Cronin, T. 199, 211

Daly, C. 74, 81, 87, 88, 308, 342
Darby, G. 271, 303
Dasgupta, S. 286, 303
Davidson, D. 106, 117, 118, 119
Della Rocca, M. 346, 348, 351, 357, 358, 360, 361, 374
Dennett, D. 193, 211

deRosset, L. 130, 169
Devitt, M. 119, 125, 242, 259
Donnellan, K. 89, 125, 135, 169
Dorr, C. 92, 125, 267, 269, 274, 303
Duhem, P. 195

Earman, J. 280, 303, 345, 349, 369, 374
Ehring, D. 290, 303
Evnine, S. 338, 342
Field, H. 286, 290, 303
Fine, K. 24, 31, 68, 69, 88, 92, 125, 226, 234, 245, 256, 259, 317, 339, 342, 343, 360, 374
Flombaum, J. 203, 211
Forrest, P. 378, 379, 389
Fowler, G. 50, 57
Frege, G. 6, 20, 21, 22, 23, 25, 31, 32, 38, 40, 76, 110, 125, 127, 169, 233, 261
French, L. 77, 88
French, S. 77, 88
Friedman, M. 81, 88

Galileo 29, 30, 31
Geach, P. 124, 202, 204, 211
Gelman, S. 188, 211
Glanzberg, M. 117, 125
Godel, K. 10, 17, 19, 24, 32
Goldman, A. 172, 186, 188, 194, 211
Goodman, N. 106, 125
Graff-Fara, D. 242, 259
Grelling, K. 26, 27, 31, 48
Grice, H. P. 96, 97, 125, 167, 169
Griffin, 202, 204, 211
Grim, P. 42, 57
Guigon, G. 366, 374
Guthrie, S. 193, 211

Hale, B. 24, 32, 130, 141, 146, 169, 343, 344, 375
Hall, N. 277, 290, 291, 302, 303
Hanley, R. 289, 303
Hardin, C. 191, 211
Hawthorne, J. 95, 107, 121, 125, 135, 212, 213, 222, 259, 265, 267, 286, 303, 304
Hegel, G. W. F. 172
Heider, F. 193, 211
Heinlein, R. 289
Hempel, C. 106, 125
Hilbert, D. 19, 20, 32, 201, 210
Hilbert, D. R. 191, 210
Hill, C. 356, 374
Hirsch, E. 92, 125, 150, 151, 169, 208, 212, 228, 259
Hitchcock, C. 366, 374
Hoeltje 306, 343
Hofweber, T. 308, 343
Horgan, T. 92, 125
Hudson, H. 49, 50, 51, 57, 222, 255, 256, 351, 358, 374
Humberstone, L. 350, 351, 374
Hume, D. 262, 263, 264, 265
Husserl, E. 326, 343
Hrbacek, K. 10, 19

Ingarden, R. 326, 338, 343

Jackson, F. 90, 125
Jech, T. 10, 19
Jeffrey, R. 17, 19
Jenkins, C. 81, 88, 306, 343
Jeshion, R. 135, 139
Johnston, M. 198, 212, 222, 224, 259
Jones, N. 222, 259
Joyce, R. 178, 179, 212

Kahneman, D. 203, 212
Kant, I. 177
Kaplan, D. 99, 110, 125, 126, 142, 143, 155, 159, 169
Keil, F. 188, 212
Keller, J. 90, 126
Kim, J. 308, 343
King, J. 96, 99, 126
Kitcher, P. 81, 88
Koethe, J. 242, 259
Konig, J. 26, 27, 32
Korman, D. 92, 95, 126
Koslicki, K. 326, 330, 336, 339, 343
Kripke, S. 93, 96, 102, 106, 107, 126, 140, 145, 152, 153, 169, 188, 189, 212, 270, 271, 304

Ladyman, J. 87, 88, 172, 212
Langford, S. 73, 81, 88
Langton, R. 270, 304
Laurence, S. 338, 344
Le Poidevin, R. 183, 212, 343, 344
Leibniz 124, 318, 345, 348, 359, 363, 364, 365, 366, 370, 374
Lepore, E. 96, 124
Leslie, S. J. 120, 121, 126, 188, 189, 190, 191, 212
Levine, S. 12, 22
Lewis, D. 46, 50, 57, 70, 81, 82, 84, 86, 88, 89, 90, 97, 101, 104, 105, 106, 107, 111, 113, 126, 130, 202, 212, 222, 224, 225, 239, 248, 249, 259, 260, 265, 267, 269, 270, 271, 275, 277, 278, 279, 281, 289, 291, 293, 303, 304, 358, 361, 374
Linnebo, O. 219, 260
Lowe, E. J. 222, 224, 225, 226, 260, 326, 339, 343, 344
Luis Borges, J. 290

Mackie, P. 95, 127
Mancosu, P. 4, 12, 19
Manley, D. 135, 169
Margolis, E. 338, 344
Markosian, N. 222, 224, 260
Marshall, N. J. 199, 211
Martin, C. B. 326
Maudlin, T. 172, 212, 266, 279, 304
McDermott, M. 290, 304
McGee, V. 33, 36, 38, 40, 42, 57, 222, 260
McLaughlin, B. 222, 260
McTaggart 181, 212, 380, 389
Melia, J. 89, 90, 127, 302, 372, 374
Menzies, P. 266, 304
Merricks, T. 95, 114, 127, 376, 378, 381, 384, 389
Meyer, U. 346, 351, 369, 373, 374
Michael, M. 95, 125
Molnar, G. 266, 304

Narenzayan, A. 194, 212
Nelson, L. 26, 31, 48
Nolan, D. 81, 84, 88, 137, 169

Oppy, G. 346, 351, 357, 359, 360, 374

Pap, A. 79, 88
Parmenides 65, 66, 88, 172
Paul, L. 112, 127, 182, 183, 212, 291, 302, 303, 304, 336, 374
Pietroski, P. 117, 127
Plato 62, 63, 64, 65, 66, 67, 68, 69, 70, 71, 72, 73, 74, 75, 77, 80, 83, 84, 85, 86, 87, 172, 317
Plotinus 172
Potrc, M. 92, 125
Priest, G. 363, 375
Prior, A. N. 140, 169, 377, 378, 379, 380, 381, 382, 383, 389

Pruss, A. 47, 53, 57, 351, 358, 359, 375
Putnam, H. 102, 106, 127, 188, 189, 212

Quine, W. V. O. 78, 83, 88, 91, 106, 127, 130, 131, 134, 139, 167, 168, 169, 195, 222, 224, 260, 306, 373, 375

Ramsey, F. 26, 27, 32
Rasmussen, J. 50
Raven, M. 306, 344
Rayo, A. 19, 42, 57
Recanati, F. 96, 127
Richard, J. 15, 26, 32
Rips, L. 191, 212
Roberts, J. 280, 303
Rosen, G. 46, 57, 90, 91, 92, 124, 306, 308, 312, 313, 314, 315, 316, 317, 318, 319, 320, 321, 322, 328, 329, 331, 332, 333, 344, 366, 375
Rosenkranz, S. 376, 379, 380, 381, 389
Ross, D. 172, 212
Royce, J. 262
Rudder-Baker, L. 251, 258, 260
Rumfitt, I. 242, 260
Russell, B. 3, 5, 6, 7, 8, 21, 22, 23, 26, 31, 32, 33, 38, 39, 40, 42, 43, 44, 46, 47, 50, 52, 55, 57, 110, 127, 219, 248, 375

Salmon, N. 110, 127
Santos, L. R. 203, 211
Sattig, T. 222, 260
Schaffer, J. 127, 172, 195, 210, 213, 300, 304, 306, 309, 310, 311, 312, 313, 314, 315, 319, 321, 322, 326, 329, 333, 342, 344, 346, 375

Schnieder, B. 306, 342, 343, 344, 360, 375
Scholl, B. 201, 203, 205, 211, 213
Schuster, R. 182, 213
Sider, Theodor 92, 100, 101, 105, 106, 118, 121, 127, 200, 213, 233, 251, 252, 260, 280, 304, 372, 375
Silverberg, R. 290
Simmel, M. 193, 211
Simons, P. 253, 260, 324, 343, 344
Soames, S. 96, 110, 127
Speaks, J. 101, 128
Spencer, J. 42, 47, 49, 52, 57
Speusippus 62
Spinoza 172, 348, 356, 358, 359, 374, 375
Stalnaker, R. 111, 128, 227, 260
Stanley, J. 96, 97, 99, 116, 117, 124, 126, 128, 242, 259, 260
Steinberg 305, 343
Sterelny, K. 119, 125
Stevenson, J. 141, 143, 144, 144, 146, 148, 161, 169
Strawson, G. 265, 304
Strawson, P. F. 167, 169, 173, 213
Street, S. 178, 179, 185, 186, 213
Studtmann, P. 69, 88
Szabo, Z. 99, 124, 126, 128

Tarski, A. 26, 32
Thomasson, A. 130, 131, 132, 135, 141, 148, 149, 151, 170, 338, 344
Tillman, C. 50, 57
Tooley, M. 266, 302, 304
Tredennick 62, 63, 65, 66, 68, 70, 85
Treisman, A. 203, 212
Trogdon, K. 306, 344

Unger, P. 221, 222, 242, 259, 260

van Fraassen, B. 81, 88
van Heijenoort, J. 31, 32
van Inwagen, P. 92, 94, 95, 100, 103, 104, 105, 112, 114, 115, 116, 122, 123, 127, 128, 130, 170, 222, 261, 269, 274, 290, 302, 304, 305, 346, 351, 355, 356, 357, 375
Varzi, A. 49, 57, 90, 128
Veres, C. 193, 210
Vignemont, F. 186, 213
von Neumann, J. 23, 32

Watson, D. 271, 303
Weatherson, B. 222, 261, 270, 305
Wettstein, H. 99, 124, 125, 126, 128, 169
White, R. 179, 181, 213
Whitehead, A. 22, 26, 32, 219, 375
Whittle, B. 10, 11, 13, 14, 15, 17, 19, 20, 21, 22, 23, 24, 25, 26, 27, 28, 29, 30, 31
Wiggins, D. 227, 229, 234, 241, 261

Wigner, E. 71, 72, 88
Williams, D. C. 326
Williams, J. R. G. 90, 121, 128
Williamson, T. 93, 102, 104, 128, 133, 134, 135, 166, 170, 233, 239, 242, 259, 260, 261, 384, 389
Wilson, J. 266, 305, 307, 308, 344
Woodward, J. 365, 366, 375
Wright, C. 24, 32, 130, 141, 146, 169, 233, 242, 261

Xenocrates 62
Xu, F. 204, 205, 205, 210, 213

Yablo, S. 90, 128
Yi, B. 130, 160

Zeno 30, 204
Zermelo, E. 23, 53
Zimmerman, D. 57, 112, 113, 128, 211, 251, 260, 261, 304, 383, 389

van Groesen, B. 41, 88
van Heijenoort, J. 31, 32
van Inwagen, P. 92, 94, 98, 100, 102, 104, 108, 112, 114, 115, 116, 122, 123, 127, 128, 136, 170, 222, 241, 249, 274, 250, 302, 304, 305, 306, 351, 376, 396, 457, 475
Varzi, A. 19, 87, 90, 128
Vann, C. 193, 211
Vigneron, C. 186, 213
von Neumann, F. 22, 32

Watson, D. 271, 305
Woolgerson, B. 222, 261, 270, 305
Wetherm, H. 94, 124, 125, 126, 128, 169
Wilde, T. 129, 151, 213
Whitehead, A. 22, 26, 32, 219, 375
Whittle, B. 10, 11, 13, 14, 15, 17, 19, 20, 21, 22, 23, 24, 25, 26, 27, 28, 29, 30, 31
Wigner, D. 227, 239, 234, 241, 261

Wigner, E. 27, 32, 68
Williams, D.C. 326
Williamson, T.K. 94, 95, 121, 128
Williamson, T. 93, 102, 104, 128, 135, 136, 135, 166, 170, 235, 236, 237, 239, 240, 261, 361, 389
Wilson, J. 260, 305, 307, 308, 344
Woodward, J. 305, 366, 375
Wright, G.H. 32, 136, 143, 144, 166, 223, 242, 261

Xenocrates 62
Xu, F. 204, 205, 205, 210, 213

Yablo, S. 90, 126
Yi, B. 126, 166

Zeno 19, 204
Zermelo, E. 23, 51
Zimmerman, D. 52, 112, 113, 125, 211, 251, 260, 261, 304, 305, 356